Beyond GDP

Beyond GDP

Measuring Welfare and Assessing Sustainability

Marc Fleurbaey

and

Didier Blanchet

OXFORD
UNIVERSITY PRESS

OXFORD
UNIVERSITY PRESS

Oxford University Press is a department of the University of Oxford. It furthers the University's objective of excellence in research, scholarship, and education by publishing worldwide.

Oxford New York
Auckland Cape Town Dar es Salaam Hong Kong Karachi
Kuala Lumpur Madrid Melbourne Mexico City Nairobi
New Delhi Shanghai Taipei Toronto

With offices in
Argentina Austria Brazil Chile Czech Republic France Greece
Guatemala Hungary Italy Japan Poland Portugal Singapore
South Korea Switzerland Thailand Turkey Ukraine Vietnam

Oxford is a registered trade mark of Oxford University Press in the UK and certain other countries.

Published in the United States of America by
Oxford University Press
198 Madison Avenue, New York, NY 10016

Library of Congress Cataloging-in-Publication Data
Fleurbaey, Marc.
Beyond GDP : measuring welfare and assessing sustainability / Marc Fleurbaey and Didier Blanchet.
p. cm.
Includes bibliographical references and index.
ISBN 978–0–19–976719–9 (cloth : alk. paper) 1. Welfare economics. 2. Gross domestic product.
3. Economic policy. 4. Social policy. I. Blanchet, Didier. II. Title.
HB846.F577 2013
330.12'6—dc23
2012038158
9780199767199

To Christine and Hélène

To Christine, Pauline, and Thomas

CONTENTS

INTRODUCTION

The Four Musketeers

Too much and for too long, we seem to have surrendered personal excellence and community values in the mere accumulation of material things. Our gross national product... counts the air pollution and cigarette advertising, and ambulances to clear our highways of carnage. It counts special locks for our doors and the jails for the people who break them. It counts the destruction of the redwoods and the loss of our natural wonders in chaotic sprawl. It counts napalm and it counts nuclear warheads, and armored cars for the police who fight the riots in our streets. . . .

Yet the gross national product does not allow for the health of our children, the quality of their education, or the joy of their play. It does not include the beauty of our poetry or the strength of our marriages; the intelligence of our public debate or the integrity of our public officials. It measures neither our wit nor our courage; neither our wisdom nor our learning; neither our compassion nor our devotion to our country; it measures everything, in short, except that which makes life worthwhile.

—Robert F. Kennedy *Address, University of Kansas, Lawrence, Kansas, March 18, 1968*[1]

The valuable capacity of the human mind to simplify a complex situation in a compact characterization becomes dangerous when not controlled in terms of definitely stated criteria. With quantitative measurements especially, the definiteness of the result suggests, often misleadingly, a precision and simplicity in the outlines of the object measured. Measurements of national income are subject to this type of illusion and resulting abuse, especially since they deal with matters that are the center of conflict of opposing social groups where the effectiveness of an argument is often contingent upon oversimplification.

—Simon Kuznets, in *National Income 1929–1932. A report to the U.S. Senate, 73rd Congress, 2nd Session. Washington, DC: US Government Printing Office, 1934 (p. 5–6)*[2]

1. The speech can be listened to at http://www.youtube.com/watch?v=77IdKFqXbUY.
2. The quote is taken from Costanza et al. (2009, p. 8).

Although the economist does not have the politician's flamboyant style, these two quotations show that the common use of GDP or GNP as the main indicator of social progress and countries' success over the last decades has been, early on, warned against by its creator and by prominent decision-makers. But even if economists cannot be accused of overselling the GDP, they should perhaps feel a special responsibility for helping to construct better alternatives.

This is the perspective from which this book is written. This does not mean that we believe that economic theory provides a ready-to-go alternative indicator. The design of good indicators of social performance should ideally be the collective endeavor of social scientists from many disciplines, and should rely on the views of the populations whose well-being is to be measured. First of all, it involves addressing hard ethical issues about distributive justice. The evaluation of individual situations and social states of affairs requires defining what should be distributed between the members of society (subjective well-being, resources, opportunities . . .), and how it should be distributed, that is, how much priority should be given to the worst-off. These two sets of issues articulate social evaluation and interpersonal comparisons, two famously difficult value-laden exercises.

While the difficult ethical issues cannot be answered once and for all and cannot be answered with the scientific authority of the standard corpus of economics and other social sciences, it is important to recognize that there are concepts and theories that do shape the questions in a remarkably helpful and clarifying way. And it so happens that welfare concepts have been developed by economists, sometimes in relation to moral and political philosophy, because of their role as advisors in the assessment of economic and social policy. In a nutshell, while the economist cannot answer the ethical questions, "welfare economics", a subfield of economic theory that we broadly construe as encompassing social choice theory and the theory of fair allocation as well as more traditional fields such as cost-benefit analysis, now provides a useful array of concepts that help *formulate* such questions. We would therefore like this book to help economists, social scientists, decision-makers, and interested persons to better identify the pros and cons of various approaches and their ethical underpinnings.

Obviously, we do not have to start from scratch, as a whole industry has set out to produce alternative indicators, following an exponential growth curve over the last three decades (as described by Gadrey and Jany-Catrice 2006). Our goal is to provide a critical examination of the main approaches. We have identified four approaches (the "four musketeers") that seek to fight the power of GDP, although, for reasons to be explained shortly, one should perhaps distinguish five approaches. The first approach proposes to gather various indicators of social performance into a hybrid, composite index, in which GDP per capita or total household income generally is one component among others such as unemployment, health, and poverty. The Human Development Index, regularly published for international comparisons since UNDP (1990), and recently revisited in UNDP (2010), is the most famous of such indicators. This approach is perhaps the simplest because it does not rely on sophisticated theory—this provides a key advantage in terms of potential popularity. It is discussed most specifically in chapter 1 of this book.

Chapter 2 is devoted to the specific issue of sustainability. While this is not exactly the same issue as measuring the well-being of the present generation, it has been quite natural for the inventors of alternative indicators to think of the hazards to future generations induced by unfettered economic growth. "Greening" GDP, or measuring the ecological "footprint" of the present generation, has become a fashionable approach in this context. This chapter therefore deals with an important aspect of the problem of going beyond GDP. It also provides a nice transition between the composite approaches discussed in chapter 1 and the monetary approaches examined in chapter 3, because various sustainability indicators have been constructed following the composite and the monetary methodologies.

The monetary approaches, as the name clearly suggests, keep the monetary metric of the GDP but seek to change the contents. A pioneering initiative in this vein has been made by Nordhaus and Tobin (1972). The monetary approaches are at the extreme opposite of the composite approaches insofar as they are most demanding in terms of economic theory background. We will therefore devote two chapters (chapters 3–4) to them. As we will explain in these chapters, there is an important distinction between the approaches that seek to put a uniform price on each dimension of well-being that GDP does not cover (or wrongly covers), and the approaches that use the monetary metric through individual willingness-to-pay and "equivalent income," allowing different values for different people. The latter offer much more flexibility, receive much better support from basic principles, and are even able to go beyond the money metric itself in order to refer to generalized opportunity sets rather than ordinary market-like budget sets. A separate discussion in two chapters appeared therefore necessary. In chapter 3 we explain the limits of the former approach (uniform pricing), but also discuss the more promising idea of keeping a role for total income as a component of an index of social welfare. The latter approach (equivalent income) is studied in detail in chapter 4, with a review of the criticisms it has been subjected to after it was first used in the late 1970s and early 1980s. We will argue that these criticisms are not insurmountable, so that the approach remains actually quite valuable.

The third approach discussed in this book involves direct measures of subjective well-being. Interest in this approach has soared in the last 20 years, mostly drawn by the development of happiness data and the application of econometric techniques to them. For an economist it is quite a revolution, in view of the long skepticism about such measures in the discipline in most of the twentieth century. In Chapter 5 we analyze the ethical underpinnings of subjective well-being indicators, their connections to psychological and philosophical background theories, their relation to economic concepts, and also the empirical strategies for possible improvements to data collection. The key issues discussed in that chapter have to do with the practical and ethical problem of comparing subjective declarations across individuals in order to estimate the distribution of well-being in a given population. Subjective well-being data are often believed to provide a direct measure of well-being, or at least a good proxy, but things are not so simple. There is a real danger that they are significantly misleading.

The fourth approach, dealt with in chapter 6, is Amartya Sen's capability approach, which has also become considerably attractive to many scholars and activists after it was first formulated in the mid-1980s (Sen 1985). Although the approach is often associated with the Human Development Index, this index is, due to data limitations for wide international comparisons, a pale reflection of the general and ambitious methodology proposed by the capability perspective. It is especially interesting to discuss this approach, not as a radically different view, but as a methodology that relates in complex ways to the approaches discussed in the preceding chapters. Although it is sometimes described as mainly focused on objective dimensions of life, it actually makes room for subjective aspects of well-being, but not as much as the equivalent income approach of chapter 4 and the subjective well-being approach of chapter 5 do. This, however, remains a matter for discussion, as the ambition to respect the values and preferences of the population whose well-being is to be measured is widely shared among the approaches described in this book.

To a substantial extent, the ideal of respecting the population's values and preferences provides the thread of the book, as each approach rebels against GDP for its failure to live by that ideal, and each approach tries to incorporate new elements that go in that direction. We will show in this book that the various approaches unequally succeed in capturing the population's values and preferences. Our conclusion will be that most if not all of these approaches deserve to be pursued, but some of them must acknowledge that they involve a substantial degree of paternalism and perfectionism, more than their advocates typically admit. While the obsession with GDP puts "the mere accumulation of material things" above "personal excellence and community values" (Kennedy), many of the alternative indicators are not more neutral and promote other values, such as good feelings or particular freedoms. Among the approaches examined in this book, the equivalent income will be shown to be the most respectful of people's goals in life—which is an advantage over the other approaches only if people's goals are respectable!

The authors of this book have been involved in the works of the Stiglitz-Sen-Fitoussi Commission,[3] whose mandate was to reconcile the diverging outlooks provided by standard indicators and by the perceptions of the population. The report of the Commission identifies various areas in which more effort should be made by statistical institutions and those who use the data. These include in particular the three approaches discussed in our chapters 4, 5, and 6, as well as the sustainability issues analyzed in chapter 2.

This book is built upon some of the work that has been done by the authors for the Commission, some of which has been published or made available on the Commission or INSEE websites (Fleurbaey 2009; Afsa et al. 2008; Blanchet, Le Cacheux, and Marcus 2009). While survey papers and committee reports provide essential elements, they often remain superficial on the technical aspects and the ethical ramifications. With this book, we seek to provide additional material for those who would like to go further and better understand the issues and the possible solutions. The problem of designing a good indicator of social progress is a tremendous opportunity to connect various areas of economics and other social sciences and is a great source of inspiration given the number and scope of debates and questions that remain open to this day.

Surveys and reports also obey certain rules of restraint and balance, whereas a book like this one is a better place to explore original ideas. While we sought to remain comprehensive, we have not hesitated to adopt a critical tone and a more personal perspective in the assessment of the various arguments and approaches, and to propose new ideas and new articulations of the various approaches.

The book is written for readers who are already familiar with the main concepts and issues rather than for readers who seek an easy introduction to the topic. But most of the text is written so as to be widely accessible to readers with an undergraduate background in economics. It should also be accessible to motivated readers with a mere elementary background in calculus, because the technical concepts from economic theory are always

3. Details about the Commission, including its downloadable report, can be found at www.stiglitz-sen-fitoussi.fr.

defined and introduced when they are used in the argument. This is not a textbook, and the text contains few formal results; it focuses on the ideas and arguments in the quest for alternative indicators.

In terms of technical difficulty, chapter 3 is the most demanding, but because it is mostly critical of the use of pricing in monetary indicators, it is also the least necessary to grasp the main messages of the book, so that it can be skipped by the reader without losing much. Note, however, that this chapter contains a constructive part, dealing with the question of writing a formula for social welfare as a function of efficiency and equity components, in which total income could appear as an element among others. Chapter 2 on sustainability can also be skipped without losing the thread in the other chapters, but obviously this does not mean that sustainability issues are less important. A reader who is especially interested in happiness or capabilities can start with chapter 5 or 6 and look at the other chapters when references are made to them.

Acknowledgments In the preparation of this book, we have benefited a lot from interactions and collaboration with many colleagues, in particular in the Stiglitz-Sen-Fitoussi Commission, which was a very stimulating experience. Our coauthors in earlier work dealing with the topics discussed here have been very influential and inspiring, although any responsibility for the shortcomings of this text should not be attributed to them. Various parts of the manuscript have greatly benefited from detailed comments, for which we are very grateful, by Angus Deaton, Koen Decancq, Juan Moreno-Ternero, Erik Schokkaert, and Giacomo Valletta. Reactions from the audience at an Urrutia-Erejalde summer school session in 2012 have also been helpful. Discussions with Geir Asheim, Larry Pervin, and Justin Wolfers are also gratefully acknowledged. Joe Jackson, Terry Vaughn, and the editorial team at Oxford University Press have been steadily helpful, efficient, and encouraging. Last but not least, our families deserve our warmest gratitude for their wonderful support during the long months of preparation of the manuscript.

CHAPTER 1

A Wealth of Indicators

1.1 INTRODUCTION

In this first chapter, we provide an introductory overview of the alternative indicators that are already available and recall the institutional and historical context in which they have been produced. This introduction sets the stage for the analysis of the foundations and possible future developments to which the bulk of this book is devoted.

A detailed and exhaustive review would, however, be impossible in a single chapter. Building alternatives to GDP is a not-so-recent industry. It started at the onset of the 1970s, and it enjoyed an exceptional boom over the last decade, fueled by both supply and demand factors. On the supply side one has the increasing availability of international data of all kinds that constitute this industry's raw material. On the demand side one witnesses the mounting dissatisfaction of citizens with the image of society returned by official statistics, calling for alternative numbers. The confluence of these two trends benefited from modern instruments of dissemination: it is now easy to post new proposals and make them accessible to a large worldwide community, sometimes bypassing the lengthy circuits of academic or technical validation. To get a feeling of how the resulting activity is burgeoning and heterogeneous, one just has to visit some dedicated websites, and *inter alia* the "wikiprogress" platform (http://www.wikiprogress.org), which is the main window of the "Global Project on Measuring the Progress of Societies," a federative project hosted by OECD, supported by several international organizations, and opened to all forms of initiatives, official or nonofficial. A glance at this site confirms the difficulty of an exhaustive presentation. Even if exhaustiveness was at hand, the proposed picture would rapidly turn obsolete.

Our ambition here remains therefore more limited. It is to give a basic idea of the main currents of thought that structure this field: Where do they come from? How do they relate to one another? What are their most emblematic representatives? What questions do they raise? To this aim, one strongly benefits from reference surveys that are already available (Boarini, Johansson, and Mira d'Ercole 2006; Gadrey and Jany-Catrice 2006) and to which the reader can refer for further details.[1]

Presenting the background of available indicators will enable us to raise and take a first look at key methodological questions that will run throughout this book. While the shortcomings of GDP are widely acknowledged, there are vivid debates about how to enrich the available information about social welfare. Two issues are particularly salient. First, there is the issue of how far from GDP one should seek to go. Modest corrections to GDP are possible, but adopting a radically new index based on totally different data, for example, an index of national happiness, is also advocated by some authors. In this vein, monetary approaches are often opposed to nonmonetary approaches, an important criticism against the former being that they too easily substitute one dimension of performance for another.

The other important debate is whether one should seek a single alternative to GDP or retain a multidimensional approach, with several indicators for different dimensions (GDP remaining possibly one of them). Aggregation has its advocates and its opponents, with theoretical and pragmatic arguments being invoked on the two sides of the debate. Elements of these debates will appear in this chapter and will motivate many parts of the book.

1.2 A BIRD'S-EYE VIEW

Let us start with a very synthetic overview, offered by figure 1.1. It tentatively orders approaches or initiatives by approximate time of apparition (on the horizontal axis) and by degree of proximity with GDP or other concepts of national accounts (along the vertical axis). A distinction is also made between indexes (gray boxes) and other elements of interest (white boxes). "Indexes" include both one-shot prototypes and indicators that have been more or less regularly produced and generally go on being

1. Vanoli's history of national accounts also offers many very informed insights on this literature, from a national accountant's point of view (Vanoli 2005).

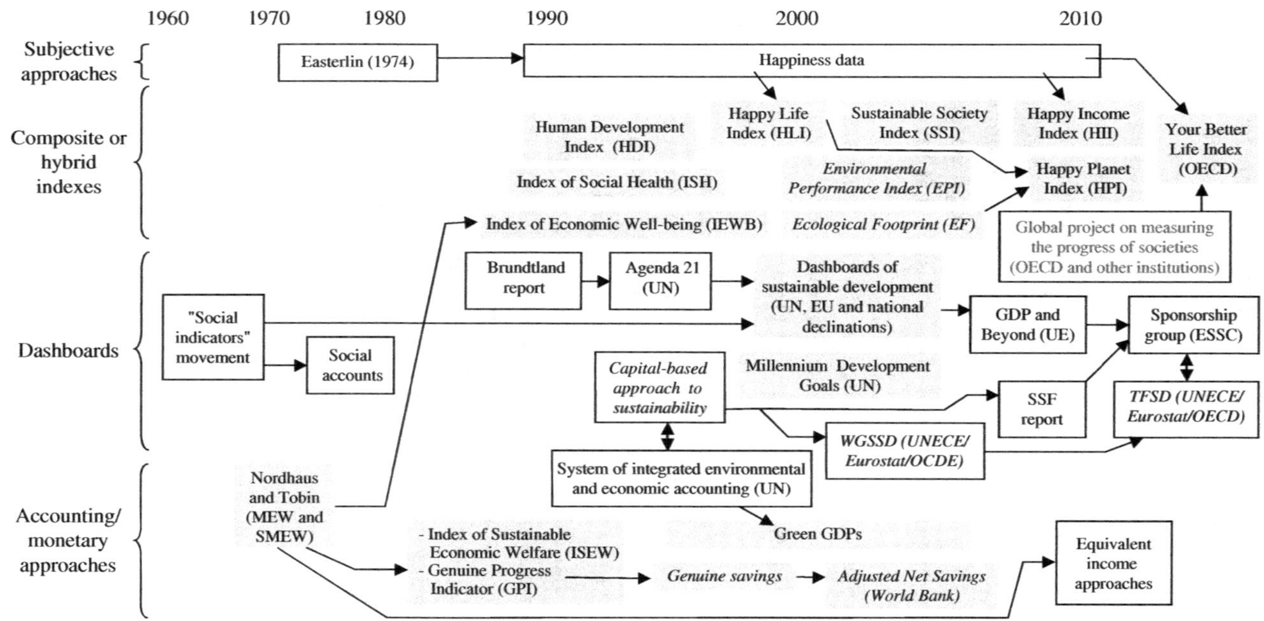

Notes: Gray boxes correspond to indexes or sets of indexes, including both one-shot prototypes and those that have benefited from some regular production. White boxes correspond to all other forms of related initiatives: reports, task forces, more or less structured research or production programs. Italics refer to indexes or initiatives excusively focussed on sustainability. Datations are *very* indicative. Arrows outline the main dependencies or filiations.
Non usual acronyms: UNECE = United Nations Economic Commission for Europe; ESSC = European Statistical System Committee, WGSSD = Working Group on Statistics for Sustainable Development, TFSD = Task Force for Measuring Sustainable Development, SSF = Stiglitz-Sen-Fitoussi report.

Figure 1.1
Alternatives to GDP : a bird's-eye view

so. The "other" category includes seminal papers, reports, working groups, formal or informal research programs, and so on. We also tried to represent some of the filiations linking these items to each other, but only the most important or specific ones. In some cases, links are so numerous that they could not be displayed. This is generally the case with federative projects that generally borrow from all preexisting trends or material.

The time origin that has been retained is 1960. It is surely not at this time that limits to GDP (or GNP) started being discovered. They had been already known for a long time. Some of them had been warned about as soon as concepts of national accounts started being coined and implemented during the 1940s. Yet the necessity of correcting or complementing GDP had no reason to strongly emerge before it had acquired its dominant position, that is, in the middle of the big expansion that followed World War II.

The first route opened at this time was on the social side. In parallel with the development and harmonization of national accounts as one of their core activities, National Statistical Organizations (NSOs) started extending the field of social statistics, mostly relying on household surveys covering the main aspects of people's living conditions: labor market outcomes, health, and so forth. The idea of integrating these social statistics into a fully integrated system of "social accounts" was pushed forward during the 1970s (Stone 1975) but failed to be applied at this stage. The reason is probably that this field is less prone to rigorous integration than stocks and flows of resources measured in monetary terms. But a current of thought had emerged, and it temporarily materialized during the 1960s for the regrouping of such statistics within sets of "social indicators," aiming at counterbalancing the increasing preeminence of GDP. In addition to various national initiatives,[2] the OECD launched an ambitious statistical program of such social indicators during the 1970s. Interest in this way of promoting social data then partially faded away, but the impulsion that had been given to statistical production remained, and more recent initiatives naturally draw upon the implicit legacy of this early movement.

2. For a history of this movement, see in particular Cobb and Rixford 1998. In the United States, regular reporting of social indicators received strong support under the Johnson administration and was then progressively abandoned during the 1970s. To take the French case as another example, interest in this question was strong at the end of the 1960s and contributed to improving the coverage and quality of social statistics, as well as developing the system of satellite accounts. But the idea of a regular and standardized reporting of such indicators progressively lost support during the 1970s, in parallel with the progressive decline of the French planification system (see Perret 2002).

It is about the same period that another step was taken, along another direction, with the publication of the seminal work by Nordhaus and Tobin (1972). This publication represented the first noticeable effort to correct GDP "from the inside," that is, in a consistent accounting framework, combining a social dimension with a partial account of environmental issues. This publication took place in a context of emerging concern for the finiteness of the resources upon which the rapid growth of post-World War II decades had been built. This concern had been spurred by the publication of the first edition of the "limits to growth" report by the Club of Rome (Meadows et al. 1972).

Here also, a period of reflux followed, however, interest in these questions turning paradoxically weaker after the first oil shock. Slow economic growth and its social consequences restored prominence to policies aiming at stimulating activity, and to GDP as the main monitoring tool. But this did not completely interrupt the quest for alternatives to GDP. The Nordhaus and Tobin endeavor had several successors still trying to make GDP closer to well-being by subtracting from it all that does not contribute to welfare and trying to reaggregate to it things that do and that are not usually captured in monetary accounts: the Index of Sustainable Economic Welfare (ISEW)[3] and the Genuine Progress Indicator (GPI) are examples that we shall briefly present later. More recently, indirect descendants of the Nordhaus and Tobin tradition are attempts to built corrected GDPs through the equivalent income approach that will be reviewed more extensively in chapter 4.

However, another very dominant strand of the literature considers that monetary valuation is inadequate for most of the components of well-being that do not spontaneously come out in monetary terms. It adopts a much simpler and more radical way of aggregating heterogenous information, the methodology of composite indexes. This methology of composite indexes is used in several domains. It is often used when one wishes to summarize complex phenomena measured in heterogeneous ways, sometimes even purely qualitative. There are composite indexes for the performance of countries in many fields: labor or product market regulation, friendliness to business activities, individual freedom, and so on. The global measurement of progress and human well-being is one of the domains where this practice is the most developed, with the emblematic example of the Human

3. Bibliographical references will not be systematically provided for all the quoted indexes. Links to the relevant information can generally be retrieved through the Wikiprogress platform.

Development Index (HDI). Some of the other examples of this kind mentioned in the upper half of figure 1.1 are the Index of Economic Well-Being (IEWB), the Social Sustainability Index (SSI), and, still more recent, the Better Life Index launched in 2011 by the OECD.

Four other points complete the picture provided by figure 1.1: indexes exclusively devoted to sustainability, the "dashboard" approach, subjective approaches to well-being, and a bunch of recent federative initiatives, often interacting or overlapping, that have developed over the very last years.

Concerning sustainability, we mentioned how oil shocks had the paradoxical effect of helping preserve a leading role for GDP. But concern for ecological constraints never disappeared and has now fully reemerged at the forefront of public preoccupations. This explains why the term "sustainable" appears in so many "generalist" composite indexes. It explains the efforts made by statisticians to elaborate a common System of Integrated Environmental and Economic Accounts (SIEEA), under the auspices of the United Nations, including some attempts to develop a "green GDP." And it has also led to the development of indexes more exclusively devoted to this sustainability issue: either essentially along the environmental dimension, such as the Ecological Footprint (EF) or the Environmental Sustainability Index (ESI), or in a more comprehensive perspective encompassing all the potential determinants of future well-being, the successive concepts of Genuine Savings (GS) or Adjusted Net Savings (ANS), the latter now implemented and regularly published by the World Bank (World Bank 2011).

This concern for sustainability and development naturally benefited from the impetus given by the publication of the very influential Brundtland report (Brundtland 1987) and the Rio summit (in 1992), whose twentieth anniversary has been very recently celebrated. The results of this new "Rio + 20" summit have been often judged disappointing in terms of political action, but it reaffirmed the need for "broader measures of progress to complement GDP" (final declaration, point 38). Now, more than the production of monodimensional indicators of the EF or ANS types, the impulse given by the Brundtland report has above all led to the development of a large variety of "dashboards," that is, sets of indicators that bring us back to the initial idea of the "social indicators" movement of the 1960s, but strongly reinforced on the environmental side. Alongside "dashboards of sustainable development" that exist in various forms and for various geographical levels, our diagram mentions the set of Millennium Development Goals (MDGs) adopted by the United Nations in 2000 (http://www.unmillenniumproject.org/goals/gti.htm). Such "dashboard" approaches are both diametrically opposed and fully complementary to the strategy of building composite indicators. This complementarity is two-sided. There is always an implicit dashboard behind any composite indicator, made of all its distinct components, and, symmetrically, it is often very tempting and relatively easy to try to summarize a dashboard by building an associated headline composite indicator that will help drawing public attention onto this dashboard.

Subjective approaches are an additional way of measuring well-being, here represented as an outsider on the upper side of the diagram, but indeed one that has counted and that has been intensively discussed over the last decade. It consists in directly measuring individual well-being through answers to questions about how people perceive their lives. This approach has a long tradition too. The seminal contribution to this literature has been roughly concomitant with the publication by Nordhaus and Tobin. It is in the middle of the 1970s that Easterlin formulated his well-known paradox (Easterlin 1974), pointing at the apparent lack of connexion between material progress measured by GDP and the flat trend for perceived well-being, as revealed by subjective data. Renewed interest in this result some 10-15 years ago has led to a considerable literature upon which chapter 5 will comment at length.

Subjective data can result in indexes that exclusively rely on them, one example being the Gallup-Healthways Well-Being Index, not reported in the graph but accessible through the Wikiprogress platform. This index goes to the point of offering a daily follow-up of Americans' health and well-being. Or subjective data can enter the composition of composite or hybrid indexes. Such is —marginally— the case for OECD's Your Better Life Index and much more substantially for the Happy Life Expectancy (HLE) index (Veenhoven 1996), which combines a subjective happiness measure with life expectancy; for the Happy Income (HI) index (Prinz and Bünger 2009), which combines the same kind of subjective measure with equivalent household income; and the HPI index, which divides the HLE by the Ecological Footprint with the objective of distinguishing those countries that can offer long happy lives with minimal pressure on the earth's resources. This latter example shows how the index-building industry can occasionally use already existing indexes as intermediate products for new ones, a possibility that can also contribute to the accumulation of competing measures.

Finally, figure 1.1 also tries to make some room for more or less recent federative initiatives, some of which are still under way. This includes the already mentioned program on "measuring the well-being and progress of societies" that has recently given birth to the "better life" initiative launched by OECD for its fiftieth anniversary. The Your Better Life Index quoted above, as the most recent of composite indicators, is a headline product of this initiative. Also worth noticing are a joint working group on "statistics for sustained development" (WGSSD) involving the OECD, the European statistical Agency (Eurostat), and the United Nations Economic Commission for Europe (UNECE/OECD/Eurostat 2008), the "GDP and beyond" communication by the European Commission in 2009 (Commission of the European Communities 2009), and the concomitant report of the Commission on Measuring Economic Performance and Social Progress (Stiglitz, Sen, and Fitoussi 2009). These three operations, which delivered their final reports roughly at the same period, have, in turn, given birth to two still ongoing task forces: a sponsorship group of the European Statistical System Committee (ESSC) and a new OECD/Eurostat/UNECE task force for measuring statistical development (TFSD) that can be viewed as a phase 2 of the former WGSSD working group.

From this first overview, one clearly sees that the problem with challenging GDP is not the lack of competitors, but rather their multiplicity. We shall now look more precisely into the details of some of these options. This closer look will suggest some reasons why, at this stage, none of them has been able to receive the global support that would have imposed it as *the* definite challenger to GDP. Leaving the specific case of purely subjective approaches for chapter 5, we shall do it under four main categories that rather naturally emerge from figure 1.1: (*a*) composite indicators of the HDI type, (*b*) monetary or quasi-monetary indicators of the "corrected GDP" type in the Nordhaus and Tobin's tradition, (*c*) synthetic sustainability indicators, and (*d*) dashboards.

1.3 AGGREGATING THE NONAGGREGATABLE?

We begin with composite indicators not because of their anteriority—they started expending much after the Nordhaus and Tobin contribution—but because of their greater conceptual simplicity. The Human Development Index (HDI) has a prominent position within this category, due to its worldwide geographical coverage and the fact of being produced by a United Nations institution, the United Nations Development Program (UNDP). Since its creation, in 1990, it has constituted a central piece of the Human Development Report published yearly by the UNDP. It has been recently "reformed" for its twentieth anniversary in 2010.

The HDI is a composite index mixing economic resources with two other dimensions, health and educational achievement, regarded as two major ingredients of development and progress. All three components are said to be given equal weight in the index, with a calibration methodology ensuring a [0,1] range of variation. Health outcomes are measured by life expectancy at birth, in years. Income was proxied by GDP per capita in the initial version of the index, replaced by Gross National Income (GNI) in the new one, the difference being that GNI excludes income that is produced within the country but that benefits residents of other countries, such as returns on capital owned by foreign investors. Using GNI instead of GDP is indeed more adequate for countries where a large share of production does not benefit the local population due to the high penetration of foreign investment. Concerning educational achievement, it was measured in the 1990–2009 version of the index by combining two statistics: the adult literacy rate, and the combined primary, secondary, and tertiary gross enrollment ratios. These two components have been replaced in 2010 by the mean years of schooling of people that have passed schooling ages (years that a 25-year-old person or older has spent in schools), and the expected years of schooling for individuals entering the schooling system, (i.e. the years that a five-year-old child will spend with his education in his whole life).

The HDI index leads to country rankings that indeed differ from those based on GDP. According to the 2011 edition, the country with the highest HDI is Norway, with a value of 0.943. This country also ranks high in terms of GDP per capita, but only in the fifth position, with a level quite far below the two GDP champions, Qatar and Luxembourg, which rank respectively 37th and 25th in terms of HDI. The most extreme case of reranking in the 2011 edition is Equatorial Guinea, which loses 90 places when moving from the GDP hierarchy to the HDI hierarchy. At the same time, as displayed on figure 1.2, HDI and GDP remain relatively well correlated, this being due both to the fact that GDP or the related concept of GNI enters the index, and to the fact that the other components of the index are themselves related, albeit in a non linear fashion, to GDP. Over its 20 years of existence, the basic HDI has been complemented by associated indexes such as the inequality-adjusted HDI or the gender inequality index, but keeping the spirit of aggregating no more than four or five elementary components.

Some of the other indexes that were mentioned on figure 1.1 are less parsimonious than the HDI or its variants in terms of number of elementary components, but are generally so because they have been developed for a smaller number of countries, and sometimes only for a single country.

Among them, the ISH, applied to the United States (Miringoff, Miringoff, and Opdyke 1999), is based on 16 social indicators, grouped by age. The Index of Economic Well-Being (IEWB), developed by L. Osberg and A. Sharpe (2002), covers current prosperity (mainly based on measures of

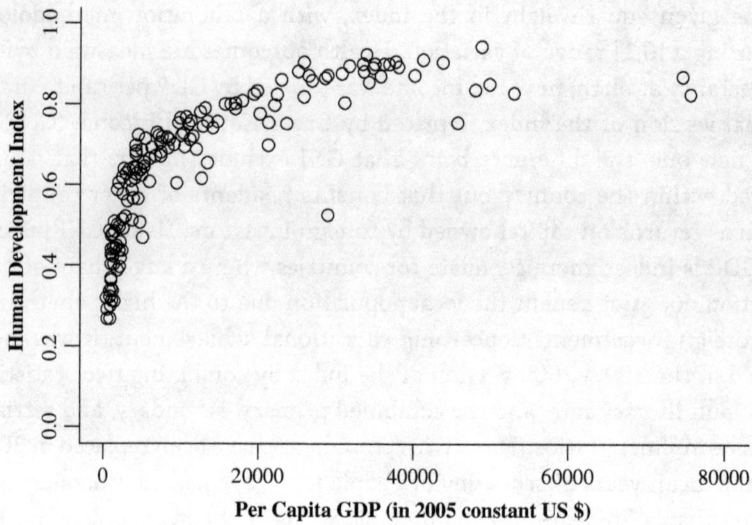

Figure 1.2
HDI versus GDP (2007 values)
Source: UNDP (2011).

consumption), wealth stocks (including natural and immaterial resources), equality, and economic security. These four broad dimensions are each fed by two to six subindexes. As an example, economic security is captured through four social risks: unemployment, illness, single parent poverty, and old-age poverty. Among the countries considered, Norway is the country that has experienced the most rapid progression from 1980 to 1999, while slow growth or even declines have been registered for Sweden, the United States, and the UK, despite significant GDP growth for the last two countries. Results are, however, partly sensitive to the choice of weighting factors. The index has been applied to some other countries. For instance, Jany-Catrice and Kampelmann (2007) revised the Index of Economic Well-Being (IEWB) for France with enhanced data over a larger time period. Their results confirm the divergence between GDP and IEWB since the end of the 1980s, largely due to the lack of improvement in inequality reduction and economic security.

The Social Sustainability Index (SSI) is also an index that aggregates a relatively large number of items (24) covering the three pillars of the Brundtlandian definition of sustainable development (van de Kerk and Manuel 2008). On the contrary, three other examples that appear in figure 1.1, and whose formulas have been already given, the HLE, the HI, and the HPI, have gone back to much simpler compositions, combining subjective well-being with either one or two additional dimensions such as life expectancy, income, and the Ecological Footprint. Subjective data have also been included in the OECD's Your Better Life Index but the dimensionality of the index is comparable to that of the IEWB or the SSI, since the subjective dimension is combined with a list of 10 more objective dimensions, each of which represented by one to three statistics: income and wealth, jobs and earnings, housing, work and life balance, health status, educations and skills, social connections, civic engagement and governance, environmental quality, personal security. All the 11 resulting dimensions, by default, are equally weighted, but a main innovation of the index is to allow testing any alternative set of weights, and see the implied changes in rankings for the 34 OECD countries covered by the index, thanks to an online interactive application.

Whatever the number of underlying dimensions and the resulting messages, what are the main problems with this approach? The methodology of composite indexes is not specific to the measurement of well-being, and, whatever the domain to which it is applied, it attracts the same criticisms concerning its lack of analytical foundations (Ravallion 2010a). The OECD has attempted a systematic examination of these limits, to help prevent excessively misleading uses of this methodology (OECD/JRC 2008).

The questions that most immediately come to mind have to do with the methodology of aggregation and the prior treatments applied to the components.[4] In the case of monetary indexes such as GDP, aggregation relies on the hypothesis that market prices more or less convey information about the way people value the elementary physical quantities that the index intends to synthetize. As will be shown in chapter 3, this hypothesis is, in fact, much less grounded than one could have believed, but it provides the feeling of aggregating things on the basis of something that is not fully arbitrary.

As soon as one leaves the field of monetary aggregates, this problem of arbitrariness becomes much more pressing, with few guidelines about how it can be managed. We shall insist here on the example of the HDI, not because it is particularly illustrative of what to do or not to do, but because it is simple to handle and well known. Since its creation, the HDI has simultaneously benefited from a high international visibility and from several critical assessments upon which it is possible to rely (Kelley 1991;

4. Another important question is data coverage or quality. It is not specific to the methodology of composite indicators, but takes a particular importance for indexes that generally try to cover large sets of countries with statistical systems that are very unevenly developed. Imputation methodologies that are used to compensate the low quality or the full absence of data cannot be neutral for the relevance of indicators.

McGillivray 1991; Srinivasan 1994; Sagara and Najam 1998; MacGillivray and White 2006; Ravallion 2010b).

The first step of the HDI methodology consists in rescaling each dimension with respect to a range of variation that is partly observed and partly conventional. In the 2011 edition, minimum and maximum values for life expectancy are set at 20 and 83.4 years respectively, the latter value being the level of life expectancy reached in Japan. For a country with an observed level of 60 years, the rescaled index of life expectancy is $(60 - 20)/(83.4 - 20) = 0.631$. This value can be interpreted as an index of relative deprivation along the life expectancy dimension, since it means that a country with a value of 60 for its life expectancy is 63.1% of the way between the worst and the best performance for this specific dimension. For the two educational indexes, minimum values are set at 0 and maximum values are respectively 13.4 for the mean number of years of schooling (the level observed in the Czech Republic in 2005) and an arbitrary 18 for the expected number of years of schooling. Concerning GNI per capita, the maximum is the 107,721 level observed for Qatar in 2010, with the minimum conventionally fixed at 100—a very low value indeed but accounting for the fact that, in countries close to this very low level, a large part of subsistence also results from nonmonetary or unreported income. This rescaling takes place after conversion to logarithms to reflect the assumed decreasing effect of GDP on well-being as GDP increases.

This is only one among various possible methodologies for all this preliminary "preparation" of the elementary components of the index. The other two main possibilities consist in standardizing variables, that is, dividing them by their standard deviations after centering around their means, or replacing values by ranks, and these choices are not neutral. For instance, using ranks will downgrade the relative performance of a country that is a strong outlier in terms of the component of interest, a property that may seem desirable in some circumstances—especially when large values are susceptible of resulting from measurement error—but not in others.

Then comes the step of aggregation *stricto sensu*, again with various possibilities. The initial version of the HDI used linear aggregation with equal weights. This version has been criticized for the induced trade-offs it allowed between components of the index, in particular between income and life expectancy. The new aggregation procedure has been presented as offering a more adequate treatment of this issue. But, according to Ravallion (2010b) the claim that it succeeds in doing so is not warranted at all. Let us examine the details briefly, dropping the education dimension that is orthogonal to this longevity/income trade-off. Using notations Y for income and *LE* for life expectancy, the two successive versions of the index boil down to

$$HDI_{old} = \frac{1}{3}\frac{LE - LE_{min}}{LE_{max} - LE_{min}} + \frac{1}{3}\frac{\ln(Y) - \ln(Y_{min})}{\ln(Y_{max}) - \ln(Y_{min})},$$

and

$$HDI_{new} = \left(\frac{LE - LE_{min}}{LE_{max} - LE_{min}}\right)^{1/3}\left(\frac{\ln(Y) - \ln(Y_{min})}{\ln(Y_{max}) - \ln(Y_{min})}\right)^{1/3}.$$

In both cases, the implicit valuation of an additional year of life, *VLE*, can be computed by equalizing to zero the global variation of the index after joint marginal changes of Y and LE. The general formula will be

$$VLE = -\left.\frac{dY}{dLE}\right|_{HDI=constant} = \left(\frac{\partial HDI}{\partial LE}\right) \Big/ \left(\frac{\partial HDI}{\partial Y}\right).$$

The application of this formula to the old and new versions of the index leads to

$$VLE_{old} = Y\,\frac{\ln(Y_{max}) - \ln(Y_{min})}{LE_{max} - LE_{min}},$$

and

$$VLE_{new} = Y\,\frac{\ln(Y) - \ln(Y_{min})}{LE - LE_{min}}.$$

The change appears nonnegligible, and its implications are not evident at first sight. In the first version of the index, aggregation led to a marginal valuation of life years that was linearly related to income. The new formula makes the dependency much stronger, due to the new $\ln(Y)$ term on the denominator, resulting in very low valuations of life years for countries close to the minimum observed income level Y_{min}. According to Ravallion's computations, in the extreme case of Zimbabwe, one year of average life expectancy is only worth \$0.51 per person under the new version of the index. In other words, if there had existed a policy allowing a \$0.51 increase in income per capita at the expense of a one year loss in average life expectancy, this policy would have been judged as increasing this country's "human development." Globally, the new index is found to have devalued longevity compared to the older version, with only very few exceptions, and it has done so much more intensively for poor countries. The ratio of the highest to the lowest VLE_{new} is 17,000. Even dropping the very extreme case of Zimbabwe, this ratio is still 1,600.[5]

The paradox of such a situation is that a methodology initially developed, inter alia, to avoid the presumed arbitrariness of monetary aggregation ends up raising exactly similar problems, and possibly in aggravated terms. Putting a money value on years of life has always generated understandable ethical reluctance, and one is tempted to welcome a composite index that apparently avoids doing such things. But there is no miracle. Aggregating GDP and life expectancy within one single scalar indicator unavoidably amounts to giving an implicit value to additional years of life, with the risk of doing so in a noncontrolled fashion. As argued by Ravallion, the apparent transparency of the indicator is illusory. The indicator is only transparent in the sense that it is easily replicable and amenable to the kind of evaluation provided above. But as long as the user does not make the effort of performing such an analysis, the indicator remains completely opaque concerning its true normative implications. And the problem does not just arise because we have GDP or GNI as one of the components of the index. The situation is not fundamentally different when none of the aggregated variables are monetary. Aggregation always implies assuming some more or less important substitution possibilities between the items that are aggregated.

Upstream from these problems comes the overarching question of the choice of the items that are to be aggregated. The question is not only "how to aggregate," it is also to know "what to aggregate." This is a stage where some theory should also be welcome, even when it can be no more than weak or very soft theory. The point is the need to be as clear as possible concerning what exactly one wants to measure, and in what way

5. On a more positive side, aggregation through geometric means can have some useful properties. Among other innovations of the revised HDI, one also finds the "inequality adjusted HDI" (IHDI) that takes into account inequalities across dimensions. A frequent limit of corrections for inequality in composite indexes is that, when aggregating subdimensions that have been separately corrected for inequality, cumulative deprivations are ignored, i.e., one neglects the fact that being relatively deprived in terms of income generally goes along with relative deprivations in the other dimensions. The correct way to proceed is to first compute individual indicators of well-being ("individual HDIs") combining the three dimensions for each individual, and then aggregate them in a way that takes their inequality into account. In some sense, the IHDI ultimately does this, because inequalities across each dimension are themselves computed according to geometric means, and the order in which geometric means are computed is neutral for the final result. Thanks to such path independence, the IHDI can be considered as using the correct form of aggregation, but it does so only under the assumption that the geometric mean is the proper way to assess individual levels of well-being, and that the geometric means also constitutes the proper way to correct for inequality.

elementary components of the index will contribute to this global objective, trying to avoid gaps and redundancies. When the objective is to measure well-being, one needs a reasonable coverage of all that indeed matters for well-being, and one must avoid combining elementary indices that measure the same thing twice. To use once again the HDI as an example, its choice of three main dimensions of well-being—monetary income, health, and education—has been presented from the start as an empirical transcription of Sen's concept of capabilities, discussed in chapter 6, that is, the fact that well-being requires access to some basic entitlements over a selected number of dimensions. But why restrict oneself to the three dimensions chosen for the HDI, excluding, for instance, economic or personal security? And what exactly means "adding" the health and education dimensions to GDP? One can argue that health and education are dimensions that are already incorporated in GDP, through levels of private and public expenditures devoted to these two items, and that the indicator may therefore suffer from double counting. The answer could be that a difference has to be made between *expenditures* on these two items and the *results* in terms of actual health or access to education, but in that case, why not remove the former from the index? An indicator whose aim is to measure a result or an outcome—actual well-being—should not incorporate elements that are only instruments for reaching this outcome.

This lack of analytical clarity concerning the divide between inputs, intermediate products, and outputs is frequent in this field. Incidentally, GDP itself is not immune to this criticism: being a summation of values-added, it has the well-known merit of avoiding double counting of intermediate products that are ultimately included in final consumption. However, adding up consumption and investment, it unduly mixes something that is undoubtedly a component of current well-being—consumption—and something that should rather be viewed as an input to tomorrow's well-being—investment. This point was taken into account by Nordhaus and Tobin, and it will reappear later in our discussion of sustainability in chapter 2.

Another good illustration of this "what to aggregate?" question is given by the Happy Planet Index, which combines "Happy Life Expectancy" and the Ecological Footprint. For someone who trusts subjective happiness data to reveal the real quality of life, it seems to make sense to first multiply the flow of happiness by an indicator of how long this flow will be enjoyed by each individual. Yet, even at this stage, questions can be raised. Are there good reasons for assuming a value of 1 for the elasticity of substitution between the two components: does 10% greater life expectancy exactly compensate for 10% less of perceived happiness? It may also be that life expectancy is one of the elements that people already incorporate in their assessment of how good their lives are, in which case a problem of double counting appears again. But the most important problem is with the division by the Ecological Footprint. There is no doubt that well-being and sustainability are two important dimensions that deserve measurement, but does this mean that it makes sense to integrate them at this point? As it stands, the indicator may make no difference at all between a low mortality / high footprint country and a high mortality / low footprint one.

1.4 CORRECTING GDP

To sum up, the problem raised by composite indexes is that, aiming at avoiding the presumed arbitrariness of monetary aggregation, they end up aggregating things in ways that are no less arbitrary, with uncontrolled consequences for resulting trade-offs between their different items.

Of course, this does not suffice to prove that a well-defined monetary aggregation is ultimately preferable to an ill-defined or undefined "nonmonetary" aggregation. Nevertheless, many economists have trod the road opened by Nordhaus and Tobin in 1972. The idea was to try to retain as much as possible of the accounting consistency of the GNP or GDP concepts, with the possibility of partly relying on other segments of the very rich production of national accounts. This approach requires monetary evaluations of all the elements that one wants to subtract from, or add to, standard GDP. This approach can be labeled "corrected GDP" or "extended accounts."

The starting point by Nordhaus and Tobin was that the best option for approaching welfare was not GDP itself, which is basically a measure of economic activity, but rather one of its subcomponents, namely global household consumption. Restarting from there, corrections proposed by the two authors were made in two steps. The first step derived a Measure of Economic Welfare (MEW) by subtracting from total private consumption a number of components that do not contribute positively to welfare (such as the costs of commuting or legal services) and by adding monetary estimates of activities that do contribute to welfare (such as leisure or work at home). The second step was to convert the MEW in a "sustainable measure of economic welfare" (SMEW) that takes into account changes in total wealth. The relation between the MEW and the SMEW is akin to that between GNP and NNP in standard national accounts: the SMEW measures the level of MEW that is compatible with preserving the capital stock, given the definition of capital stock retained by the builders of the index.

To convert the MEW into the SMEW, an estimate of total public and private wealth was computed that included reproducible capital, nonreproducible capital (limited to land and net foreign assets), educational capital (based on the cumulated cost of years spent in education by people belonging to the labor force) and health capital, based on a method of permanent inventory with a depreciation rate of 20% per year.

Nordhaus and Tobin provided an evaluation of the SMEW for the United States over the 1929–1965 period, compared not to GDP but rather to gross *national* product (GNP) which, at that time, was the indicator privileged by National Accounts. Two major conclusions emerged. First, levels for the SMEW were significantly higher than those of GNP, due to the large positive contribution of leisure. Second, consistent messages were delivered by both GNP and the SMEW when considering the overall direction of socioeconomic progress, even if the magnitudes differed. Over the period considered, the growth rate for the SMEW was about two-thirds of total GNP growth.

Nordhaus and Tobin's conclusion was that, despite its limits, GNP growth remained a not-so-inadequate guide for policy. But they remained cautious to present their work as being no more than a point of departure. Some further initiatives took place during the 1980s, such as the Economic Aspect of Welfare index (EAW) proposed by Zolotas (1981). The issue was then reopened in the late 1980s by Cobb and Daly (1989), who proposed the index of sustainable welfare (ISEW), further refined by Cobb and Cobb (1994). The ISEW has much in common with the MEW or the SMEW but with two important additions: (*a*) an evaluation of natural resource depletion, measured as the investment necessary to generate a perpetual equivalent stream of renewable substitutes, and (*b*) the distribution of income. Nordhaus and Tobin had themselves acknowledged in their paper that the distributional issue was one of the dimensions missing from their index. On the other hand, the initial ISEW did not include any monetary evaluation of leisure time, perceived as being too fragile.

A very similar indicator has been proposed since 1995 by the nongovernmental organization Redefining Progress, the Genuine Progress Indicator (GPI) (see, for instance, Talberth, Cobb, and Slattery 2006). ISEW and GPI have been often presented as alternative names for the same index.[6]

Messages delivered by these indexes depart from the one that resulted from Nordhaus and Tobin's seminal paper. The levels of these indexes are lower than the MEW due to the exclusion of leisure time, and they are

6. Posner and Costanza (2011) provide a list of 25 applications of this ISEW/GPI methodology covering a total of 21 countries.

also lower than GDP due to the incorporation of natural resource depletion and of income distribution. The magnitude of the gap varies across countries: Bleys (2005) and Gadrey and Jany-Catrice (2006) show that the gap between the ISEW and GDP is much higher for the UK and the United States than for Sweden, essentially due to different levels of income inequality. Even more important, growth of the ISEW and the GPI is much less than that of GNP or even negative. This has led some authors to argue in favor of a so-called threshold hypothesis according to which GDP growth contributes to welfare only up to a certain level, beyond which GDP and welfare move in opposite directions (Max-Neef 1995).

Another couple of much more recent papers can also be related to the Nordhaus-Tobin tradition. Fleurbaey and Gaulier (2009)[7] and Jones and Klenow (2010) develop monetary approaches based on the notion of "equivalent income," the theoretical justification of which will be discussed at length in chapter 4. When individuals differ along nonincome dimensions, reference levels for these dimensions are chosen, and equivalent incomes (or consumptions) are computed, that is, the monetary amounts that, associated with reference conditions, would render people indifferent with their current position.[8] These amounts can be evaluated by different methods: marginal willingnesses to pay as revealed by market prices (e.g., using wages as a way to value leisure) or calibration of structural utility functions, as done, for instance, for the valuation of years of life.[9] Equivalent incomes or consumptions within each country are then aggregated in a way that takes inequality into account. Nonmonetary dimensions considered by Jones and Klenow are leisure and overall life expectancy, and their work applies to a set of 143 countries, with a quantification of changes recorded between 1980 and 2000. Fleurbaey and Gaulier cover only 24 OECD countries for year 2004 but include additional nonmonetary items such as life expectancy in good health, employment status (unemployment is supposed to represent a larger loss in well-being than the sole income loss) or the composition of households (a given income leads to higher well-being in larger households that benefit from economies of scale).

In both cases, correlation with GDP remains strong, but corrections made for leisure contribute to a large reduction of the gap between the

7. The French institute CEPII has recently published updated figures (Lettre du CEPII, n° 312, 2011).

8. In fact, the methodology adopted by Jones and Klenow (2010) produces rankings that are inconsistent with preferences due to the use of different references for different countries (see section 4.1).

9. On this latter point, both studies rely on earlier work by Becker, Philipson, and Soares (2005).

United States and European countries. Covering developed as well as developing countries, Jones and Klenow also observe that the relative situation of the latter is pushed downward due to their higher mortality level. Over time, increases in life expectancy account for a large share of the global growth of their well-being indicator.

An important difference between the equivalent income approach and the monetary indexes reviewed earlier in this section is that the former relies on an estimation of the population preferences over the various dimensions that affect well-being, whereas the latter rely only on market or imputed prices. This difference will play an important role in this book, and it motivates our treatment of the foundations of the various monetary approaches in two separate chapters (3 and 4). Incidentally, the main shortcoming of the equivalent income computations in Fleurbaey and Gaulier (2009) and Jones and Klenow (2010) is that they do not have sufficient data about individual preferences and therefore provide only illustrative prototypes of this methodology.

The monetary approaches involve complex imputations or estimations and therefore lack the simplicity and apparent transparency that has done so much for the success of the HDI. But we have seen that this transparency could prove illusory. There is therefore a strong case in favor of looking closely at more elaborate approaches of this kind, and this will indeed be an important focus of this book.

1.5 SUSTAINABILITY ASSESSMENT: WEAK OR STRONG?

Let us move to the more specific question of assessing sustainability. This sustainability dimension was already present in some of the indicators that we have mentioned. Such was already the case in Nordhaus and Tobin's proposal, since this proposal was twofold: an index of economic welfare (MEW), and an index of *sustainable* economic welfare (SMEW). Adopting such a dual approach was not for the simple sake of providing two numbers where one could have done the job. In Nordhaus and Tobin's conceptual framework, a clear distinction had to be drawn between measuring how well we currently live (MEW) and how well we can or could live in a way compatible with sustainability, that is, a standard of living susceptible of being reproduced by future generations (SMEW). There is no reason at all for the two indicators to coincide, and it is precisely the difference between these two indicators that matters for sustainability. Either the MEW is lower than the SMEW, in which case sustainability is warranted, or it is not. In the first case, we can even enjoy the consumption possibilities that are currently offered to us more intensively without condemning future generations to be less well-off than we would be. If the MEW is higher than the SMEW, this is the signal we are living above our means. This clearly illustrates that the SMEW, by nature, is not a sufficient sustainability statistic; it makes sense only by comparaison with the MEW.

This point has been unfortunately somewhat forgotten in subsequent attempts at the development of indexes. The quest for the ideal single number able to fully replace GDP has sometimes led to the favoring of SMEW-like indexes as useful summary measures of both current and future living conditions, without paying attention to the strong loss of information that such an aggregation implies (Neumayer 2000). This criticism applies to the ISEW/GPI indexes that were direct heirs of the SMEW. It applies as well to attempts at building "green GDPs". Greening GDP is often intuitively perceived as being the natural way of correcting the environmental limits of standard GDP, but, even if this correction were easy to perform—and such is not the case—the kind of message that such a correction sends us about sustainability is much more limited than often believed. Green GDPs would admittedly reorder somewhat the hierarchy of countries in terms of economic performance, with "dirty" ones downgraded by several places. But, in itself, observing that such or such country's green GDP is only 95% or 90% of its standard GDP does not send any message about whether this country's current standard of living can or cannot be maintained in the future.

This basic limit of green GDP helps explain why progress has been so slow on this aspect of green accounting. The point is not only that building green GDPs is demanding, it is also that the expected informational gain is not very evident. And this criticism can also be applied to some of the composite indexes that can be found on the market. The HDI is immune to such a criticism, as it clearly presents itself as an index of current economic achievement, with no prospective content. The last human development report (2011), whose main theme was sustainaibility, does not deviate from this. It clearly separates the two dimensions of measuring the HDI and assessing how far current HDIs are sustainable. This is indeed the right question to ask if you adhere to the choice of the HDI as an adequate index of current well-being. But "green HDIs" have nevertheless been proposed elsewhere (Desai 1994; Lasso de la Vega and Urrutia 2001; Costantini and Monni 2004), simply complementing the current HDI with emissions of some pollutants using the same rescaling and agregation technique described above. Clearly, messages sent by such indexes are not easy to analyze. For sure, a country with a high HDI that emits large amounts of pollutants will see once again its ranking decrease due to this addition, but will this drop adequately measure how far this country negatively contributes to the future well-being of mankind? Does the index send us a more exact message about which countries are "sustainable" and which are not? And the same kind of problem has been already mentioned concerning the Happy Planet Index: two countries having respectively a low life expectancy and a low footprint and a high value for both may end up classified in a similar way, while their positions clearly need to be differentiated.

On the whole, the issue of sustainability is therefore much better addressed by returning to Nordhaus and Tobin's original way of raising the problem: measuring how well we are or how much we consume is one thing, measuring whether this corresponds to overconsumption is another. This being posited, there are two ways to proceed. Either one follows Nordhaus and Tobin's choice of a (MEW, SMEW) combination, or, more directly, once a MEW-like indicator of current well-being has been chosen, we complement it with an indicator or with some indicators that directly inform about its sustainability, that is, the difference SMEW − MEW or any acceptable proxy (or proxies) of it.

What have been the attempts in this direction? In this category, some room can be made again for one composite index, the ESI (Environmental Sustainability Index) or the EPI (Environmental Performance Index) (Estes et al. 2005). The ESI aggregates 76 variables into 21 intermediate indicators, such as air and water quality, waste reduction, and greenhouse gas emissions. The EPI is a reduced form of ESI, based on 16 indicators (outcomes) and is more policy oriented. Now, such a compilation of information just allows ranking countries according to the efforts they make in favor of environmental sustainability, and, incidentally, this is done in disputable ways: the ESI and the EPI both have biases in favor of the "sustainability" of more advanced countries just because of the relative weight they give to institutions and policies that help promote environmental protection. Such institutions or policies matter, but they are not by themselves guarantees that these countries do less harm to the environment than other countries. Globally, neither the EPI nor the ESI really quantifies how far such and such country is from sustainability, even from the sole environmental viewpoint. As things stand, the pure question of sustainability is addressed by only two indicators, and with very contrasting results, Adjusted Net Savings (ANS) and the Ecological Footprint (EF).

Adjusted Net Savings is the name that we will use here for an indicator that, depending upon authors, has been also labeled "genuine savings" (Pearce, Hamilton, and Atkinson 1996; Hamilton and Clemens 1999) or "genuine investment" (Arrow et al. 2004). The ANS denomination is the one used by a World Bank team that started, in 2004, a program of systematic compilation of this concept for all countries, and it is this latter denomination that we shall use hereafter (World Bank 2011). Whatever the denomination, the principle is the same. It consists in computing an extended notion of national savings that combines net capital accumulation in the usual sense of the term with various kinds of dissavings such as consumption of nonrenewable fossil resources, degradations of the environment, compensated, on the positive side, by the accumulation of knowledge or human capital. This index can also be understood as the net variation of an encompassing concept of global or "inclusive" wealth combining all the different assets that matter for production and quality of life. This way of thinking about sustainability is often presented as the "capital-based approach to sustainability." Adjusted Net Savings can also be amended to incorporate consequences of purely exogenous technical progress or of population change. Technical progress can help sustain growth or well-being even when the global capital stock is declining. Concerning population change, the practice is to consider that sustainability requires maintaining inclusive wealth per capita, meaning that a positive population growth rate must be compensated for by larger savings (Arrow, Dasgupta, and Mäler 2003b).

Much more will be provided in chapter 2 concerning the analytical foundations and the limits of this indicator. At this stage, we shall just recall the main qualitative criticisms that have been addressed to this way of measuring sustainability (see, e.g., Dietz and Neumayer 2004). The main criticisms can be gathered under three headings.

- A first point is that merging variations of very different assets into a single monetary figure requires putting money values on each of them, that, a system of relative prices, and such prices are difficult to compute in an adequate way. In fact, as we have already argued concerning the implicit valuations hidden within the HDI, this problem will be shared by any form of aggregate sustainability indicator. But it is necessarily more striking for an index whose results are expressed in money units. How is it managed by builders of the index, and what are the problems raised by their way of doing it? For some assets, prices are directly observable on the market. But, even for these, we have no guarantee that these prices convey the right information on the long-term collective value of these assets. This is especially the case for the few environmental assets for which markets exist. Such markets are very probably working in very inefficient ways, due in particular to large externalities. And there are also many assets for which there are no markets at all, hence no observable price. Simply excluding these assets from the computation is of course unacceptable, but incorporating them requires relying on imputed prices, and the difficulty is knowing on which basis these imputed prices can be evaluated.

- The second difficulty is closely related to the first one. It corresponds to the weak/strong sustainability debate.[10] Taken literally, the additive nature of the ANS suggests that any level of natural capital depreciation can potentially be offset by a sufficiently high rate of physical or human capital accumulation. In other words, the index assumes that there always exists a possibility of substituting produced capital goods to natural ones, even when stocks for the latter become very low. Such a vision does not fit with the *strong* view of sustainability according to which minimal critical stocks of natural resources are necessary for the simple maintenance of human life, a fortiori for the maintenance of a certain level of well-being. Because it fails to incorporate this constraint, the ANS criterion is said to provide only a necessary condition for sustainability, not a sufficient one. It is in that sense that it is generally understood as a *weak* sustainability criterion. Here also, the problem is not specific to the fact of having adopted a monetary index, and chapter 2 will show that it is not insurmountable in theory. As soon as prices are imputed rather than observed in the market, it is always possible to greenwash the index more intensively by adopting very high prices for all those "green" assets whose stocks are supposed to be close to critical values that would make their preservation really crucial. But a central theme of chapter 2 will be the difficulty of doing so in indisputable ways.
- The third main difficulty appears when ANS estimates are compared across countries (see, e.g., Everett and Wilks 1999). The most striking result from the systematic computation of ANS indicators performed by the World Bank is that problems of unsustainability essentially arise in developing countries. Figure 1.3 indeed displays a positive association between the ANS expressed as a fraction of current GDP and the current level of GDP. Most of the countries with negative values for this ANS are countries with GDP levels lower than $10,000 per inhabitant in 2005. The typical case is a poor country that draws most of its income from the exploitation of an exhaustible natural resource. In such an economy, the only way to ensure long-run sustainability is to reinvest a sufficient share of this rent into other productive assets, the returns of which will progressively compensate for the decline of incomes provided by the

10. For a more complete view on this debate, see Neumayer (2004).

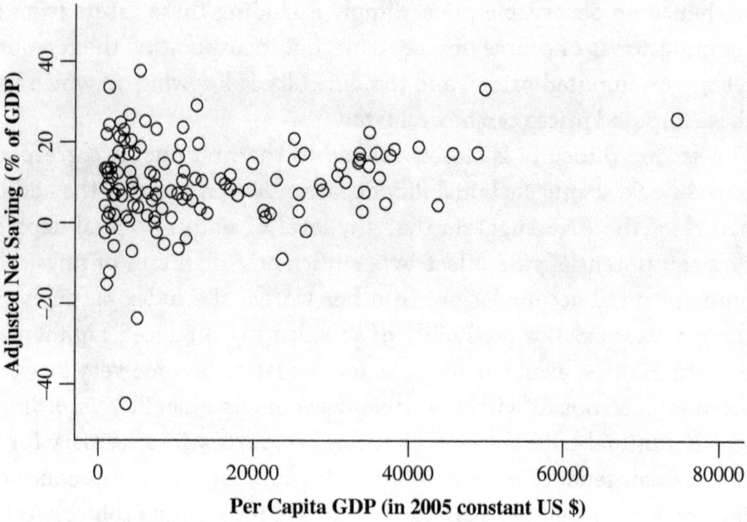

Figure 1.3
Adjusted Net Savings (2005–2099 values) and GDP (2007 values)
Source: World Bank (2011) and UNDP (2011).

vanishing natural resource. This is the so-called Hartwick rule for sustainability (Hartwick 1977). Unsustainable poor countries are countries that do not try or, more realistically, cannot afford to conform to this rule. Admittedly, there can be some elements of truth in the message that such countries are on unsustainable paths. At least until recently, economic growth indeed appeared more fragile or unstable in many less developed countries than in already developed ones. But, if we focus on environmental issues, the idea that there is no sustainability problem in developed countries is strongly at odds with the idea that they are the major contributors to environmental problems such as global warming.

All this explains why many have a marked preference for the completely opposite messages conveyed by the Ecological Footprint. The EF compares each country's direct or indirect pressure on natural resources either to its own resources or to the average of resources available per head at the worldwide level (Wackernagel and Rees 1995). This indicator is generally considered as being much more in line with the strong view of sustainability, that is, the idea that sustainability requires a separate preservation of all environmental assets, whatever the accumulation of other produced assets. It also conveys a message more in line with the idea that developed countries' modes of consumption bear a large responsibility in the degradation of the world ecosystem (Figure 1.4). It also shows how rapidly the situation

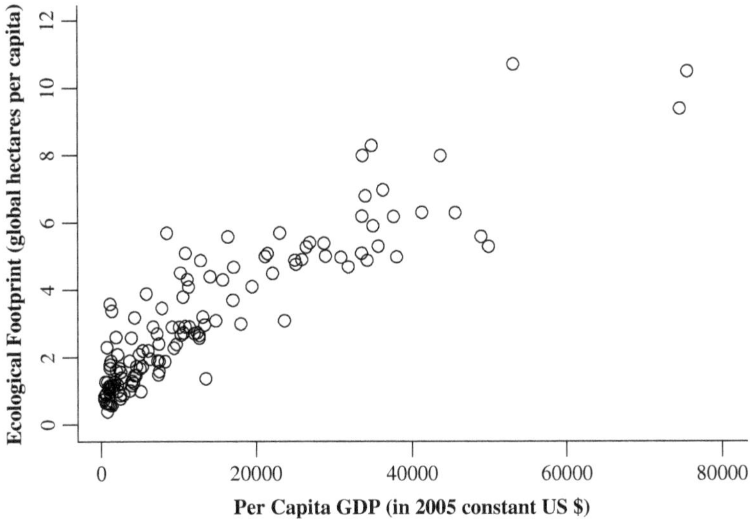

Figure 1.4
Ecological Footprint and GDP (2007 values)
Source: Global Footprint Network (2010) and UNDP (2011).

seems to have deteriorated over the last decades. At the worldwide level, a global footprint that still remained below the regenerating capacity of the ecosystem in the 1960s is now far over this capacity, a strong message of unsustainability indeed that does not show up with the ANS considered at the worldwide level.

But several criticisms have been also addressed to this indicator.[11] They can be classified under two headings, internal or external. Internal criticisms admit the general idea of the index but discuss the details of its implementation. It is beyond the scope of this chapter and of the whole volume to discuss these practical issues at length, but one must recall that, exactly as is done by monetary indicators, the Ecological Footprint needs some rules for weighting different forms of pressure on the environment. This is the inescapable price to pay for aggregation, and the fact of aggregating things in a unit that is not monetary —global hectares— changes the nature of the problem only in appareance, not in reality.

11. A forum had been devoted to the Ecological Footprint in volume 32 of *Ecological Economics*. Several other papers have been devoted to the index since then by the same journal and by other outlets. The interested reader can find a very extensive bibliography in Wiedmann and Barrett (2010), who also include a review of perceptions and policy uses of the footprint based on a questionnaire submitted to a panel of some 50 experts.

Without going into details, a few consequences of the accounting rules adopted by EF are worth emphasizing. First, in some respect, the index is less green than one could expect. For instance, it does not really incorporate the pressure on arable land due to excessively aggressive agricultural techniques. More precisely, since resources in arable land are postulated to be exactly equal to the arable land actually used by agriculture, weighted by its current average yield, this component of the footprint is mechanically balanced at the worldwide level. The only message delivered by the indicator on this aspect of sustainability is that very densely populated countries overconsume their arable land while sparse populations do not. Such a message is not necessarily interesting: it is not a sign of unsustainability per se that countries with different land endowments specialize in a way consistent with their endowments. This is all the more true at the intranational level: it is natural for a city to "consume" more land than the actual surface that it covers. It is only once everything is consolidated that a message of sustainability or unsustainability can be delivered, but, once again, this will unfortunately not be the case here due the convention of equalizing land resources to those that are actually used at the worldwide level.

Second, by focusing on renewable resources, it also ignores how sustainability is threatened by the consumption of fossil resources. For instance, in the EF, oil consumption raises a problem for sustainability only through its consequences on CO_2 emissions, valued according to the number of hectares of forest that would theoretically be needed to absorb these emissions. In fact, at the end of the day, it is essentially this factor that explains the explosion of the footprint over the last decades, other components of the index being, by contrast, surprisingly flat. This suggests isolating this important factor and then looking for better ways of capturing imbalances along the other dimensions. Indeed, over the last years, the concept of carbon footprint has started taking precedence over the initial EF indicator (Wiedmann and Minx 2008), and footprint-like approaches have started being developed for some other items not initially covered by the EF, such as the water footprint (Hoekstra 2009).

As far as external criticism is concerned, discomfort with this index points to its complete ignorance of possibilities offered by substitution with other factors of production—the weak/strong sustainability debate once again—or through technical progress. Critics argue that even if substitution possibilities between produced and nonproduced assets are not infinite, they are real, and that indicators that neglect them give an overly pessimistic view of future eco-environmental prospects. One can also point out that an indicator that focuses on natural resources is no more sufficient than the ANS for sustainability. For instance, an economy that has a very parsimonious use of its natural resources but that stops investing in physical capital or in education is on a path that is no more sustainable than an economy that does exactly the opposite. Indicators such as the EF miss this aspect of sustainability, because they only focus on the environmental dimension. It is precisely one of the attractive aspects of the ANS approach that it tries to combine both environmental and nonenvironmental dimensions of development.

In a nutshell, also considering the EPI/ESI,[12] sustainability is probably the domain where a consensus seems the most out of reach. The situation appears much more difficult than for current well-being. In this latter case, although alternatives to GDP can lead to significant corrections, they generally do not result in a complete reversal of the hierarchy of countries: the high correlation between GDP and the HDI shown by figure 1.2 is illustrative of that. When one turns to sustainability, one is confronted by two completely opposite paradigms. One might seek a way of picking up what seems to make sense on both sides. But subsuming the opposition under one single metaindicator looks problematic. The alternative strategy is to let the divergent indicators live their own lives, improving them whenever needed, but putting them on comparable levels, as incorporting two distinct and complementary views of sustainability that are not reducible to one another. It is then the responsibility of civil society or of policymakers to see how one can cope with these contradictory signals. This is precisely the philosophy of the last approach we need to examine, which consists in equipping users with multidimensional dashboards combining indicators of various sorts.

1.6 COPING WITH MULTIDIMENSIONALITY: DASHBOARDS

As already emphasized, the "dashboard" approach to measuring well-being or its sustainability has a long tradition that can be traced back to the social indicators movement of the 1960s. After the period of setback that followed the first oil shock, interest in this way of presenting statistics came into favor again during the 1990s, now with a stronger focus on environmental issues, and, as mentioned, international organizations have played a large role in this reemergence. The main outcome of the Rio summit in 1992 was the adoption of Agenda 21, whose fortieth chapter invited signatory countries to develop quantitative information on their

12. For a more detailed comparative analysis that simultaneously covers the ANS, the EF, and ESI/EPI, see Pillarisetti and van den Bergh (2010).

actions and realizations along the three "Bruntlandian" pillars of economic efficiency, social equity, and environmental sustainability. The direct result of this recommendation has been a work program launched in 1995 by the United Nations Commission on Sustainable Development (UNCSD), which first came out with a preliminary list of 134 indicators, later reduced to 58 indicators after some pilot-testing conducted between 1996 and 1999. The third revision of this list (UN Department of Economic and Social Affairs 2007) now includes about 50 core indicators completed by an equivalent number of "other" indicators.

Several parallel or related initiatives took place at some other international levels. The OECD, again, has been active in the field by continuing the publication of the list of social indicators it started to publish in the 1970s and by developing a new set of key environmental indicators whose publication started in 2001. At the European level, the European Council adopted its own strategy for sustainable development in 2001, later revised in 2006, leading to still another Dashboard of Sustainable Development, with 11 key indicators and a complete list of about 100 indicators. National actions have followed or preceded this general movement, albeit in a somewhat scattered way. A review made for Eurostat in 2004 among members of the European Union showed large variations across countries at this time: between 14 and 218 indicators for the broadest versions of their country-specific dashboards, and between 14 and 25 for their narrower versions focusing on headline indicators —when such versions existed.

To illustrate what dashboards are and to help discuss their pros and cons, table 1.1 fully reproduces the contents of the UNCSD dashboard, in its 2007 version. What are the merits of this methodology? First, under the presentation adopted in the UNCSD dashboard, messages from GDP, while not hidden, are very clearly relegated to a nonprominent place. Second, from the point of view of statisticians, dashboards are a good way to advertise the many facets of their production, without the problematic step of trying to summarize this information in the form of composite indexes. This does not mean that aggregation is fully ruled out, but it is left to final users. Official statisticians prefer not to be in charge of saying by how much income must be weighted against additional years of life or other nonmonetary aspects of well-being. This is supposed to be a matter of personal values, not of scientific judgment. As mentioned above, the possibility of testing different weighting factors has been already proposed by Osberg and Sharpe (2002). Modern communication tools allow doing this in a much more systematic way, with clients of statistical websites being able to perform their own online aggregations and vizualise their results in various forms. We have seen that it is the strategy followed by OECD with

Table 1.1. AN ILLUSTRATIVE DASHBOARD: THE UNCSD INDICATORS OF SUSTAINABLE DEVELOPMENT, THIRD REVISION

Theme	Subtheme	Core indicator	Other indicator
Poverty	Income poverty	Proportion of population living below national poverty line	Proportion of population below $1 a day
	Income inequality	Ratio of share in national income of highest to lowest quintile	
	Sanitation	Proportion of population using an improved sanitation facility	
	Drinking water	Proportion of population using an improved water source	
	Access to energy	Share of households without electricity or other modern energy services	Percentage of population using solid fuels for cooking
	Living conditions	Proportion of urban population living in slums	
Governance	Corruption	Percentage of population having paid bribes	
	Crime	Number of intentional homicides per 100,000 population	
Health	Mortality	Under-five mortality rate	
		Life expectancy at birth	Healthy life expectancy at birth
	Health care delivery	Percentage of population with access to primary health care facilities	Contraceptive prevalence rate
		Immunization against infectious childhood diseases	
	Nutritional status	Nutritional status of children	
	Health status and risks	Morbidity of major diseases such as HIV/AIDS, malaria, tuberculosis	Prevalence of tobacco use
			Suicide rate
Education	Education level	Gross intake ratio to last grade of primary education	Lifelong learning
		Net enrolment rate in primary education	
		Adult secondary (tertiary) schooling attainment level	
	Literacy	Adult literacy rate	

Continued

Table 1.1. (continued)

Theme	Subtheme	Core indicator	Other indicator
Demographics	Population	Population growth rate	Total fertility rate
		Dependency ratio	
	Tourism		Ratio of local residents to tourists in major tourist regions and destinations
Natural hazards	Vulnerability to natural hazards	Percentage of population living in hazard prone areas	
	Disaster preparedness and response	Human and economic loss due to natural disasters	
Atmosphere	Climate change	Carbon dioxide emissions	Emissions of greenhouse gases
	Ozone layer depletion	Consumption of ozone depleting substances	
	Air quality	Ambient concentration of air pollutants in urban areas	
Land	Land use and status		Land use change
			Land degradation
	Desertification		Land affected by desertification
	Agriculture	Arable and permanent cropland area	Fertilizer use efficiency
			Use of agricultural pesticides
			Area under organic farming
	Forests	Proportion of land area covered by forests	Percentage of forest trees damaged by defoliation
			Area of forest under sustainable forest management
	Coastal zone	Percentage of total population living in coastal areas	Bathing water quality

Source: United Nations 2007

Table 1.1. (continued)

Theme	Subtheme	Core indicator	Other indicator
Oceans, seas, and coasts	Fisheries	Proportion of fish stocks within safe biological limits	
	Marine environment	Proportion of marine area protected	Marine trophic index
		Area of coral reef ecosystems and percentage live cover	
Freshwater	Water quantity	Proportion of total water resources used	
		Water use intensity by economic activity	
	Water quality	Presence of faecal coliforms in freshwater	Biochemical oxygen demand in water bodies
			Wastewater treatment
Biodiversity	Ecosystem	Proportion of terrestrial area protected, total and by ecological region	Management effectiveness of protected areas
			Area of selected key ecosystems
			Fragmentation of habitats
	Species	Change in threat status of species	Abundance of selected key species
			Abundance of invasive alien species
Economic development	Macroeconomic performance	Gross domestic product per capita	Gross saving
		Investment share in GDP	Adjusted Net Savings as percentage of gross national income (GNI)
			Inflation rate
	Sustainable public finance	Debt to GNI ratio	
	Employment	Employment-population ratio	Vulnerable employment
		Labor productivity and unit labor costs	
		Share of women in wage employment in the nonagricultural sector	

Continued

Table 1.1. (continued)

Theme	Subtheme	Core indicator	Other indicator
	Information and communication technologies	Internet users per 100 population	Fixed telephone lines per 100 population
			Mobile cellular telephone subscribers per 100 population
	Research and development		Gross domestic expenditure on R&D as a percentage of GDP
	Tourism	Tourism contribution to GDP	
Global economic partnership	Trade	Current account deficit as percentage of GDP	Share of imports from developing countries and from LDCs
			Average tariff barriers imposed on exports from developing countries and LDCs
	External financing	Net Official Development Assistance (ODA) given or received as a percentage of GNI	Foreign direct investment (FDI) net inflows and net outflows as percentage of GDP
			Remittances as percentage of GNI
Consumption and production patterns	Material consumption	Material intensity of the economy	Domestic material consumption
	Energy use	Annual energy consumption, total and by main user category	Share of renewable energy sources in total energy use
		Intensity of energy use, total and by economic activity	
	Waste generation and management	Generation of hazardous waste	Generation of waste
		Waste treatment and disposal	Management of radioactive waste
	Transportation	Modal split of passenger transportation	Modal split of freight transport
			Energy intensity of transport

its Your Better Life Index. This is part of a more general communication strategy developed by statistical (national or international) organizations to reconqueer the confidence of citizens after years of progressive deterioration due to the increasing gap between official statistics and individual perceptions of socioeconomic change.

Furthermore, beyond being a convenient way to promote existing statistics, dashboards are also one way to help develop new ones. Trying to implement a comprehensive dashboard of socioeconomic development helps in identifying gaps in statistical production, or needs for improved international harmonization of statistics. Dashboards also have the advantage of being relatively easy to tailor to the needs of policymakers or to the requests of representatives of civil society: their development can be participatory, especially for dashboards developed at a local level.

But the main drawback of dashboards comes from their richness. The natural criticism of these dashboards is their very hybrid character and the fact that their composition often looks arbitrary. One can also be worried about the lack or harmonization of dashboards, the frequent changes that occur in their compositions, or the fact that they deliver too much information to be efficient communication tools, even when their main messages are summed up in a limited set of headline indicators.

1.7 THE CORE QUESTION: HOW FAR CAN AGGREGATION GO?

What lessons can be retained from this introductory chapter? As announced in its preamble, we have the confirmation that the problem with challenging GDP is not the lack of competitors nor the fact that this research field has been left abandoned for decades — quite the opposite. Initiatives have mushroomed after the stream of "social indicators" and Nordhaus and Tobin's seminal work in the 1960–1970s. Initatives have emerged from various horizons, carried through or sponsored by academics, international organizations, and various nongovernmental organizations. The resulting landscape is quite intricate and heterogeneous, still evolving, and we did not in this chapter pretend to offer a thorough visit to all its recesses. The aim was mainly to provide an illustrated taxonomy of its main elements.

Hopefully, this has been enough to reveal the problems that are at stake. The major one is to find an acceptable compromise in terms of aggregation. At one extreme, extensive dashboards allow full pictures of the performance of countries in many respects. They are useful, but their choice of avoiding any loss of information is both their strength and their limit.

The impossibility of deriving any clear synthetic message from such large dashboards explains the recurrent tendency to go back to the much simpler messages provided by GDP. If the situation remains that of having GDP on one side, and plethoric dashboards on the other, it is likely that the former's preeminence will remain durably uncontested. Single numbers have a natural power of attraction against which excessively rich sets of detailed figures cannot compete.

Is there conversely some scope for arranging the heterogeneous information of existing dashboards in a way that could provide a better challenger to GDP? What has been said on limits of composite indicators casts some doubts about the relevance of this track. It is therefore likely that the optimal solution lies somewhere in between, with an intermediate level of aggregation that will preserve complementary points of views on items that are the most difficult to reduce to one another. But this requires two things: a clear view of what are the few dimensions of well-being and its durability that deserve separate measures, and, since aggregation will remain necessary within each of these dimensions, what rules can be followed to have it done as appropriately as possible. Can aggregation still be done in monetary units, as Nordhaus and Tobin proposed, or would other metrics be more appropriate? These questions will provide the main thread for all subsequent chapters, starting with the domain that is perhaps the most contentious, sustainability.

CHAPTER 2

Measuring Sustainability

2.1 INTRODUCTION

Most of this book is about improving measures of *current* well-being. Yet chapter 1 showed that a large share of the literature on alternatives or complements to GDP is also concerned with the *sustainability* issue or, more generally, with *intertemporal* aspects of well-being. The present chapter is the only one we shall devote to these questions, but this is compensated for by our choice of putting it early in our argumentation. Three main reasons explain this choice.

The first one is the intrinsic importance of the topic. It would be of low interest to promote a better monitoring of current well-being if this was fully at the expense of the well-being of future generations. This interplay between current development or current well-being and sustainability was at the heart of the Bruntland report by the end of the 1980s (Bruntland 1987), and it still remains one of its most popular messages. Much closer to us, it has been the general theme of a recent Human Development Report (UNDP 2011), the idea being to explore trade-offs and synergies between the maximization of current HDIs and long-run prospects, especially in the environmental dimension. GDP has been repeatedly blamed for being blind to all these matters; therefore alternatives to it must address this sustainability dimension. It is important not to treat it as subsidiary.

The second reason for an early examination is one of clarification. A central idea of this chapter is that, because of its importance and its specificities, the measurement of sustainability has to be done separately from the measurement of current well-being. This might seem to go without saying, yet it has not always been the position adopted by the literature. Several proposals proceed as if the proper challenger of GDP has to be an index of *sustainable well-being*, hence mixing in a single figure the two ideas of measuring well-being and its sustainability. Reasons for not following this route must be exposed before proceeding any further.

The third reason is that this issue of sustainability allows a first look at a question that will occupy a large share of this volume, the opposition between monetary and nonmonetary approaches to well-being. In fact, chapter 1 showed that this issue combined with the previous one provides a way to classify alternatives to GDP along two axes. The first axis opposes those indicators that try to measure well-being and its sustainability at the same time and those that clearly separate these dimensions—as advocated here. The second axis contrasts indicators whose results are expressed in monetary equivalents and indicators relying on other metrics. This double classification leads to four classes, and none of them is empty.

Within the first class, the seminal example of a comprehensive monetary index of well-being incorporating a sustainability dimension was Nordhaus and Tobin's "sustainable measure of economic welfare" (SMEW). Green GDPs also belong to this category. Still monetary, but exclusively focused on sustainability, hence belonging to the second class, were the concepts of "Genuine Savings" and "Adjusted Net Savings." Next, the very popular notion of ecological footprint has been described as representative of a nonmonetary approach of the third class that exclusively sends messages about sustainability, and not at all about current well-being. According to this footprint indicator, best-performing countries are often very poor ones that one would hardly identify as success stories in terms of current well-being. But several other composite indicators tend to reaggregate these two notions of current well-being and sustainability.

Beyond or besides all this, dashboards of sustainable development that have flourished since the early 1990s under the "Agenda 21" program, by nature, mix all these ways to look at the problem, as they generally combine monetary and nonmonetary components and components devoted either to development—that is, current well-being and its short-term trends—or to its long-run sustainability.

This opposition between monetary and nonmonetary indicators is often assimilated to the one between weak and strong views of sustainability. Let us focus on the two indicators clearly dedicated to sustainability *stricto sensu*, Adjusted Net Savings and the Ecological Footprint. We have already seen how different the messages delivered by these two indicators are. This is confirmed again by figure 2.1. The correlation that is depicted is between the ANS and the concept of ecological surplus rather than the Ecological

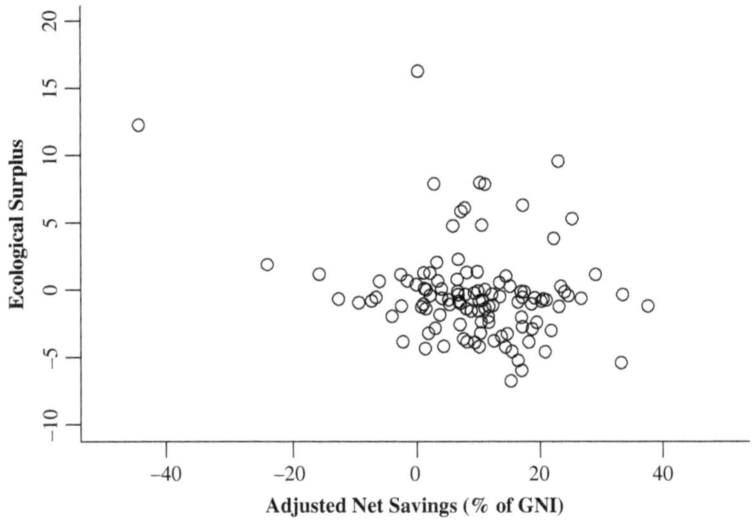

Figure 2.1
Divergent messages from two sustainability indicators
Reading: Adjusted Net Savings is the generalized notion of savings including depreciation of natural resources and the net accumulation of human capital: all these items are expressed in monetary units, and the result is expressed in % of gross national income (GNI). The ecological surplus is the difference between each country's average bio-capacity and its consumption of renewable resources. It is expressed in "global hectares per capita". A negative value means that a country consumes more than its endowment.
Source: Values for both indexes are taken from the 2011 human development report (UNDP, 2011).

Footprint, in order to have two indexes expected to move in the same way. Yet the correlation, if any, appears to be rather negative: countries presented as sustainable by one of the indicators are often on nonsustainable paths from the point of view of the other. This is often taken as a typical illustration of the weak/strong sustainability controversy, with the monetary ANS showing excessive optimism about the possibility of replacing depleting natural resources by physical or human capital, and the footprint representing the opposite bias, fully ignoring opportunities offered by technical progress. The possibilities of overcoming this opposition will be the other major topic of this chapter.

More precisely, the organization of the chapter will be the following. We shall first discuss the shortcomings of approaches in terms of either intertemporal or sustainable well-being. We shall start with the way the intertemporal dimension of well-being comes up in the assessment of *individual* well-being, how it suggests measuring well-being in terms of global wealth and how concepts of sustainable consumption or well-being derive from this idea. Notions such as net domestic product (NDP) or green GDP are economy-wide counterparts of these concepts, and we shall examine why such an approach raises more problems than expected, arguing definitely in favor of measuring sustainability separately.

Then, we shall focus on the second divide, that is, between monetary and nonmonetary approaches, but not without some rephrasing. Manichaean objections to the monetary approach will have to be left aside. Opposing "monetary" evaluation is legitimate when this term is a synonym for naive trust in all price signals sent by markets. But monetary evaluation does not reduce to this. Once we escape this narrow view, monetization just becomes a conventional way of expressing the relative weights we give to components of sustainability. This is not at all to say that the choice of units is fully indifferent. Some units tell more to the user, depending on the question at stake, and one reason for the success of the Ecological Footprint is to have adopted a metric often perceived as better suited for measuring pressure on the earth's resources. Yet the fundamental problem comes ahead of this issue. Before choosing an aggregation unit, one needs to know to what extent aggregation itself is possible, given the great variety of factors that shape long-run socioeconomic and environmental perspectives.

It is on this point that a large part of our discussion will focus, and the conclusion will be ambivalent. On the positive side, we shall explore approaches that have the potential advantage of subsuming the weak/strong opposition. This confirms that monetary approaches are not by construction unable to capture the strong view of sustainability. We shall even exhibit an example in which some applications of this monetary approach may deliver messages that, in some sense, appear *too* strong. On the negative side, the conclusion will emphasize the very theoretical nature of all that can be proposed for fully adequate sustainability indexes. These theoretical developments are thus readable in two ways: either as showing the lines along which the quest for a universal sustainability indicator could go, or as the proof that this quest is akin to that of the holy grail, and that we'd better reorient ourselves toward more pragmatic second-best solutions, theory having the more modest role of helping in the design of these.

Two last points must be made before starting. First, this chapter can be viewed at best as an introduction to the sustainability literature, which is huge and often very technical. We did not attempt to be fully comprehensive in our assessment of this literature. The reader interested in further details will strongly benefit from much more comprehensive surveys, such as Pezzey and Toman (2003),[1] Heal and Kriström (2005), and Asheim (2007).

Second, the issue of sustainability is often assimilated to the question of "greening" macroeconomic indicators. There is indeed a large overlap

1. A related volume by the two same authors also gathers some of the most important pre-2000 papers published on this issue (Pezzey and Toman 2002).

between these two topics, and environmental illustrations are going to be used throughout this chapter. Yet neither of these two questions strictly reduces to the other. Greening economic indicators is already a necessity from the point of view of *current* well-being, when it is affected by environmental features that are not captured in usual aggregates. This question is implicitly or explicitly covered in other chapters of this volume. Conversely, assessing sustainability involves many facets that are not environmental but are fundamental for the longevity of our living standards: replacement or accumulation of productive capital (human or nonhuman, tangible or intangible capital) and the evolution of factors such as institutions. In this chapter, we concentrate on this general issue of sustainability, in this broad acceptation that encompasses both environmental and nonenvironmental dimensions.

2.2 WEALTH AND SUSTAINABLE WELL-BEING

2.2.1 Discounting future streams of well-being?

Measuring sustainability is one way to introduce long-term economic prospects into our assessment of socioeconomic well-being. It is not the only one, and some other ways to address the question have played a role in designing some of the indicators briefly recalled in the introduction of this chapter. Our first task is to discuss how these approaches relate to one another.

The question can be introduced by analogy with the way the time dimension arises in the assessment of individual well-being. For a given individual, there are obvious reasons for pushing measures of well-being beyond the current period. Consider two individuals of the same age, enjoying the same satisfaction for the current period, but with individual i facing poor prospects for the rest of his life, while individual j knows in advance that he will benefit from expanding opportunities, for instance because he is at the onset of a career in a category of jobs offering high returns to experience.

There are obvious reasons for incorporating such information in measures of well-being applied to these two individuals. A standard way of evaluating the prospective intertemporal well-being of an individual observed at time t is the discounted sum of his future utilities, that is, in the tradition of Yaari (1965):

$$v(t) = \int_t^{\infty} u(c(\tau))s(\tau|t)e^{-\lambda(\tau-t)}d\tau. \tag{2.1}$$

In this expression, $s(\tau|t)$ is the probability of surviving until time τ given that one is alive at t (expected to become zero past a certain time horizon), $c(\tau)$ is the vector of consumption flows or other sources of utility or disutility at time τ, $u(.)$ is the resulting level of instantaneous well-being, and λ is a subjective discount factor. Lowercase letters are used to emphasize the fact that, at this stage, we are considering individuals rather than collectivities. This is not the only way to aggregate future utilities and to account for individual lifetime uncertainty—see Bommier (2006) for an alternative view—but entering this debate is not essential for our purpose.

Another question, if we compare the well-being of persons of different ages, is how to correct for the fact that these people are expecting different amounts of remaining years of lives, and of lives that may be of different qualities. Without any such correction, the prospective well-being of people of older ages would appear mechanically lower, unless we incorporate in our valuations of these people's lives some account of what they have also achieved in the past. An intertemporal utility function that is basically designed to model how individuals plan the rest of their lives is only half-suited for a proper valuation of their whole existences. But let us also keep aside this second difficulty.

Even then, in practice, one seldom estimates (2.1) as it stands, and statistical evaluations tend to use a related concept of monetary wealth. To be exhaustive, this concept of wealth should include not only current assets $k(t)$ but also the discounted flow of future net incomes $y(t)$, with a discount factor that is now an interest rate r, that is, a technical transformation rate between consumptions at different periods:

$$w(t) = k(t) + \int_t^{\infty} y(\tau)s(\tau|t)e^{-r(\tau-t)}d\tau = \int_t^{\infty} c(\tau)s(\tau|t)e^{-r(\tau-t)}d\tau. \quad (2.2)$$

The justification of this way of proxying welfare is the positive link that will exist between $w(t)$ and $v(t)$ under the assumption of a fixed r. The question here is to know how to translate such concepts for a collectivity. Formally, lowercase letters are replaced by uppercase letters, and the typical intertemporal function of social welfare takes the form

$$V(t) = \int_t^{\infty} U(C(\tau))e^{-\mu(\tau-t)}d\tau, \quad (2.3)$$

while a concept of global wealth represents the global intertemporal budget constraint of the economy:

$$W(t) = K(t) + \int_t^{\infty} Y(\tau)e^{-r(\tau-t)}d\tau = \int_t^{\infty} C(\tau)e^{-r(\tau-t)}d\tau. \quad (2.4)$$

A recent applied example of this way of considering long-term well-being is the Stern review on climate change (Stern 2007), where the consequences of global warming and of policies aiming at its prevention were assessed with an indicator that is a hybrid between (2.3) and (2.4). A lively debate has followed over the pertinent choice of the discount factor μ, Stern having been criticized for a choice giving excessive weight to the very distant future. As will be made clear later, this rate of time preference plays a role in sustainability indexes that is a bit different from the one it has played in this debate, but given the recurrence of this debate, a short reminder of what is at stake is necessary here.

First, it was of course not unintentional that, moving from (2.1) to (2.3), we changed notations, replacing the individual discount factor λ by a collective discount factor μ. The reason is that there are no arguments in favor of adopting similar values in the two contexts. At the individual level, λ is introduced to acccount for the short-sightedness attested in people's behavior. In fact, already at this individual level, it is debatable whether we should take this impatience into consideration when assessing welfare. If we consider again two individuals i and j with the same instantaneous utility functions $u(.)$ but such that $\lambda_i \gg \lambda_j$, it is not obvious that we must consider individual i as less well-off just because of his higher degree of time impatience. It is also debated whether time preference reflects myopia and justifies paternalistic evaluations of individual well-being by public agencies.

This moral objection to discounting is all the more valid at the collective level. There are definitely no reasons to use a characteristic of individual psychology as a benchmark for weighting levels of welfare across cohorts. Many authors, going back to Ramsey (1928), have argued that the only acceptable value at the collective level should be $\mu = 0$, if we want to respect interpersonal and intergenerational impartiality. In fact, the basic motive for not doing so and keeping a positive μ in equation (2.3) is practical: it is to avoid nonconvergence of infinite integrals.

One traditional rationalization of $\mu > 0$ is that it accounts for a risk of extinction of mankind: we must weight future generations according to the probability that they will exist or not (Dasgupta and Heal 1974). If we follow this tradition, we see that $e^{-\mu(\tau-t)}$, rather than being the counterpart of $e^{-\lambda(\tau-t)}$ in (2.1), is rather to be considered as the equivalent of the survival function $s(\tau|t)$, just shifting from individual survival to the global survival of mankind. Yet, as in (2.1), this is not necessarily the only way to take into account this nonzero risk of extinction (Bommier and Zuber 2008), and, second, it is difficult to rely on this argument for attributing a precise value to μ.

A second point is that the pure rate of time preference of equation (2.3) must be distinguished from the social discount rate of equation (2.4). This is true in the short run when we approximate r by the market interest rate, which has no reason to exactly reflect μ. And this remains true in the long run, when market references are no longer available, and r must be imputed. Two important additional parameters of the social discount rate are the expected general rate of growth for the economy and the degree of preference for intergenerational equity. High expected growth can provide a justification for less effort in favor of future generations even if one is equally concerned about their well-being. This will be the case if we trust that unabated general economic progress will make them, on the whole, much better off than we are. From that point, there are various possibilities to complicate the picture: for instance, the introdution of risk aversion, if the continuation of economic progress is increasingly uncertain as we move away from the present (Weitzman 2001; Gollier 2012), or the fact that discount factors to be applied to various policy issues may be heterogenous: if such and such environmental resource is expected to become increasingly scarce in the future and, for this reason, becomes highly constraining for the well-being of our descendants, decisions that affect the future path of this resource cannot be based on the same relative valuation of the future as the decision of building a new factory or investing in some other kind of basic public infrastructure. Such an argument has been used in defense of actualization choices made in the Stern review (Sterner and Persson 2008; see also Guesnerie 2005).

The question of relative prices will find a strong echo when we examine later the dynamics of accounting prices to be used for weighting sustainability components against each other. And the uncertain character of future economic growth reminds us that, as soon as it is the future that we want to quantify, uncertainty cannot be ignored. Ideally, it is not indexes that we should produce, but distributions of probabilities for these indexes, or indexes with a probabilistic interpretation—something clearly at odds with standard statistical production.

Yet, at this stage, a more basic point is enough for skepticism about the feasibility and relevance of statistical indicators in the spirit of (2.3) and (2.4). Their usefulness for theoretical work is not questionable. And it is also relevant to try to use them for cost-benefit analysis of current policies, as attempted by the Stern review for global warming prevention. But the question here is different. Our aim is to enlarge the set of regular statistical indicators to overcome their limitations. This commands indicators that can be implemented on a regular basis and that speak to users. Discounted social well-being is a concept that is clearly off these marks. If we want to assess prospective well-being according to (2.3), what is required is much more than incorporating the projected costs of a phenomenon like global warning in otherwise mechanical projections of GDP growth; we need to build a full projection of social well-being incorporating all the facets of this well-being and its determinants. According to Samuelson's (1961) wording, this involves putting a considerable amount of "futurity" in our evaluation of well-being that will make it both difficult to interpret and probably not very credible.

One can read a large part of the subsequent literature as successive attempts to overcome this problem, with indexes still oriented toward the measurement of the future, but in a way that is more commensurable with statistics pertaining to the current socioeconomic situation, and avoiding reliance on the kind of long-term projections that are required to properly fill the requirements of (2.3) and (2.4). Our recurrent question will be whether these attempts have been successful—our recurrent answer will be that they have not.

2.2.2 From intertemporal well-being to sustainable consumption

Let us first address the problem of the lack of commensurability. Some users of statistics are fond of those that can come out in impressively huge numbers, and such would be the case with sums of prospective levels of income or well-being. But figures are much more understandable when they are comparable with quantities we are used to manipulating in our day-to-day lives, such as yearly individual incomes, savings ratios, and so on. There is actually one way to rescale the amounts given by (2.3) and (2.4), which is to convert them into equivalent permanent flows of well-being and income, that is, the constant levels of these variables that provide exactly the same discounted sum. Their expressions are respectively

$$\bar{U} = \mu \int_t^\infty U(C(\tau))e^{-\mu(\tau-t)}d\tau \tag{2.5}$$

and

$$\bar{C} = r\int_t^\infty C(\tau)e^{-r(\tau-t)}d\tau = r\left[K(t) + \int_t^\infty Y(\tau)e^{-r(\tau-t)}d\tau\right]. \tag{2.6}$$

The latter concept can be interpreted as sustainable consumption, that is, the maximal level of immediate consumption that can be forever perpetuated without violating the intertemporal budget constraint combining current assets and the flow of future incomes. At first sight, (2.5) or (2.6) only solve our problem of rescaling but without offering any solution to our "futurity" problem, to name it as Samuelson did. Evaluations still require full projections of either $C(\tau)$ or $Y(\tau)$, even in the more elementary case of $\bar{C}$.

But what makes or has made the attractiveness of the constant-equivalent concept is that, at least in some cases, it can be reexpressed in terms that do not seem to request more than data obtainable from current observations. In fact, under such conditions, $\bar{C}$ can be equated with concepts already available in standard national accounts, such as net domestic product (NDP), from which the concept of green GDP mentioned in the introduction to our chapter is a kind of generalization.

This point was made by Weitzman (1976), whose contribution can be read from two symmetric points of view: either as providing a way to evaluate (2.6), or as providing national accountants with a justification for NDP computations. Why such a justification is welcome is worth emphasizing. As is the case for GDP, NDP is a hybrid concept that adds up something that directly contributes to current well-being, that is, consumption, and something that does not, that is, savings. It seems to do it more correctly than GDP because it subtracts from output the share of capital that disappears every year, but adding up consumption and net savings still looks like adding up apples and oranges.

To be more precise, such an addition makes sense from the point of view of measuring economic activity: what is consumed and what is saved are both outputs of current economic activity, and it is legitimate to add them up if it is total activity that we want to measure. But, in that case, there is no rationale for deducing capital depletion: the energy we devote to replacing depleted capital is also a form of economic activity, it generates employment and incomes that will be reinjected in the economy, and it has to be counted as such. Hence NDP is a concept that looks less natural than expected.

The way to rehabilitate NDP from the well-being perspective is to consider that savings, while not contributing to current well-being, constitute our current contribution to future well-being, precisely the kind of things we want to include in our intertemporal approach. If so, it is clearly net savings that matter: capital destruction has to be counted negatively because, contrary to savings, it has a negative impact on well-being prospects.

This identity between NDP and sustainable consumption is completely trivial in the case of a single all-purpose good that is used for both consumption and investment. In that case, with δ the depreciation rate for capital, consuming $Y - \delta K$ at time t ensures that the capital stock will be unchanged at the start of period $t + dt$, warranting an indefinite replication of the process. This exactly responds to the definition of Hicksian income, as "the maximum value [an individual] can consume during a week, and still expect to be as well off at the end of the week as he was at the beginning" (Hicks 1946, p. 174).

The contribution by Weitzman goes one point further, retaining the scalar representation for consumption $C(t)$, allowing for a multiplicity of capital goods, yet restricting attention to the case of an optimizing economy—which is going to be a strong limitation. Let the stocks of capital goods be denoted $K_k(t)$, $k = 1, \ldots, m$, possibly including stocks for various forms of natural capital. The law of motion for these capital goods is

$$\dot{K}_k(t) = g_k(K(t), C(t)), \tag{2.7}$$

meaning that changes in capital stocks in an elementary time period depend on initial values for stocks of all these capital goods (the vector $K(t)$) and the current consumption behavior.

We then consider that the economy works as if it was maximizing the utility function (2.3). Let $\pi_k(t)$ denote the costate variable associated with the flow equation (2.7). The optimization problem admits the Hamiltonian

$$H(\tau) = U(C(\tau))e^{-\mu(\tau-t)} - \sum_k \pi_k(\tau)g_k((K(\tau), C(\tau)),$$

and the optimal path, in addition to (2.7), must satisfy $\partial H/\partial C = 0$ and $\dot{\pi}_k = -\partial H/\partial K_k$.

Let us then call $V^*(t)$ the optimal value that is so attained for $V(t)$, which is a function of initial capital endowments $K(t)$. From standard results we know that

$$\partial V^*(t)/\partial K_k = \pi_k.$$

This corresponds to the usual interpretation of costate variables: they measure the social intertemporal benefit of additional units of each of the m capital goods at time t, that is, their current values or prices in an efficient competitive economy. This directly leads to

$$\dot{V}^*(t) = \sum_k \pi_k(t)\dot{K}_k(t). \tag{2.8}$$

But along an optimal path that is time-consistent, this variation of V^* over time can also be computed by differentiating (2.3) with respect to t, which yields

$$\dot{V}^*(t) = -U(C(t)) + \mu \int_t^\infty U(C(\tau))e^{-\mu(\tau-t)}d\tau = -U(C(t)) + \mu V^*(t). \tag{2.9}$$

Hence, combining (2.5), (2.8), and (2.9),

$$\bar{U} = \mu V^*(t) = U(C(t)) + \sum_k \pi_k(t)\dot{K}_k(t), \tag{2.10}$$

which shows that we have an identity between three concepts:

- A level of permanent utility $\bar{U}$ that would provide exactly the same amount of global utility as the path expected to be followed by the economy.
- A "return" at rate μ on the $V^*(t)$ indicator if we reintrepret it as the inclusive wealth of this economy, in the usual interpretation of wealth as the future flow of benefits to be derived from initial endowments.
- A quantity close to the concept of net domestic product—a valuation of current consumption plus net changes in capital endowments valued at current optimizing prices. The identity with NDP is even exact if we assimilate $U(C(t))$ with $C(t)$.

At first sight, this allows a simultaneous satisfaction of the two requisites expressed at the end of subsection 2.1.2. First it solves the problem that we had with the order of magnitude of $V(t)$: global utility discounted until the end of times is now scaled down to something comparable to current well-being. Second, we are apparently able to do so without having to compute the full sequence of future utility levels, since this indicator can be computed on the sole basis of current observations: current consumption $C(t)$, current changes in stocks of all the different kinds of capital goods $\dot{K}_k(t)$, and current coefficients $\pi_k(t)$ for the valuation of these changes.

But how far does this solution really go? Three questions can be raised. Is this NDP? Does it tell us whether our current mode of living is sustainable or not? Does it at least tell us what level of consumption would be sustainable? Unfortunately, answers to these three questions will all prove negative. Let us look at each of them in turn.

The first one is the easiest to answer. Potential differences with NDP as computed by national accountants have probably been obvious to the reader as the demonstration proceeded. The identification requires an assimilation of global monetary consumption with current well-being; it also assumes that capital flows measured by national accounts indeed include all forms of capital that matter for long-term well-being. It assumes, finally, that prices revealed by capital markets or imputed by national accountants correspond to the optimizing prices $\pi_k(t)$. All these conditions are indeed crucial.

Second, does this new index tell us something about sustainability, that is, whether our children will live as well as we do or not? The reason for the negative answer is simple. Let us temporarily admit that $\bar{U}$ is a proper measure of the level of well-being that could be eventually sustained for ever. This information is clearly insufficient to know on which kind of path we actually are.

Figure 2.2 illustrates the problem with the horizontal line characterizing this long-term sustainable well-being. Knowing this level is only part of the answer to the question of sustainability. The real point is to know whether we are currently above or below this value: in itself, the $\bar{U}$ indicator does not tell us whether we are in the situation of path B, where excess initial consumption, although compatible with short-term growth, will ultimately force future generations to reduce their standard of living below the current one, or the situation of path C, where current behavior is frugal enough to allow the prospect of permanent increases for all future generations.

To this, one could object that, even if $\bar{U}$ is not the full answer to the sustainability issue, it is an important component of it: if we provide simultaneous measures for $U(C(t))$ and $\bar{U}$ to the public or the policymaker, we can let them check by themselves whether $U(C(t)) \lesseqgtr \bar{U}$. But this way of presenting results may be a source of confusion, as it is the case when adjusted GDPs or other so-called measures of sustainable well-being are taken as substitutes rather than complements to measures of actual GDP or well-being. There is less ambiguity with pairs of indicators more specifically dedicated to measuring, respectively, current well-being and prospects concerning its future growth or decline.

But there is more than that. Even if we were adopting the $(U(C(t)), \bar{U})$ way of presenting the current state of society and its prospects, the problem

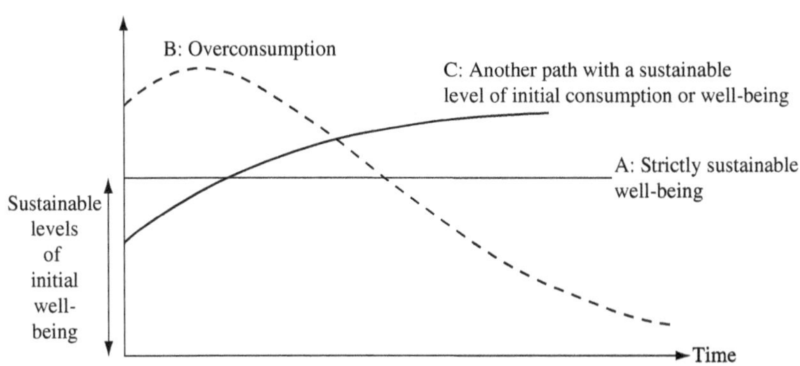

Figure 2.2
Sustainable and nonsustainable paths

is that we cannot even say that $\bar{U}$ represents a sustainable standard of living. In fact, it is not as such that it has been presented in (2.10). A constant flow that *would* provide the same global amount of intertemporal utility as $V^*(t)$ is not necessarily one that can be realized in practice.

The best way to show this is to provide a counterexample that, at the same time, will synthetize all the points raised up to now in an illustrative way. This counterexample will be the one of a simple cake-eating economy (Hotelling 1931) whose income only derives from the exploitation of an exhaustible resource. Dropping subscript k, which becomes useless in this single-asset framework, the optimization problem of this economy reads

$$\max_{c(\tau)} \int_t^{\infty} U(C(\tau))e^{-\mu(\tau-t)}d\tau \tag{2.11}$$

under the constraint

$$\dot{K}(\tau) = -C(\tau)$$

with $K(t)$ the initial stock and the condition $K(\tau) \geq 0$ for all τ.

The Hamiltonian becomes

$$H(\tau) = U(C(\tau))e^{-\mu(\tau-t)} - \pi(\tau)C(\tau).$$

Since K does not directly appear in the Hamiltonian, the dynamics of $\pi(\tau)$ reduce to $\dot{\pi} = -\partial H/\partial K = 0$, that is, $\pi(\tau) = \pi$. Assuming a log utility function, maximization of H with respect to C then leads to

$$C(\tau) = \frac{e^{-\mu(\tau-t)}}{\pi},$$

and, after adjusting π to get a full exhaustion of the initial stock as $t \to \infty$,

$$C(\tau) = \mu K(t)e^{-\mu(\tau-t)}.$$

From this expression for the optimal path of consumption, we let the reader check that we get

$$V^*(t) = (\log(\mu K(t)) - 1)/\mu, \tag{2.12}$$

hence

$$\bar{U} = \mu V^*(t) = \log(\mu K(t)) - 1.$$

This expression expresses the fact that this economy, if managed optimally, generates a global amount of intertemporal well-being positively related to the initial stock $K(t)$. It will even approximately correspond to this stock if μ is low enough to allow a linear approximation to (2.12), and we can associate with that an equivalent permanent level of well-being $\bar{U}$. Yet this is not at all a *sustainable* well-being, for the simple reason that such an economy cannot benefit from any positive sustained level of consumption. Given its bounded resources and the impossibility of substituting any other factor for this resource, no positive value of C can be sustained in the long run. This very simple example exactly shows the limits of the $\bar{U}$ concept. It is just one way to reexpress the integral $V^*(t)$ in terms of a flow of current well-being, but without any guarantee that permanently benefiting from such a flow is an option for this economy.

What would be needed to better characterize this economy? The information on $U(C(t))$ remains economically significant if we want to assess how satisfied its members currently feel compared to members of some other economies. However, from the point of view of sustainability, the information that really matters is the fact that such a level of consumption is necessarily obtained at the expense of future generations and that, for this reason, sustainability is out of reach. To send this message, it is enough to say that we have $\dot{K}(t) < 0$ and, in this very simple case, without the need to compute relative prices for the variations of the different K_k's. It is this kind of approach to sustainability that we shall now discuss. It is undoubtedly much better fitted to the issue. However, as we shall see, it still leaves many problems unsolved, for the simple reason that we have already mentioned. Assessing sustainability necessarily involves making projections about the future because it is illusory to believe that all the information that we need about the future is already present in current observations. No sustainability index can escape this obvious constraint.

2.3 THE SAVINGS APPROACH: A REFERENCE FRAMEWORK

2.3.1 Shifting the focus to sustainability: why?

Let us take stock. Until now, we have explored two kinds of indicators that, in fact, are very close to each other, $V(t)$ and $\bar{U} = \mu V(t)$, the only difference being the rescaling factor μ. Both of them summarize the global path of future utility flows but with no clear message concerning the way it is going to be distributed across future cohorts. This lack of concern for intergenerational distribution is at its peak when we assimilate current well-being with global consumption, that is, $U(C(\tau)) = C(\tau)$, in which case we are completely indifferent about who consumes how much.

Alternative forms for the current welfare function will give some more weight to the way resources are shared between generations: this was already the case with the logarithmic form used in our Hotelling example, and the way to push this concern further is generally to rely on the more general form $U(C(\tau)) = C(\tau)^{1-\gamma}/(1-\gamma)$, where γ measures aversion to intertemporal inequality, the logarithmic form corresponding to the particular case $\gamma = 1$. However, even this category of indicators may still fail to distinguish between the three kinds of profiles given in figure 2.2, despite the fact that they exhibit a fundamental difference: on path B, contrary to path C, current behavior forces some future generation's well-being to stay below the present generation's. This is what the sustainability issue is about.

One pause may be necessary at this stage, to end up our comparison with the question of individual intertemporal well-being that we used as our point of departure. Why do we raise this question of sustainability in the collective context while it is seldom raised at the individual level? Where is the difference? After all, we could insist as well on testing whether utility paths are ascending or declining over their life cycles for individuals, and we do it sometimes, for instance when examining individual prospects concerning elements of welfare such as retirement benefits. But, abstracting from this, the question appears less relevant in the individual case because it is usually considered that inequalities in $u(c(t))$ at this individual level are, above all, a matter of individual choice. Consider two individuals i and j born the same year with the same initial endowments at time t and facing the same future income prospects. If individual i chooses to consume most of his resources right now, neglecting his future needs, while individual j chooses to potspone consumption to later stages of life, this can be considered individual choices that should not count when comparing these two individuals' well-being. Eventually, if the path followed by i drives him into deep proverty, society will help him, but it will do so in a minimal and reluctant way if it considers that all this just results from shortsightedness, and not from the fact that this individual has been disadvantaged, from the beginning, by nature or social determinism.

The situation is clearly different in the collective case. Here, intertemporal inequalities can no longer be viewed as freely assumed intrapersonal inequalities across different periods of one's life. It is now different people from different generations who are compared to each other, and we can consider it our moral duty not to impose on future generations any form of sacrifice that we do not accept for ourselves. It is exactly what the concept of sustainability tries to capture. It will only provide a very partial classification criterion for the set of future paths of our society, that is, a binary classification between paths for which current well-being will be always at least as great as the current level and those for which it won't. And there is also a risk that the first group of paths may be an empty one: such was the case in our Hotelling example, and, at the end of the day, one can argue that such is necessarily the case in a very long-run perspective. The later the better, but mankind will necessarily disappear from the surface of the earth one day or later. As a consequence, sustainability will have to be thought of only relative to some time horizon and will probably have to be compounded with other criteria if we want to choose among the different sustainability paths available from now on. Yet this criterion undoubtfully deserves a large place in our attempts to build alternatives or complements to GDP. It is on this criterion that we shall now focus, with the help of the conceptual apparatus developed in the previous section.

2.3.2 Sustainability in imperfect but predictable economies

From our previous discussion, we have seen that we have one candidate for assessing sustainability, which is an index measuring evolutions of stocks of all the kinds of goods that are expected to matter for future well-being. In the Weitzman case, we have seen how to weight these different evolutions, using co-state variables π_k determined along the optimizing path of the economy. But this assumption of optimality is clearly problematic, and it is all the more so in the domain of long-term eco-environmental change, where potential sources of inefficiency are numerous. There is a crude need for indicators that do not require this optimality assumption.

What we shall now explore is one proposition for avoiding this optimality assumption along the lines proposed in a series of papers by Arrow, Dasgupta, and Mäler (Dasgupta and Mäler 2000; Dasgupta 2001; Arrow, Dasgupta, and Mäler 2003a). Fortunately enough, it does not require a more complex apparatus, because some of the previous results can be easily extended to any form of trajectory potentially followed by the economy. It suffices to consider that, from the initial state $K(t)$, both $K(\tau)$ and $C(\tau)$ are expected to evolve according to a trajectory consistent with the laws of motion (2.7), without requiring this trajectory to be optimal in any sense of the term. If the aim is to evaluate the sustainability of current consumption behavior, we shall for instance characterize this trajectory by a constant C with the implied evolutions for K. In the Hotelling example examined above it would lead to the exhaustion of the natural resource in finite time, with consumption forced to adjust suddenly to zero at this point. Or, alternatively, it could correspond to a path of progressive exhaustion, but starting from an initial level higher than the optimal one, then compensated with a faster rate of decrease, that is,

$$C(\tau) = \mu' K(t) e^{-\mu'(\tau - t)},$$

with $\mu' > \mu$.

Let us examine what we get if we choose the latter form of nonoptimality. The new value function associated with this nonoptimal path will be

$$\begin{aligned} V(t) &= \int_t^{\infty} \left[\log(\mu' K(t)) - \mu'(\tau - t)\right] e^{-\mu(\tau - t)} d\tau \\ &= \frac{1}{\mu}\left[\log(\mu' K(t)) - \frac{\mu'}{\mu}\right], \end{aligned} \tag{2.13}$$

with which an equivalent permanent flow of utility will still be associated, now equal to

$$\bar{U} = \mu V(t) = \log(\mu' K(t)) - \frac{\mu'}{\mu}. \tag{2.14}$$

From this expression, it is still possible to compute an imputed price for capital corresponding to the contribution of a marginal increase in $K(t)$ to intertemporal well-being, that is,

$$\pi(t) = \frac{\partial V(t)}{\partial K(t)} = \frac{1}{\mu K(t)},$$

which, in this specific case, is the same whatever the degree of nonoptimality of the expected path, and that, incidentally, still satisfies the relation

$$\pi(t)\dot{K}(t) = \bar{U} - U(t) = -\frac{\mu'}{\mu}.$$

In other words, we still have an indicator consistent with the message that the current consumption level is not sustainable, based on a valuation of capital that does not refer anymore to the optimizing values of program (2.11), and that can be interpreted in terms of a gap between the current utility level and the constant level that would ensure the same global level of discounted well-being.

All this can be generalized. We do so by reintroducing multiple capital goods, as in the Weitzman approach, and it is not costly to also consider a multiplicity of "consumption goods." The general formulation for the renewal of capital good i, will thus become

$$\dot{K}_k(t) = R_k(K_1(t), \ldots, K_m(t), C_1(t), \ldots, C_p(t)). \tag{2.15}$$

Such a formulation means that all forms of consumptions and all existing stocks of capital goods can simultaneously contribute to changes of these stocks, that is, a fairly general setting. Then, given initial conditions $K_1(t), \ldots, K_m(t)$ we consider a "program," that is, a projected joint trajectory of $C_1(t), \ldots C_p(t)$ and $K_1(t), \ldots K_m(t)$ respecting (2.15). To this program, a value function can be associated:

$$V(K_1(t)\ldots, K_m(t)) = \int e^{-\mu(\tau-t)} U(C_1(\tau)\ldots, C_p(\tau), K_1(\tau)\ldots, K_m(\tau))d\tau,$$

introducing the possibility of having current well-being $U(.)$ depend not only on consumption flows but also on amenities provided by the current stocks of the different capital goods. Then, as before, we can write the change over time of V as

$$\dot{V}(t) = \sum_k \pi_k \dot{K}_k(t), \tag{2.16}$$

with

$$\pi_k = \frac{\partial V}{\partial K_k} \tag{2.17}$$

interpreted as an accounting price for the i-th capital good.

In what sense can we now consider that (2.16) is a sustainability indicator? The basic result is that $\dot{V}(t) \geq 0$ is a necessary condition for having a path where the current level of well-being is sustained. The proof is immediate using the other characterization of $\dot{V}(t)$, that is:

$$\dot{V}(t) = -U(t) + \mu V(t).$$

It just requires writing that being at a sustainable initial level of well-being implies $U(\tau) \geq U(t)$ for all τ, hence

$$V(t) \geq \int e^{-\mu(\tau-t)} U(t)d\tau = U(t)/\mu,$$

which directly implies $\dot{V}(t) \geq 0$.

As a consequence, a negative value of $\dot{V}(t)$ warns us that, at some point in time, well-being will fall below its current value, a test of nonsustainability. This test is generally presented as only partial in the sense that it only provides a *necessary* condition for sustainability, but cannot ensure that sustainability is respected. Indeed, for a given μ, drops in $U(\tau)$ that occur over a sufficiently remote or a sufficiently short period of time may very well remain compatible with a positive $\dot{V}(t)$ if there are some compensating positive changes of $U(\tau)$ at other periods.

But this limit can be partly overcome if we assume that μ is a parameter of the indicator that the index builder is allowed to adjust. Let us consider trajectories that violate sustainability in the sense that $U(\tau) < \psi U(t)$ with $\psi < 1$ for all $\tau > \tilde{\tau}$, with U bounded by U_{max} over the $[t, \tilde{\tau}]$ interval. This implies

$$V(t) < (\tilde{\tau} - t)U_{max} + \frac{1}{\mu}\psi U(t),$$

hence

$$\dot{V}(t) = -U(t) + \mu V(t) < \mu(\tilde{\tau} - t)U_{max} + (\psi - 1)U(t),$$

which can be made negative by choosing

$$\mu < \frac{(1 - \psi)U(t)}{(\tilde{\tau} - t)U_{max}}.$$

Thus, in such a case, there exists a $\tilde{\mu}$ such that, for all $\mu < \tilde{\mu}$, $\dot{V}(t)$ will be negative and send the proper message of nonsustainability. Here μ has no normative meaning, contrary to what we have when discounted well-being is used to compare the costs and benefits of policies that affect the future path of the economy. The situation is different here because we are just in an index-building framework, in search of an index summarizing the shape of the expected utility path: adjusting the value of μ can be seen as tuning the resolution of the index to explore more or less remote segments of this social welfare path.

2.3.3 An example

Let us illustrate the properties of this approach with an example that will be just a little more complex that the simple Hotelling model considered up to now. This example will mix characteristics of the standard Solow growth model with the existence of a natural resource that, contrarily to the Hotelling case, is a renewable one, but with a threshold effect: beyond some level of pressure, the resource cannot renew itself at a rate compensating for its depreciation. Instead of using subscripts to denote the various capital goods, let $K(t)$ and $S(t)$ denote the stocks of these two kinds of capital, $K(t)$ being the standard capital good and $S(t)$ the stock of the natural resource. We first write down a Cobb-Douglas global production function:

$$Y(t) = K(t)^{\alpha},$$

with $K(t)$ being accumulated according to the net investment equation:

$$\dot{K}(t) = Y(t) - C(t) - \delta K(t) = \sigma Y(t) - \delta K(t),$$

where $C(t)$ is consumption of the produced good at t and where σ and δ are respectively the savings rate and the depreciation rate. We know that such a pattern of evolution for K implies an equilibrium capital stock K^* computed by equalizing $\dot{K}$ to zero. We get.

$$K^* = \left(\frac{\sigma}{\delta}\right)^{\frac{1}{1-\alpha}}. \tag{2.18}$$

From the pure point of view of K and Y, an economy that starts from a capital stock lower than K^* will be on an ascending path. Conversely, if it starts from $K(t) > K^*$, this means that it saves too little to maintain its production. This can for instance occur if it has inherited a large capital stock due to high savings by previous generations, and suddenly moves to a less frugal behavior with lower savings, or if it is confronted to an increasing rate of obsolescence for its capital. In both cases, we can anticipate that the current well-being of the population will not be sustainable.

Let us now turn to natural resources. We could have introduced them as an additional input for producing $Y(t)$. This would have meant an explicit modeling of their rate of extraction. Let us rather choose a more compact modeling that consists in assuming that productive activity has a negative externality on S, and that this negative effect directly affects well-being by introducing $S(t)$ in the utility function. This negative externality of production on $S(t)$ will be supposed to creep in only beyond some threshold. Below a value $Y = Y^*$, even if some of this natural resource is consumed or damaged in the process, we assume that its spontaneous rate of regeneration is sufficient to keep its stock constant. But, above Y^*, the natural resource starts depreciating irremediably, at a rate that increases with Y. More precisely, we write

$$\dot{S}(t) = -\lambda(Y(t))S(t),$$

where $\lambda(.)$ is zero before Y^*, increases from 0 to λ_{max} between Y^* and a second threshold of Y^{**}, then remains permanently at this value of λ_{max}.

The last step is to define current utility as a function of $C(t)$ and $S(t)$. Here also the specification is Cobb-Douglas, that is, $U(t) = C(t)^{\epsilon} S(t)^{\eta}$. With this definition of current utility and a discount rate of μ, intertemporal utility writes down

$$V(t) = \int_t^{\infty} e^{-\mu(\tau-t)} C(\tau)^{\varepsilon} S(\tau)^{\eta} d\tau.$$

Given this definition of $V(t)$ and the laws of motion for all parameters of the economy, it is possible to compute the sustainability indicator at each period according to (2.16) for different values of μ. For numerical illustrations, this index will be expressed as a fraction of total current well-being, consistent with the fact that accounting prices in (2.17) are expressed in utility units, hence

$$\Sigma(t) = [\pi_K(t)\dot{K}(t) + \pi_S(t)\dot{S}(t)]/U(t).$$

This Σ-indicator is the theoretical counterpart of ANS that one could try to construct empirically for this stylized economy, but using the exact imputed prices that are correctly associated with the "program" that we consider. Due to this use of "correct" prices, it could have deserved as well the denomination of "Genuine Savings" used earlier in the literature.

We shall benchmark this indicator against two "nonmonetary" indicators focusing on the environmental dimension. The first one, Φ_1, will simply be the current rate of change for the natural resource $\dot{S}/S$, while the second, Φ_2, will try to be closer in spirit to the concept of ecological surplus. To this end, we use the fact that the threshold value Y^* can be interpreted as an environmental carrying capacity, that is, the maximum level of production that we can have without degrading our resources in an irreversible way. This second indicator at time t will be the relative difference between Y^* and $Y(t)$:

$$\Phi_2(t) = 1 - \frac{Y(t)}{Y*}.$$

It will be negative if the economy produces more than what is compatible with the preservation of its natural assets, and positive in the opposite situation.

The three indicators $\Sigma(t)$, $\Phi_1(t)$, and $\Phi_2(t)$ are to be interpreted in the same qualitative way, with negative values announcing that current well-being is unsustainable either in the short run or the long run. Since all these indicators are expressed in relative terms, their order of magnitude will roughly fall into comparable brackets, and this will make graphical illustrations easier. $\Sigma(t)$ and $\Phi_2(t)$ have the additional property that they can also be positive, but such positive values will have different meanings. For $\Sigma(t)$ it will necessarily result from a positive accumulation of produced capital, while for $\Phi_2(t)$, this will simply mean that the economy is living below the carrying capacity of its environment.

Let us now compare the properties of these indicators under a scenario of environmental collapse for a society that is unable to control its production and consumption so that they stay a level that is compatible with the preservation of its natural resources. Assumptions are the following. Initial stocks are equal to one both for produced and for natural capital. The Cobb-Douglas production function has a coefficient $\alpha = \frac{1}{3}$. Under the initial conditions, output Y is equal to 1 and consumption to 0.8. With a constant savings rate of $\sigma = 0.2$ combined with the depreciation rate of $\delta = 0.05$ this economy converges to the long-run capital level given by (2.18), that is, $K^* = 8$, implying a long-run production level of 2 and a long-run consumption level of 1.6.

From the pure point of view of consumption and production, the initial conditions are therefore perfectly sustainable, and, neglecting the environmental side of the coin, this sustainability would be correctly reflected in the positive net savings rate of this economy, initially equal to $\sigma Y - \delta K = 0.15$. This conventional measure of savings progressively approaches zero as society comes closer to its long-run standard of living, but always from above. The predicted path for $C(t)$ appears on the upper line of figure 2.3a, which gives the main projected outcomes for this economy, that is, C, S, and U.

Now, on the environmental side, this expansion of production starts leading to nonrenewal of the natural resource when $Y(t)$ passes the first threshold Y^*, which has been fixed here at 1.5, with a depreciation rate for this natural capital that progressively increases until a maximum value of $\lambda_{max} = 0.25$, reached when $Y(t)$ passes the second threshold of $Y^{**} = 3$. With such values, net depletion of the natural resource starts at $t = 18$, and the negative consequences of this depletion on current well-being start outweighing the positive impact of the increasing $C(t)$ in $t = 27$. After that,

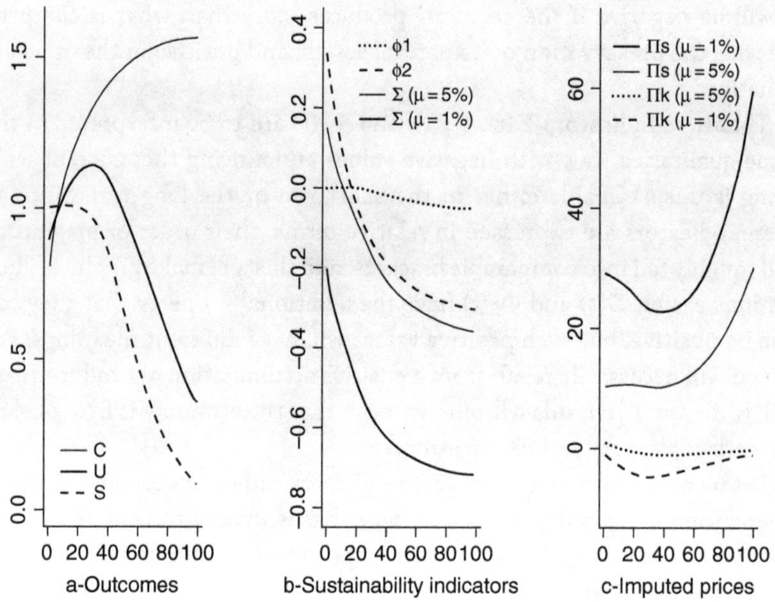

Figure 2.3
The behavior of three indicators under a scenario of environmental collapse

this society that blindly ignores the environmental consequences of its economic expansion sees its level of current well-being $U(t)$ decline inexorably, as illustrated by the two bottom lines of figure 2.3a. Such an evolution is certainly not optimal, but the goal here is not to discuss this inefficiency and the reasons for it. It is only to assess how well the indicators warn us about this situation of unsustainability.

This is what is shown in figure 2.3b. All indicators warn about future unsustainability, since they all end up with negative values, but with degrees of anticipation that differ. In fact, under the specification retained here, the two physical indicators Φ_1 and Φ_2 do not anticipate the collapse very well. Both of them fall below zero when the natural resource starts being depleted, that is, before current utility $U(t)$ itself starts declining, but much later than first signals of nonsustainability sent by the Σ indicator, which is here provided for two values of the discount factor μ, to illustrate the impact of this discount factor. Once again, the choice of this parameter does not need to be understood as expressing an attitude about how the welfare of different generations has to be weighted. It can be seen as a technical parameter that can be tuned to make the indicator as long-sighted as one wishes. Here, choosing $\mu = 0.01$ against $\mu = 0.05$ is sufficient to immediately deliver the message that the projected path does not satisfy $U(\tau) \geq U(0)$ for all τ.

How does the indicator achieve this result? Elements are provided in figure 2.3c. One explanation could have been that, from the start, we attribute a high value to natural capital. It is actually the case that this initial valuation is high, because the imputed price π_S incorporates from the beginning the fact that natural capital matters for well-being and will increasingly do so due to its increasing relative scarcity. Expectedly, it then skyrockets when $S(t)$ actually starts declining. However, under initial conditions, this cannot explain the message of nonsustainability delivered by the indicator, since this imputed price is applied to a physical variation $\dot{S}(t)$ that is initially equal to zero. The explanation can only come from the fact that the indicator attributes a negative value to produced capital, immediately incorporating the negative consequences that the accumulation of this capital good will have on long-run well-being, as shown on the bottom line of figure 2.3c.

To sum up, the Σ index has interesting properties, and even the potential for dominating the other two. In particular, a proper evaluation of accounting prices is able, *in theory*, to fully anticipate the consequences of environmental externalities of economic growth. In that sense, its use is not confined at all to the assessment of situations of "weak" sustainability where capital accumulation is always able to offset consequences of a deteriorating environment. In the context simulated here, accelerating capital accumulation in the hope of compensating losses of natural capital will aggravate the negative signal provided by Σ, given the negative value of the shadow price π_k.

2.4 THE SAVINGS APPROACH: MANY PROBLEMS REMAIN

Let us recap. We have the potential for an indicator that complements both GDP and any alternative measure of current welfare. The way it could work is the following. GDP measures economic activity but is not equivalent to welfare. A specific measure of current welfare $U(t)$ is asked to tell us the level of current well-being that goes with this current level of GDP: some components contribute to welfare, others may not, and this current measure of welfare can be affected by many other factors that are not captured by GDP. The quest for such an index will be the purpose of the next four chapters. But it would be counterproductive to ask this measure to look further in the future. This task must be left to another indicator devoted to measuring the global direction of the change between today and tomorrow, tomorrow being here understood as a long-term perspective, and this is what the Σ index seems to offer.

To further illustrate how such a set of indexes (GDP, $U(t)$, and Σ) could work in practice, let us look at their expected behavior in the case of a sudden shock to produced or natural capital. It is a repeated criticism of GDP that, in such a case, it can send apparently irrelevant messages. If the consequence of the shock is to intensify economic activity because of repairing needs and if GDP is erroneously interpreted as an indicator of well-being, then the shock will be presented as a blessing, which is obvious nonsense.

This paradox disappears when the signal given by GDP is put back in its right place within this suggested set of indicators. Several subcases can be considered:

- If the shock is to produced capital (i.e., a storm or an earthquake) and if the economy reacts by trying to reconstitute lost capital, it can do so in two ways: either by increasing production—hence an increase in work intensity—or by increasing its savings—hence a drop in consumption. The first case may indeed lead, as initially considered, to more GDP, but the $U(t)$ index will prevent us from reading this as pure good news. Increased work effort or reduced consumption will show up as a decline in the utility index, sending the correct message that the initial catastrophe was definitely not a blessing. However, under this kind of reaction, the Σ index can correctly tell us that, thanks to this temporary effort, sustainability is not threatened: the current generation pays its share of the bill generated by the catastrophe.
- If the economy does not react by trying to reconstitute the capital that has been lost and maintains its ordinary standard of living without any additional production effort, then the message can be a decrease in activity due to the fact that less capital has been available for production, but there will be no registered change in current well-being if consumption goes on unabated. The message on sustainability then depends upon the initial situation of the economy and the magnitude of the shock. If the economy, before the shock, was on a more than sustainable path, then the lack of defensive reaction to the shock can remain compatible with sustainability. But if it was close to strict sustainability, and if the shock is large, then the Σ index should tell us that sustainability is no longer the case. This is the correct expression of the fact that the bill will have to be paid, sooner of later.
- If the shock is to natural capital, the typology of messages is the same. If the society has the possibility to restore the initial level of this capital either by positive actions or by temporarily reducing its consumption, we can have the same kinds of messages about global economic activity (possibly increasing), current well-being (stable or declining), and

sustainability (maintained or no more warranted). In the less favorable case where the damage to the environnement is definitive and cannot be repaired, in principle, increasing activity is not an option. The choice is only between reducing current well-being or threatening its sustainability.

2.4.1 Monetization in practice

So much, however, for positive messages. It cannot have escaped the reader how demanding an implementation of this theoretical framework would be. It is only in appearance that the Σ indicator looks like an indicator requiring no more than current observations of flows and values. It creates the illusion that we can measure sustainability in the way an accountant can assess the financial viability of a firm or the way a household can assess whether it overconsumes its resources. In practice, there are very few of the components of this indicator that are directly measured or even measurable. Variations of stocks of the various physical, natural, or immaterial assets that matter for future well-being seem to be the least difficult part of the job, especially in view of the fact that it is only variations that are requested, not full measures of global stocks. But even for things as simple as the variation of the different forms of produced capital, we know that measurement is already imperfect. In particular, depreciation is measured on relatively conventional grounds, due to the lack of systematic inventories of equipments.

The problem is increasingly difficult as we move away from this apparently simple case. Consider the intermediate case of human capital, which represents an important part of empirical versions of the ANS. A proxy that is sometimes used is gross education expenditures, but this is obviously a very poor proxy. It does not take into account that human capital is embodied in individuals and depreciates as these individuals get older; it also neglects that a given level of education expenditures can be more or less efficient in generating human capital. An alternative approach is to directly try to evaluate the stock of human capital as the aggregation of the expected discounted flows of earnings that existing individuals can expect to draw over the remainder of their working lives given their current ages, employment positions, and skills (Jorgenson and Fraumeni 1989). Then it suffices to examine how this stock changes over time.

This methodology fulfills some of the requirements of sustainability assessment. It measures human capital not by the money that has been invested in its accumulation but by its actual earnings potential: an expensive but inefficient education system will not be considered as automatically generating large amounts of human capital. This also takes into account depreciation or obsolesence: shorter remaining working lives yield a lower valorization of current skills. If properly implemented, it can even correctly account for negative shocks to human capital formation that can threaten sustainability. For instance, a sudden drop in the efficiency of the schooling system should lead to an inflexion in the accumulation of skills and associated earnings potential. In a similar fashion, an economic crisis, if it is expected to have long-lasting effects on the earnings potential of people losing their current jobs, should be recorded as having a negative impact on the global savings index.

But all this remains limited in several ways. First, it focuses on contributions of human capital accumulation to productive and earning capacities, a point that can be discussed if we consider that education also contributes to well-being in ways that are not valued by labor markets—that is, the equivalent of the amenity effects that were postulated in the model above in the case of natural capital. And despite the fact that it apparently relies on current observations—distributions of skills in the labor force and current measures of economic returns to these skills—it already corresponds to a projection of the return on these skills in the future. Believing that such returns are to remain constant in the long run is an assumption; it is not an empirical fact.

The necessity to ground the indicator on projections rather than just current observations is all the more obvious for components K_k that represent natural capital. For part of this natural capital, stocks are not necessarily fully known—think of yet undiscovered mineral resources—but flows are, and, for such goods, we benefit from market valuations. Combining these two pieces of information on flows and prices for evaluating $\pi_k \dot{K}_k$ means assuming that observed prices properly reflect how $\dot{K}_k$ impacts the future discounted flow of well-being, and exactly for the value of the discount rate that we want to use for our index. If not, we have to reconstruct the valuation of $\dot{K}_k$ on the basis of full projections of $U(t)$ and the resulting discounted sum $V(K_1(t)\ldots, K_m(t))$ exactly as we would spontaneously do for those natural goods for which no markets exist and for which imputation is the only way to provide valuation.

In addition, the stylized example proposed above has shown that the full implementation of the proposed framework not only requires we perform imputation for goods without markets or with notoriously inefficient markets, but also for all other goods, since the absence or inefficiency of some markets potentially biases the information provided by the whole system of prices. In the example provided, this went to the extreme point of requiring a negative valuation for the accumulation of produced capital. This stylized example was admittedly conceived so as to yield such a result, but it is sufficient to prove that the problem exists. And this example also shows that the fact of not needing more than measures of *changes* in stocks is itself illusory. To get the proper estimate of how to value a given change in the stock of good k, we generally need to know the magnitude of the stock, and in fact of the stocks of all forms of capital goods. Computing derivatives of the form $\partial V(K_1(t)\ldots, K_m(t))/\partial K_k$ cannot be done without knowing the whole state $(K_1(t)\ldots, K_m(t))$ of the socio-eco-environmental system and how it determines the entire future path of this system.

In short, no miracle happened. Unless we believe the fiction that all the relevant information about future trends is adequately reflected in current observed prices, there is no way to measure any characteristic of the future without making predictions, and a basic prerequisite of any projection is a full knowledge of the current state of the system that we need to predict, combined with a full knowledge of the rules governing its future evolution. All this puts a strong demand on index builders and raises, in turn, additional questions.

First, the ultimate utility of the index one seeks to construct has to be clarified. If the purpose is to know whether the predicted path for $U(t)$ crosses the horizontal line $U = U(0)$ downward at some point in the future, direct inspection of a graph of $U(t)$ is sufficient, once it has been projected. No index is needed for that. Let us, however, ignore this argument. It is not uncommon to have summary indicators synthetizing the full results of extensive projection exercises: such is, for instance, the case of many sustainability indicators used in the financial or fiscal domain. The main point is more fundamental. It is the fact that such perfect predictions are not possible, just because of the several forms of uncertainties that need to be dealt with.

More precisely, three main forms of uncertainty can be roughly distinguished. One can primarily think of the global class of "technological" uncertainties, reflecting the fact that parameters governing economic-environmental interactions are far from being known with certainty. Even if they were known with precision for the current period, they can evolve over time in unpredictable ways, due to various external shocks. A second category could be labeled "normative" uncertainty: we wonder about the preservation of a level $U(0)$ for the next generations but without being sure of the shape of their future preferences. The last category is what could be called "behavioral indeterminacy." The Σ approach proceeds as if future behavior were fully predetermined. Yet, even without the other two forms of uncertainties, several future paths remain possible for the system. The fact of choosing only one of these paths (the "program") may make the

Σ indicator less appropriate than it looks at first sight. It is on this last point that we shall concentrate first.

2.4.2 Behavioral indeterminacy, or when "weak" indicators can turn out too strong

The choice of a reference "program" is a standard practice for projection exercises. Projections are predictions of the "what if" type. The Σ approach cannot be blamed for also applying this approach. The reference scenario can be, for example, a "business as usual" (BAU) scenario assuming the indefinite prolongation of current behavior. In that case, the role of the indicator is to provide a summary statement of where such a BAU scenario drives us. But BAU scenarios are generally accompanied by variants, including scenarios where behavior or policies change at some future points in time. The "what if?" inquiry naturally goes along with questions of the "what else?" type.

The simple pedagogical example developed above gives a strong and simple example of how important this point can be. The attentive reader may have noticed a paradox of the "what if" scenario used in this example. It describes as "unsustainable" the initial consumption/savings behavior because of the ultimate consequences of its permanent application all over the prediction horizon. Formally, it is fully correct to say that "if" the same accumulation behavior goes on unabated, it will ultimately trigger an irreversible deterioration of the environment and of living conditions. Yet this message ignores alternative options. For instance, since we start with a level of production lower than the environmental threshold Y^*, it is possible to accumulate capital and enlarge production capacity at the same pace up to this threshold, then suddenly reduce accumulation to replacement needs and benefit after that from enhanced consumption opportunities without entering the regime of permanent environmental degradation. Thus, it is totally unfair to say that people living at time $t = 0$ and saving at the assumed rate of 20% are transmitting an unsustainable state of affairs to their descendants, as was done in subsection 2.3.3 with the most farsighted version of the Σ index (i.e., with $\mu = 0.01$). The reverse is the truth. By saving more than required for capital replacement, these people improve the opportunities of people who live just after them, and they do so without compromising the opportunities of people coming even later. No immediate irreversibility is created by the fact of accumulating capital at early stages of development as long as we stay below the environmental threshold.

This result is worth insisting upon, for it clearly shows how simplistic it is to associate "monetary" and "weak" approaches to sustainability. Here, a so-called "weak" indicator sends messages of unsustainability at periods where it should not: it appears too strong. This shows that, despite its elegance and apparent evidence, the Σ approach to sustainability still misses important points. It is not the "capital" approach to sustainability that is in question. What is at stake is too narrow a way of predicting consequences of current accumulation or decumulation of capital goods. The exact question about sustainability should not be to know whether one specific potential path for U is always above the initial value $U(0)$. The question must be enlarged to the whole set of paths that remain open to future generations once current consumption choices have been made. Following the words of Pezzey (1997), we need to shift to a more resourcist view of sustainability, without any ambition to predict how these resources will be effectively used by future cohorts. A similar view can be found in Asheim (2007).

Hamilton and Clemens (1999) and Pezzey (2004) have noted that the Σ index still provides a test of unsustainability that covers all possible future paths (not just a particular program) when the current actions in t are part of a program that maximizes the intertemporal objective $V(t)$. When $U(t) > \bar{U}$, it is then truly impossible for future generations to maintain $U(t)$ over all periods, no matter what they do. Indeed, if it were possible, future generations could then follow a feasible path with a greater $\bar{U}$, therefore a greater $V(t)$, in contradiction to the optimality assumption. This observation is interesting, but one should look for a better test, namely, a test that applies to suboptimal situations and that provides a necessary and sufficient condition of sustainability, not just a necessary condition.

Although this is rare in the literature, we believe that formalizing this approach to sustainability is easier in discrete time, because of the need to clearly separate the state of the world and the resulting opportunities at the beginning of period 1 compared to those that existed at the beginning of period 0. Let us adapt our notations to this discrete time framework. K_t will again be the vector of "capital" goods that matter for well-being and that are available at the beginning of period t. A_t will be the set of "actions" chosen by people during the same discrete period t. These "actions," in particular, include consumption behavior. The set they can be chosen from is delimited by the current availability of capital goods, that is, a constraint of the form $A_t \in \Phi(K_t)$. Such actions, combined with the capital stocks available at the beginning of the period, determine what levels of capital stocks will be available at the beginning of the next period, through an equation $K_{t+1} = f(A_t, K_t)$, which is the discrete time equivalent to equation (2.7) of our inital continuous time problem. The same variables also determine current utility $U(A_t, K_t)$, assuming once again an amenity value for capital goods.

Based on all these definitions, we can determine $\Phi(K_1)$ the set of future actions and resulting capital stocks $(A_1, A_2, \ldots, K_2, K_3, \ldots)$ that will be feasible starting with the stocks K_1, that is, the set of opportunities that remain open once actions have been chosen for period 0. Within this set we can compute the maximum level of well-being U such that at least one element of $\Phi(K_1)$ satisfies $U(A_t, K_t) \geq U$ for all $t \geq 1$—this is formally equivalent to applying the maximin criterion to the selection of paths, but there is no assumption that the maximin path is followed. Let $V(K_1)$ denote this value of U: it represents the upper bound of what K_1 can offer to the least well-off of future generations. A natural definition of sustainability is then to say that the current utility level $U(A_0, K_0)$ is sustainable if it is less or equal to $V(f(A_0, K_0))$, that is, if we maintain for every future generation the *possibility* of living as well as we do. This requires no a priori assumption concerning what future generations will really do with these possibilities. For instance, egoistic people living at period 1 may choose to overconsume what they inherited, forcing strong drops in utility levels for some of their descendants. Alternatively, if these persons are strongly altruistic, they may deliberately adopt a standard of living lower than the initial $U(A_0, K_0)$ in order to widen the opportunities offered to their own children or grandchildren. In both cases, the resulting trajectories will violate our initial definition of sustainability, the one that was illustrated by figure 2.2, since these trajectories will at some point fall below the initial utility level of $t = 0$. But people that lived in period 0 cannot be held liable for this. The only requirement we must have for the generation living at $t = 0$ is that their behavior does not force such future welfare reductions.

Incidentally, this approach is compatible with both a monetary or "footprint" way of formulating sustainability, confirming than the choice between the two metrics is more a matter of presentation than a question about fundamental principles. The monetary version comes out if we use monetary units to express utility levels: $V(K_1) - U(A_0, K_0)$ can be interpreted as a sustainability gap, with the dimensionless alternative of the relative gap $V(K_1)/U(A_0, K_0) - 1$. But we can as well use this framework for a generalized version of the global footprint. Let λ be a parameter such that $V(f(A_0, \lambda K_0)) = U(A_0, K_0)$. This parameter λ represents in which proportion the initial capital endowment has to be increased in order to ensure sustainability for unchanged values of initial actions A_0. A value that is greater than one will indicate that we are living beyond what can be sustainably warranted given the true capital stocks K_0.

Such an approach has obvious links with the maximin approach to intergenerational equity, introduced early on in the debate on natural resources by Solow (1974) and Hartwick (1977), although the idea is not to assume that society behaves in a way that maximizes this criterion, exactly as we relaxed the optimality criterion when we moved from the Weitzman argument to the elaboration of the Σ index.[2]

It also has very close ties with the so-called viability approach of dynamical systems (Aubin 1991). A system is said to be viable as long as there remains at least one trajectory from the current point that does not violate a set of predefined constraints for variables of interest. Here the constraint consists in forbidding drops of the future utility level U_t below its current level U_0. Needless to say, however, shedding the assumption of a unique reference "program" in this way does not simplify the practical implementation of the index. Even in simple deterministic settings, the definition of viable trajectories or "viability kernels" is not immediate (see examples in Bene, Doyen, and Gabay 2001; Martinet and Doyen 2007; or Baumgärtner and Quass 2009). At this stage, we are clearly far from being able to translate it literally for the building of applied sustainability indicators.

2.4.3 Technological and normative uncertainties

What if we add the fact that all of this takes place in an uncertain environment, which we labeled as technological uncertainty? Whatever the basic principles upon which sustainability indicators are constructed, uncertainty means that they can give no more than a likelihood that we are or are not on an unsustainable path, with the symmetrical potential errors of warning us unnecessarily of problems that will not materialize or, on the other hand, letting us believe that we are on a sustainable path when we are not. This issue is discussed in Asheim and Brekke (2002) and Cairns and Long (2006).

Let us sketch out how this can be done within the framework of the last subsection. Consider again the maximin "value" of the capital stock that is left for the beginning of period 1, $V(K_1)$, and assume that this value has a cumulative distribution function $F(v)$. In this case, $1 - F(U(A_0, K_0))$ gives us the probability that the current level of well-being $U(A_0, K_0)$, under actions A_0, will be sustainable in the future.

We can also be interested in more global aspects of the distribution of outcomes of current actions. For instance, current policy A_0 may give a

2. Asheim, Buchholz, and Withagen (2003) provide a very useful analysis of the Hartwick approach and connect it to the question of sustainability.

lower global probability of unsustainability than policy A'_0 but, in case of unsustainability, may have much more negative consequences. One may think, for instance, of investment in a technological innovation expected to act as a subtitute for the exhaustion of some natural resources. In a majority of cases, this innovation can be expected to be a big help in sustaining current well-being, but, in some rare catastrophic cases, it may make our descendants much worse off than would have been the case without it, hence the necessity of an arbitrage. It is only if $F(v) \leq F'(v)$ for all v that policy A_0 can be viewed as definitely preferable to policy A'_0.

Of paramount difficulty here is the fact that the problem is more than just putting probability distributions on parameters of an otherwise consensual model of socio-eco-environmental interactions. We are in a situation of more radical uncertainty: uncertainty does not apply only to the parameters of the model that govern these interactions, it applies to the structure of the model itself. It applies also to the measurement of current stocks, and even to the list of these natural assets whose stocks and future evolutions have to be taken into account. It should come as no surprise that there is no way for sustainability indexes to avoid such difficulties. And these are clearly difficulties that bring us once again well beyond the problems usually faced by statisticians whose ordinary job essentially consists in measuring the current state of the world. Already at this level, there can be measurement problems and divergences in the way to properly measure the current state of affairs. But trying to quantify sustainability adds the dimension of assessing the future, and heterogeneity of beliefs concerning this future come into play with all the consequences one can guess.

A still more fundamental source of uncertainty comes from our third proposed dimension of uncertainty, the normative one. Intuitively, there can be as many definitions of sustainability as there are definitions of what we want to sustain, and it is what we mean here by "normative" uncertainty that applies both to current and future preferences. The Σ indicator is completely dependent on the choice made for function U, and this is clearly not a minor problem. This applies as well to the alternative approach of the previous subsection, where this U function kept a similar role. Empirically, one can try to infer the form of U from current observations of how people value environmental factors compared to economic ones. Since this cannot be done from observed prices, we must rely on other means, such as contingent valuations, or direct measures of the impact of environmental amenities on indexes of subjective well-being. This is going to be the question addressed in chapters 4 and 5.

But the prospective problem remains. Can contingent evaluations or subjective measures established today in a certain eco-environmental setting be used to predict the valuations of future generations in settings that may have become very different? It may be for instance that our descendants will become very sensitive to the relative scarcity of some environmental goods to which we pay little attention today because they currently remain very abundant. Should the precaution principle command to immediately put a high value on these items just because we think that our descendants may wish to do so? On the contrary, some antienvironmentalists may argue that future generations may be completely indifferent to the disappearance of some environmental amenities that we currently value only because we are used to doing so. This brings the additional complexity stemming from the possible path dependence of function U. For instance, just to be provocative, a strict Easterlinian believing that people permanently adapt their aspirations to their realizations could argue that $U(t)$ is nothing else than a constant and, under such an assumption, any growth or degrowth path is a path of sustained well-being. Such is, of course, not the position we wish to defend—see chapter 5—but it puts in crude light how relative the definition of sustainability may be.

To give another aspect of this normative problem, one can also mention the importance of knowing how U aggregates individual preferences, that is, the distributive dimensions of current well-being. If for instance one considers that a headline indicator of current well-being must be the disposable income of the bottom 80% of the population, or of the bottom 50%, rather than total disposable income, then indicators of sustainability must be adapted to such an objective function. In a world with natural tendencies to increasing inequalities within countries, messages concerning sustainability will differ depending on the goal that the present generation adopts. A specific attention to distributional issues may even suggest enlarging the list of "capital" goods to be taken into account: "sustainability" of well-being for the bottom x% of the population may require some specific investment in institutions that help protect this population from poverty, which implies also considering such institutions as forms of "assets."

2.4.4 An additional problem: the cross-national dimension of unsustainability

Distributive questions also arise when addressing the international dimension of the question. The need for a global view of sustainability is beyond discussion and is central in debates about climate change. This will be our last point in this chapter.

Primarily, the quest of alternatives to GDPs takes place in the perspective of building "national" or "domestic" indicators that will be used to compare countries' performances to one another. Such indicators remain nation-based. This is not to say that the level of well-being for people living in country A at time *t* is not under the influence of what is done in other countries at the same period. Socioeconomic and environmental policies followed by all partners or competitors of country A affect well-being in this country. For instance, weak labor regulations adopted in country B may create labor market problems in country A. Or pollutions that cross the border from B to A may have adverse impacts on health in country A. Yet, as long as it is *current* well-being that is our concern, we do not need to look across the borders to capture these effects. In principle, we directly observe these consequences within country A: a high unemployment rate, low wages, poor health, and so on.

Moving to the assessment of sustainability, things become more complicated. The future well-being of country A can be affected by choices currently made in country B or made later by this same country, with consequences that are not immediately observable to the statisticians of country A. The way to deal with such interactions is another source of divergence between sustainability indicators such as the ANS and the Ecological Footprint. Depending on which index is chosen, the least developed or the most developed countries are the most severely concerned with unsustainability, the former because of underinvestment in physical and natural capital or because of a poor management of their natural resources, the latter because of their high standard of living that puts pressure on the world ecosystem and natural assets. The viability approach leans on the side of ANS, as it evaluates whether future generations of a given country have the means to maintain their living standards.

Advocates of the ANS can defend the first view by arguing that, if markets work properly, the pressure that developed countries exert on other countries' resources is reflected in the prices they pay for importing these resources. If, despite the cost of these imports, they are still able to have a positive ANS, this means that they invest enough to compensate for their consumption of natural resources. It is then the responsibility of exporting countries to reinvest the income from their exports in sufficient quantities if they want to be themselves on sustainable paths.

Yet prices are informative only under an assumption of efficient markets. If markets are not efficient and if the natural resource is underpriced, then the importing countries benefit from an implicit subsidy and the exporting ones are taxed. This means that effective sustainability of the former is overestimated, while the sustainability of the latter is underestimated. And this problem will be all the more crucial when there are no markets at all, or in the presence of strong externalities.

As for the single-country case, we cannot accept an approach ignoring problems raised by externalities or an inefficient functioning of markets. But the task is not easy. Consider the following, extremely stylized two-country example. Physical capital is ignored. Production takes place with labor as the only input, but with external effects on the stock of a natural resource that is now a global public good with free access and available in quantity $S(t)$ at time t. We also neglect the spontaneous regeneration of this good. It is therefore treated as an exhaustible resource.

We assume that the two countries produce and consume at each period in quantities $C_1(t) = C_2(t)$, but with different technologies. Country 2 uses a clean technology that has no impact on $S(t)$, while country 1 uses a "dirty" one that leads to a depreciation of $S(t)$ by an amount proportional to $C_1(t)$, that is, $dS(t) = -\lambda C_1(t)$.

Last, we push further the asymmetry by assuming that it is only country 2 that is affected by this loss in $S(t)$, for instance with a current utility function of the same form as before, that is, $U_2(C_2, S) = C_2^{\mu} S_1^{-\mu}$. Country 1 is completely indifferent to the level of $S(t)$, for instance because its geographical characteristics fully protect it from the consequences of a declining $S(t)$. Its instantaneous utility function may therefore be $U_1(C_1, S) = C_1$. With such a setting it is natural to redefine countries 1 and 2 as being respectively "the polluter" and "the polluted."

What can be the transcription of the general rules presented in this two-country setting? One possibility consists in computing country-specific accounting prices for $S(t)$, this difference reflecting the fact that the two countries suffer differently from variations in $S(t)$. If V_1 and V_2 are the intertemporal utilities for the two countries, we therefore define $\pi_1 = \partial V_1/\partial S$ and $\pi_2 = \partial V_2/\partial S$. Next, given that the depreciation of $S(t)$ is global, it is the overall variation of $S(t)$ over time that must be deducted from each country's Σ weighted with the country-specific accounting prices. We therefore get

$$\Sigma_1(t) = \pi_1(t)dS(t) = -\pi_1(t)\lambda C_1(t), \tag{2.19}$$

and

$$\Sigma_2(t) = \pi_2(t)dS(t) = -\pi_2(t)\lambda C_1(t). \tag{2.20}$$

It is easy to guess that $\pi_1(t)$ will be identically equal to zero: the polluter is not impacted by changes in $S(t)$; hence it gives no value to this asset and it considers itself sustainable. On the other hand, the polluted will give a positive value $\pi_2(t) > 0$ to this asset, and its standard of living is not sustainable. The viability indicators would deliver the same message.

From a certain point of view, these results make sense. It is true that the polluter is on a sustainable path while the polluted is not. But from another point of view, the message to policymakers is misleading. Country 2 can do nothing to restore its sustainability. It is only a change in the polluter's technology that can help restore sustainability for the polluted country.

The solution to this paradox is not necessarily to throw away indicators like (2.19) and (2.20)—the information they convey is not meaningless—but rather to combine them with another set of indicators that would not assess each country's own sustainability, but rather the contributions of the different countries to global unsustainability. If we rewrite more generally dS_1 and dS_2, the contributions by each country to the deterioration of the global stock (with $dS_2 = 0$ in our particular example), (2.19) and (2.20) are rewritten as

$$\Sigma_1(t) = \pi_1(t)[dS_1(t) + dS_2(t)],$$

$$\Sigma_2(t) = \pi_2(t)[dS_1(t) + dS_2(t)],$$

and we see immediately that the elements of these two equations can be rearranged as

$$\Sigma_1'(t) = [\pi_1(t) + \pi_2(t)]dS_1(t), \tag{2.21}$$

and

$$\Sigma_2'(t) = [\pi_1(t) + \pi_2(t)]dS_2(t). \tag{2.22}$$

In this alternative formulation, the global accounting price $\pi(t) = \pi_1(t) + \pi_2(t)$ can be interpreted as a global impact of a given change in the global stock dS on an aggregate index of intertemporal well-being $V = V_1 + V_2$, and the contribution of each country to global sustainability or unsustainability is equal to its own contribution to dS, weighted by this implicit price. This is, for instance, the line that is followed when one estimates contributions of countries to climatic change using their respective levels of GHG emissions, valued at a common price supposed to reflect global worldwide damages from the marginal ton of CO_2.

The double accounting system (2.19–2.20) and (2.21–2.22) illustrates that unsustainability and contributions to global unsustainability are two different things that both deserve measurement. A country with a highly negative dS_i and $\pi_i = 0$ can be sustainable while strongly contributing to global unsustainability, and the reverse can be true as well.

Now, one cannot hide that all this requires, in turn, many disputable assumptions. There are, for instance, two additivity assumptions, which are respectively the additivity of the dS_i's and the idea that $V = V_1 + V_2$ has some sense as a global well-being index, that is, that national well-beings can be aggregated in an utilitarian way. And this way of tackling the multidimensional aspect of sustainability still raises the main general problem that we have met all through this chapter, that is, our ability to fully project long-term consequences of changes in S, now in a simultaneous way for all countries in the world.

2.5 CONCLUSION: WHERE TO GO FROM HERE?

Popular wisdom says that problems that are clearly laid out are half resolved. Is it the case here? Yes and no. For those longing for a single headline indicator of sustainability immune to any form of contestation, the answer sounds clearly negative. We stopped less than halfway to such a dream. Many obstacles have surged on the road that seem unsurmountable, at least within the realm of ordinary statistical production. The basic reason now sounds obvious. Informing about sustainability is informing about the future. It is not a pure measurement issue, it is one of global prediction. Yet, on a more constructive side, breakthroughs are very significant. Even if the ultimate goal stays out of reach, we come back with several recommendations for what could be second-best solutions. Let us recapitulate the main messages.

First of all, we know much better what we need to measure and what for. Theoretical detours have helped identify objectives that are not very interesting to pursue. Aiming at a statistical transcription of the concept of discounted social well-being is probably a waste of time. The alternative concepts of sustainable standard of living or constant equivalent standard of living do not appear very relevant either, despite looking more appealing at first sight. They correspond to what statisticians have instinctively tried to build under the denomination of green GDP, and greening GDP has often been perceived as the natural answer to the lack of concern of standard GDP for sustainability issues. But it is probably not fortuitous that these efforts have not been very successful so far.

The reason is deeper than the difficulty of gathering all the necessary information. It is that the return to such an investment is not warranted. We do not know exactly how such an indicator could be used if it happened to be built systematically. It would admittedly produce some interesting revisions of country rankings, favoring countries that are able to produce more with lower pressure on the earth's resources, but, in itself, this indicator says nothing about sustainability. Even if it were a measure of sustainable consumption—and we have seen that this is not a warranted view—it would inform about sustainability only once compared to actual consumption. Messages are definitely clearer if we can directly communicate the results of this comparison, and this is what sustainability indicators should be about. What we need are indicators of overconsumption of resources or indicators of savings/dissavings.

If we address the problem along this line, it then splits into two subproblems. The first one is the identification of all those assets that matter for future well-being, their current stocks, and the measurement of how they evolve over time. This remains within the competence of statisticans, and it is indeed on this front that most of their efforts are currently oriented.

The second step is where difficulties become insurmountable. It is about synthetizing all this information. Some factors generally go on being accumulated—produced physical capital, human capital, intangible capital such as knowledge or institutions—while other capital goods are depleted, generally natural capital, either in a reversible way, or fully irreversibly, as it is the case for exhaustible ressources. It is when we come to aggregating all this information that we are caught up by the "futurity" problem raised by Samuelson more than 50 years ago. A confortable solution would have been be to assume that people acting on markets are correctly informed about how these assets will matter for future well-being and do manage this information in an optimal way. Current-price aggregation of the usual kind would then have been one solution to consider. But such a belief about the clearsightedness of markets is unreasonable. The burden of the evaluation is thus shifted to the index builder, and what we ask him is a considerable task. We ask him to provide the correct assessment of what counts, be it in monetary or nonmonetary terms.

In such a situation, it is not surprising to find room for very different assessments of sustainability, reflected by the various indicators of this kind already available. These differences simply reflect different beliefs about how future well-being will be generated. What are the prospects for substituting such and such produced resource for natural resources that are becoming excessively scarce? When are we going to cross thresholds beyond which such and such renewable resource starts deteriorating in an irreversible way? What are the environmental externalities of such and such aspects of our production process? How do these externalities cross the borders of the different countries for which we are asked to build sustainability indicators? Or, to move away from the sole eco-environmental field, do our institutions evolve in a direction that is favorable to future quality of life? Here the statistician is urged to convert himself into a multidisciplinary prospectivist. The task is daunting. It is easily understandable why answers to this request, until now, have essentially consisted in providing building blocks for this global prospective, and not the full vision.

Within such a state of affairs, the second-best solution for statisticians emerges relatively neatly, that is, focusing on what they think they can do, the production of well-structured and as focused as possible dashboards of information on these assets and their dynamics, completed where possible with relevant information about what we think to be critical thresholds for the stocks of these assets. Efforts toward more comprehensive messages on sustainability are not at all to be given up, and the choice of final metrics for expressing their results remains open: it can be done in monetary terms or following some generalized version of the "footprint" way of quantifying sustainability. But problems encountered in the two cases are roughly the same. Due to the many assumptions required for such exercises, they clearly fall into another branch of activity, more exploratory and more open to controversy. We shall come back to these messages in the general conclusion of the volume.

Now, another clarification provided by this chapter is that there can be no sustainability assessment without a prior consensus about what we want to sustain, that is, what content we give to the notion of current social well-being. This is the question addressed in the four next chapters.

CHAPTER 3

A Price for Everything?

The project of correcting GDP has been often understood as adding or subtracting terms that have the same structure as GDP, that is, monetary aggregates computed as quantities valued at market prices or at imputed prices in case market prices are not available. For instance, in their seminal work, Nordhaus and Tobin set out to compute "a comprehensive measure of the annual real consumption of households. Consumption is intended to include all goods and services, marketed or not, valued at market prices or at their equivalent in opportunity costs to consumers" (1972, p. 24).

As we will see in this chapter, economic theory is much less supportive of this approach than usually thought by most users of national accounts. Many official reports swiftly gloss over the fact that economic theory has established total income as a good index of social welfare under some assumptions (which are usually left unspecified). To be sure, there is a venerable tradition of economic theory that seeks to relate social welfare to the value of total income or total consumption. Surveys of this tradition can be found in Sen (1979) and Slesnick (1998). As a matter of fact, the assumptions under which one can say something about social welfare from total income or total consumption are extremely restrictive. Most of the theory, moreover, deals with the limited issue of determining the sign of the welfare change for a given population. The theory is silent about the magnitude of the change, not to mention the level of welfare itself. It is also silent about comparisons across populations with different preferences. In this perspective, the widespread use of GDP per capita, corrected or uncorrected, as a cardinal measure allowing percentage scaling of differences and variations across countries and generations should be seen as lacking foundations in economic theory.

At this point it is worth asking what is needed actually. Certainly, policy debates need an ordinal ranking of the social and economic consequences of various policy options. This is the minimum. There are, however, contexts in which different populations are considered. First, in the long run different policies may generate different populations with predictably different habits and preferences. Is it better, for instance, to encourage rural or urban lifestyles by urban development policies? Second, the evaluation of growth over the long run involves different generations, while international comparisons of living standards involve very different populations across the world. Is the population better off in the United Kingdom or in Japan? This question is meaningful but cannot be answered without a measure that covers variations in preferences. There are, moreover, contexts in which rankings are not sufficient and one would like a cardinal scale. The measurement of growth and the comparison of living standards naturally require the ability to evaluate some differences as larger than other differences. It seems important, for instance, to know if the improvement in social welfare has slowed down (if it has not decreased) after the first oil crisis.

In this chapter we review old and recent arguments for and against monetary aggregates as social welfare indicators. Although the topic of this chapter is the approach that consists in "correcting" national income by adding or subtracting elements of nonmarketed consumption, valued at imputed prices, it will not be a surprise that most of the attention will be on the core problem of using national income as a measure of social welfare, even when no corrections are needed. The problems and difficulties in this "easy" case are obviously at least as severe in the difficult case in which corrections are needed. Sections 3.1 and 3.2 examine two different revealed-preference arguments that can be used to link the sign of welfare variations with the evolution of total consumption at market prices. Section 3.3 reviews the theory of index numbers, which has the more ambitious goal of providing cardinal measures of welfare. Section 3.4 is about the more modest, but perhaps more promising, idea of decomposing social welfare into factors separately representing efficiency and equity. Section 3.5 introduces the problem of imputing prices for nonmarketed goods and computing a "full income."

Because this chapter is, apart from section 3.4 on the decomposition of social welfare, mostly critical, it can be skipped by the readers who are already convinced that a notion of total income cannot be a good proxy for social welfare. This is also the most demanding chapter in terms of economic theory background.

3.1 A REVEALED PREFERENCE ARGUMENT

The cornerstone of the theory of national income as a proxy for social welfare is the $p\Delta X \gtrless 0$ criterion, where p is the initial price vector and ΔX the change in total consumption.[1] This is equivalent to checking if the Laspeyres index[2] of total consumption, $p\left(X+\Delta X\right)/pX$, is greater than 1. This approach is inspired by a similar criterion for individual welfare. We first review the idea at the individual level, before examining how it can be extended to the social level.

3.1.1 The argument for an individual consumer

Consider a consumer who consumes a bundle $x \in \mathbb{R}_+^\ell$ at market prices $p \in \mathbb{R}_{++}^\ell$ and is free to choose any bundle x' such that $px' \leq px$. Obviously, x is *at least as good as* any such x' for the consumer, because if one of them were better, the consumer could have picked it.

Moreover, if local nonsatiation is satisfied (which means in every vicinity of every bundle there is a strictly preferred bundle), x must be *strictly preferred* to any bundle x' such that $px' < px$. Indeed, if x was as good as some x' such that $px' < px$, one could find a bundle x'', strictly better than x and x', in a vicinity of x' that is small enough so that $px'' < px$.

Now consider a change from x to x' and from p to p'. Under what conditions can one say that the change represents an increase in welfare, if one assumes that the consumer's preferences have not changed? If $p'x' \geq p'x$, x' is at least as good as x by the first observation, and, under local nonsatiation, it is strictly better if $p'x' > p'x$. Conversely, the inequalities $px \geq px'$ and $px > px'$ betray a (weak or strict) decrease in welfare. There is a gray area in which the change in welfare is not determined by this methodology, namely, when $p'x' < p'x$ and $px < px'$.

This is illustrated in figure 3.1, which depicts the typical consumer choice of the most preferred bundle in a budget set.[3] In the figure, one has $px > px'$, and indeed x is revealed preferred to x' but, as $px < px''$, x'' can be

1. The expression $p\Delta X$ is the inner product $\sum_k p_k \Delta X_k$, where k is the commodity label.

2. The Laspeyres index of quantities uses the prices of the initial period; the Laspeyres index of prices uses the quantities of the initial period. The corresponding Paasche indices use the final values instead. See subsection 3.3.1, equations (3.10) and (3.11).

3. The curve is an indifference curve; the line delineates the budget. The consumer can afford all bundles below or on the line, but not the bundles above.

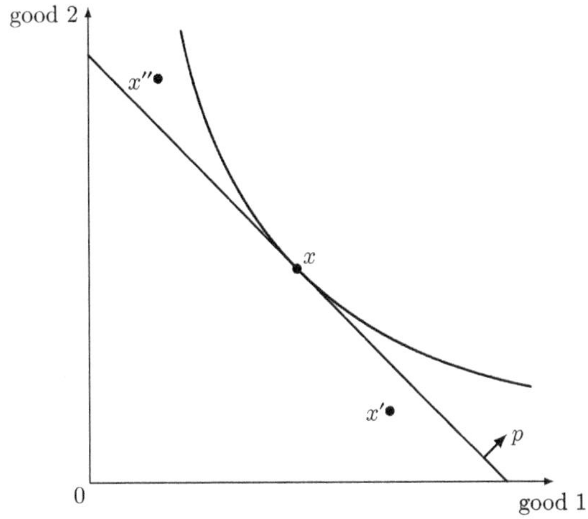

Figure 3.1
The revealed preference argument for a consumer

better or worse than x depending on the precise location of the consumer's indifference curve.

When the changes are infinitesimal (i.e., $x' = x + dx$, $p' = p + dp$), the gray area vanishes if the consumer has preferences that are representable by a differentiable utility function $u(x)$ and if x is interior, that is, $x \in \mathbb{R}^{\ell}_{++}$. Indeed, in this case, the price vector p is proportional to the gradient of u at x,[4] or, in economic terms, relative prices $p_k/p_{k'}$ are equal to marginal rates of substitution $(\partial u/\partial x_k) \,/\, (\partial u/\partial x_{k'})$. This implies that the differential du is proportional to pdx and therefore has the same sign as pdx: $du \geq 0 \Leftrightarrow pdx \geq 0$. Note the importance of the interiority assumption here. If the consumer did not consume some of the goods, $pdx > 0$ would be compatible with a decrease in satisfaction.

Before examining how this revealed preference argument has been extended to social welfare, let us ponder its limitations. These limitations come primarily from the assumptions. The assumption that the consumer freely chooses in a budget set excludes rationing and nonmarketed (in particular, nonexcludable) public goods. The assumption of local nonsatiation excludes the situation of people who donate part of their income. Their welfare cannot be examined in terms of personal consumption, and one must

4. In simple terms, as can be seen on figure 3.1, at x the slope of the indifference curve is identical to the slope of the budget line. The gradient of u, $(\partial u/\partial x_1, \partial u/\partial x_2)$, is by definition a vector that is orthogonal to the indifference curve, while the price vector (p_1, p_2) is orthogonal to the budget line. Therefore, these two vectors must be proportional.

include the donation itself as a consumption (of generosity), which raises all sorts of ethical problems because it is debatable whether other-regarding preferences deserve as much attention in social evaluation as self-centered preferences. The assumption that preferences do not change is essential and reveals that this approach has nothing to say about comparisons involving different consumers with different preferences. Even consumers who have the same preferences about consumption commodities may not be comparable in such simple terms, because there may be other determinants of welfare (e.g., health) that are missing in the framework. The assumption of an interior consumption is obviously unrealistic, as every consumer buys only a very small fraction of the available commodities.

The limitations also come from the result itself, which has to do with the sign of welfare change. No indication of the magnitude of the change is obtained, although the observation that du is *proportional* to pdx suggests that slightly more could be squeezed out of the reasoning—for example, for small changes $2dx$ has twice the effect of dx on utility.[5] No indication about how to measure welfare in a cardinal way is given. The market value of consumption cannot be declared a measure of welfare from this reasoning. Finally, let us notice that extending this result to a setting with time and uncertainty is far from obvious. With a set of complete markets and a fully rational consumer, one can evaluate his ex ante lifetime welfare with this methodology. But with or without complete markets, the connection between welfare and the market value of per period consumption (or income) is not immediate, as it has been discussed in the previous chapter.

3.1.2 Extending the argument to social welfare through a representative agent

How can one extend this revealed preference argument from individual income or consumption to national income? Assume that social welfare for a society of n members is defined as the value of a social welfare function applied to individual utilities $W(u_1(x_1), \ldots, u_n(x_n))$. The aim is to link this magnitude to the market value of total consumption $X = x_1 + \cdots + x_n$, more precisely, to the criterion $pX > pX'$.

Two ways of establishing such a link have been proposed. One approach consists in considering a "representative agent" who consumes X and whose demand behavior mimics the aggregate demand of the society under

5. One can perhaps view the theory of index numbers (discussed in section 3.3) as exploiting this idea.

consideration. It is customary in macroeconomics to identify the preferences of the representative agent with social welfare. The transposition of the revealed preference argument is then immediate because society is simply identified with this macroeconomic individual. This approach, however, is quite discredited, as explained in Kirman (1992).

To begin with, the existence of a representative agent is rare. In particular, when income is redistributed across individuals and prices remain unaltered, it is generally unlikely that aggregate demand remains unchanged (individual Engel curves, which describe the relation between demand and income for given prices, should be linear and parallel), but a representative agent must keep the same demand. As it turns out, the condition of linear and parallel Engel curves is actually necessary and sufficient for the existence of a representative agent when prices are also allowed to vary.[6]

The existence of a representative agent is less unlikely when the variations of incomes and prices are restricted. For instance, Dow and Werlang (1988) and Jerison (2006) assume that income shares are determined by a function ("distribution rule") that depends only on the price vector and total income: letting M denote total income, the distribution rule is a vector-valued function $f(p, M)$ such that $\sum_{i=1}^{n} f_i(p, M) = M$, and $f_i(p, M)$ is individual i's income. The representative agent is then studied under the assumption that income shares never deviate from the distribution rule. Even under this restriction, the existence of the representative agent[7] is not guaranteed in general. Studying cases in which a representative agent exists, and assuming a fixed distribution rule, these authors show the following interesting facts.

First, it may happen that the representative agent prefers X to X' while all the individuals weakly prefer their bundle in X' to their bundle in X, or that the representative agent weakly prefers X to X' while all the individuals weakly prefer their bundle in X' to their bundle in X and at least one individual has a strict preference. This is called a "Pareto-inconsistent" representative agent. The examples showing such a possibility are not very simple (see the quoted references). But the problem is not limited to pathological preferences because almost any preferences over X can be those of a Pareto-inconsistent representative agent.

Second, however, if $pX > pX'$, that is, if X is revealed preferred to X' by the choice made under p by the representative agent, then at least one

6. See Deaton (1980, pp. 150–151).

7. The existence of the representative agent requires the Slutsky matrix of the aggregate demand function to be symmetric and negative semidefinite (see Varian 1992, chap. 08, for explanations, and (3.16) for the definition of the Slutsky matrix).

individual prefers his bundle in X to his bundle in X'. Indeed, if $pX > pX'$, necessarily $px_i > px_i'$ for at least one $i \in \{1, \ldots, n\}$ because $pX = \sum_{i=1}^{n} px_i$ and $pX' = \sum_{i=1}^{n} px_i'$. The fact that $px_i > px_i'$ implies that i prefers x_i to x_i' (assuming local nonsatiation). But obviously, it may be that only one individual agrees with the representative agent.

Third, if the representative agent is Pareto consistent (i.e., is not Pareto inconsistent), then its preferences can be represented by a social welfare function $W(u_1(x_1), \ldots, u_n(x_n))$. In order to see this point, it is more convenient to take the pairs (p, M) as the objects of preferences. For the representative agent, preferences over (p, M) are like ordinary indirect preferences of an agent who has to choose under the budget constraint $pX \leq M$: (p, M) is preferred to (p', M') if the bundle chosen under the former budget is preferred to the bundle chosen under the latter. For individuals $i = 1, \ldots, n$, preferences over (p, M) can also be defined. They are deduced from the distribution rule $f(p, M)$, which determines the income m_i of each i, and from their indirect preferences over (p, m_i): (p, M) is preferred to (p', M') by i if choosing from the budget $(p, f_i(p, M))$ is better than choosing from the budget $(p', f_i(p', M'))$. Let $v_i(p, M)$ denote a utility function representing i's preferences over (p, M), and let $V(p, M)$ denote the representative agent's preferences over (p, M).

If the representative agent is Pareto consistent, one has $V(p, M) = V(p', M')$ whenever $v_i(p, M) = v_i(p', M')$ for all i. One can then define a social welfare function W as follows: for every vector $(\hat{u}_1, \ldots, \hat{u}_n)$ such that there is (p, M) for which $v_i(p, M) = \hat{u}_i$ for all i, let $W(\hat{u}_1, \ldots, \hat{u}_n) = V(p, M)$. This function is well defined because for any other (p', M') for which $v_i(p', M') = \hat{u}_i$ for all i, necessarily $V(p', M') = V(p, M)$. In addition, this function must be strictly increasing over the domain of vectors $(\hat{u}_1, \ldots, \hat{u}_n)$ such that there is (p, M) for which $v_i(p, M) = \hat{u}_i$ for all i.

This result connecting the representative agent to a Paretian social welfare function is, however, limited because the function is defined only for a given distribution rule. For another distribution rule the representative agent would typically have different preferences. Moreover, the function need not satisfy good ethical properties apart from satisfying the Pareto principle.

This last remark can be illustrated with an example. Consider an economy with two goods in which individual 1 only likes good 1 and the other individuals only like good 2. The distribution rule is such that $m_1 = .9M$, while $m_i = .1M/(n-1)$ for $i = 2, \ldots, n$. The aggregate demand of good 1 is $X_1 = .9M/p_1$ and can be obtained with Cobb-Douglas preferences, for the representative agent, that are represented by the function $(X_1)^{.9}(X_2)^{.1}$. Let us measure individual i's utility $\hat{u}_i$ by the quantity consumed of the good he likes. This is the natural measure here. One then sees that the representative agent's preferences, formulated as a social welfare function over individual utilities, can be written

$$\left(\hat{u}_1\right)^{.9}\left(\hat{u}_2\right)^{\frac{.1}{n-1}}\cdots\left(\hat{u}_n\right)^{\frac{.1}{n-1}}. \tag{3.1}$$

Obviously, the social welfare function is directly influenced by the distribution rule and gives more weight to the "rich" individual. In this example, the distribution rule is optimal for the social welfare function (3.1). But other social welfare functions could rationalize the representative agent's preferences, because the variation of $\left(\hat{u}_1,\ldots,\hat{u}_n\right)$ is restricted by the distribution rule. For instance, the function $\left(\hat{u}_1\right)^{.9}\left(\hat{u}_2\right)^{.1}$, which ignores all agents $i=3,\ldots,n$, works just as well under the given distribution rule, which clearly is not optimal for this social welfare function. Observe that this social welfare function is not even Paretian. Dow and Werlang (1988) and Jerison (2006), with different arguments, show that a Pareto-consistent representative consumer may exist even when the distribution rule is not optimal for *any* social welfare function.

3.1.3 Extending the argument to social welfare with an optimality assumption

The bottom line of the previous subsection is that unless the distribution rule is assumed to be optimal for a reasonable social welfare function, there is no reason to give much ethical credit to a Pareto-consistent representative agent. As it turns out, optimality of the distribution underlies the second approach to be examined here. This approach provides a different justification to the "$pX \geq pX'$" criterion.

Due to Samuelson (1956), it consists in assuming that X is optimally distributed, in the sense that $(x_1,\ldots,x_n)$ maximizes $W(u_1(x_1),\ldots,u_n(x_n))$ subject to the constraint $x_1+\cdots+x_n=X$. Under this assumption there is a welfare function that depends on total consumption and coincides with social welfare:

$$W^*(X)=\max W(u_1(x_1),\ldots,u_n(x_n)) \quad \text{s.t. } x_1+\cdots+x_n=X. \tag{3.2}$$

It is much like a utility function and can serve to apply the revealed preference argument to total consumption for the evaluation of market allocations, if one assumes that W is increasing in each argument (Pareto principle).

This is shown by connecting this approach to the previous one, as the social optimality of the distribution is a sufficient (but not necessary) condition for the existence of a Pareto-consistent representative agent. For a given (p, M), find some X that maximizes $W^*(X)$ under the constraint $pX \leq M$. This is equivalent to maximizing $W(u_1(x_1), \ldots, u_n(x_n))$ under the constraint that $p\,(x_1 + \cdots + x_n) \leq M$ and letting $X = x_1 + \cdots + x_n$. Pick a corresponding optimal distribution of consumption $(x_1, \ldots, x_n)$. One may then define the distribution rule by setting $f_i(p, M) = px_i$. When the prevailing market price vector is p and when individual income is $f_i(p, M)$, x_i must be optimal for i. If not, there would be a better x'_i for i satisfying $px'_i \leq f_i(p, M)$, and one could thereby find an alternative allocation $(x'_1, \ldots, x'_n)$ satisfying the constraint $p\left(x'_1 + \cdots + x'_n\right) \leq M$ and yielding greater social welfare than $(x_1, \ldots, x_n)$ by the Pareto principle. But this would be in contradiction with the optimality property that served to choose $(x_1, \ldots, x_n)$.

Under this distribution rule, therefore, there is a representative agent because the sum of individual demands x_i coincides with the maximization of $W^*(X)$ under the constraint $pX \leq M$. The representative agent's preferences are then represented by the function W^*. Moreover, it is obviously Pareto consistent because of the connection between W^* and the Paretian W, and its corresponding social welfare function is ordinally equivalent to W over the relevant range of vectors $\left(\hat{u}_1, \ldots, \hat{u}_n\right)$, that is, the vectors such that there is an optimal $(x_1, \ldots, x_n)$ for which $u_i\,(x_i) = \hat{u}_i$ for all i.

These preliminary considerations make it possible to formulate and prove the message of this second approach. If $(x_1, \ldots, x_n)$ is, under prices p, a market allocation that optimally distributes X according to the social welfare function W, and if $pX \geq pX'$, then necessarily social welfare measured by W is at least as great at $(x_1, \ldots, x_n)$ as at any distribution of X'. This is because X is the representative agent's choice under the budget constraint defined by p and $M = pX$, and the inequality $pX \geq pX'$, by the standard revealed preference argument, implies $W^*(X) \geq W^*(X')$, which itself implies

$$W(u_1(x_1), \ldots, u_n(x_n)) = W^*(X) \geq W^*(X') \geq W(u_1(x'_1), \ldots, u_n(x'_n))$$

for all $(x'_1, \ldots, x'_n)$ such that $X' = x'_1 + \cdots + x'_n$.

Under the same assumptions, plus the assumption that at least one individual's preferences satisfy local nonsatiation, it holds that if $pX > pX'$, then social welfare is greater at $(x_1, \ldots, x_n)$ than at any distribution of X'. This is due to the fact that W^* then also satisfies local nonsatiation.

The limitation of this second approach is that it is not realistic to assume that consumption or wealth can be redistributed at will by lump-sum transfers (as is implicit in positing that the only constraint is $x_1 + \cdots + x_n = X$), and that the status quo (in the application of the revealed preference argument) is always socially optimal. Dropping either of these two assumptions invalidates the approach. When the status quo is not optimal, an improvement in social welfare is even compatible, obviously, with a decrease in total consumption, not just a decrease in the *value of* total consumption. A smaller cake better distributed may be socially preferable to a larger cake badly distributed.

When redistribution is made by distortionary taxes, even if the distribution is optimal under the constraint of using such taxes (this constraint may itself be due to imperfect information about the individuals' characteristics), the revealed preference argument fails as well. Indeed, at a second-best optimum the social marginal value of income[8] for different individuals typically remains unequal, so that a change of allocation that favors individuals with greater social marginal value may improve social welfare even if the market value of total consumption is reduced. Concretely, what usually happens is that the poor retain a greater social marginal value of income at the social optimum because redistribution is less successful with such taxes than with lump-sum transfers. Then, a change of allocation that increases the value of their consumption less than it decreases that of richer people may improve social welfare and nonetheless reduce the market value of total consumption at the initial prices.

The conclusion should be clear. Under reasonable assumptions, total income, or the market value of total consumption, has no direct connection with social welfare. The revealed preference argument is already quite limited at the individual level, as has been emphasized above. At the social level, distribution simply cannot be ignored and severely restricts the possibility of using income as a proxy for welfare.

8. Consider the social welfare function defined on individual indirect utilities:

$$W\left(v_1\left(p, m_1\right), \ldots, v_n\left(p, m_n\right)\right).$$

The *social marginal value of income* for *i* is defined as

$$\frac{\partial W}{\partial v_i}\frac{\partial v_i}{\partial m_i},$$

i.e., it measures the change in social welfare induced by giving one more dollar to individual *i*.

3.2 A VARIANT OF THE REVEALED PREFERENCE ARGUMENT

Sen (1976) examines a variant of the revealed preference argument. If consumer preferences are convex, at any bundle x there is a price vector p such that for all bundles x', $px' < px$ implies that x is preferred to x'. In figure 3.1, for instance, p can be chosen endogenously so as to obtain a line of equation $px' = cst$ that is tangent to the indifference curve at bundle x.

This argument does not assume that x maximizes utility in the budget set, which means that the vector p need not coincide with market prices. In fact some components of x may not even be marketed.

As explained by Sen, this argument can be immediately extended to social welfare if social welfare is measured by a function $\overline{W}(x_1, \ldots, x_n)$ that is defined directly on quantities and if this function is quasi-concave. But the corresponding price vector $\bar{p}$ must then have $n\ell$ components (like the arguments of $\overline{W}$), each component $\bar{p}_{ik}$ weighting the consumption of a particular commodity k consumed by a particular individual i.

If $(x_1, \ldots, x_n)$ is a market allocation in which all individuals face the same ℓ-dimensioned price vector $p \in \mathbb{R}^{\ell}_{++}$ and freely choose in their budget set, and if the social welfare function is Paretian, then the $n\ell$-vector $\bar{p}$ can be chosen such that the ratios $\bar{p}_{ik}/\bar{p}_{il}$ (individual i, commodities k and l) are the same for all i and are simply equal to the relative market price p_k/p_l. The computation of the inner product $\bar{p} \cdot (x_1, \ldots, x_n)$ then simply boils down to $\alpha_1 px_1 + \cdots + \alpha_n px_n$, for a vector of weights $(\alpha_1, \ldots, \alpha_n)$ which embodies distributional preferences.

The criterion obtained with this approach can then be formulated as meaning that for any quasi-concave function $\overline{W}(x_1, \ldots, x_n)$, a market allocation $(x_1, \ldots, x_n)$ is at least as good as another allocation $(x'_1, \ldots, x'_n)$ whenever $\sum_{i=1}^{n} \alpha_i px_i \geq \sum_{i=1}^{n} \alpha_i py_i$, for a suitable vector of weights $(\alpha_1, \ldots, \alpha_n)$ that may depend on $(x_1, \ldots, x_n)$.

The main limitation of this approach is that the weights $(\alpha_1, \ldots, \alpha_n)$ generally depend on the allocation in a complex way. For instance, if the function $\overline{W}(x_1, \ldots, x_n)$ is derived from a social welfare function $W(u_1(x_1), \ldots, u_n(x_n))$, the weight α_i must be proportional to the social marginal value of i's income, $\frac{\partial W}{\partial u_i} \frac{\partial v_i}{\partial m_i}$ (where $v_i(p, m_i)$ is the indirect utility function, and $m_i = px_i$). Another limitation, in the context of seeking theoretical foundations for national accounts, is that national income bears no direct relation with $\sum_{i=1}^{n} \alpha_i px_i$. The weights seem to complicate the picture considerably.

Sen examines a way to address both issues. First, total income can appear in a decomposition formula. If the weights are scaled so that $\alpha_1 + \cdots + \alpha_n = n$, the sum can be decomposed into two terms:

$$\sum_{i=1}^{n} \alpha_i px_i = pX \times \frac{\alpha_1 px_1 + \cdots + \alpha_n px_n}{pX}, \tag{3.3}$$

the second term being less than unity if $(\alpha_1, \ldots, \alpha_n)$ and $(px_1, \ldots, px_n)$ are inversely ranked, that is, in case of inequality aversion over expenditures.

As an example of such a weighting system, Sen suggests taking weights that are simply proportional to the ranks (giving rank 1 to the richest, and so on) of the individuals in $(px_1, \ldots, px_n)$. The second term of the decomposition then takes a familiar form. Indeed, if one assumes that $px_1 \leq \cdots \leq px_n$, one obtains

$$\frac{\alpha_1 px_1 + \cdots + \alpha_n px_n}{pX} = \frac{2}{n+1} \frac{npx_1 + \cdots + ipx_i + \cdots + 1px_n}{pX}.$$

For large numbers the ratio $(2i-1)/(2j-1)$ is not very different from i/j, so that for a large n,

$$\frac{\alpha_1 px_1 + \cdots + \alpha_n px_n}{pX} \simeq 1 - G(px_1, \ldots, px_n), \tag{3.4}$$

where $G(px_1, \ldots, px_n)$ is the Gini coefficient, which can be defined as follows:

$$G(px_1, \ldots, px_n) = 1 - \frac{(2n-1)\, px_1 + \cdots + (2i-1)\, px_i + \cdots + 1px_n}{npX}.$$

More precisely, one computes that

$$\frac{\alpha_1 px_1 + \cdots + \alpha_n px_n}{pX} - \left(1 - G(px_1, \ldots, px_n)\right)$$
$$= \frac{1}{n}\left(1 - \frac{\alpha_1 px_1 + \cdots + \alpha_n px_n}{pX}\right),$$

an expression that is in effect small when n is large.

This proposal provides simple and intuitive weights and includes total income in a decomposition of the social welfare criterion. Such rank-order weights, unfortunately, are difficult to reconcile with a Paretian social welfare function approach. Hammond (1978) shows that the partial ordering of allocations generated by this approach (i.e., fixing the proportional rank-order weights assigned to various ranks and applying the revealed preference argument for all possible market prices) is compatible with a Paretian social welfare function $\overline{W}(x_1, \ldots, x_n) = W(u_1(x_1), \ldots, u_n(x_n))$ only if all individual Engel curves are linear and identical. As Hammond's result holds for a larger set of fixed rank-order weights than the proportional weights, and his proof contains imperfections, a proof of the generalized result is provided in appendix B.

It is striking that the restriction that is obtained is almost the same as (actually, is stronger than) the condition needed to have a representative agent (namely, parallel linear Engel curves). The conclusion is that this approach, which appears initially promising because it is applicable to nonmarket goods, does not go very far. The difficulty is to find the relevant weights, and the "easy" case of a market allocation reveals that there is no simple way to define the distributional weights on individual incomes if one wants the evaluation to be compatible with the Pareto principle, that is, to respect individual preferences.

Another limitation of revealed preference approaches is that, not only is the criterion incomplete and therefore silent in some comparisons, but when it is conclusive, it only indicates the sign of welfare change. One does not get a *quantitative* evaluation of welfare change, as would be obtained with an index number such as GDP in volume terms. It is only in a decomposition like equation (3.3) that one can give a quantitative meaning to the evolution of total consumption at certain well-defined prices. More direct attempts to obtain cardinal indices can be found in the theory of index numbers, to which we turn in the next section. The idea of making total income appear in a decomposition of social welfare will be explored further in a later section.

3.3 THE THEORY OF INDEX NUMBERS

Initiated by Fisher (1922), the theory of index numbers seeks to define price and quantity indices in the hope of being able to compare monetary values in a meaningful way when prices and quantities change across the situations to be compared. Compared to the revealed preference approach, it offers the perspective of measuring the size of changes, not just their sign.

After Fisher's seminal contribution, it has burgeoned in three directions. The first is a direct axiomatic study of index numbers, which does not directly make a link with welfare concepts but is nevertheless inspired by the revealed preference argument reviewed above; the second seeks approximations of true welfare criteria by simple price-quantity statistics; the third is the conceptually and ethically more ambitious, but data-greedy, money-metric utility. Here we examine the first two approaches, as the money metric is the topic of the next chapter.

3.3.1 An axiomatic approach

The axiomatic approach consists in defining desirable properties for the price and quantity indexes $P(p^1, p^0, x^1, x^0)$ and $Q(p^1, p^0, x^1, x^0)$ (where p^t and x^t denote the price and quantity vectors at $t = 0, 1$). The problem can be formulated as follows. The monetary value index p^1x^1/p^0x^0 is not meaningful for the evaluation of changes in quantities or welfare when prices change, and therefore one seeks to decompose it into separate summary indexes for prices and for quantities.

Here are three examples of desirable properties. The first refers to the decomposition idea and says that the product of the price index and the quantity index must equal the monetary value index. The second refers to the revealed preference argument and says that when the price vector is unchanged, the quantity index must equal the value index. The third says that reversing time should yield inverse values of indexes.

$$P(p^1, p^0, x^1, x^0)\, Q(p^1, p^0, x^1, x^0) = \frac{p^1x^1}{p^0x^0}; \tag{3.5}$$

$$Q(p, p, x^1, x^0) = \frac{px^1}{px^0}; \tag{3.6}$$

$$Q(p^1, p^0, x^1, x^0)\, Q(p^0, p^1, x^0, x^1) = 1. \tag{3.7}$$

Diewert (1992b) provides a list of 21 axioms of this sort and shows that the pair of Fisher indexes

$$P^F(p^1, p^0, x^1, x^0) = \left(\frac{p^1x^0}{p^0x^0}\frac{p^1x^1}{p^0x^1}\right)^{1/2}, \tag{3.8}$$

$$Q^F(p^1, p^0, x^1, x^0) = \left(\frac{p^0x^1}{p^0x^0}\frac{p^1x^1}{p^1x^0}\right)^{1/2}, \tag{3.9}$$

satisfies all of them and is the only one to do so. Observe for instance that (3.7) is satisfied neither by the Laspeyres indexes, defined as

$$P^L(p^1, p^0, x^1, x^0) = \frac{p^1x^0}{p^0x^0}, \quad Q^L(p^1, p^0, x^1, x^0) = \frac{p^0x^1}{p^0x^0}, \tag{3.10}$$

nor by the Paasche indexes

$$P^P(p^1, p^0, x^1, x^0) = \frac{p^1x^1}{p^0x^1}, \quad Q^P(p^1, p^0, x^1, x^0) = \frac{p^1x^1}{p^1x^0}. \tag{3.11}$$

Diewert's characterization of the Fisher index is quite simple. In addition to (3.5) and (3.7) and the requirement that the indexes be strictly positive, the characterization relies on the following properties, which impose symmetry among the weights of periods 0 and 1:

$$P(p^1, p^0, x^1, x^0) = P(p^1, p^0, x^0, x^1), \tag{3.12}$$

$$Q(p^1, p^0, x^1, x^0) = Q(p^0, p^1, x^1, x^0). \tag{3.13}$$

Here is a variant of his argument adapted for the quantity index.

$$\begin{aligned}
\frac{p^1x^1}{p^1x^0}\frac{p^0x^1}{p^0x^0} &= \frac{p^1x^1}{p^0x^0}\frac{p^0x^1}{p^1x^0} \quad \text{by rearranging the terms at the denominator} \\
&= \frac{P(p^1, p^0, x^1, x^0)\, Q(p^1, p^0, x^1, x^0)}{P(p^1, p^0, x^0, x^1)\, Q(p^1, p^0, x^0, x^1)} \quad \text{by (3.5)} \\
&= \frac{Q(p^1, p^0, x^1, x^0)}{Q(p^1, p^0, x^0, x^1)} \quad \text{by (3.12)} \\
&= \frac{Q(p^1, p^0, x^1, x^0)}{Q(p^0, p^1, x^0, x^1)} \quad \text{by (3.13)} \\
&= Q(p^1, p^0, x^1, x^0)^2 \quad \text{by (3.7).}
\end{aligned}$$

Taking the square root on both sides, one obtains the Fisher quantity index. From (3.5) one then derives the Fisher price index.

A great advantage of this approach is that it can be applied to aggregate quantities just as well as to individual consumption. The counterpart is that the connection to welfare is hard to make. One would like the quantity index to reflect welfare variations. In order to appreciate the required properties, it is convenient to try them on a true hedonic index in the case of individual welfare. In order to make things as easy as possible, suppose that the consumer's preferences are homothetic, with an indirect utility function equal to $m/\beta(p)$, for a linearly homogeneous function $\beta(p)$.[9] This indirect utility can then serve as a quantity index by taking

$$Q(p^1, p^0, x^1, x^0) = \frac{p^1x^1/\beta(p^1)}{p^0x^0/\beta(p^0)}. \tag{3.14}$$

9. A linearly homogeneous function satisfies $\beta(\lambda p) = \lambda\beta(p)$ for $\lambda \in \mathbb{R}_{++}$. Homothetic preferences are such that x is at least as good as y if and only if λx is at least as good as λy, for all $\lambda \in \mathbb{R}_{++}$. For instance, Cobb-Douglas preferences represented by $x_1^\alpha x_2^{1-\alpha}$ are homothetic and induce the indirect utility function $m/\beta(p)$ with $\beta(p) = p_1^\alpha p_2^{1-\alpha}$.

There seems to be little harm in having a price index that derives from (3.5). With the true index (3.14) one would obtain

$$P(p^1, p^0, x^1, x^0) = \frac{\beta(p^1)}{\beta(p^0)},$$

which makes a lot of sense. Let us now examine if the other properties are satisfied. First, observe that this price index satisfies (3.12), although (3.12) is problematic for a reason to be explained shortly.

The quantity index (3.14) satisfies (3.6) and (3.7) without any problem, which seems to confirm that these properties are sensible. The difficulties, however, come with (3.13), which cannot be satisfied by this quantity index.

One might try to defend (3.13) on the grounds that if it reflects welfare, the quantity index should primarily depend on quantities and not so much on prices. But this property reveals a problem. If the index is applied to market situations reflecting maximization in a budget set, it may not be possible to obtain the configurations (p^0, x^1) and (p^1, x^0). This problem concerns both (3.12) and (3.13). The true index (3.14) is applicable only to situations in which p^t is the supporting price of x^t, that is, in which relative prices in p^t correspond to the marginal rate of substitutions at x^t.

One way out of the difficulty consists in redefining the true index, for any arbitrary situation, by taking the supporting price vector $p(x)$. One then obtains a pair of indexes that satisfy (3.12) and (3.13) readily because they only depend on quantities and prices, respectively:

$$Q(x^1, x^0) = \frac{p\left(x^1\right)x^1/\beta\left(p\left(x^1\right)\right)}{p\left(x^0\right)x^0/\beta\left(p\left(x^0\right)\right)}, \quad P(p^1, p^0) = \frac{\beta(p^1)}{\beta(p^0)}.$$

This pair satisfies (3.5) whenever p^t is the supporting price of x^t for $t = 0, 1$. The other axioms of the characterization are fully satisfied. Yet this does not correspond to the Fisher index. The difference comes only from the fact that the characterization requires (3.5) to be satisfied in all situations.

If one wants (3.5) to be satisfied, one can use it to define the price index, which then gives the pair of indexes

$$Q(x^1, x^0) = \frac{p\left(x^1\right)x^1/\beta\left(p\left(x^1\right)\right)}{p\left(x^0\right)x^0/\beta\left(p\left(x^0\right)\right)}, \quad P(p^1, p^0, x^1, x^0) = \frac{p^1x^1}{p^0x^0Q(x^1, x^0)}.$$

Obviously, one then loses (3.12).

In conclusion, the fact that the Fisher index does not coincide in general with a true index of welfare implies that the seemingly nice axioms of its characterization are problematic. A similar analysis would be obtained with social welfare instead of consumer welfare.

3.3.2 Approximating welfare changes

The second branch of the theory of index numbers seeks indexes that depend only on price and quantity data but are good proxies for welfare change at the individual level. From the revealed preference argument invoked in section 3.1, it is well known that x^1 is revealed preferred to x^0 if the Paasche index satisfies $Q^P(p^1,p^0,x^1,x^0) > 1$ and that x^0 is revealed preferred to x^1 if the Laspeyres index satisfies $Q^L(p^1,p^0,x^1,x^0) < 1$. In market situations reflecting maximization in a budget set, it is impossible to have $p^1x^1 > p^1x^0$ and $p^0x^0 > p^0x^1$ at the same time. Therefore $p^1x^1 > p^1x^0$ implies $p^0x^0 \leq p^0x^1$, so that the Fischer index satisfies $Q^F(p^1,p^0,x^1,x^0) > 1$. Similarly, $p^0x^0 > p^0x^1$ implies $p^1x^1 \leq p^1x^0$, so that $Q^F(p^1,p^0,x^1,x^0) < 1$. In other words, the Fisher index never fails to track situations of revealed preferences that are identified with the Laspeyres and the Paasche indexes. So far, however, no progress has been made beyond the revealed preference argument.

Along the same vein, Diewert (1976, 1992a), following Hicks (1941) and discussing Weitzman (1988), develops a more ambitious approach. Let $e(p,u)$ denote the individual expenditure function (i.e., the minimum expenditure needed to obtain utility level u when market prices p prevail). The equivalent variation and compensating variation are respectively equal to

$$EV(p^1,p^0,x^1,x^0) = e(p^0,u(x^1)) - e(p^0,u(x^0)),$$

$$CV(p^1,p^0,x^1,x^0) = e(p^1,u(x^1)) - e(p^1,u(x^0)).$$

Each of these magnitudes correctly records if individual utility has increased or decreased when moving from x^0 to x^1 — this holds true for the expression $e(p,u(x^1)) - e(p,u(x^0))$ for any arbitrary price vector p, because the function $e\left(p,u\right)$ is increasing in u.

If these situations are obtained by maximization in a budget set, then for $t = 0,1$, $p^tx^t = e(p^t,u(x^t))$, and by Shephard's Lemma, for all goods k,

$$x_k^t = \frac{\partial e}{\partial p_k^t}(p^t,u(x^t)). \tag{3.15}$$

Let S^t denote the $\ell \times \ell$ Slutsky matrix, whose kk' term is defined as

$$S^t_{kk'} = \frac{\partial e}{\partial p^t_k \partial p^t_{k'}}(p^t, u(x^t)). \tag{3.16}$$

Let us now study how to approximate the EV and CV expressions. When prices are not too different, a second-order Taylor expansion of $e(p^0, u(x^1))$, for instance, yields:

$$\begin{aligned} e(p^0, u(x^1)) &\simeq e(p^1, u(x^1)) + \sum_k \left(p^0_k - p^1_k\right) \frac{\partial e}{\partial p^1_k}(p^1, u(x^1)) \\ &+ \frac{1}{2} \sum_{k,k'} \left(p^0_k - p^1_k\right) \left(p^0_{k'} - p^1_{k'}\right) \frac{\partial e}{\partial p^1_k \partial p^1_{k'}}(p^1, u(x^1)) \\ &\simeq p^1 x^1 + \left(p^0 - p^1\right) x^1 + \frac{1}{2} \left(p^0 - p^1\right)' S^1 \left(p^0 - p^1\right), \end{aligned}$$

where the second line uses (3.15) and (3.16), and $\left(p^0 - p^1\right)'$ denotes the row vector transposed from the column vector $p^0 - p^1$.

A second order approximation of the equivalent and compensating variations can then be computed as follows:

$$\begin{aligned} EV(p^1, p^0, x^1, x^0) &\simeq p^1 x^1 + \left(p^0 - p^1\right) x^1 + \frac{1}{2} \left(p^0 - p^1\right)' S^1 \left(p^0 - p^1\right) - p^0 x^0 \\ &\simeq p^0 \left(x^1 - x^0\right) + \frac{1}{2} \left(p^0 - p^1\right)' S^1 \left(p^0 - p^1\right); \qquad (3.17) \\ CV(p^1, p^0, x^1, x^0) &\simeq p^1 x^1 - p^0 x^0 - \left(p^1 - p^0\right) x^0 - \frac{1}{2} \left(p^1 - p^0\right)' S^0 \left(p^1 - p^0\right) \\ &\simeq p^1 \left(x^1 - x^0\right) - \frac{1}{2} \left(p^1 - p^0\right)' S^0 \left(p^1 - p^0\right). \qquad (3.18) \end{aligned}$$

Note that the first-order terms do not depend on preferences and have signs consistent with the comparison to one of the Laspeyres and Paasche quantity indexes, respectively. The second-order terms, however, cannot be derived from price and quantity information and depend on information about preferences. Obviously, one should always bear in mind that such approximations are valid only if the prices p^0 and p^1 are not too different (large differences in quantities and utilities are allowed).

Diewert's approach consists in seeking functional forms for the expenditure functions that are *(i)* flexible enough so that they provide good approximations to the second order of any twice differentiable expenditure function, and *(ii)* simple enough so that the corresponding (exact) equivalent variation depends only on price and quantity data. The obtained measure of equivalent variation is called "superlative" by Diewert.

For instance, he shows that the expenditure function defined as

$$e(p,u) = \left[p'Apu^2 + 2\,(pa)\,(pb)\,(u-\alpha)\,(u-\beta)\right]^{1/2}, \tag{3.19}$$

where A is a $\ell \times \ell$ symmetric matrix, a and b are ℓ-vectors, and α, β are real numbers, is flexible enough to approximate any twice continuously differentiable expenditure function to the second order at any particular point p, u such that $u > 0$ and $p \in \mathbb{R}^{\ell}_{++}$.[10]

Now assume that $\alpha = u^0$, $\beta = u^1 \neq u^0$, that A is normalized so that $p^{0\prime}Ap^0 = 1$, and that a is normalized so that $p^0a = 0$. (As shown by Diewert, such assumptions are compatible with (3.19) approximating any twice continuously differentiable expenditure function to the second order at the point $\left(p^0, u^0\right)$, provided that $u^0 > 0$ and $p^0 \in \mathbb{R}^{\ell}_{++}$.) Under these assumptions, the equivalent variation for (3.19) is equal to an expression that relies only on prices and quantities and involves the Fisher quantity index:

$$p^0x^0\left[\left(\frac{p^0x^1}{p^0x^0}\frac{p^1x^1}{p^1x^0}\right)^{1/2} - 1\right]. \tag{3.20}$$

This last point is easy to show. Under the assumed normalizations, one has $e(p^0, u) = u$, so that

$$EV(p^1, p^0, x^1, x^0) = u^1 - u^0 = p^0x^0\left(\frac{u^1}{u^0} - 1\right). \tag{3.21}$$

From (3.15), and using $e(p^t, u(x^t)) = p^tx^t$, one computes

$$x^t = \frac{Ap^t\left(u^t\right)^2}{p^tx^t},$$

implying

$$\frac{p^0x^1}{p^0x^0}\frac{p^1x^1}{p^1x^0} = \frac{p^0Ap^1\left(u^1\right)^2/p^1x^1}{p^0x^0}\,\frac{p^1x^1}{p^1Ap^0\left(u^0\right)^2/p^0x^0} = \left(\frac{u^1}{u^0}\right)^2, \tag{3.22}$$

where the last equality relies on the fact that by symmetry of A, one has $p^0Ap^1 = p^1Ap^0$. Putting (3.22) into (3.21), one obtains (3.20).

It is important to emphasize that there are many flexible functions yielding different formulas for the equivalent variation. For instance, with

10. See Diewert 1992, Th. 1, p. 573.

another function one can obtain a formula that involves the arithmetic mean of the Laspeyres and Paasche quantity indexes, instead of their geometric mean as in the Fisher index:[11]

$$p^0x^0\left[\frac{1}{2}\frac{p^0x^1}{p^0x^0}+\frac{1}{2}\frac{p^1x^1}{p^1x^0}-1\right]. \tag{3.23}$$

It is puzzling that different expressions, which equally pretend to be good approximations of the equivalent variation, may have different signs in certain cases. Even when the Laspeyres and Paasche indexes are arbitrarily close to unity, their geometric mean can be lower than unity while their arithmetic mean is greater. It is equally puzzling that the true second-order approximations in (3.17) and (3.18) involve terms that vary with individual preferences and do not just depend on quantities and prices. How can (3.20) and (3.23) then be claimed to approximate welfare changes?

The explanation of this apparent contradiction in the arguments is that the approximation is made by Diewert at the initial situation (p^0, u^0) only. Each formula for the equivalent variation is correct only when the true expenditure function is exactly equal to the contemplated flexible function at the situation (p^0, u^1), for which there is no guarantee of approximation. Otherwise there is an error term, which converges to zero when u^1 tends to u^0 but may remain larger than the welfare change throughout. Therefore, no matter how close the two situations are, a formula like (3.20) or (3.23) may not give the correct sign, let alone the magnitude, of the welfare change.

Note that in the derivation of (3.20) it is apparently "assumed" that $\beta = u^1$, but this is misleading because it does not mean that any value of u^1 is admissible. Quite to the contrary, the various normalizations imply that u^1 has a specific value, namely, $p^0x^0Q^F(p^1, p^0, x^1, x^0)$, as can be seen from (3.22). While these normalizations are compatible with the flexible function approximating the true expenditure function at (p^0, u^0), they may impose a serious discrepancy over the estimation of $e\left(p^0, u^1\right)$. This is the cost for obtaining an expression of $e\left(p^0, u^1\right)$ that depends only on prices and quantities.

All in all, no approximation result can circumvent the hard fact that price and quantity data cannot completely determine the sign of welfare changes, even locally. One must also note that this approach applies only to individual consumption welfare, not to total consumption and social welfare.

11. See Diewert (1992a, p. 577).

In conclusion, the theory of index numbers, in the two approaches described here, does deliver interesting concepts, but it fails to provide measures that adequately reflect individual well-being and social welfare. It certainly does not provide a justification for the use of total income as a measure of social welfare.

3.4 DECOMPOSING WELFARE

If total income cannot be used as a reasonable proxy for social welfare, one can still hope to give it a role as a factor of social welfare along other aspects. In particular, we have seen that distribution is bound to matter and is not represented in total income. But could it be that variations in total income reflect variations in social welfare when the distribution factor stays constant? This idea inspires the project of finding a convenient decomposition of social welfare in which total income appears as one term, as in Sen's decomposition (3.3). It would be nice to be able to say that when a certain monetary measure of social welfare is worth, say, 73% of total income, this means that inequity in the distribution dampens the contribution of total income to welfare by 27%.

3.4.1 A first decomposition, with the social expenditure function

Pollak (1981) introduced the notion of social expenditure function. The usual definition of this function takes the standard form of an expenditure function and computes the minimum amount of (total) expenditure needed under a given price vector p to attain a given level of (social) welfare w:

$$\bar{V}(p,w) = \min p\,(x_1 + \cdots + x_n) \quad \text{s.t. } W(u_1(x_1),\ldots,u_n(x_n)) \geq w. \qquad (3.24)$$

One can then define the corresponding "money-metric" social welfare function, for which, in the arguments, the physical allocation is substituted for the level of social welfare:

$$V(p,x_1,\ldots,x_n) = \bar{V}(p, W(u_1(x_1),\ldots,u_n(x_n))) \qquad (3.25)$$

Equivalently,

$$V(p,x_1,\ldots,x_n) = \min p\left(x_1' + \cdots + x_n'\right)$$
$$\text{s.t. } W(u_1(x_1'),\ldots,u_n(x_n')) \geq W(u_1(x_1),\ldots,u_n(x_n)).$$

Under mild regularity conditions, these functions are well defined and, for a given p, the V function is ordinally equivalent to $W(u_1(x_1), \ldots, u_n(x_n))$.

Being expressed in monetary units, its evolution in time can be compared to that of GDP, no matter what social welfare function $W(u_1(x_1), \ldots, u_n(x_n))$ is adopted. But this does not provide a justification for GDP itself. When $(x_1, \ldots, x_n)$ is a market allocation with prices p, one always has

$$V(p, x_1, \ldots, x_n) \leq pX,$$

because equality between the two terms is obtained when the allocation is socially optimal (given X), and strict inequality is obtained when the distribution is not optimal. When $(x_1, \ldots, x_n)$ is not a market allocation with prices p, one still has $V(p, x_1, \ldots, x_n) \leq pX$, but a strict inequality remains possible even if $(x_1, \ldots, x_n)$ is an optimal distribution of X.

For a market allocation, Jorgenson (1990) therefore proposes the following decomposition:

$$V(p, x_1, \ldots, x_n) = pX \times \frac{V(p, x_1, \ldots, x_n)}{pX}. \tag{3.26}$$

The additive variant of this decomposition,

$$V(p, x_1, \ldots, x_n) = pX + \left(V(p, x_1, \ldots, x_n) - pX\right),$$

has also been proposed by Jorgenson and Slesnick (see Slesnick 1998, p. 2152). This decomposition can accommodate a wide variety of social welfare functions $W(u_1(x_1), \ldots, u_n(x_n))$.

Using decomposition (3.26) for the analysis of variations (across time or space) raises a complication when prices change. If one wants to compare a market allocation described by p, $(x_1, \ldots, x_n)$ with another allocation described by p', $(x'_1, \ldots, x'_n)$, one can then write

$$\frac{V(p, x'_1, \ldots, x'_n)}{V(p, x_1, \ldots, x_n)} = \frac{pX'}{pX} \times \frac{V(p, x'_1, \ldots, x'_n)/pX'}{V(p, x_1, \ldots, x_n)/pX}.$$

The first term nicely features the Laspeyres quantity index. The second term, unfortunately, may be less than 1 even if the distribution is optimal in both allocations, because one typically has $V(p, x'_1, \ldots, x'_n) < pX'$ if $p' \neq p$. A related problem is that this formula is not symmetric. If one took p', $(x'_1, \ldots, x'_n)$ as the benchmark, one would obtain the decomposition

$$\frac{V(p',x_1,\ldots,x_n)}{V(p',x'_1,\ldots,x'_n)} = \frac{p'X}{p'X'} \times \frac{V(p',x_1,\ldots,x_n)/p'X}{V(p',x'_1,\ldots,x'_n)/p'X'},$$

in which the two terms are not the inverses of the terms of the previous decomposition.

This observation reveals a limitation of (3.26). The function $V(p,x_1,\ldots,x_n)$ is ordinally equivalent to W when p is fixed. For the comparison of a wide array of allocations, one should therefore fix a reference price vector $\tilde{p}$ and use it throughout. This is not a problem for the first term of the decomposition, which would then behave like a constant-price index of quantity. But, as observed above, the second term of the decomposition accurately measures inequity only if p is the prevailing price at the allocation $(x_1,\ldots,x_n)$.

A further limitation of the decomposition must be mentioned. Jorgenson and Slesnick call the first term in (3.26) the "efficiency" term and the second one the "equity" term. This terminology is slightly misleading because pX could be quite inefficient, for instance if the production sector did not make use of the technology efficiently. It might also happen that the allocation $(x_1,\ldots,x_n)$ is an inefficient distribution of X, for instance if rationing occurred on the market. In this case, the second term would partly measure the degree of distributive inefficiency of the allocation and not just inequity in the distribution.

This remark makes it interesting to consider a related kind of decomposition, which has been proposed by Graaff.

3.4.2 A second decomposition, in terms of efficiency and equity

Graaff's decomposition does not involve total income as an element, but it provides interesting ideas that will be exploited in the next subsection. Graaff (1977) computes an efficiency index as the smallest fraction of any producible bundle that maintains everyone at current satisfaction, normalizes social welfare as the smallest fraction of any producible bundle that maintains social welfare at its current level, and measures an equity index as the ratio of normalized social welfare over efficiency. Then normalized social welfare is the product of the efficiency and equity indexes.

Let us examine these notions in more detail. We retain the assumption that the social welfare function is increasing in individual utilities, and that individual preferences satisfy local nonsatiation. A key element of the decomposition is the Scitovsky set, which contains the vectors of total consumption that can be distributed so as to maintain all individuals' current satisfaction. It is formally defined as

$$\mathbf{S}(x_1,\ldots,x_n) = \Big\{X' \in \mathbb{R}^\ell_+ \mid \exists (x'_1,\ldots,x'_n),\ x'_1 + \cdots + x'_n = X', \\ u_i(x'_i) \geq u_i(x_i)\ \forall i\Big\},$$

which is equivalent to computing the Minkowski sum[12] of the individual upper contour sets $\left\{x'_i \in \mathbb{R}^\ell_+ \mid u_i(x'_i) \geq u_i(x_i)\right\}$.

Let the production possibilities be described by a production set $\mathbf{P} \subset \mathbb{R}^\ell_+$. Graaff's index of efficiency is defined as

$$\begin{aligned}\varepsilon(x_1,\ldots,x_n) &= \min \lambda \ \text{ s.t. } \exists X' \in \mathbf{P}, \lambda X' \in \mathbf{S}(x_1,\ldots,x_n),\\ &= \min \lambda \ \text{ s.t. } \lambda \mathbf{P} \cap \mathbf{S}(x_1,\ldots,x_n) \neq \varnothing.\end{aligned}$$

This index is equal to 1 when it is impossible, under the prevailing production possibilities, to raise the satisfaction of one individual without decreasing the satisfaction of anyone. It therefore tracks inefficiency in production, when X is not on the upper boundary of $\mathbf{P}$. It also tracks inefficiency in the distribution, when $(x_1,\ldots,x_n)$ could be redistributed so as to increase everyone's satisfaction.

This index bears some similarity with Debreu's (1951) coefficient of resource utilization, which is the smallest fraction of the resources available before production that would have made it possible, given the technology and the preferences, to maintain everyone at current satisfaction. Unlike Graaf's index, Debreu's coefficient depends on the role of commodities as net inputs or net outputs in production.

The measure of social welfare used by Graaff is not exactly the social expenditure function. It involves the Bergson set, which contains the vectors of total consumption that can be distributed so as to maintain social welfare. It is formally defined as

$$\begin{aligned}\mathbf{B}(x_1,\ldots,x_n) &= \left\{\begin{array}{c} X' \in \mathbb{R}^\ell_+ \mid \exists (x'_1,\ldots,x'_n),\ x'_1 + \cdots + x'_n = X' \\ W(u_1(x'_1),\ldots,u_n(x'_n)) \geq W(u_1(x_1),\ldots,u_n(x_n)) \end{array}\right\},\\ &= \left\{X' \in \mathbb{R}^\ell_+ \mid W^*(X') \geq W(u_1(x_1),\ldots,u_n(x_n))\right\}.\end{aligned}$$

The lower boundaries of Bergson sets correspond to the indifference map of the function W^*. Interestingly, the Bergson set is also the union of the Scitovsky sets corresponding to a given level of social welfare:

12. The Minkowski sum of two sets A and B is the set of elements $a + b$, where $a \in A$ and $b \in B$.

$$\mathbf{B}(x_1,\ldots,x_n) = \bigcup_{\substack{(x'_1,\ldots,x'_n) \text{ s.t.} \\ W(u_1(x'_1),\ldots,u_n(x'_n)) \geq W(u_1(x_1),\ldots,u_n(x_n))}} \mathbf{S}(x'_1,\ldots,x'_n).$$

The lower boundaries of Scitovsky sets, also called Scitovsky curves, do not form an indifference map because they cross. But if one restricts attention to a set of utility vectors $(u_1,\ldots,u_n)$ that all dominate each other for all components, the corresponding Scitovsky curves do not cross.

Graaff's index of social welfare is defined in the same way as the efficiency index, with the Bergson set taking up the role of the Scitovsky set:

$$\begin{aligned}\Gamma(x_1,\ldots,x_n) &= \min \lambda \;\text{ s.t. } \exists X' \in \mathbf{P}, \lambda X' \in \mathbf{B}(x_1,\ldots,x_n), \\ &= \min \lambda \;\text{ s.t. } \lambda \mathbf{P} \cap \mathbf{B}(x_1,\ldots,x_n) \neq \varnothing.\end{aligned}$$

This index is equal to 1 when it would be impossible to increase social welfare under the current production possibilities.

The ingredients of the decomposition are illustrated in figure 3.2. The P curve is the upper frontier of the production set (i.e., any aggregate bundle on or below this curve can be produced), the S curve is the lower boundary of the Scitovsky set for allocation $(x_1,\ldots,x_n)$ (i.e., any aggregate bundle on or above this curve can be distributed so as to give every $i = 1,\ldots,n$ his satisfaction at x_i), and the B curve is the lower boundary of the Bergson set (i.e., any aggregate bundle on or above this curve can be

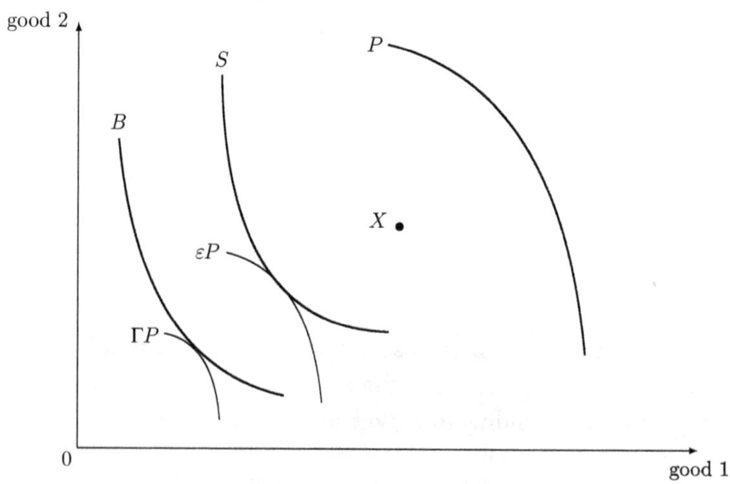

Figure 3.2
Graaff's decomposition of social welfare

distributed so as to yield as much social welfare as at $(x_1, \ldots, x_n)$). Note that the B curve is also the indifference curve at the level $W(u_1(x_1), \ldots, u_n(x_n))$ for the function W^* defined in (3.2).

One always has $\mathbf{S}(x_1, \ldots, x_n) \subset \mathbf{B}(x_1, \ldots, x_n)$, because maintaining everyone's satisfaction obviously maintains social welfare for a Paretian social welfare function, while it may be possible to maintain social welfare with other allocations in which some individuals endure a loss of satisfaction. When $(x_1, \ldots, x_n)$ is efficiently distributed (in the sense that no other distribution of X would be better for someone and worse for no one), X belongs to the lower boundary of $\mathbf{S}(x_1, \ldots, x_n)$. When it is optimally distributed for W, X belongs to the lower boundary of $\mathbf{B}(x_1, \ldots, x_n)$.

Graaff's equity index is the ratio of the social welfare and equity indexes:

$$\eta(x_1, \ldots, x_n) = \frac{\Gamma(x_1, \ldots, x_n)}{\varepsilon(x_1, \ldots, x_n)},$$

which is always less or equal to 1 by virtue of the inclusion $\mathbf{S}(x_1, \ldots, x_n) \subset \mathbf{B}(x_1, \ldots, x_n)$. It is equal to 1 when $(x_1, \ldots, x_n)$ is an optimal allocation for W, in which case all three indices are actually equal to 1, due to local nonsatiation that forces any Pareto-efficient production plan to be on the upper boundary of the production set. In summary, the decomposition is then

$$\Gamma(x_1, \ldots, x_n) = \varepsilon(x_1, \ldots, x_n) \times \eta(x_1, \ldots, x_n). \tag{3.27}$$

The equity index may be less than 1 even if $(x_1, \ldots, x_n)$ is an optimal distribution of X for W, which is somewhat disturbing. This will occur when the allocation is not fully efficient, so that social welfare would be maximized with another production plan in the production set. The lower boundaries of the Scitovsky and the Bergson set typically coincide only at X, when $(x_1, \ldots, x_n)$ is an optimal distribution of X for W. If the reduced set $\Gamma(x_1, \ldots, x_n)\mathbf{P}$ intersects $\mathbf{B}(x_1, \ldots, x_n)$ at a different point than X, it is typically the case that $\Gamma(x_1, \ldots, x_n)\mathbf{P}$ does not intersect $\mathbf{S}(x_1, \ldots, x_n)$, so that $\Gamma(x_1, \ldots, x_n) < \varepsilon(x_1, \ldots, x_n)$.

Another unpalatable feature of Graaff's decomposition is that his measure of normalized social welfare depends on the production set $\mathbf{P}$, unlike Pollak's social expenditure function. This implies that situations involving different production sets cannot be compared. For instance, if technical progress makes it possible to increase social welfare, and social welfare is increased accordingly, the index $\Gamma(x_1, \ldots, x_n)$ may remain unchanged. The size of the pie is just not part of the picture. In particular, this decomposition does not include total expenditure and the vector X itself plays little role in it. This approach therefore cannot serve the purpose of this section, but it provides the inspiration for the next subsection.

This is an area where research can still make progress. In the next two subsections we propose two new decompositions.

3.4.3 A new decomposition, based on Bergson curves

Taking inspiration from the decompositions proposed by Graaff, Jorgenson, and Slesnick, let us seek a better decomposition that would avoid the drawbacks pinpointed for these decompositions. Figure 3.3, similar to figure 3.2, illustrates a typical configuration (with a somewhat pessimistic outlook for efficiency and equity in order to better visualize the different curves). The lines with negative slopes represent bundles of equal value at reference prices $\tilde{p}$.

Let us take the Pollak function $V(\tilde{p}, x_1, \ldots, x_n)$ as the measure of social welfare. Apart from the fact that it has a convenient monetary scale, it also has the advantage of being independent of the technology, which makes it easy to compare allocations obtained under different technologies. The magnitude $V(\tilde{p}, x_1, \ldots, x_n)$ is represented on the figure, taking good 1 as numeraire.

The benchmark, ideal situation to which actual welfare should be compared can be constructed as the maximum level of social welfare obtainable with the production set

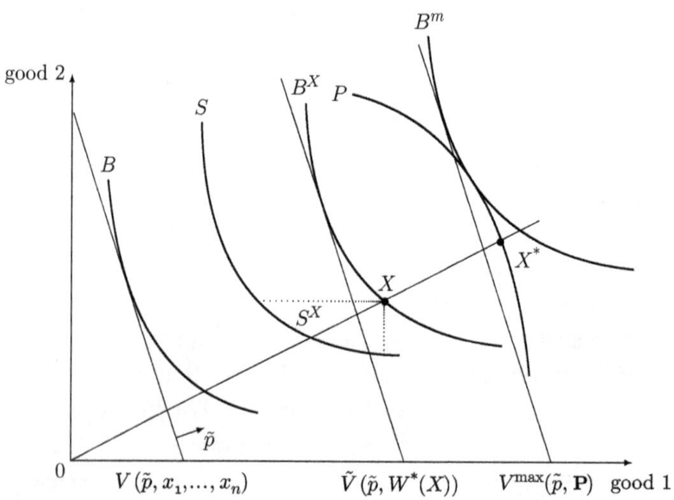

Figure 3.3
Decomposing social welfare

$$V^{\max}(\tilde{p}, \mathbf{P}) = \max \bar{V}(\tilde{p}, W^*(Y)) \text{ s.t. } Y \in \mathbf{P}.$$

This quantity is also represented in figure 3.3. The curve B^m is the highest indifference curve for W^* that intersects the production set.

The starting point of the decomposition is the product

$$V(\tilde{p}, x_1, \ldots, x_n) = V^{\max}(\tilde{p}, \mathbf{P}) \times \frac{V(\tilde{p}, x_1, \ldots, x_n)}{V^{\max}(\tilde{p}, \mathbf{P})}, \qquad (3.28)$$

in which the second term, typically less than 1, encapsulates inefficiency and inequity.

In order to see why $V^{\max}(\tilde{p}, \mathbf{P})$ is the appropriate benchmark, note that the ideal situation is obtained when the production set and the Bergson set are tangent. This is a situation in which all indices of efficiency and equity should equal 1, so that social welfare must then be equal to the benchmark magnitude from which, in the decomposition, inefficiency and inequity would deduct some amount in a nonideal situation. Conversely, this means that the benchmark magnitude must equal the highest Bergson curve that is tangent to the production set. Indeed, fix a Bergson curve (an indifference curve for W^*) and consider various possible optimal allocations belonging to different production sets that would each be tangent to this curve. The benchmark magnitude must then be the same for all these situations, as it must be equal to social welfare at this Bergson curve.

Now let us examine how to decompose the second term of (3.28) into efficiency and equity terms. A first term that can play a role is $\bar{V}(\tilde{p}, W^*(X))$, that is, the maximum social welfare that could be obtained with an optimal distribution of X. The indifference curve of $W^*(X)$ is the curve B^X on the figure. The ratio

$$\chi\,(x_1, \ldots, x_n) = \bar{V}(\tilde{p}, W^*(X))/V^{\max}(\tilde{p}, \mathbf{P})$$

then measures the welfare loss due to the suboptimality of the production plan X. It does not involve the way X is distributed, but only the fact that a better plan could be found in the production set. It is not just a measure of productive efficiency, because it also accounts for the suboptimality of the direction of X. This ratio may be less than 1 even if X lies on the production frontier (i.e., the upper boundary of $\mathbf{P}$).

If X is inefficiently distributed, it is as if part of X was wasted before the distribution, so that the actual quantity distributed lies on the part of curve S that lies below X. Let this part of the curve, identifiable in the figure by dotted lines below X, be denoted S^X. The lowest level of welfare that could be obtained with an optimal distribution of resources taken from S^X, namely,

$$V^{\min}(\tilde{p}, S^X) = \min \bar{V}(\tilde{p}, W^*(Y)) \text{ s.t. } Y \in S^X,$$

yields an interesting quantity to be used in a measure of distributive efficiency. Let

$$\delta\,(x_1, \ldots, x_n) = V^{\min}(\tilde{p}, S^X)/\bar{V}(\tilde{p}, W^*(X)).$$

Such an index measures the gap between the level of welfare attainable with X and the level that is attainable with what is actually used of X, given distributive inefficiencies.

It is equal to 1 when X is efficiently distributed and therefore lies on the curve S, so that S^X reduces to the singleton $\{X\}$. For this property of $\delta\,(x_1, \ldots, x_n)$ to be satisfied, it is important to take $V^{\min}(\tilde{p}, S^X)$ rather than $V^{\min}(\tilde{p}, S)$ in the definition of the ratio. Taking the latter would induce an index $\delta\,(x_1, \ldots, x_n)$ that is generally lower than 1 when X is efficiently but not socially optimally distributed.

Finally, equity can be measured by the ratio

$$\xi\,(x_1, \ldots, x_n) = V(\tilde{p}, x_1, \ldots, x_n)/V^{\min}(\tilde{p}, S^X).$$

This ratio is equal to 1 when the distribution of X is optimal. It is also equal to 1 when the distribution is inefficient but the individual shares are optimal, so that there is $Y \in S^X$ on the Bergson curve for $(x_1, \ldots, x_n)$. This is a case in which one could throw away part of X but keep the same distribution of utilities and obtain a socially optimal distribution of the remaining quantities.

In summary, one obtains the following decomposition:

$$V(\tilde{p}, x_1, \ldots, x_n) = V^{\max}(\tilde{p}, \mathbf{P}) \times \chi\,(x_1, \ldots, x_n) \times \delta\,(x_1, \ldots, x_n) \times \xi\,(x_1, \ldots, x_n). \tag{3.29}$$

This decomposition appears to avoid the main drawbacks listed for the previous decompositions. It relies on a notion of social welfare that respects preferences, that clearly separates distributive equity from distributive efficiency and productive optimality, unlike (3.26), and that does not depend on the technology, unlike (3.27). Its equity index is always equal to 1 when X is optimally distributed, a property that neither (3.26) nor (3.27) satisfied. Moreover, its index of distributive efficiency is always equal to 1 when X is efficiently distributed.

One nice property of Graaff's decomposition (3.27) can also be retrieved. When the production set and the Scitovsky set are tangent, its index of efficiency $\varepsilon(x_1, \ldots, x_n)$ is equal to 1. As a matter of fact, our new index of productive optimality $\chi(x_1, \ldots, x_n)$ can be decomposed into an index of productive efficiency and an index of directional optimality. The former may be defined as $\pi(x_1, \ldots, x_n) = \bar{V}(\tilde{p}, W^*(X))/\bar{V}(\tilde{p}, W^*(X^*))$, where X^* is the expansion of X that lies on the production frontier (see the figure). Taking the product of the two indexes of productive and distributive efficiency, $\pi(x_1, \ldots, x_n)\, \delta(x_1, \ldots, x_n)$, the desired property is then retrieved.

A limitation of this decomposition is that it is conceived for a very special model of private goods and is not easily extendable to a setting with nonmarket goods (such as public goods or personal nontransferable characteristics) and unequal productive skills.

In the context of a search for a decomposition featuring total income as a particular term, however, the decomposition (3.29) is not successful. It does not display the market value of X as a specific term. However, the product of the first two terms is equal to

$$V^{\max}(\tilde{p}, \mathbf{P}) \times \chi(x_1, \ldots, x_n) = \bar{V}(\tilde{p}, W^*(X)),$$

which is not too different from $\tilde{p}X$ when the supporting price vector of the curve B^X at X is not too different from $\tilde{p}$. Rigorously, however, this is not the same thing, and the difference may be substantial in some cases.

The fact that the money-metric social value of X rather than a simple market value of X at suitable prices appears in this decomposition may, perhaps, reveal a deep difficulty. It appears intrinsically hard to make pX an interesting term in the analysis of social welfare.

3.4.4 Another decomposition, for small variations

In this last decomposition, we consider a richer setting in which individual utility $u_i(x_i, y_i)$ is determined by market commodities x_i and nonmarket goods y_i. The latter can also include leisure when individuals have unequal skills and labor time cannot be transferred between individuals without affecting the production. Let $v_i(p, y_i, m_i)$ denote the indirect utility function, defined as the maximum utility $u_i(x_i, y_i)$ that i can obtain when buying x_i with income m_i under prices p, for a fixed y_i:

$$v_i(p, y_i, m_i) = \max\left\{u_i(x_i, y_i) \mid px_i \le m_i\right\}.$$

For small variations, assuming continuous differentiability of u_i, a rather simple decomposition of social welfare can be obtained. It relies on the assumption that market commodities x_i are always bought on a market in which all individuals face the same price vector p.

The starting point is to notice that, at a market allocation, for a small change (dp, dx_i, dy_i, dm_i), the variation in utility is equal to

$$dv_i = \frac{\partial v_i}{\partial m_i}(pdx_i + w_i), \tag{3.30}$$

where

$$w_i = \sum_l \frac{\partial v_i/\partial y_{il}}{\partial v_i/\partial m_i} dy_{il}$$

is the willingness-to-pay to incur the change in the vector y_i (l is the label of dimensions of y_i).[13]

Letting $\beta_i = \frac{\partial W}{\partial v_i}\frac{\partial v_i}{\partial m_i}$ denote the social marginal utility of m_i, one can write

$$\begin{aligned} dW(v_1(p, y_1, m_1), \ldots, v_n(p, y_n, m_n)) &= \sum_{i=1}^{n} \frac{\partial W}{\partial v_i} dv_i \\ &= \sum_{i=1}^{n} \beta_i (pdx_i + w_i). \end{aligned}$$

13. Equation (3.30) is proved as follows. By definition,

$$dv_i = \sum_k \frac{\partial v_i}{\partial p_k} dp_k + \sum_l \frac{\partial v_i}{\partial y_{il}} dy_{il} + \frac{\partial v_i}{\partial m_i} dm_i.$$

By Roy's identity, which remains valid in the presence of a given y_i,

$$x_{ik} = -\frac{\partial v_i/\partial p_k}{\partial v_i/\partial m_i},$$

and by definition, $dm_i = pdx_i + x_i dp$. One therefore has

$$\begin{aligned} dv_i &= -\frac{\partial v_i}{\partial m_i} \sum_k x_{ik} dp_k + \sum_l \frac{\partial v_i}{\partial y_{il}} dy_{il} + \frac{\partial v_i}{\partial m_i} dm_i \\ &= \frac{\partial v_i}{\partial m_i} pdx_i + \sum_l \frac{\partial v_i}{\partial y_{il}} dy_{il}, \end{aligned}$$

from which it is immediate to derive (3.30) by factorizing $\partial v_i/\partial m_i$.

This makes it possible to compute the following decomposition (letting $\bar{\beta}$ denote the mean $\frac{1}{n}\sum_{i=1}^{n}\beta_i$ and $\bar{w}$ the mean $\frac{1}{n}\sum_{i=1}^{n}w_i$):

$$dW(u_1(x_1),\ldots,u_n(x_n)) = \bar{\beta}\, pdX + \bar{\beta}\, n\bar{w}$$
$$+\sum_{i=1}^{n}\left(\beta_i-\bar{\beta}\right)\left(pdx_i - pdX/n\right)+\sum_{i=1}^{n}\left(\beta_i-\bar{\beta}\right)\left(w_i-\bar{w}\right). \quad (3.31)$$

The formula uses the fact that the mean of a product equals the product of the means plus the covariance.

The last two terms in the decomposition (3.31) depend on the correlation between the social priority of individuals and the variation in their situation and is quite intuitive for a distributional term. Each term is positive if the individuals whose situation improves more than average tend to have a greater β_i coefficient.[14]

This decomposition is very simple, additive, and features *pdX* as a component. It nicely distinguishes the effects of changes in the pie and changes in the distribution, both for market and for nonmarket goods. One could argue that it makes it legitimate to focus on the evolution of total expenditure at constant prices, provided it is explicitly stated that distributive issues and nonmarket dimensions are ignored. Obviously, it suggests that the most interesting approach is to compute the four terms rather than just one, because a positive evolution in *pdX* may hide ominous developments in nonmarket dimensions and in the distribution.

The difficulty in implementing this decomposition is that one needs not only data on the joint distribution of (x_i, y_i), but also the weights β_i, which depend on the calibration of utilities. This is where the equivalent income concept discussed in the next chapter will appear particularly useful because it provides a calibration of utilities that delivers interpersonal comparisons across individuals with different preferences.

To conclude this section, the quest for a good decomposition of social welfare turns out to be a rather complex and intriguing task. Among the decompositions introduced in this section, (3.29) and (3.31) appear the most interesting. The former, which can be applied to any conception of social welfare, contains aggregate terms that are similar but not identical

14. Such terms should not be confused with the "distributional characteristic" (Feldstein 1972a, 1972b; Atkinson and Stiglitz 1980) that plays an important role in the analysis of optimal indirect tax or public pricing. The distributional characteristic depends on the correlation between β_i and the *level* rather than the *variation* of consumption of a commodity.

to total income. The latter, for small variations, does feature total income (at fixed prices) and is also compatible with any social welfare function.

The field of social welfare decomposition deserves more research. It would be nice to obtain axiomatic justifications of specific decompositions, and to be able to identify terms that embody particular efficiency notions and especially particular equity notions. Another decomposition will be introduced in the next chapter, involving a specific calibration of utility and with equity defined as inequality aversion with respect to such calibrated utilities.

One can dream that in the near future, implementing these decompositions with real-life statistics would become a routine and would inform the evaluation of social progress by showing the contribution to social welfare made by efficiency and equity components of the social situation.

3.5 SPECIFIC PROBLEMS WITH IMPUTED PRICES AND FULL INCOME

In most of this chapter (i.e., except in the last subsection and in a small part of section 3.2), we have assumed away the presence of nonmarketed goods or similar considerations that would obviously call for a correction to income before looking for a link between income and welfare, at the individual level. The fact that in absence of these difficulties, the link has already proved hard to establish, especially at the social level, suggests that the idea of refining the concept of total income by making such corrections is not very promising. Refinements are usually elaborated for concepts that are successful in the simplest case, not for concepts that are already flawed in the simplest conditions. It is, however, worth examining how such corrections affect the relation between income and welfare.

The addition of the shadow price of nonmarketed goods is usually said to yield a measure of "full income." The principle of computation of full income is very simple and can be illustrated in the case in which there are only two goods, a generic marketed good called "income" (taken as the numeraire) and a nonmarketed good y (e.g., health, leisure, safety, environmental quality). Consider a consumer whose income is m and who consumes the quantity y of the other good. He has a marginal rate of substitution r that measures how much of m he is willing to pay in order to have an additional unit of y.

Full income is then defined as the magnitude $m + ry$. The concept, illustrated in figure 3.4, is natural if one seeks to find the market-like hypothetical situation that is the closest to the actual situation of this consumer.

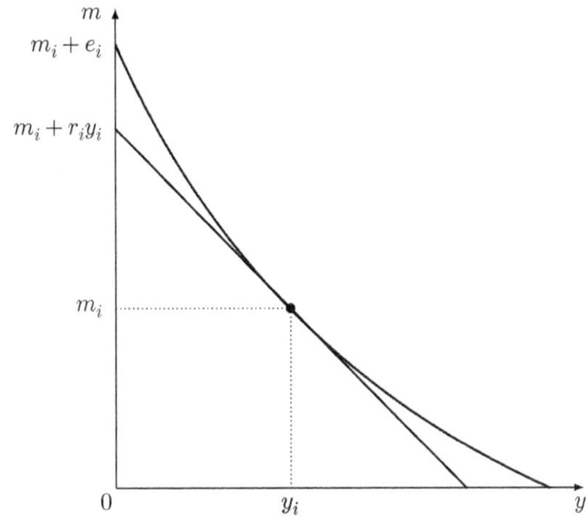

Figure 3.4
Full income

Assuming that preferences are convex, one sees that if this consumer could buy both goods on the market at the price vector $(1, r)$, with total income $m + ry$, he would indeed take the bundle (m, y) as a best choice.

The notion of full income is often invoked in relation to leisure. Although there is a labor market, it requires some imagination to consider that a worker "buys" his leisure on a market at a posted price of leisure. In particular, the net wage varies with the amount of leisure, and many workers are not really free to choose their preferred quantity of labor in their budget set. It is therefore interesting to seek to estimate the true shadow value of leisure.

Once the analysis is cast in the framework of consumption bundles (m, y) at prices $(1, r)$, the analysis of the previous sections can be unfolded again. Not much is changed at the individual level. For instance, the revealed preference argument is still valid. If $m + ry \geq m' + ry'$, the individual is at least as well off with (m, y) as with (m', y').

The only nuance one could think of is that there might be a difference, for the evaluation of welfare, between a free choice in a budget set of a full bundle (m, y) and being constrained on y, or choosing (m, y) from an opportunity set with a shape different from a typical budget set. This issue is ignored in the typical consumer preferences, which only care about the final bundle consumed. If individual preferences were enriched so as to care about the opportunities and not just the final bundle, the analysis could be developed again in a richer space.

At the social level, however, there is an important new problem. The shadow price r is specific to the particular individual situation that is examined. In particular, different individuals will have different shadow prices. One cannot therefore talk about "the" shadow price of leisure or health. This considerably complicates the implementation of monetary measures based on prices.

Given such practical complexity, it is not a big step to move beyond the use of the "pricing" methodology and to move to a "willingness-to-pay" methodology, as will be done in the next chapter. The difference between the two methodologies is illustrated in figure 3.4, where $m_i + e_i$ denotes the level of income that renders the individual indifferent between enjoying the current bundle (m_i, y_i) and obtaining instead the income increment e_i without any quantity of y.[15] It turns out that most of the problems implied by measuring welfare with prices are avoided when one relies instead on willingness-to-pay. From figure 3.4, it is intuitive that a measure like $m_i + e_i$, which is based on the indifference curve, is more precise than a measure like $m_i + r_i y_i$, based on a local marginal rate of substitution. This alternative approach will be explored further in chapter 4.

We conclude this section by briefly noting that there is an extension of Samuelson's optimality result to the setting with nonmarket goods. Suppose that $(x_1, \ldots, x_n) \in \mathbb{R}^{n\ell}_{++}$ is a market allocation at prices p, with $px_i > 0$ for all i, while $(y_1, \ldots, y_n) \in \mathbb{R}^{n\ell'}_{++}$ is a nonmarket allocation of other goods, with shadow price vectors $(r_1, \ldots, r_n)$. Individual preferences are assumed to be locally nonsatiable and representable by differentiable utility functions. If $(x_1, \ldots, x_n)$ is an optimal distribution of X given $(y_1, \ldots, y_n)$ for a social welfare function $W(u_1(x_1, y_1), \ldots, u_n(x_n, y_n))$ that is quasi-concave and differentiable in the quantities of commodities, then for all allocations $(x'_1, \ldots, x'_n), (y'_1, \ldots, y'_n)$ such that

$$\sum_{i=1}^{n} px_i + r_i y_i \geq \sum_{i=1}^{n} px'_i + r_i y'_i,$$

one has

$$W(u_1(x_1, y_1), \ldots, u_n(x_n, y_n)) \geq W(u_1(x'_1, y'_1), \ldots, u_n(x'_n, y'_n)).$$

15. The distinction between shadow prices and willingness-to-pay vanishes for infinitesimal variations, as in the computation of decomposition (3.31), where willingness-to-pay w_i relies on shadow prices computed with marginal rates of substitution between m_i and y_{il}.

This is proved by showing that, in a social budget set defined by the condition

$$\sum_{i=1}^{n} px_i' + r_i y_i' \leq M,$$

with $M = \sum_{i=1}^{n} px_i + r_i y_i$, the allocation $(x_1, \ldots, x_n), (y_1, \ldots, y_n)$ is optimal for the objective $W(u_1(x_1, y_1), \ldots, u_n(x_n, y_n))$ because of quasi-concavity with respect to quantities.

Indeed, by differentiability the fact that $(x_1, \ldots, x_n)$ is an optimal distribution of X implies that for some $\lambda > 0$, for all individuals i, all goods k, either $\frac{\partial W}{\partial u_i} \frac{\partial u_i}{\partial x_{ik}} / p_k = \lambda$ or $\frac{\partial W}{\partial u_i} \frac{\partial u_i}{\partial x_{ik}} / p_k < \lambda$ and $x_{ik} = 0$.

By definition of shadow prices, one has for all k, l such that $x_{ik} > 0$,

$$\frac{\frac{\partial u_i}{\partial x_{ik}}}{p_k} \geq \frac{\frac{\partial u_i}{\partial y_{il}}}{r_{il}},$$

with equality when $y_{il} > 0$.

Now consider an infinitesimal change to the allocation $(x_1, \ldots, x_n)$, $(y_1, \ldots, y_n)$. It induces

$$\begin{aligned} dW &= \sum_i \frac{\partial W}{\partial u_i} \left(\sum_k \frac{\partial u_i}{\partial x_{ik}} dx_{ik} + \sum_l \frac{\partial u_i}{\partial y_{il}} dy_{il} \right) \\ &= \sum_i \frac{\partial W}{\partial u_i} \left(\sum_k \frac{\partial u_i}{p_k \partial x_{ik}} p_k dx_{ik} + \sum_l \frac{\partial u_i}{r_{il} \partial y_{il}} r_{il} dy_{il} \right) \\ &\leq \lambda \sum_i \left(p dx_i + r_i dy_i \right), \end{aligned}$$

where the last inequality comes from the fact that for all i, $\frac{\partial W}{\partial u_i} \frac{\partial u_i}{p_k \partial x_{ik}} \leq \lambda$ and $\frac{\partial W}{\partial u_i} \frac{\partial u_i}{r_{il} \partial y_{il}} \leq \lambda$.[16]

This proves that $(x_1, \ldots, x_n), (y_1, \ldots, y_n)$ is optimal in the defined budget M, because $\sum_i (p dx_i + r_i dy_i) = 0$ when the equality $M = \sum_{i=1}^{n} px_i + r_i y_i$ is preserved, and quasi-concavity with respect to quantities has been assumed.

16. More precisely, if $x_{ik} = 0$ and $\frac{\partial W}{\partial u_i} \frac{\partial u_i}{p_k \partial x_{ik}} < \lambda$, then $dx_{ik} \geq 0$ and $\frac{\partial W}{\partial u_i} \frac{\partial u_i}{p_k \partial x_{ik}} dx_{ik} < \lambda dx_{ik}$; if $x_{ik} > 0$, then $\frac{\partial W}{\partial u_i} \frac{\partial u_i}{p_k \partial x_{ik}} = \lambda$ and $\frac{\partial W}{\partial u_i} \frac{\partial u_i}{p_k \partial x_{ik}} dx_{ik} = \lambda dx_{ik}$. The same holds for y_i. Note that the argument extends easily to the case in which y_{il} must belong to a compact interval. When it is equal to the higher bound, one can have $\frac{\partial W}{\partial u_i} \frac{\partial u_i}{p_k \partial y_{il}} > \lambda$, but then $dy_{il} \leq 0$, which implies $\frac{\partial W}{\partial u_i} \frac{\partial u_i}{p_k \partial y_{il}} dy_{il} \leq \lambda dy_{il}$.

The argument is then completed by observing that any alternative allocation $(x'_1,\ldots,x'_n)$, $(y'_1,\ldots,y'_n)$ that belongs to the same budget set $\sum_{i=1}^{n} px'_i + r_i y'_i \leq M$ yields at most as good an outcome as the optimal $(x_1,\ldots,x_n)$, $(y_1,\ldots,y_n)$.

In summary, the fact that $(x_1,\ldots,x_n)$ is optimally distributed (with nonnegative income for every individual) given $(y_1,\ldots,y_n)$ is enough to make sure that the trade-offs embodied in the price vector $(p,r_1,\ldots,r_n)$ reflect the true trade-offs for the social objective.

3.6 CONCLUSION

In conclusion, economic theory does not provide much support for relying on the market value of total consumption as a proxy for social welfare. The revealed preference argument justifies an incomplete criterion based on the Laspeyres and Paasche indexes (i.e., based on the inequality $pX > pX'$) only under stringent assumptions of social optimality that have no chance of being realized in a world of imperfect information. The decomposition approach, however, does deliver interesting insights about how to separate efficiency from equity in the analysis of social welfare, and there are interesting decompositions featuring the market value of consumption. In particular, (3.31) seems promising and makes it possible to disentangle the welfare effect of total expenditures, nonmarketed goods, and inequalities.

A limitation of the revealed preference approaches is that they are conceived for the evaluation of changes affecting a given population. They do not help much in comparisons across different populations across countries or across generations. Sen (1976) does raise the issue explicitly and shows that, under the additional principle that only the statistical distribution of individual situations matters, not the size of the population, his approach can be extended to comparisons between populations in a limited way. Specifically, one can then check if the population in one country is better off than if it were served the *distribution* of consumption of another country. Concretely this is done by checking if

$$\alpha_1 px_1 + \cdots + \alpha_n px_n > \alpha_1 px'_1 + \cdots + \alpha_n px'_n,$$

where the subscripts $1,\ldots,n$ refer to n-quantiles instead of concrete individuals. The same methodology can be adapted to the $pX > pX'$ criterion, which then simply has to be formulated in per capita terms, as well as to the decompositions listed in a previous section.

But this sort of comparison does not address the challenge of comparing populations with different preferences. It is for instance possible to find in some cases that country A is better off (in its eyes) than country B and that country B is also better off (in its eyes) than country A.

This problem is related to another general limitation of most of the approaches described in this chapter, namely, their silence about how to make interpersonal comparisons. In particular, the various approaches assuming that the distribution is optimal, or that it is described in a separate term in a decomposition such as (3.26), make it possible to focus on total consumption without even specifying further the distributive judgments. The function $\overline{W}(x_1, \ldots, x_n)$ or $W(u_1(x_1), \ldots, u_n(x_n))$ that is referred to in these constructions could be based on many different sorts of evaluation of individual well-being.

That can be viewed as an advantage because it makes a focus on total expenditure compatible with many different distributive principles. But as soon as one wants to also evaluate the distribution, it creates a danger. Indeed, formulas such as (3.26) and (3.31) naturally suggest taking the monetary value of individual consumption as the measure of individual well-being, and this is indeed done explicitly in (3.4). It is, however, important to be aware that the theory presented so far does not give any reason to adopt this measure of individual well-being. Independent arguments are needed.

Here is an example of such an argument. In the theories of justice proposed by Rawls (1971) or Dworkin (2000), social justice consists in allocating resources in a fair way, letting individuals make use of the resources at their disposal according to their own conception of the good life. If one ignores differences in internal resources (talent, disabilities), the fair distribution is that which maximizes the share of resources of those who have the least—the market valuation appearing convenient for the comparison of resource shares. Recall, however, that Rawls's list of primary goods includes nonmarketed items such as basic freedoms, the powers and prerogatives of positions of responsibility, and the social bases of self-respect. Wealth is only one item, but an important one. In sum, provided that the other aspects of resources such as basic freedoms and status are well distributed, individual wealth is then a suitable measure for interpersonal comparisons. The market value of individual consumption can then be defended as a reasonable proxy for comparisons of wealth.

If personal abilities and needs are unequal, however, this line of argument no longer supports the market value of consumption as a proper metric. A practically important example concerns the valuation of leisure time, which is part of consumption broadly construed and is unequally accessible to individuals with different wage rates on the labor market. As shown in the previous section, the revealed preference argument suggests using individuals' net wage rate as the proper valuation of leisure time. But one should resist the temptation to compare full incomes (i.e., earnings plus the value of leisure) across individuals without a suitable deflator that corrects for their unequal opportunities. One cannot simply consider that those with a greater full income are better off, and that it would be nice to reduce inequalities in full incomes. In fact, equalizing full incomes across individuals would imply that those with greater productivity would have strictly smaller budget sets than those with lower productivity (because their leisure is more expensive), in a strange reversal from the laissez-faire situation. Moreover, they would typically be forced to work at their highest wage rate in order to pay their taxes, implying what Dworkin (2000) called a "slavery of the talented." The literature on fairness has proposed various reasonable ways of comparing the resource shares of individuals with unequal productivity. More generally, there are interesting ways to extend the notion of wealth to the case of unequal needs and abilities. These issues will be addressed in more detail in chapters 4 and 6.

The conclusion of this one is that putting uniform prices on the different dimensions of individuals' lives is too simple an approach if one wants to respect individual preferences.

CHAPTER 4

Equivalent Income, or How to Value What Has No Price

The previous two chapters have been devoted to approaches that involve prices. In both chapters it has been shown that the link between income, wealth, or the market value of consumption on the one hand and individual well-being or social welfare on the other hand is not simple. Chapter 2 shows that supplementing the market value of consumption with the value of net investment in order to assess the sustainability of current welfare is fraught with difficulties. In chapter 3 the link between total income and social welfare has been analyzed in detail and has been shown to be loose, even when nonmarket dimensions of welfare are ignored. Putting a price on everything is not a promising way of going "beyond GDP."

In this chapter we study another approach, which involves willingness-to-pay instead of prices and shadow prices. It involves measuring individual well-being by "equivalent income," also called "money-metric utility," and using this measure in social welfare functions of the classical form. The distinction between the approaches studied in this chapter and the previous one may seem like a technical detail more than a paradigm shift. In particular, equivalent incomes are still measured in monetary units. To economists and statisticians, this is an advantage because such a measure seems amenable to convenient mathematical and statistical computations. But many people in search of alternative indicators would consider this a drawback of the measure, on the grounds that the monetary scale is reductionist or even fetishistic. Measuring the beauty of life in dollars and euros seems vulgar. It is therefore a great attractive feature of happiness indicators or of the capability approach that they are directly formulated in terms of the important aspects of life, such as emotions, health, education, and self-respect.

In this chapter we will argue that the notion of equivalent income deserves careful attention. It is one of the most fascinating concepts of economic theory because of its connection to different parts of welfare economics that seldom talk to one another. It appeared at least twice, in very different contexts. The first appearance was in the classical works about consumer surplus and index numbers. After the expenditure function and similar concepts were introduced by Hicks (1956) and McKenzie (1957), it is really with Samuelson (1974) and Samuelson and Swamy (1974) that the idea of using the money metric as a specific representation of preferences was brought to the fore. Interestingly, Samuelson was actually afraid that the monetary scale could entice analysts to make wild computations such as sums of money-metric utilities over a population, without probing the dubious ethical implications. A wave of studies and applications of the concept followed,[1] accompanied by the extension of the concept to include nonmarket characteristics (such as household composition).[2] The enthusiasm, however, was quickly dashed by social choice theorists who defended the superior Bergson-Samuelson social welfare function[3] and criticized the use of equivalent incomes in social evaluation as "arbitrary and capricious ethics" (Donaldson 1992, p. 93). More precisely, social choice theorists pointed out the dependence of the measure on reference prices (Blackorby, Laisney, and Schmachtenberg 1994) and the possibility of antiegalitarian implications (Blackorby and Donaldson 1988). It seems that, although criticism emanating from social choice theorists has never been powerful enough to deter practioners from using consumer surplus and compensating variations in welfare analysis, it has seriously undermined the interest of the profession in the (much superior) equivalent income.

1. See in particular McKenzie and Pearce (1976, 1982), Deaton (1980), Deaton and Muellbauer (1980), Willig (1981), Diewert (1983), King (1983), McKenzie (1983), Weymark (1985), and other references cited in Blackorby et al. (1994) and Ahlheim (1998).

2. Hammond (1994) also studied the extension to public goods and externalities.

3. The "Bergson-Samuelson social welfare function" is the usual name of the classical function

$$W(u_1(x_1), \ldots, u_n(x_n)),$$

although Bergson (1938) and Samuelson (1947) have also introduced the function that depends directly on quantities:

$$\bar{W}(x_1, \ldots, x_n).$$

As we will explain in this chapter, the equivalent income made another appearance in economics, namely, in the theory of fair allocation, as a special case of the "equivalence" approach. What is exciting at this point is that in the context of the theory of fair allocation, the ethical foundations of the approach are much firmer. In particular, the development of the theory of fair social choice sheds new light on the social choice theorists' criticism against the equivalent income. It becomes even possible to argue that rather than being inferior to the Bergson-Samuelson approach, money-metric utilities provide one of the best ways to construct Bergson-Samuelson social welfare functions!

This chapter is organized as follows. The first section recalls the definition of money-metric utilities and equivalent incomes, and the second section explains the various criticisms raised against it by social choice theorists. The third section shows how the notion can be viewed under a new light in the context of the theory of fair allocation and the theory of fair social choice, and how this makes it possible to rebut or at least downplay the criticisms listed in the second section. The fourth section introduces a new decomposition of social welfare (in the style of the decompositions discussed in section 3.4) that makes use of equivalent incomes. The last section concludes.

4.1 MONEY-METRIC UTILITY AND EQUIVALENT INCOME

In section 3.3 we reviewed two branches of the theory of index numbers that seek to produce proxies for welfare variations in terms of price and quantities. Samuelson (1974) and Samuelson and Swamy (1974) recognized that, if one wants to obtain an index that really reflects welfare, the index has to depend on individual preferences and not just on prices and quantities. Several ideas have followed this vein. Their own proposal is the money-metric utility function

$$e\left(\tilde{p}, u(x)\right) = \min\left\{\tilde{p}x' \mid u(x') \geq u(x)\right\}, \tag{4.1}$$

which is derived from the expenditure function

$$e(p, u) = \min\left\{px' \mid u(x') \geq u\right\}$$

and computes the minimal expenditure required to obtain the same satisfaction as with x at reference prices $\tilde{p}$—it is therefore measured in monetary units. See figure 4.1 for an illustration.

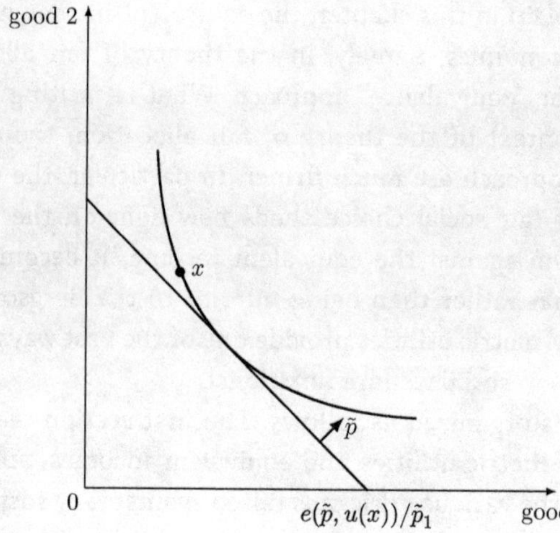

Figure 4.1
The money-metric utility

This measure is closely linked to the equivalent variation and compensating variation mentioned in subsection 3.3.2. However, a problem with *EV* and *CV* is that the reference price they rely on is different for different pairwise comparisons, creating a problem of chaining. When $EV(p^1, p^0, x^1, x^0) > 0$ and $EV(p^2, p^1, x^2, x^1) < 0$, for instance, one can infer nothing about the welfare change from $\left(p^0, x^0\right)$ to $\left(p^2, x^2\right)$ from the value of these two equivalent variations. In contrast, if the same reference $\tilde{p}$ is used consistently, then one has

$$e(\tilde{p}, u(x^2)) - e(\tilde{p}, u(x^0)) = \left[e(\tilde{p}, u(x^2)) - e(\tilde{p}, u(x^1))\right] + \left[e(\tilde{p}, u(x^1)) - e(\tilde{p}, u(x^0))\right].$$

It therefore appears important, for comparisons involving many alternatives, to use the same reference price throughout, as stressed in McKenzie (1983). This is the simple idea that motivates the money-metric utility.

In applied evaluations of living standards, unfortunately, many approaches adopt reference parameters that are specific to the situation, as in cost-benefit analysis.[4] For instance, Usher (1973) and Becker, Philipson, and Soares (2005) compute the income growth that would be equivalent,

4. For a critique of traditional methods of cost-benefit analysis such as the sum of compensating variations or equivalent variations, see Boadway and Bruce (1984) and Blackorby and Donaldson (1990).

for average preferences, to the combination of income growth and increase in life expectancy that has been observed over a certain period of time. Jones and Klenow (2010) make international comparisons that involve computing the change in per capita income that would be needed in every country to bring it to the welfare level of the United States if it kept its own nonmarket characteristics. One can even note that when McKenzie (1983) advocates evaluating reforms with the status quo providing the reference parameters, this guarantees a consistent ordering of reforms, but consistency is not guaranteed across evaluation exercises when the status quo changes. Indeed, the problem with such variable parameters is that they may generate inconsistent evaluations: Starting from a certain initial status quo, a sequence of improvements may lead back to it, because the reference parameters change through the process. It is therefore highly desirable to fix the parameters for a large class of evaluations.

Another famous proposal in the same vein as the money-metric utility is the "ray" utility function, defined by the property that the individual is indifferent between x and $u_{\tilde{x}}(x)\tilde{x}$, for a reference bundle $\tilde{x}$. This utility is unitless but corresponds to fractions of a bundle and can therefore be treated like a quantity index. This function was introduced, in the context of finding an index representation of preferences, by Malmquist (1953) and Kannai (1970) and used, in the context of finding social welfare functions based on ordinal noncomparable individual preferences, by Samuelson (1977) and Pazner (1979). See figure 4.2 for an illustration.

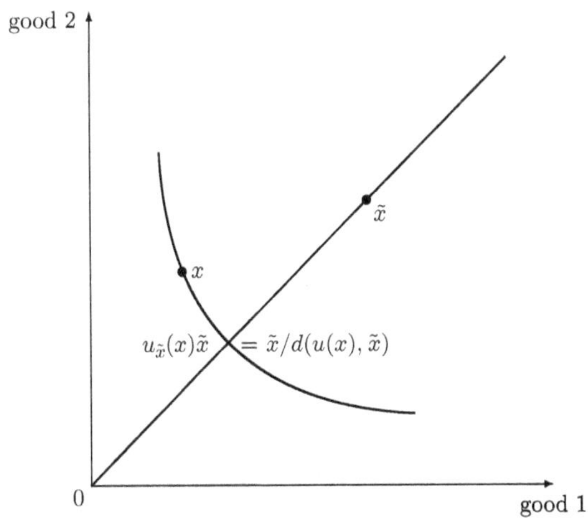

Figure 4.2
The ray utility and the distance function

The ray utility is also linked to the "distance function" studied in Deaton (1979), which can be defined by the formula $d(u, \tilde{x}) = 1/u_{\tilde{x}}(x)$, where x is any bundle giving the individual utility level u (for any given utility function $u(x)$). Interest in the distance function comes in particular from the fact that

$$d(u, \tilde{x}) = \min\left\{p\tilde{x} \mid p \in \mathbb{R}^{\ell}_{++},\ e(p, u) \geq 1\right\}$$

while

$$e(p, u) = \min\left\{p\tilde{x} \mid \tilde{x} \in \mathbb{R}^{\ell}_{++},\ d(u, \tilde{x}) \geq 1\right\},$$

yielding interesting duality properties (e.g., one can retrieve compensated inverse demand functions and shadow prices from d in a similar fashion as one can obtain compensated demand from e, as recalled in (3.15)).[5]

This approach is more demanding because it requires data on preferences, not just on prices and quantities. The counterpart is that, contrary to the previous approaches, these indexes do always reflect preferences. Another interesting feature is that they can serve for comparisons between different individuals with different preferences, if an ethical justification can be provided for such comparisons.

Now consider a richer framework in which individual i consumes a bundle (x_i, y_i) made of market commodities x_i and other nonmarketed dimensions y_i (such as public goods and personal characteristics and functionings). The money-metric utility is then equal to the expenditure in x_i needed to reach the utility level $u_i(x_i, y_i)$ under a reference price vector $\tilde{p}$ and with reference $\tilde{y}$:

$$e_i\left(\tilde{p}, \tilde{y}, u_i(x_i, y_i)\right) = \min\left\{\tilde{p}x' \mid u_i(x', \tilde{y}) \geq u_i(x_i, y_i)\right\}. \tag{4.2}$$

It seems that, according to the most common practice, one talks about "money-metric utility" when x_i is the sole object of preferences and y_i is absent, as in (4.1), and about "equivalent income" in the presence of the other dimensions captured in y_i. Really, the two notions are the same, and we will use the terms interchangeably.

5. The compensated, or Hicksian, demand function $x(p, u)$ determines the commodities demanded by the consumer when prices p prevail and his utility is maintained at level u. The compensated inverse demand function is the function $p(x, u)$ determining the price vector (normalized by the expenditure px) that induces demand x when the consumer's utility is maintained at u. The shadow price at x, as already explained in section 3.5, is the price vector p that induces the consumer to demand x when his income is px.

The distinction between the variables p and y in the arguments of $e_i(.)$ is, in fact, a matter of intuitive presentation because from the point of view of individual well-being, prices are just another aspect of the environment and are essentially identical to any other form of public bad. This can be seen most clearly if one looks at the indirect money-metric utility. Let m_i denote i's income (or wealth), so that indirect utility is defined as[6]

$$v_i(p, y_i, m_i) = \max \left\{ u_i(x_i, y_i) \mid px_i \leq m_i \right\}.$$

The indirect money-metric utility is then

$$e_i\left(\tilde{p}, \tilde{y}, v_i(p, y_i, m_i)\right) = \min \left\{ m \mid v_i(\tilde{p}, \tilde{y}, m) \geq v_i(p, y_i, m_i) \right\},$$

or, equivalently, is the solution m^* to the equation

$$v_i(\tilde{p}, \tilde{y}, m^*) = v_i(p, y_i, m_i). \tag{4.3}$$

In this equation it is transparent that the distinction between p and y is not important from the individual's viewpoint—although, of course, prices are a specific form of public bad because they reduce the usefulness of income in a special way, as revealed by the fact that v_i is homogeneous of degree zero in (m_i, p).

Figure 4.3 illustrates (4.3) for the case in which there is only one dimension of y, while p is ignored (or fixed at 1).[7]

This equation also makes it intuitive why the expression "equivalent income" is adequate. The equivalent income for i is the level of income that, combined with reference parameters for the nonincome dimensions of life, would give i the same satisfaction as the current situation. If i is indifferent between his current situation and an income of 120 combined with the reference $\tilde{p}, \tilde{y}$, his equivalent income is 120.

The above equation also makes it clear that equivalent income is a utility, that is, a representation of preferences, in the standard circumstances of locally nonsatiable preferences. A better situation for i raises $v_i(p, y_i, m_i)$, which requires raising the unknown m in $v_i(\tilde{p}, \tilde{y}, m)$ because v_i is increasing in income.

6. It is implicitly assumed here that the price vector p is the same for all individuals, but the definitions would be identical if personalized prices p_i were considered.

7. This figure is essentially the same as figure 3.4, and one sees that $m_i + e_i$ in that figure corresponds to taking $\tilde{y} = 0$ as the reference.

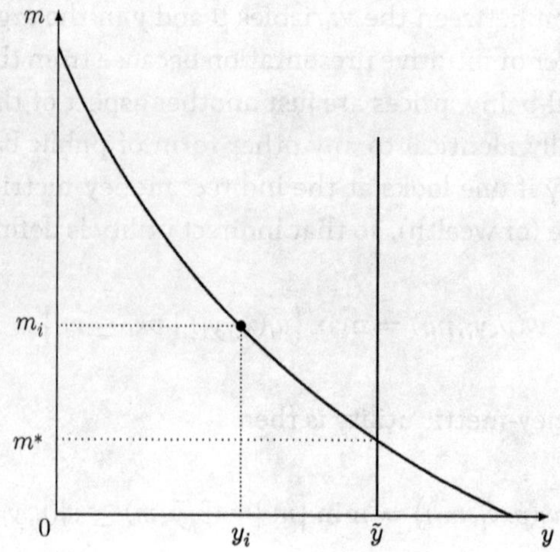

Figure 4.3
Equivalent income

4.2 KNOCKOUT CRITICISMS?

Let us now turn to the criticisms raised against this calibration of utilities. Five main objections are worth considering. They are presented in this section and critically examined in the following section.

4.2.1 Not welfarist enough

The first critique is that equivalent income does not incorporate sufficient information about subjective welfare, as it only depends on ordinal preferences. "A variation of one's intensities of pleasure or welfare cannot, therefore, find any reflection in this numbering system as long as the ordering remains unchanged" (Sen 1979, p. 11). In particular, if two individuals i and j have the same ordinal preferences and enjoy the same situation (p, y, m), they will have the same equivalent income even though it may happen that i is ecstatic whereas j feels miserable.

This is a very important criticism, which calls for a serious examination of the foundations of interpersonal comparisons of well-being. Do ordinal and noncomparable preferences provide enough information about individual situations for the purpose of determining who is better off and who is worse off, or for weighing gains and losses accruing to different individuals? The dominant tradition in social choice theory claims that interpersonal comparisons require additional data in the form of utility functions that incorporate comparable information.

As we have seen, however, equivalent income is a utility function that is measured in monetary terms, so that from a purely computational standpoint, there is no difficulty in making any operation over, and any comparison of, equivalent incomes. This is why, in the first place, equivalent income appeared so attractive and convenient to many applied analysts. The objection raised by Sen is, therefore, not that equivalent income is not amenable to algrebraic operations and comparisons, but that such comparisons would not be ethically sound because the information contained in such utility numbers lacks some relevant data about subjective well-being. The key ethical question is therefore whether it is reasonable to judge that two individuals i and j are equally well off when they have the same ordinal preferences and enjoy the same situation (p, y, m). The objection is that, at least in some cases, such a judgment is not reasonable.

4.2.2 Too welfarist

An almost opposite criticism is that the equivalent income measure does not sufficiently reflect physical differences in individual situations (Kolm 2004). When two individuals have different preferences, their indifference curves can cross, so that the agent with a lower equivalent income may actually be better off in some dimensions of the vector (p, y, m) and worse off in none. For instance, it is possible that $m_i > m_j$ and $y_i = y_j$, but that when solving the equations

$$v_i(\tilde{p}, \tilde{y}, m_i^*) = v_i(p, y_i, m_i)$$
$$v_j(\tilde{p}, \tilde{y}, m_j^*) = v_j(p, y_j, m_j),$$

one obtains $m_i^* < m_j^*$. This can happen only when $\tilde{p}, \tilde{y}$ is different from p, y_i, and when i's willingness-to-pay for a change from p, y_i to $\tilde{p}, \tilde{y}$ is greater than j's willingness-to-pay. Indeed, one can rewrite the equations in terms of willingness-to-pay for $\tilde{p}, \tilde{y}$:

$$v_i(\tilde{p}, \tilde{y}, m_i - WTP_i) = v_i(p, y_i, m_i)$$
$$v_j(\tilde{p}, \tilde{y}, m_j - WTP_j) = v_j(p, y_j, m_j),$$

so that $m_i - WTP_i < m_j - WTP_j$ is compatible with $m_i > m_j$ if $WTP_i - WTP_j > m_i - m_j$.

The phenomenon is illustrated in figure 4.4, which focuses on ordinary commodities x (assuming $y_i = y_j = \tilde{y}$). In the figure, i has a greater income than j but a lower equivalent income.

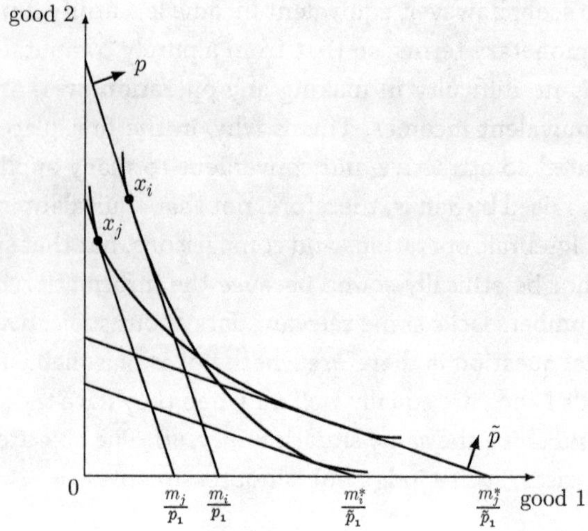

Figure 4.4
A violation of dominance

Once again, this criticism requires a clarification of the foundations of interpersonal comparisons. Is it necessary to judge that any individual with $(p, y, m + \delta)$ is better off than any individual with (p, y, m) when $\delta > 0$, independently of their preferences? By extension (assuming continuity of the measure of well-being), is it necessary to judge that any individual at a given situation (p, y, m) is as well off as any other individual at the same situation, independently of their preferences, which means that well-being at any given situation (p, y, m) is independent of preferences?

The symmetry with the previous objection is interesting. The previous objection said that two individuals at the same situation (p, y, m) and with identical preferences are not necessarily equally well off. This second objection is that two individuals at the same situation (p, y, m) are equally well off even if they have different preferences. The equivalent income measure of well-being occupies an apparently uncomfortable middle ground, by implying that two individuals at the same situation (p, y, m) are equally well off when they have the same preferences but may not be equally well off if they have different preferences.

Ironically, one of the most famous advocates of the claim that any individual with $(p, y, m + \delta)$ is better off than any individual with (p, y, m) when $\delta > 0$, independently of their preferences, is Sen again. When examining how to perform interpersonal comparisons of functionings and capabilities, Sen (1985) proposes a partial ordering based on the "intersection principle." This principle says that when everyone considers a situation to be preferable than another, any individual at the former situation must be judged better off than any individual at the latter situation. In particular, when functionings and capabilities are measured in such a way that more is always better, an individual who enjoys more than another in some dimensions and less in no other dimension must be considered better off, independently of the concerned individuals' preferences. Applied to our particular example, this principle implies that enjoying a greater income and the same level for other dimensions guarantees a greater well-being, independently of preferences.

4.2.3 Potentially regressive

The third critique has to do with the distributive consequences of using individual equivalent incomes as the utility arguments of a social welfare function. The problem is that equivalent incomes may fail to be concave in x when used as direct utility functions and fail to be concave in m when used as indirect utility functions. This will induce antiegalitarian policy implications even if the social welfare function is quasi-concave in equivalent incomes and therefore displays aversion to inequality in equivalent incomes.

To illustrate this point, observe that a failure of concavity with respect to m in the indirect equivalent income function will generate a configuration like this:

$$e\left(\tilde{p},\tilde{y},v(p,y,m)\right) - e\left(\tilde{p},\tilde{y},v(p,y,m-\delta)\right) < e\left(\tilde{p},\tilde{y},v(p,y,m+\delta)\right) - e\left(\tilde{p},\tilde{y},v(p,y,m)\right), \quad (4.4)$$

for a small $\delta > 0$.

The antiegalitarian implication of this concavity failure is derived as follows. Consider two individuals who share this same equivalent income function. Imagine moving them from the initial situation in which both enjoy (p,y,m), and therefore have the same level of equivalent income, to a situation in which δ is transferred from one to the other. If the social welfare function W is symmetric, approximately the same weight is given to the change of both individuals (for a small δ), so that the change is an improvement in the contemplated case because the gain to one (the right-hand side in (4.4)) is greater than the other's loss (the left-hand side in (4.4)). The inequality aversion incorporated in W cannot counterbalance this effect when δ is small enough, unless W gives absolute priority to the worst off.

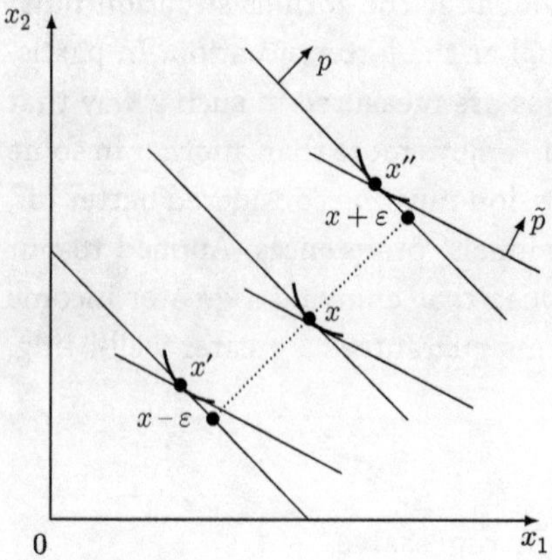

Figure 4.5
A concavity failure

When does a concavity failure occur? When $(\tilde{p}, \tilde{y}) = (p, y)$, one has

$$e(\tilde{p}, \tilde{y}, v(p, y, m)) = m,$$

which is a concave function of m. The problem appears only when $(\tilde{p}, \tilde{y}) \neq (p, y)$. But it appears for most preferences. Indeed, Blackorby and Donaldson (1988) show that concavity failures are bound to occur for at least some reference parameters whenever individual preferences are not homothetic with respect to x.

We can even show a local form of their result. A concavity failure in the form of (4.4) occurs at any bundle around which the income expansion path (i.e., the curve of the x bundles chosen for a fixed p and variable m) is not a straight line.

This is illustrated in figure 4.5, which, like figure 4.4, focuses on ordinary commodities x, assuming $\tilde{y} = y$. Let $m = px$, $\delta = p\varepsilon$. One sees that $v(p, y, m) = u(x, y)$, $v(p, y, m - \delta) = u(x', y)$, and $v(p, y, m + \delta) = u(x'', y)$. Moreover, $\tilde{p}$ is chosen so that $e(\tilde{p}, \tilde{y}, u(x, y)) < \tilde{p}x$, $e(\tilde{p}, \tilde{y}, u(x', y)) > \tilde{p}(x - \varepsilon)$, $e(\tilde{p}, \tilde{y}, u(x'', y)) > \tilde{p}(x + \varepsilon)$. As a consequence,

$$\begin{aligned} e(\tilde{p}, \tilde{y}, v(p, y, m)) - e(\tilde{p}, \tilde{y}, v(p, y, m - \delta)) &= e(\tilde{p}, \tilde{y}, u(x, y)) - e(\tilde{p}, \tilde{y}, u(x', y)) \\ &< \tilde{p}\varepsilon, \end{aligned}$$

whereas

$$\begin{aligned} e(\tilde{p}, \tilde{y}, v(p, y, m + \delta)) - e(\tilde{p}, \tilde{y}, v(p, y, m)) &= e(\tilde{p}, \tilde{y}, u(x'', y)) - e(\tilde{p}, \tilde{y}, u(x, y)) \\ &> \tilde{p}\varepsilon, \end{aligned}$$

which implies (4.4).

In this example, a concavity failure occurs only for some $\tilde{p}$. But one can modify this example. Take preferences with perfect complementarity and imagine an expansion path that zigzags, turning to one direction (say, the north) first and then to the other direction (say, the east). One then obtains a concavity failure around *some* bundle for *all* $\tilde{p} \neq p$ (assuming again $\tilde{y} = y$).

When the consumption set for x is the nonnegative orthant and individual preferences are continuous and homothetic in x, then for every

y there is a homogeneous utility function representing the preferences: $u(\lambda x, y) = \lambda u(x, y)$. The corresponding indirect utility function is linear in $m : v(p, y, m) = mv(p, y, 1)$. The expenditure function is the inverse function of v (swapping the roles of utility and income) and therefore is written as $e(p, y, u) = u/v(p, y, 1)$. One then obtains that equivalent income is linear in m, whatever the reference parameters:

$$e\left(\tilde{p}, \tilde{y}, v(p, y, m)\right) = m\frac{v(p, y, 1)}{v(\tilde{p}, \tilde{y}, 1)}.$$

This is therefore the only case in which the equivalent income function is concave in m for all reference parameters.

4.2.4 Reference dependent

The fourth criticism is concerned with the role of the parameters $\left(\tilde{p}, \tilde{y}\right)$. There are two forms of this criticism. The weak form is that such parameters introduce arbitrariness in the computation of equivalent incomes. To make this point, Blackorby and Donaldson (1988), Donaldson (1992), and Blackorby, Laisney, and Schmachtenberg (1994) use the following example. Ignoring y to simplify the presentation, consider a two-good setting in which $u_i(x_1, x_2) = x_1$ and $u_j(x_1, x_2) = x_2$. One then has $e_i\left(\tilde{p}, u_i\right) = \tilde{p}_1 u_i$ and $e_j\left(\tilde{p}, u_j\right) = \tilde{p}_2 u_j$, so that a social welfare function W applied to equivalent incomes would be the same as a social welfare function written as a function of utilities as follows:

$$W\left(\ldots, \tilde{p}_1 u_i, \ldots, \tilde{p}_2 u_j, \ldots\right).$$

If no guidelines can be provided for the choice of the reference prices, it appears that the weights of individuals i, j in social evaluation will be arbitrary.

The strong form of the criticism is that "ethically-consistent welfare prescriptions are reference price-independent," which is the title of Blackorby, Laisney, and Schmachtenberg (1994). In their Theorem 1 (p. 250), they have a formal statement and proof of this striking and impressive sentence. The framework is a finite population $i = 1, \ldots, n$, each individual having an indirect utility function $v_i(p_i, m_i)$—the parameters y are absent. Price vectors can be individual-specific or common to all individuals. Here again, we will restrict attention to the case in which the price vector is the same p

for all i. The equivalent income approach takes the form of a social welfare function applied to equivalent incomes:

$$W\left(e_1\left(\tilde{p}, v_1(p, m_1)\right), \ldots, e_n\left(\tilde{p}, v_n(p, m_n)\right)\right).$$

Ethical consistency is defined as a property of $(W, v_1, \ldots, v_n)$ and consists of the existence of a Bergson-Samuelson social welfare function $W^*(u_1, \ldots, u_n)$ such that for all $(m_1, \ldots, m_n, p), (m'_1, \ldots, m'_n, p')$,

$$W\left(e_1\left(\tilde{p}, v_1(p, m_1)\right), \ldots, e_n\left(\tilde{p}, v_n(p, m_n)\right)\right) \geq W\left(e_1\left(\tilde{p}, v_1(p', m'_1)\right), \ldots, e_n\left(\tilde{p}, v_n(p', m'_n)\right)\right)$$

if and only if

$$W^*\left(v_1(p, m_1), \ldots, v_n(p, m_n)\right) \geq W^*\left(v_1(p', m'_1), \ldots, v_n(p', m'_n)\right).$$

The proof of their Theorem 1 is then simply based on the observation that $\tilde{p}$ does not appear in the second term of this equivalence.

Unfortunately for their argument, the definition of ethical consistency is ambiguous because it contains no quantifier for $\tilde{p}$. There are several possible ways of making the definition meaningful. One is to require that the equivalence must hold for all $\tilde{p}$:

> $(W, v_1, \ldots, v_n)$ are ethically consistent if there exists a Bergson-Samuelson social welfare function $W^*(u_1, \ldots, u_n)$ such that for all $\tilde{p}$, for all $(m_1, \ldots, m_n, p), (m'_1, \ldots, m'_n, p')$ ... (the remainder as above).

This appears to be what the authors have in mind, given the proof of their theorem. However, it is hard to see why such a notion of ethical consistency is compelling. Suppose for instance that it so happens that for some particular $\tilde{p}$, for all i, $v_i(p, m_i) = e_i\left(\tilde{p}, v_i(p, m_i)\right)$. Then ethical consistency is achieved for this particular $(W, v_1, \ldots, v_n)$ by simply taking $W^* = W$. But it is not clear why one should be concerned with other values of $\tilde{p}$ in $e_i\left(\tilde{p}, v_i(p, m_i)\right)$, because if $v_i(p, m_i)$ is the proper measure of individual utility, this gives a special ethical salience to the corresponding value of $\tilde{p}$.

A second way to make the definition sensible is to move the expression "for all $\tilde{p}$" toward the beginning of the definition:

> $(W, v_1, \ldots, v_n)$ are ethically consistent if for all $\tilde{p}$ there exists a Bergson-Samuelson social welfare function $W^*(u_1, \ldots, u_n)$ such that for all $(m_1, \ldots, m_n, p), (m'_1, \ldots, m'_n, p')$ ... (the remainder as above).

With this formulation, ethical consistency is always satisfied because the expression $e_i\left(\tilde{p}, v_i(p, m_i)\right)$ is increasing in $v_i(p, m_i)$, and the requirement then becomes innocuous.

More generally, one wonders why ethical consistency should be defined as a property of $(W, v_1, \ldots, v_n)$ rather than the fully specified criterion

$$W\left(e_1\left(\tilde{p}, v_1(p, m_1)\right), \ldots, e_n\left(\tilde{p}, v_n(p, m_n)\right)\right).$$

Since this criterion satisfies the Pareto principle and provides a complete ordering of all the situations to be evaluated, it seems ethically consistent in the most natural sense of this expression. In conclusion, it is hard to make sense of the idea that one can "prove" that ethical consistency requires independence of the reference price.

This leaves us, however, with the weak form of the criticism. This weak form, if considered valid, is enough to make it worthwhile seeking conditions under which the evaluation with equivalent incomes is indeed independent of the reference parameters. Blackorby, Laisney, and Schmachtenberg (1994) note that, in the framework that has just been introduced in the previous paragraphs, independence of the reference price implies that the evaluation of social situations described by $\left(m_1, \ldots, m_n, p\right)$ is also independent of the price vector p. Indeed, under independence of the reference price, for every $\tilde{p}$, one has

$$\begin{aligned} W\left(e_1\left(\tilde{p}, v_1(p, m_1)\right), \ldots, e_n\left(\tilde{p}, v_n(p, m_n)\right)\right) \\ \geq W\left(e_1\left(\tilde{p}, v_1(p, m_1')\right), \ldots, e_n\left(\tilde{p}, v_n(p, m_n')\right)\right) \end{aligned}$$

if and only if, taking $\tilde{p} = p$,

$$W\left(m_1, \ldots, m_n\right) \geq W\left(m_1', \ldots, m_n'\right).$$

This shows that the comparison between $\left(m_1, \ldots, m_n, p\right)$ and $\left(m_1', \ldots, m_n', p\right)$ is actually independent of p.

The problem is then equivalent to finding out under what conditions on W and $v_1, \ldots, v_n$ an evaluation based on $W\left(v_1(p, m_1), \ldots, v_n(p, m_n)\right)$ is independent of p. This problem has been studied by Roberts (1980) and Slesnick (1991) and, for the case of personalized prices, by Slivinsky (1983). Under some mild regularity and Pareto conditions, it turns out that independence of p implies that individual preferences must be identical and homothetic.[8] Once again, stringent conditions are therefore obtained. As Roberts's and Slesnick's proofs contain imperfections, the argument is developed in appendix B.

4.2.5 Arrow's coup de grâce

In summary, equivalent income has been criticized for being insufficiently *and* excessively welfarist, insufficiently egalitarian, and substantially arbitrary. Can it survive such deadly blows? To this list of criticisms one should add the devastating message of Arrow's impossibility theorem of social choice (Arrow 1951), which has discouraged many economists from seeking a reasonable criterion for the evaluation of individual and social situations. In a nutshell, this theorem is usually interpreted as implying that there is no reasonable social evaluation methodology that respects individual ordinal preferences and does not rely on extra utility information. As the equivalent income approach satisfies these two conditions, it is a direct target of the theorem, and a potential victim.

Let us briefly recall the setting and the conditions that form the components of the impossibility theorem. The problem is to define an ordering (a complete and transitive binary relation) on a given set of alternatives, as a function of the individual preferences (orderings) about these alternatives. Three conditions are proved to be incompatible when there are at least three alternatives, at least two individuals, and the domain of possible individual preferences is sufficiently rich: (1) Weak Pareto: An alternative unanimously preferred to another must be ranked above it. (2) Independence: The ranking of any pair of alternatives must depend only on how these two alternatives (at the exclusion of the others) are ranked in individual preferences. (3) Nondictatorship: No individual can impose his strict preference on the social ordering for all possible profiles of individual preferences.

Arrow's theorem is often presented in textbooks in an abstract framework with unspecified alternatives, but the theorem is equally valid in an economic model with standard consumer preferences. It is actually in such a model that an intuition for the result can be given most easily.

Consider, then, a simple model with two individuals consuming two goods, bread and water. Suppose that when only bread is available, the distribution (10,10) is preferred to (5,20). That is, giving ten units of bread

8. In the case of personalized prices, preferences must be homothetic and the social welfare function must be of the Cobb-Douglas form.

to each individual is better than having individual 1 starve with five units while individual 2 wastes 20 units.

Arrow's result consists in showing that under Weak Pareto and Independence, it is then necessary, when only water is available, to prefer the distribution (20,5) to the distribution (10,10)! This means that individual 1's interest is again given priority, even though in this case the inequality is reversed. Such a result comes from the fact that, under Weak Pareto and Independence, the only possibility is to have collective orderings that reflect the preferences of only one individual, in this example individual 1. Why is it so?

The argument is the following. There exist preferences such that individual 1 prefers 20 units of water to 10 units of bread, and 5 units of bread to 10 units of water. There also exist preferences such that individual 2 prefers 20 units of bread to 10 units of water, and 5 units of water to 10 units of bread. These preferences are illustrated in figure 4.6; they are not pathological.

When such preferences prevail, by Weak Pareto the distribution (20,5) of water is better than the distribution (10,10) of bread, because both individuals prefer the former, and similarly the distribution (5,20) of bread is better than the distribution (10,10) of water.

When such preferences prevail, it is still the case that when only bread is available, the distribution (10,10) is preferred to (5,20), because by Independence this only depends on the individuals' preferences over these two allocations (individual 1 prefers the former, individual 2 prefers the latter), which have not changed. Therefore, by transitivity of the social ordering one must conclude that the distribution (20,5) of water is better than the distribution (10,10) of water. Moreover, this conclusion does

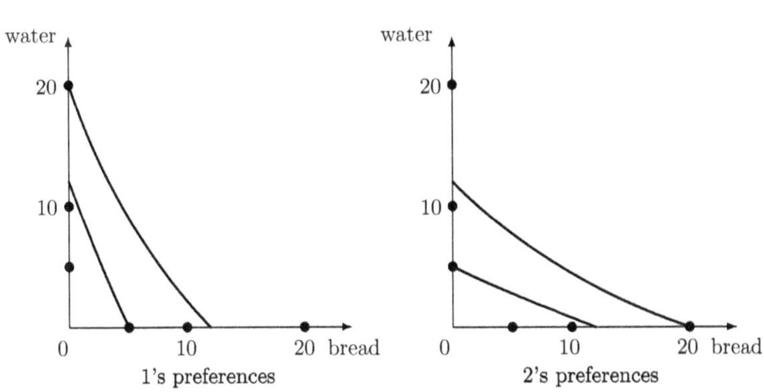

Figure 4.6
Arrow's theorem illustrated

not hold only under these particular preferences; it must be valid whenever individual 1 prefers the latter and individual 2 prefers the former, which is always the case with standard monotonic preferences.

From this starting point it is then an easy step to show that individual 1's preferences are always given priority in all conflicts about the allocation of bread and water, which violates the Nondictatorship requirement.

Of course, one could have started with the opposite assumption that when only bread is available, the distribution (5,20) is preferred to (10,10). By a similar reasoning, one would then have found individual 2 to be a "dictator." And if the two distributions were equivalent, one could modify them slightly so that one of the two individuals prevails in the conflict of interests, and the path to dictatorship would be rushed down again. The full argument is developed in appendix B.

The impossibility theorem has had a profound influence on welfare economics. "This starkly negative finding became a major stumbling block to the empirical implementation of an explicit social welfare function" (Slesnick 1998, p. 2139). "The apparent innocuousness of Arrow's assumptions, the strength of his result and its apparent robustness to further inquiry have seemed to many to undermine the whole idea of measuring social welfare" (Blundell, Preston, and Walker 1994, p. 29) In particular, Arrow's theorem was especially targeted at criteria that, like equivalent income, are based only on individual ordinal noncomparable preferences. As a consequence, the theory of social choice after Arrow (which is well described, e.g., in Sen 1999b) has focused on interpersonal comparisons of utility. It has led many economists to believe that the impossibility can only be escaped by relying on interpersonally comparable information about individual utilities, and that measures of individual well-being that, like equivalent income, involve only ordinal noncomparable information about individual preferences are condemned to be useless.

The popularity of the idea that a measure of well-being exclusively based on ordinal noncomparable information about individual preferences cannot serve for social evaluation is probably reinforced by the obvious observation that social evaluation does indeed require an interpersonally comparable measure of individual *well-being*. This observation does not require a theorem. How could one define social priorities without being able to identify the worst off in the population? But interpersonal comparisons can be made in various metrics, such as income, wealth, equivalent income, capabilities, or similar notions for which an index may or may not need information about ordinal preferences and information about subjective utility. In particular, we have seen that equivalent income is a utility function that is easy to manipulate and compare across individuals thanks to the fact that it is expressed in monetary units. Yet it is constructed on the sole basis of ordinal noncomparable information about individual preferences. This shows that ordinal noncomparable information about preferences does not preclude interpersonal comparisons of some measure of well-being.

For a measure like equivalent income, therefore, the challenge of Arrow's theorem does not lie in its ordinal noncomparable informational basis. What is at stake is that a social welfare function applied to equivalent incomes,

$$W\left(e_1\left(\tilde{p},\tilde{y},v_1(p,y_1,m_1)\right),\ldots,e_n\left(\tilde{p},\tilde{y},v_n(p,y_n,m_n)\right)\right),$$

defines a social ordering function that must violate some of Arrow's axioms. If the social welfare function is increasing in every individual's equivalent income, it satisfies Weak Pareto and Nondictatorship. But Arrow's Independence is not satisfied, because the ranking of two allocations depends on the expenditure functions at the reference parameters $\tilde{p},\tilde{y}$. This means that the ranking of two allocations will be determined by the comparison of two other allocations, in which individuals choose from hypothetical budget sets at prices $\tilde{p}$ and obtain the same satisfaction as in the two allocations to be ranked. The key question to ask is therefore whether such violation of Arrow Independence is problematic. As we will see in the next section, the theory of fair allocation suggests that it is not.

4.3 FAIRNESS TO THE RESCUE

The theory of fair allocation offers new insights into the problem of social evaluation. While the attraction of a monetary measure such as equivalent income seemed suspect in welfare economics, fairness is explicitly defined in this theory in terms of equality of resources. Why be interested in equality of resources? The pioneers such as Kolm (1972), Varian (1974), and Pazner and Schmeidler (1974, 1978) were, presumably, simply seduced by intuitive concepts such as no-envy (an allocation is envy-free if no individual would rather consume another's bundle than his own),[9] which seem to capture the idea that every individual can have what he wants and which provide a natural normative extension to the theory of general equilibrium. But theories of justice based on principles of equality of resources have been developed by Rawls (1971, 1982) and Dworkin (1981, 2000) and appear to provide additional justifications to the approach. As alluded to

9. A precise definition is given later on.

in the conclusion of chapter 3, the general idea of such theories is that individuals have a variety of goals in their life, which are essentially incommensurable, and that the duty of just social institutions is only to give them equal means to pursue their specific ends. Such theories have been criticized by the authors who propose alternative theories of justice in terms of equality of opportunities (Arneson 1989; Cohen 1989; Sen 1992; Roemer 1998), but even these alternative theories share the idea that there is a division of labor between social institutions and individual responsibility. The debate between these various theories, in the application to welfare economics, will be examined in more detail in chapter 6. Here it should be emphasized that the theory of fair allocation is generally formulated in terms of resources, but many of its concepts are easily extended to more general spaces of goods. As will be explained in the first subsection below, the key problem of this theory is to define equality in a setting in which individuals have heterogeneous preferences over multiple dimensions of goodness (which may or may not be ordinary commodities).

The theory of fair allocation was initially developed in a form that made difficult a connection to the theory of social choice and the more classical branches of welfare economics. Indeed, the theory of fair allocation focused on finding a fully efficient and equitable allocation, whereas welfare economics and the theory of social choice sought evaluation criteria that would assess any arbitrary allocation. The recent development of a theory of "fair social choice" (Fleurbaey and Maniquet 2011b) makes it easier to understand the links and differences between the various approaches.

The purpose of this section is the following. Assuming that there are sufficient reasons to be interested in some general idea of equality of resources, it presents some concepts of fairness that provide an interesting generalization of money-metric utility. In this light, the criticisms listed in the previous section can be revisited and, by and large, rebutted.

4.3.1 The equivalence approach in fair allocation theory

The theory of fair allocation[10] makes great use of a class of "egalitarian-equivalent" criteria that bear a striking similarity to the equivalent-income approach. But the equivalence approach in fair allocation is more general than the equivalent income. In fact, before introducing this approach, it is useful to present the general problem tackled by the theory of fair allocation.

10. For a general survey of this theory, see Thomson (2011).

Consider a space Z with finitely many dimensions and assume that individual situations are represented by vectors z_i in this space. Assume moreover that individuals have complete, transitive, continuous, and monotonically increasing preferences, denoted R_i, in this space. That is, $z_i R_i z_i'$ means that individual i weakly prefers z_i to z_i'. Let $z_i I_i z_i'$ denote the configuration in which individual i is indifferent between z_i and z_i'. For any set $A \subset Z$, let $z_i I_i A$ denote the situation in which i is indifferent between z_i and the best element(s) of A for R_i.[11] The central problem for the theory of fair allocation is to define equality in z in such a framework. The difficulty lies in the heterogeneity of individual preferences over the multiple dimensions of Z.

Let us start with the simple case in which Z has only one dimension. In this case, all individuals have the same preferences (more is better), and the definition of equality in z seems simple. Equality is achieved when $z_i = z_j$ for all i, j.

A slightly more complicated case is when Z has multiple dimensions, but individuals are still assumed to share the same preferences. Then, equality in z is defined as the situation in which $z_i I_i z_j$ for all i, j. This can serve as a useful benchmark for notions of equality that cover more complex cases. In fact, requiring $z_i I_i z_j$ for all i, j sharing the same preferences remains a useful test in cases in which not all individuals have identical preferences.

Note that one could retain the definition of equality as $z_i = z_j$ for the general case of heterogeneous preferences, but it would be a stupid notion of equality because the differences in preferences call for a reallocation of z that better suits everyone's tastes. This is why a more general notion of equality is needed.

The theory of fair allocation has developed two general notions of equality that are substantially different. The first is the concept of no-envy, which says that equality is achieved when the allocation is envy-free, that is, when $z_i R_i z_j$ for all i, j. When individuals have the same preferences, $z_i R_i z_j$ and $z_j R_j z_i$ imply that $z_i I_i z_j$, so that this notion is consistent with the definition of equality for the benchmark case of identical preferences.

The concept of no-envy is closely associated with market institutions. A competitive equilibrium in which all individuals have the same budget generates an envy-free allocation, because for all i, j, z_j belongs to i's budget set and therefore $z_i R_i z_j$. Conversely, it has been proved by Varian (1976) and Champsaur and Laroque (1981) that, when preferences are sufficiently diverse in a continuum of individuals, every allocation that is Pareto efficient and envy-free is a competitive equilibrium with equal budgets.

11. That is, there is $z_i^* \in A$ such that $z_i I_i z_i^*$ and for all $z \in A$, $z_i^* R_i z$.

This close link between no-envy and market institutions makes envy-free allocations share some unpalatable features of the market. It is well known that, in a market economy, changes in the general environment that create new possibilities for the economy (technological innovation, reduction of trade barriers) generally alter the relative prices and wages and make some people lose even when, in principle, everyone could gain from the change. It has been proved that, similarly, a general change that appears good may in some cases make it impossible to preserve Pareto efficiency and envy-freeness without harming some individuals.[12]

This drawback makes it worthwhile looking at the second general notion of equality, introduced by Pazner and Schmeidler (1978). In its simplest form, it seeks to obtain a configuration in which for some z_0, one has $z_i I_i z_0$ for all i. The situation is then such that the allocation $(z_1, \ldots, z_n)$ is *equivalent*, in the sense of Pareto, to the allocation $(z_0, \ldots, z_0)$, which is egalitarian in the simplest sense. This is how this approach gets its name of the equivalence approach.

Pazner and Schmeidler (1978), for the case in which z_i is the commodity bundle x_i, propose to seek z_0 among the bundles proportional to total consumption X. Egalitarian-equivalence is then achieved when for some $\lambda > 0$, for all i, $x_i I_i \lambda X$. This is the same as seeking equality of the ray utilities u_X.[13]

Clearly, when individuals have the same preferences, $z_i I_i z_0$ and $z_j I_j z_0$ imply $z_i I_i z_j$, which shows that the benchmark test is, once again, satisfied. While it would generally be inefficient to seek to give the same z_0 to every individual, seeking a situation that is equivalent to it is much better because one may then cater to the diversity of individual preferences and obtain a situation that is equivalent to an allocation $(z_0, \ldots, z_0)$ that is high in individual preferences and would not be feasible.

It is also intuitive why the drawbacks of market-like institutions tend to be avoided with this alternative approach. If policy always seeks to achieve the highest equivalent $(z_0, \ldots, z_0)$, a general change in the economy parameters that makes it possible to raise $(z_0, \ldots, z_0)$ will make everyone gain because the equivalence $z_i I_i z_0$ means that a greater z_0 corresponds to a better z_i in i's preferences.

The link between this approach and the concept of equivalent income is not too difficult to imagine. The social criterion based on the function

$$W\left(e_1\left(\tilde{p}, \tilde{y}, v_1(m_1, p, y_1)\right), \ldots, e_n\left(\tilde{p}, \tilde{y}, v_n(m_n, p, y_n)\right)\right)$$

12. See Chichilnisky and Thomson (1987); Moulin and Thomson (1988).
13. Ray utility has been defined in section 4.1.

evaluates the situation $((m_1, p, y_1), \ldots, (m_n, p, y_n))$ by looking at the Pareto-equivalent situation $((m_1^*, \tilde{p}, \tilde{y}), \ldots, (m_n^*, \tilde{p}, \tilde{y}))$. Indeed, recall from (4.3) that i is indifferent between (m_i, p, y_i) and $(m_i^*, \tilde{p}, \tilde{y})$ if and only if

$$m_i^* = e_i\left(\tilde{p}, \tilde{y}, v_i(m_i, p, y_i)\right).$$

A Paretian and inequality-averse function W applied to $(m_1^*, \ldots, m_n^*)$ is the natural way to evaluate the equivalent situations of the form $((m_1^*, \tilde{p}, \tilde{y}), \ldots, (m_n^*, \tilde{p}, \tilde{y}))$.

There are, however, different ways of making the connection between equivalent income and the equivalence approach in fair allocation. What has been done in the previous paragraph consists in defining the "z_i" of the theory of fair allocation as the bundle (m_i, p, y_i) and exploiting the equivalence $v_i(m_i, p, y_i) = v_i(m_i^*, \tilde{p}, \tilde{y})$ in terms of indirect preferences.

Another interesting way comes back to direct preferences and interprets z_i as the consumption bundle (x_i, y_i), in which x_i is commodity consumption and y_i encapsulates the nonmarket dimensions of consumption. This is worth doing because it shows that the notion of equivalent income can be generalized.

Indeed, so far we have defined the equivalence approach in terms of simple equivalent bundles z_0. In a more general form of the approach developed by Thomson (1994), equivalent situations take the form of a collection of nested sets $(B_\lambda)_{\lambda \in \mathbb{R}_+}$ such that $\lambda \leq \lambda'$ if and only if $B_\lambda \subseteq B_{\lambda'}$. An individual's situation z_i is evaluated by computing the "equivalent set" in the collection. This is the set B_λ that would yield the same satisfaction (if i could freely choose from B_λ) as the current allocation, that is, the solution B_λ to the following equation:

$$z_i I_i B_\lambda.$$

Individual situations are therefore compared in terms of equivalent sets, which can be carried out unambiguously as these sets are nested: the larger, the better—assuming away satiation. Such a measure respects individual preferences as whenever $z_i R_i z_i'$, the corresponding indexes λ and λ' must satisfy $\lambda \geq \lambda'$.

This is more general than the previous definition in terms of equivalent bundle z_0. The bundle approach can be retrieved, for instance, by considering sets

$$B_\lambda = \{z \in Z \mid z \leq \lambda z_0\}.$$

Given this background, when z_i is defined as the bundle (x_i, y_i), the notion of equivalent income may be defined as referring to the equivalent sets

$$B_\lambda = \left\{(x,y) \in Z \mid \tilde{p}x \leq \lambda,\ y = \tilde{y}\right\}.$$

This makes it clear that using budget sets as the equivalent sets is not the only possibility. In fact, even budget sets need not be linear in the presence of taxes, rationing, and personal constraints on the consumption set.

This generalization is particularly interesting because it establishes a connection with the idea of evaluating individual situations in terms of opportunity sets. This idea was invoked by early theorists of the money-metric approach (e.g., Deaton 1980; Deaton and Muellbauer 1980) and has become very popular in recent theories of justice and related applications to economics. Chapter 6, which deals with the capability approach, will explore these ideas in greater depth.

The main point of this subsection is that the equivalent income approach is a particular example of the general equivalence approach. Let us now see how the objections against equivalent income that were listed in the previous section can be reassessed in this light.

4.3.2 Arrow Independence is not compelling

As we have seen, a criterion based on equivalent incomes does not satisfy Arrow's axiom of Independence, and this is true of the equivalence approach in general. This implies that either the equivalence approach is flawed or Independence is not compelling.

To get a sense that the latter is the more plausible conclusion, observe that while many economists have been mystified by the elegance of Arrow's theorem and accepted the consensual view about the "apparent innocuousness of Arrow's assumptions" (Blundell, Preston, and Walker 1994), a great majority of economists have remained interested in the concept of willingness-to-pay. But Independence precludes the use of willingness-to-pay, which involves considering a hypothetical situation in which the individual is brought back to his initial satisfaction by paying (or receiving) some amount of money. Most economists have also remained interested about marginal rates of substitutions, for instance in order to check if an allocation is efficient. But Independence forbids checking if an allocation is efficient when it is compared to another, because marginal rates of substitution can be computed only by looking at other allocations in the neighborhood of the contemplated allocation.

Willingness to pay and marginal rates of substitution involve information about the indifference curves of individuals in the situations under consideration. It is indeed very natural to take account of indifference curves, and this has been argued convincingly by Hansson (1973), Mayston (1974), and Pazner (1979). Observe that in order to compute the equivalent income of an individual, it is enough to know his indifference curve at the current situation. Strikingly, this is also enough to apply the no-envy concept and any of the equivalence notions of the theory of fair allocation, as well as all the notions of cost-benefit analysis such as compensating and equivalent variations, willingness-to-pay, and the like.

Therefore one can argue that a measure of well-being in terms of equivalent income uses the typical sort of information about individual preferences that one finds in prominent approaches of welfare economics. Arrow's impossibility is obtained by excluding the sort of information that appears most naturally useful for welfare evaluation.

However, Arrow's theorem provides a nice way to describe the difference between two approaches in welfare economics that introduce two different sorts of additional information about well-being. Independence says that the ranking of two alternatives should depend only on how they are ranked by individual preferences. This requirement can be logically decomposed in two components:[14]

Ordinal Noncomparability: The ranking of two alternatives should depend only on individual preferences.[15]

Binary Independence: The ranking of two alternatives should depend only on individual utilities at these two alternatives.

Together, these two requirements imply Arrow's Independence, because the only thing that individual utilities at two alternatives tell us about preferences is which alternative is preferred to the other. Conversely, Independence implies each of them.

Arrow's impossibility can be escaped by relaxing either of these two requirements. Relaxing Binary Independence is the route followed by the theory of fair allocation and the equivalence approach, because knowledge

14. See, e.g., Roemer (1996); Fleurbaey and Mongin (2005).

15. Arrow's theorem was introduced in subsection 4.2.6 in a framework in which individual utilities were not defined and only preferences were considered, but nothing would change if utilities were defined in the background.

of indifference curves at two allocations cannot be retrieved from a pair of utility figures. But these approaches retain Ordinal Noncomparability, as they are constructed on the basis of individual preferences over personal bundles.

The other route has been followed by a branch of social choice theory initiated by Sen (1970) and d'Aspremont and Gevers (1977). Social welfare functions of the form $W(u_1, \ldots, u_n)$, in which the same function W is applied to whatever profile of individual utilities is prevailing, satisfy Binary Independence because the evaluation of a situation only depends on utility levels at this allocation. They require interpersonally comparable information about individual utilities and therefore drop Ordinal Noncomparability.

This second route has somehow managed to be widely considered the only escape from Arrow's theorem, in spite of the development of the theory of fair allocation that exemplified the other route.[16] As mentioned in subsection 4.2.6, perhaps the obvious fact that interpersonal comparisons of some measure of well-being are needed has fed the belief that interpersonal comparisons *of utility* are necessary.

Another source of confusion is that a criterion based on

$$W\left(e_1\left(\tilde{p}, \tilde{y}, v_1(p, y_1, m_1)\right), \ldots, e_n\left(\tilde{p}, \tilde{y}, v_n(p, y_n, m_n)\right)\right)$$

can also be described as involving utility functions, namely, $e_i\left(\tilde{p}, \tilde{y}, v_i(p, y_i, m_i)\right)$, and the function W satisfies Binary Independence and violates Ordinal Noncomparability with respect to these utilities. This shows that there are two possible ways to describe the equivalent income approach in the context of Arrow's impossibility.

The first way is to say that Binary Independence is dropped and information about indifference curves is introduced, while Ordinal Noncomparability is retained. The alternative way is to say that specific interpersonally comparable utility functions are constructed and introduced in a standard social welfare function. What must be added is then

16. It has often been alleged that the theory of fair allocation obtains positive results because, contrary to social choice theory, it does not construct full rankings but only seeks to determine the subset of optimal allocations. This explanation cannot be accepted because the selection of a subset of allocations is, formally, equivalent to defining an ordering. The theory of fair allocation has actually also developed fine-grained rankings just like social choice theory. The correct explanation for its positive results is the violation of Independence by all of the solutions proposed in this theory. More on this issue can be found in Fleurbaey, Suzumura, and Tadenuma (2005).

that these utility functions are computed on the sole basis of ordinal noncomparable individual preferences.

Either description is acceptable and dispels the mistaken idea that exogenous data about interpersonally comparable utilities are needed in order to make social evaluation. The first way directly says that information about indifference curves is enough to construct reasonable social welfare functions. The second way says that interpersonally comparable utilities can be constructed with purely ordinal data. They concur in questioning the soundness of Arrow's Independence requirement.

4.3.3 References need not be arbitrary

Let us now turn to the objection that the choice of reference parameters $(\tilde{p}, \tilde{y})$ is crucial and arbitrary. For the equivalence approach more generally, what is at stake is the choice of reference sets $(B_\lambda)_{\lambda \in \mathbb{R}_+}$. The generality of the equivalence approach is helpful here as it suggests that the literature that criticizes the money-metric utility for being dependent on the reference price vector does not fully pursue the logic of its own critique. This literature accepts taking budget sets at given prices as the class of reference sets $(B_\lambda)_{\lambda \in \mathbb{R}_+}$. But this too should be questioned if one really wants the analysis to be independent of the reference. Conversely, if one accepts working with budget sets, why not see if some reference prices are more plausible than others?

More directly, the answer to this objection is that if the equivalence approach depends on reference parameters, it can avoid arbitrariness by developing an ethical theory of the choice of reference. Some interesting reflections about this choice were offered, for instance, by Willig (1981). If the market prices are adopted as the reference, this means that equality of ordinary incomes is considered to be satisfactory as a social goal. But if an individual with a special orientation of tastes is considered to be disadvantaged because what he likes is more expensive, one can adopt lower prices than the market for his preferred goods and obtain the conclusion that equality of ordinary incomes still leaves him somewhat disadvantaged (because at the average level of income he could be just as satisfied with a lower income if his preferred goods were less expensive).

To illustrate, recall the example in which $u_i(x_1, x_2) = x_1$ and $u_j(x_1, x_2) = x_2$, so that a social welfare function W applied to equivalent incomes is the same as a social welfare function written as a function of utilities as follows:

$$W\left(\ldots, \tilde{p}_1 u_i, \ldots, \tilde{p}_2 u_j, \ldots\right).$$

If the market prices are adopted as references, then $\tilde{p}_1 u_i, \tilde{p}_2 u_j$ are i's and j's expenditures. If a lower $\tilde{p}_1$ is adopted, this implies that i's well-being is only equal to the fraction $\tilde{p}_1/p_1$ of his expenditures.

One may worry that these considerations show that one needs an external criterion to determine interpersonal comparisons. Instead of letting the reference parameters decide who is better off, it seems that an a priori evaluation determines how to pick the reference. This is true and, in fact, normal. An ethical theory of the choice of reference is needed and must naturally rely on additional principles that are not already in the general definition of equivalent income. In the example of the previous paragraph, the considerations that guide the choice of reference prices have to do with finding the prices such that at such prices, ordinary incomes would provide a good metric of well-being. Although there may be some hesitation about the correspondingly appropriate values of the reference prices, it is very unlikely that any price vector would appear equally plausible. Instead of exposing an "arbitrary and capricious ethics," this example shows that there are well-defined considerations that must decide the choice of reference.

Other examples in the literature on fair social orderings show in a more precise way that natural axioms of fairness may force the adoption of certain reference parameters. For instance, in a framework in which individual situations are described by a private contribution $x_i \in \mathbb{R}$ and a certain level of public good $y \in \mathbb{R}_+$, Maniquet and Sprumont (2004) characterize a criterion that evaluates individual situations as follows: one computes the level of public good that, absent any contribution, would give the same satisfaction to the individual as the situation under consideration. Formally, the index λ is the solution to the equation

$$(x_i, y) I_i (0, \lambda).$$

This method is an example of the equivalence approach with sets $(B_\lambda)_{\lambda \in \mathbb{R}_+}$ defined as (assuming monotonic preferences that are decreasing in x_i and increasing in y)

$$B_\lambda = \{(x, y) \in \mathbb{R}_+ \times \mathbb{R}_+ \mid y \leq \lambda\}.$$

In their characterization, the choice of such reference sets is driven by a quite intuitive axiom saying that if i and j are such that $x_i < 0 < x_j$ (i.e., i is subsidized while j pays a contribution), it is an improvement to reduce j's contribution and i's subsidy by the same amount.

Another example is found in Fleurbaey and Maniquet (2006). The setting there has consumption $c \geq 0$ and leisure $l \in [0,1]$, individuals being endowed with unequal productivities and heterogeneous preferences over consumption and leisure. The evaluation proposed in that paper relies on the reference sets

$$B_\lambda = \left\{(c,l) \in \mathbb{R}_+ \times [0,1] \mid c \leq \lambda l\right\},$$

which correspond to budget sets without taxes delimited by a given wage rate λ.

This choice of reference sets is based on an axiom saying that when all individuals have the same productivity, the laissez-faire allocation is a best allocation among all feasible allocations.

These are just examples, and the literature on fair social orderings is far from providing a complete theory of references for all settings. But the possibility of such a theory seems well established by these examples.

It is worth mentioning that in the two articles that have just been quoted, the adoption of the equivalence approach is not a postulate but a consequence of the axiomatic analysis. In the literature on fair allocation, one rarely sees the analysis proceeding by first adopting the equivalence approach and then asking what the reference sets should be. Instead, it is the combination of efficiency and equity axioms that imposes both the approach and specific reference sets.

The general principle underlying the choice of reference parameters in the three examples discussed in this subsection is the following. When can one say something about the comparison of individual situations without looking at individual preferences? The idea that laissez-faire is optimal when all individual are equally productive means that equality is, in this case, achieved in the absence of redistribution, no matter what individual preferences may be. Similarly, in the public good example, the situation $x_i < 0 < x_j$ is taken to represent unfairness independently of individual preferences.

This is intuitive. If a situation $\left((p,y_1,m_1),\ldots,(p,y_n,m_n)\right)$ must be evaluated by looking at the Pareto-equivalent situation $\left((\tilde{p},\tilde{y},m_1^*),\ldots,(\tilde{p},\tilde{y},m_n^*)\right)$ and computing $W\left(m_1^*,\ldots,m_n^*\right)$, the adequate value for $\left(\tilde{p},\tilde{y}\right)$ must be such that income becomes a suitable measure of well-being when an individual enjoys $\left(\tilde{p},\tilde{y}\right)$. The idea that income is the proper measure of well-being under $\left(\tilde{p},\tilde{y}\right)$ is, combined with the Pareto principle, the cornerstone of the equivalent income approach.

The examples provided here pertain to special models in which the reference emerges from the structure of the model. For concrete applications of the equivalent income approach, a theory of the reference, which takes account of further ideas introduced later in this book, is developed in appendix A.

4.3.4 The right dose of welfarism

It is at this point that the criticisms having to do with welfarism (subsections 4.2.1–4.2.2) can be addressed. One says that income is never the proper measure of well-being because important subjective data are missing. The other incriminates the possibility that an individual having more of every commodity and functioning can be deemed worse off.

As far as subjective data are concerned, the answer lies in the observation that elements of subjective well-being may be the objects of preferences. In principle, any object of preference that pertains to an individual's personal situation can be incorporated in the analysis by putting it in y_i, the nonmarket aspects of *i*'s situation. If certain mental states are important to an individual, such as avoiding anxiety or enjoying peace of mind, there is no difficulty, at least in theory, in putting them in y_i along other dimensions. One does observe that people care about their mental health and their psychological comfort; it would indeed be strange to bracket such things out of welfare analysis. It is therefore a mistake to believe that a monetary measure neglects subjective well-being.

The fact that a measure like equivalent income respects individual preferences implies that subjective aspects of well-being will be given a particular weight in the measure corresponding to the priority that individuals themselves give it. If *i* cares about his contentment but also about his career and is willing to endure more stress in order to get better career achievements, a purely hedonic measure might record a reduction of well-being although *i* himself considers that his situation has improved. Therefore, not only does the equivalent income approach take account of subjective well-being, it gives it a weight that respects the individual's own priorities.

Subjective well-being will be discussed at great length in the next chapter. There are indeed many interesting developments in the empirical study of happiness and satisfaction, which provide a lot of material to think about the appropriate methodology to take account of subjective well-being in social evaluation.

The objection that a monetary measure is too materialistic often refers to special needs, too. Again, there is no difficulty of putting special needs in y_i, if individuals have preferences about such characteristics. A branch of the theory of fair allocation has actually been developed to deal with special needs and handicaps.[17] Rather than throwing the fairness approach, it has extended it in order to take account of individual preferences over these aspects of well-being.

The key message at this point should be that *equivalent* income is very different from *ordinary* income. When solving the equation

$$v_i(p, y_i, m_i) = v_i(\tilde{p}, \tilde{y}, m_i^*),$$

with m_i^* as the unknown, one takes account of whatever benefit or disadvantage is contained in y_i, insofar as this is seen as a benefit or disadvantage by i himself. The monetary scale used by equivalent income does not give more importance to money and income than the individual himself does.

This respect for individual preferences sometimes creates a problem for the computation of equivalent incomes. Consider an individual who is enjoying more than the reference $\tilde{y}$ for a particular dimension and considers this to be incommensurably more important than having a greater income. One then has

$$v_i(p, y_i, m_i) > v_i(\tilde{p}, \tilde{y}, m_i^*)$$

for all values of m_i^*, so that his equivalent income can be considered to be infinite. Nevertheless, it may not be obvious that this individual is better off than most people in the population, because he may suffer disadvantages in other important dimensions that would deserve to be addressed by public policy.

What the methodology of equivalent income assumes is that variations in individual situations are sufficiently mild that they are commensurable, in the eyes of the concerned individuals, to variations in incomes. Whether this is the case or not is ultimately an empirical, not an ethical, question. If it turned out to be the case that income is not a suitable metric because it is not important enough in the eyes of the population, this would not imply that the equivalence approach is altogether unsatisfactory. It may simply mean that another variant of the equivalence approach would be preferable, with different reference sets in which the main variation occurs for another dimension than income, or for a combination of dimensions.

4.3.5 Bundle dominance is unacceptable

Let us now turn to the opposite criticism, namely, that a better bundle in all dimensions always reflects a better situation, independently of individual

17. See overviews in Fleurbaey (2008) and Fleurbaey and Maniquet (2011a).

preferences. This objection is problematic because it ultimately implies that two individuals with the same bundle (m, p, y) are equally well off, independently of their preferences. This throws away any idea of respecting individual preferences. Conversely, if the same bundle may correspond to more or less well-being depending on the concerned individual's preferences, it may happen, as with the equivalence approach, that an individual with a better bundle but a less good fit with preferences is worse off than another.

These considerations can be illustrated as follows. Suppose, as in subsection 4.3.1, that individual situations are represented by vectors in some space Z, and that all reasonable preferences are strictly monotonic. In this context, Sen's intersection principle (see subsection 4.2.3) can motivate a dominance principle stipulating that an individual having more in all dimensions is better off. All monotonic individual preferences do indeed agree with this principle. But another natural way to respect individual preferences, especially if one wants to avoid paternalism, is to say that two situations that are ranked in a certain fashion by an individual should be evaluated in the same fashion when they are given to this individual.

Formally, interpersonal comparisons can be encapsulated in a transitive but not necessarily complete ranking $\succeq$ of situations (individual vectors) $z \in Z$, the expression $(z_i, i) \succeq (z_j, j)$ meaning that i in situation z_i is at least as well off as j in situation z_j (and $\succ, \sim$ denote the corresponding strict and equivalence relations). The expression $z_i R_i z_i'$ still means that z_i is at least as good as z_i' for i's preferences (with $z_i I_i z_i'$ denoting indifference).

The dominance and nonpaternalism principles can then be formulated as follows.

Dominance: For all i, j, all $z_i, z_j \in Z$, if $z_i \gg z_j$ then $(z_i, i) \succ (z_j, j)$.
Nonpaternalism: For all i, all $z_i, z_i' \in Z$, $(z_i, i) \succeq (z_i', i)$ if and only if $z_i R_i z_i'$.

Now, it turns out that under mild assumptions, these two requirements are incompatible whenever there are individuals with different preferences. Because one can then find $z_i, z_i', z_j, z_j' \in Z$ and i, j such that $z_i \gg z_j$, $z_j' \gg z_i'$, $z_i I_i z_i'$ and $z_j I_j z_j'$. (This is illustrated in figure 4.7.) By the dominance principle, $(z_i, i) \succ (z_j, j)$ and $(z_j', j) \succ (z_i', i)$, but by nonpaternalism, $(z_i, i) \sim (z_i', i)$ and $(z_j, j) \sim (z_j', j)$, which violates transitivity.

This result implies that one of the two requirements must be relaxed. It is natural to give priority to nonpaternalism, because respecting individuals' preferences over their own situation should be more important than following their preferences over interpersonal comparisons. One can nonetheless try to preserve as much as possible of the dominance principle as is compatible with nonpaternalism. A restricted dominance principle, for example, would apply only to a subset of bundles. In contrast, it can be extended to apply to a wider set of dominance configurations, because compatibility with nonpaternalism allows it.

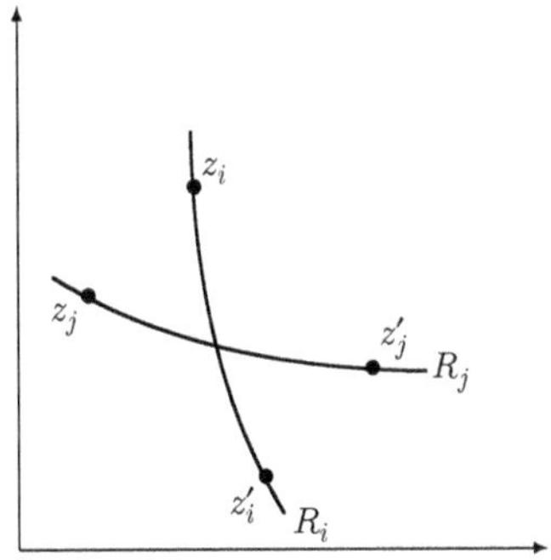

Figure 4.7
The tension between dominance and nonpaternalism

Restricted dominance: For some subset $A \subseteq Z$, for all i, j, all $z_i, z_j \in Z$, if $z_i \geq z_j$ then $(z_i, i) \succeq (z_j, j)$.

Under mild regularity conditions, the combination of this restricted dominance principle with nonpaternalism implies that the ranking $\succeq$ must be of the equivalence sort (Fleurbaey et al. 2009). More precisely, the subset A over which dominance applies has to be a monotone path (an increasing curve in Z), and interpersonal comparisons must be performed as follows: $(z, i) \succeq (z', j)$ if and only if $a \geq b$, where $a, b \in A$ are defined by $zI_i a$ and $z' I_j b$.

Indeed, taking for granted that A is a monotone path, imagine the following configuration: $z_i I_i a$, $z_j I_j b$, and $a, b \in A$, $a \geq b$. By the nonpaternalism principle, $(z_i, i) \sim (a, i)$ and $(z_j, j) \sim (b, j)$. By the restricted dominance principle, $(a, i) \succeq (b, j)$. Therefore, by transitivity, $(z_i, i) \succeq (z_j, j)$.

Conversely, assume $z_i I_i a$, $z_j I_j b$, and $(z_i, i) \succeq (z_j, j)$. By transitivity, $(a, i) \succeq (b, j)$. By restricted dominance, $(a, i) \sim (a, j)$. Therefore, $(a, j) \succeq (b, j)$, which, as A is a monotone path and preferences are strictly monotonic, requires $a \geq b$ in view of nonpaternalism.

The only difficulty in the full argument is to show that for all $a, b \in A$, necessarily $a \geq b$ or $a \leq b$ (that is, A is a monotone path). See Fleurbaey et al. (2009) for details.[18]

Note that even if the dominance principle is, formally, restricted to a set of measure zero, it will still occur very often that an individual enjoying more in all dimensions than another is deemed better off. The dominance principle, even restricted in this way, retains a great deal of influence on the evaluation.

This simple formalism actually suggests in a very intuitive way why the intersection principle proposed by Sen is not compelling. When everyone considers z_i to be better than z_j, this simply means that $z_i R_k z_j$ for all k. But

18. An extension of this reasoning to equivalent sets B_λ can be found in Fleurbaey (2007).

why should that imply that $(z_i, i) \succeq (z_j, j)$ independently of R_i, R_j? Even if there is unanimity in the population to say, "I would prefer to be a banker and earn \$500,000 rather than be a banker and earn \$400,000," there is no reason to conclude that a devoted artist would be better off in the former situation than a born banker in the latter. Individual goals matter, and the fit between the contents of one life and one's goals is important. The comparisons that are made by people in the intersection principle are intrapersonal comparisons for fixed preferences; they have little reason to induce conclusions about interpersonal comparisons involving different preferences.

Perhaps the attraction of the intersection principle comes from the impression that if a life is better in all respects, that should include a better fit between preferences and contents. But this is not what the intersection principle says. It does not ask individual opinions about $(z, i) \succeq (z', j)$, but only about zR_iz'. The latter involves personal preferences; the former is an ethical question that underlies the very issue to be addressed in the construction of a good measure of well-being. We will come back to this issue when discussing the capability approach in chapter 6.

The unrestricted dominance principle is so unappealing that one may wonder if the restricted dominance principle, which is satisfied by the equivalence approach and characterizes it in combination with nonpaternalism, is worth retaining as well. For instance, with the equivalent income, individuals who are in the same situation $(\tilde{p}, \tilde{y}, m)$ are considered equally well off independently of the fit between this situation and their preferences. Isn't this objectionable?

This is a sensible criticism, which can be addressed by two refinements of the equivalent income approach that proceed as follows. A first refinement consists in combining different reference values and compute a weighted average:

$$\sum_{\tilde{p},\tilde{y}} e_i\left(\tilde{p}, \tilde{y}, v_i(p, y_i, m_i)\right) f(\tilde{p}, \tilde{y}). \tag{4.5}$$

(An integral instead of a sum may be used if a continuum of reference values is considered.) In this way, a better fit between preferences and a particular situation $(m, \tilde{p}, \tilde{y})$ will increase the equivalent income at other values of the reference paramaters and will therefore be recorded in the average.

This multireference equivalent income is still a correct representation of individual preferences and shares most of the features of the single-reference equivalent income. In particular, it still allows taking account of needs and personal characteristics that influence individual satisfaction.

The main difference is that the multireference equivalent income takes account of more information about the indifference curve than the single-reference equivalent income. It therefore introduces a greater sensitiveness to individual preferences. Figure 4.8, a variant of figure 4.3, illustrates this property. If the indifference curve of the individual rises as in the figure (dotted curve), which corresponds to a better fit between preferences and the situation, this is not recorded with the single reference $\tilde{y}$, but it is if $\tilde{y}'$ is also used in a multireference equivalent income, because a weighted sum of m^* and $m^{*\prime}$ increases.

Another possible refinement, for the choice of $\tilde{y}$,[19] consists in picking the reference $\tilde{y}$ that represents the ideal value of y for the individual, for a fixed income. In this way different individuals may have different references that respect their own ideal in terms of y. For instance, individuals who like working may have a reference leisure that is smaller than the individuals who dislike working. This personalization of the reference is particularly attractive. It implies that restricted dominance is respected along paths that are specific to the preferences, and only for individuals having the same path (in particular, individuals having the same preferences). Figure 4.9 illustrates this choice of personalized reference that depends on each preference and, for each preference, on each indifference curve.

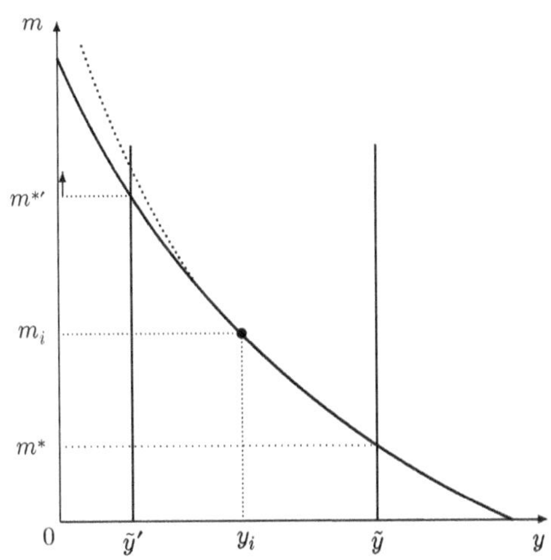

Figure 4.8
Equivalent income with multiple references

19. For reasons discussed in appendix A, for $\tilde{p}$ another approach is needed.

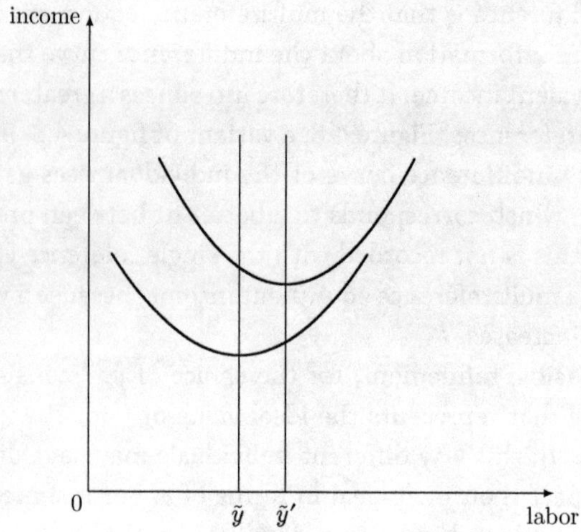

Figure 4.9
Personalized reference for two indifference curves

Formally, this second refinement means that one computes a minimum equivalent income, defined as

$$\min_{\tilde{y}} e_i\left(\tilde{p}, \tilde{y}, v_i(p, y_i, m_i)\right).$$

It is worth mentioning that, even if the reference may change with each preference and even with each indifference curve, one still obtains a good representation of preferences, because $\min_{\tilde{y}} e_i\left(\tilde{p}, \tilde{y}, u_i\right)$ is increasing in u_i.

Note that this can be viewed as the limit of the weighted sum (4.5) when a concave transform φ is applied to equivalent incomes and its degree of concavity tends to infinity:

$$\sum_{\tilde{y}} \varphi\left(e_i\left(\tilde{p}, \tilde{y}, v_i(p, y_i, m_i)\right)\right) f(\tilde{y}).$$

Giving a special priority to the low values of $e_i\left(\tilde{p}, \tilde{y}, v_i(p, y_i, m_i)\right)$ when the references $\tilde{y}$ are spanned appears a natural way to focus on the least favorable evaluation of individual situations, and the most respectful of individual aspirations. Appendix A provides additional justifications for this approach.

4.3.6 Egalitarianism is demanding

Let us take stock. The equivalence approach violates Arrow Independence, but this is acceptable, and it shares this feature with other popular approaches. Reference dependence is not a drawback if a theory is proposed for the choice of good references. While such a theory is in its infancy, it can no longer be said that the reference has to be totally arbitrary. Subjective well-being, far from being neglected, is incorporated inasmuch as individuals care about it, which seems the most respectful way to do so. Violations of dominance, far from being a problem, are the natural consequence of taking account of the fit between life and goals, and one may even argue that the single-reference equivalence approach retains too much of the dominance principle.

One criticism remains to be examined, namely, the problem of concavity failures. The possibility that a social welfare function defined on money-metric utilities may not be quasi-concave in the quantities of commodities consumed, or in ordinary incomes, actually finds an echo in a result from the fair allocation literature.[20]

Consider any social ordering function that ranks two allocations on the sole basis of individual indifference curves at these allocations—this is a weak form of independence, due to Hansson (1973) and therefore called Hansson Independence, which is satisfied by the equivalence approach (including social criteria based on money-metric utilities) and other approaches as well, as explained in subsection 4.3.2. Assume in addition that it satisfies the following principle of transfer: if two individuals have identical preferences and one of them consumes more of every commodity than the other, then the allocation is improved if a transfer proportional to the difference between the two bundles is made in order to reduce (but not eliminate) the inequality—this principle of transfer is satisfied by any quasi-concave social welfare function that is symmetrical for individuals with identical preferences. Assume finally that the social ordering satisfies the Strong Pareto principle, which says that an allocation is at least as good as another if it is at least as good for every individual, and that it is strictly better if, in addition, it is better for at least one individual. Then the result says that the social ordering must give absolute priority to the worst off when one considers two individuals with identical preferences but unequal consumptions.

The argument that proves this result is illustrated in figure 4.10, borrowed from Fleurbaey and Maniquet (2011b, chap. 3). Consider the two individuals i, j at the initial allocation z_i, z_j. Suppose that their indifference curves are as in the figure and that their preferences are identical. By Strong Pareto, the allocation z_i^1, z_j^1 is equally good. A transfer from j to i can be

20. For a detailed presentation of various forms of this result, see Fleurbaey and Maniquet (2011b, chap. 3).

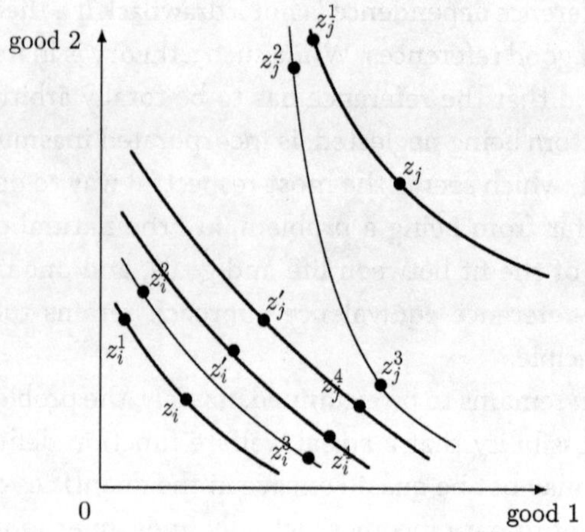

Figure 4.10
Absolute priority to the worst off

made to produce allocation z_i^2, z_j^2, which constitutes an improvement. By Strong Pareto again, allocation z_i^3, z_j^3 is as good as z_i^2, z_j^2. A transfer can again be made and produce allocation z_i^4, z_j^4. By transitivity, this allocation is better than the initial allocation z_i, z_j while by Strong Pareto it is as good as the allocation z_i', z_j'. In conclusion, moving from z_i, z_j to z_i', z_j' is good, even though one observes that this represents a big loss of consumption for *j* and a small gain for *i*. Now, this has been obtained only for a special configuration of preferences. But by Hansson Independence, the only information that matters for the comparison of z_i, z_j and z_i', z_j' is contained in the indifference curves at these allocations. Therefore, whenever indifferences of *i* and *j* at z_i, z_j and z_i', z_j' do not cross, one can construct intermediate indifference curves as in the figure[21] and conclude that improving the situation of the worst off is always good.

In practice social orderings satisfying this property are of the maximin or leximin type. Blackorby and Donaldson's (1988) examples of violation of quasi-concavity are valid only for social welfare functions with finite aversion to inequality in money-metric utilities. Granting absolute priority to the worst off is indeed the only way to avoid a violation of quasi-concavity,

21. When every point of the indifference curve at z_j is above the whole indifference curve at z_j', the intermediate indifference curve that contains z_j^2 and z_j^3 cannot be simultaneously close to z_j^1 and z_j^4, and an additional step is needed in the argument. See Fleurbaey and Maniquet (2011b).

and the result that has just been described confirms and extends this conclusion. What the result shows is that the necessity of giving absolute priority to the worst off does not hold only for the equivalent income approach, but for any approach that evaluates well-being on the basis of indifference curves.

Is this a negative result? The literature on fair social choice tends to view it as a positive result because it forces a specific degree of inequality aversion and therefore reduces the range of acceptable social orderings, with a novel argument in favor of the Rawlsian priority for the worst off. Moreover, it appears that the maximin is not very restrictive because with various fairness principles it is possible to evaluate individual situations in many ways. For instance, even laissez-faire policies can be justified by maximin criteria if individual situations are measured taking the endowments of the individuals as justified benchmarks.[22]

For those who really abhor the idea of giving absolute priority to the worst off, the result is useful in pointing to the various conditions that have to be relaxed. If the Pareto principle is considered sacrosanct, only two possibilities emerge.

The result can be first escaped by relaxing Hansson Independence, but not much is known about how to define a reasonable social criterion in this way. The potential complexity of criteria that need information about a large part of the indifference map in order to evaluate a particular situation is quite unattractive.

The transfer principle can also be questioned. Although Blackorby and Donaldson take it as axiomatic that quasi-concavity is a basic condition of ethics,[23] one could argue that the violations of the transfer principle induced by a criterion of the equivalent income sort are not necessarily shocking. Consider the equivalent income computed as the income that would be equivalent to an individual if his health were good (i.e., the reference is "good health"). Imagine two individuals with mediocre health.

22. Intuitively, imagine that an individual's situation is measured by the gap between the value of his consumption and the value of his endowment. The competitive equilibrium ensures that the gap is null for everyone, which achieves equality in terms of such gaps. The criterion yielding this result, however, is not of the equivalence kind (see Fleurbaey and Maniquet 2011b, chap. 7, for details).

23. They quote Samuelson (1956) as saying that quasi-concavity of the social welfare function is "the foundation for the economics of the good society." It is plausible that Samuelson thought so, but in the quoted phrase he was only referring to the Bergson curves as a useful tool for welfare economics: "Future publications will show how these social indifference contours can be used to throw light on international trade policy and on the methodological problems of the older and newer welfare economics. The foundation is laid for the 'economics of a good society'" (p. 22).

Suppose that their ordinary incomes in allocation x are $(100, 200)$ and their equivalent incomes $(80, 150)$. Imagine that a regressive transfer between them would produce a new situation with ordinary incomes $(90, 210)$ and equivalent incomes $(75, 190)$. If one considers that, for two healthy individuals, the distribution $(75, 190)$ is better than $(80, 150)$, it is only logical, by Pareto indifference, that for the less than healthy individuals under consideration, the regressive transfer yields an improvement. This is intuitively defensible if one observes that the regressive transfer triggers a reduction in both individuals' willingness-to-pay for good health, especially for the beneficiary of the transfer, who then benefits doubly (more income and lower concern for his bad health). This example also suggests that, in practice, such violations of the principle of transfer are unlikely to occur in dramatic proportions if the aggregator has enough inequality aversion.

In conclusion of this subsection, it appears that concavity failures are a pervasive problem for measures of well-being that use information about local indifference curves only. Whether this justifies giving absolute priority to the worst off or accepting certain limited violations of inequality aversion is the ethical issue facing those who want to keep the equivalent income methodology.

4.4 SOCIAL WELFARE DECOMPOSITION

Before concluding this chapter, we briefly come back to the issue of decomposing social welfare into components reflecting different ethical goals such as efficiency and equity. The equivalent income offers an interesting calibration of utilities that lends itself nicely to a sum-inequality (rather than efficiency-equity) decomposition, with the market value of total consumption as one element of the decomposition.

We first need to introduce the notion of "equally-distributed equivalent." Consider a social welfare function $W(u_1, \ldots, u_n)$, assumed to be increasing in each argument. Following Kolm (1968) and Atkinson (1970), the equally distributed equivalent $E(u_1, \ldots, u_n)$ is defined as the amount of utility that, equally given to all individuals, yields the same social welfare as the distribution $(u_1, \ldots, u_n)$. Formally, $E(u_1, \ldots, u_n)$ is equal to the solution e^* to the equation

$$W(e^*, \ldots, e^*) = W(u_1, \ldots, u_n).$$

As the solution e^* increases with the value of $W(u_1, \ldots, u_n)$, the function $E(u_1, \ldots, u_n)$ is ordinally equivalent to $W(u_1, \ldots, u_n)$. For inequality averse social preferences, $E(u_1, \ldots, u_n)$ is less than the average utility. This makes it possible to write the decomposition

$$E(u_1, \ldots, u_n) = \frac{1}{n}\sum_{i=1}^{n} u_i \times \frac{E(u_1, \ldots, u_n)}{\frac{1}{n}\sum_{i=1}^{n} u_i}, \tag{4.6}$$

in which the second term, which lies between 0 and 1, captures distributional preferences.

The first term, average utility, is not, apparently, a function of total income, but this can be remedied as follows, with the help of equivalent incomes as defined in (4.2).

We retain the framework in which individual utility $u_i\left(x_i, y_i\right)$ depends on marketed commodities x_i and nonmarket goods y_i. It is important that equivalent income $e_i\left(\tilde{p}, \tilde{y}, u_i\right)$ takes account of the fact that individuals may differ in other aspects than market consumption. Under these conditions, it is reasonable to consider that inequality in such indexes of well-being is undesirable—a condition that is needed to make use of the equally distributed equivalent.

Therefore we now assume that social welfare is computed as

$$W\left(e_1\left(\tilde{p}, \tilde{y}, u_1\right), \ldots, e_n\left(\tilde{p}, \tilde{y}, u_n\right)\right),$$

with an inequality-averse W function to which decomposition (4.6) can be applied.

The average value of these utilities, $\frac{1}{n}\sum_{i=1}^{n} e_i\left(\tilde{p}, \tilde{y}, u_i\right)$, which would then appear as the first term in decomposition (4.6), can itself be decomposed by observing that one has

$$\begin{aligned} e_i\left(\tilde{p}, \tilde{y}, u_i(x_i, y_i)\right) &= e_i\left(\tilde{p}, y_i, u_i(x_i, y_i)\right) \\ &\quad + e_i\left(\tilde{p}, \tilde{y}, u_i(x_i, y_i)\right) - e_i\left(\tilde{p}, y_i, u_i(x_i, y_i)\right). \end{aligned} \tag{4.7}$$

The first term is not too different from $\tilde{p}x_i$ when $\tilde{p}$ is close to the prevailing market price vector p. The second term measures the welfare impact of the gap between y_i and the reference $\tilde{y}$. This decomposition can be used in the analysis of the first term of (4.6), but also in the second term, as it may be interesting to separate the impact on inequalities of differences in x and differences in y.

As in the previous chapter, we do not obtain a simple monetary value like $\tilde{p}x_i$ but a money-metric value. Again, this reveals the difficulty of connecting prices with welfare, budget lines with indifference curves, when prices are not fixed.

One can, however, use a price index and decompose the first term of (4.7) into

$$e_i\left(\tilde{p}, y_i, u_i(x_i, y_i)\right) = px_i \frac{e_i\left(\tilde{p}, y_i, u_i(x_i, y_i)\right)}{e_i\left(p, y_i, u_i(x_i, y_i)\right)} = \frac{px_i}{P_i},$$

where $P_i = e\left(p, y_i, u_i(x_i, y_i)\right) / e\left(\tilde{p}, y_i, u_i(x_i, y_i)\right)$ is a price index—this kind of index is called a true Könus index in the literature.[24]

The aggregate term $\sum_{i=1}^{n} e_i\left(\tilde{p}, y_i, u_i(x_i, y_i)\right)$ can then be written as a deflated value of total expenditure:

$$\sum_{i=1}^{n} e_i\left(\tilde{p}, y_i, u_i(x_i, y_i)\right) = \frac{\sum_{i=1}^{n} px_i}{P},$$

where the price index P is determined by

$$P = \frac{\sum_{i=1}^{n} px_i}{\sum_{i=1}^{n} \frac{px_i}{P_i}} = \left[\frac{1}{\sum_{i=1}^{n} px_i} \sum_{i=1}^{n} px_i \frac{1}{P_i}\right]^{-1},$$

that is, P is a harmonic mean of the individual P_i, weighted by px_i.[25]

In summary, the decomposition of social welfare is then as follows:[26]

$$\left(\frac{\frac{1}{n}\sum_{i=1}^{n} px_i}{P} + \frac{1}{n}\sum_{i=1}^{n}\left[e_i\left(\tilde{p}, \tilde{y}, u_i(x_i, y_i)\right) - e_i\left(\tilde{p}, y_i, u_i(x_i, y_i)\right)\right]\right)(1 - I), \tag{4.8}$$

where I is the inequality index

$$I = 1 - \frac{E\left(e_1\left(\tilde{p}, \tilde{y}, u_1(x_1, y_1)\right), \ldots, e_n\left(\tilde{p}, \tilde{y}, u_n(x_n, y_n)\right)\right)}{\frac{1}{n}\sum_{i=1}^{n} e_i\left(\tilde{p}, \tilde{y}, u_i(x_i, y_i)\right)},$$

24. Under perfect complementarity, $P_i = px_i/\tilde{p}x_i$. In all cases, it satisfies the property that px_i/P_i is equal to the value of the expenditure function at reference price $\tilde{p}$.

25. One also has

$$P = \sum_{i=1}^{n} \frac{e_i\left(\tilde{p}, y_i, u_i(x_i, y_i)\right)}{\sum_{j=1}^{n} e_j\left(\tilde{p}, y_j, u_j(x_j, y_j)\right)} P_i,$$

i.e., the social price index is also the arithmetic mean of the P_i, weighted by $e_i\left(\tilde{p}, y_i, u_i(x_i, y_i)\right)$.

26. Deaton (1980) proposes a similar decomposition, with all terms assembled in multiplicative fashion.

which can itself be further decomposed into inequalities due to x and inequalities due to y, as suggested earlier. Although this decomposition does not separate the various components of efficiency and equity as (3.29) does, it contains ethically relevant terms:

- Average income suitably deflated, representing the contribution of x to aggregate welfare
- Contribution of y to aggregate welfare
- Inequalities (which can themselves be decomposed into x and y contributions).

Figure 4.11 illustrates this decomposition, in the simple case of a single nonincome variable, as in figures 4.3 and 4.8. There are two individuals, one of which enjoys the reference $\tilde{y}$. The gap between average income and average equivalent income measures the loss due to the fact that i has a lower y_i, and the gap between average equivalent income and social welfare measures the loss due to inequalities in equivalent incomes.[27]

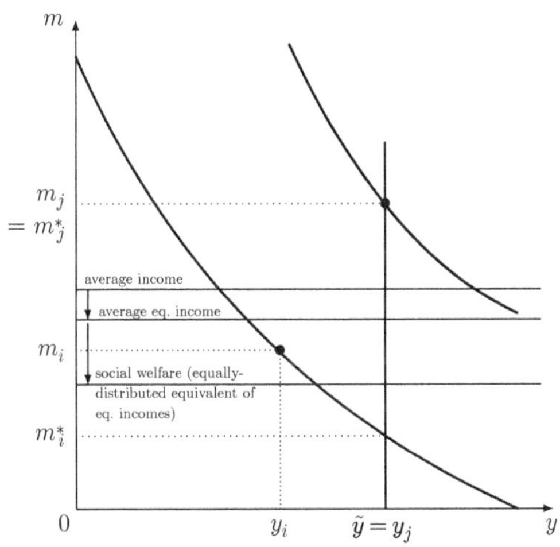

Figure 4.11
Social welfare decomposition

27. In the figure, the level of social welfare cannot be deduced from the displayed data, as it also depends on the degree of inequality aversion embodied in the social welfare function.

4.5 CONCLUSION

In conclusion, even though the money-metric approach has been criticized for being inferior to the classical Bergson-Samuelson social welfare function, one can argue that it should be considered among the best candidates for a measure of well-being to include in a Bergson-Samuelson social welfare function. Bergson (1954) and Samuelson (1947) themselves recommended seeking ethical principles pairing indifference curves of different individuals in order to make sensible interpersonal comparisons. After all, one should not forget that the money-metric approach was introduced by Samuelson (1974), and in his 1977 article he takes the (similar) ray utility as an illustration of his approach.[28]

The reference to willingness-to-pay in the computation of equivalent incomes does not mean that everything is marketable or that "a dollar is a dollar," and it does not push us back into the pitfalls of the old cost-benefit analysis. It simply amounts to comparing individuals in a simple hypothetical world in which they are all equal over the nonincome dimensions and differ only in the income dimension. This hypothetical world is constructed so that all individuals are indifferent between their current situation and their "equivalent" situation in the hypothetical world. It then makes sense to compare them in terms of income because, when they all enjoy the reference levels for nonincome dimensions, their preferences over these dimensions no longer seem relevant for such comparisons. This approach is compatible with giving priority to the worst off, and its main motivation is respecting individuals' preferences over the dimensions of life.

The main criticisms that have been raised against the money-metric utility are not decisive, and the emergence of the equivalence approach in the theory of fair allocation justifies renewed interest in the notion of equivalent income, viewed as a special case of the equivalence approach. The latter even appears as the only possible methodology if one seeks a method of measurement of well-being that respects individual preferences while considering that there are certain situations of dominance in which comparisons can be made in terms of bundles. We have seen that the dominance principle, however, is questionable even when restricted to special situations. This led us to suggest that multireference and personalized-reference variants of the equivalent income might provide a more comprehensive measure of well-being than the standard single-reference concept. This idea is further studied in appendix A.

28. See Fleurbaey and Mongin (2005) for a detailed analysis of the Bergson-Samuelson approach and the controversies around it.

The problem of concavity failures is perhaps the most intriguing. It has been recalled here that this problem concerns a large class of measures of well-being, not just the equivalence approach. For those who want to retain the equivalent income methodology and use a criterion like

$$W\left(e_1\left(\tilde{p},\tilde{y},v_1(m_1,p,y_1)\right),\ldots,e_n\left(\tilde{p},\tilde{y},v_n(m_n,p,y_n)\right)\right),$$

this poses a dilemma between giving absolute priority to the worst off, that is, letting W be the maximin function (or adopt the leximin ordering), and accepting that in certain situations the criterion may display a preference for inequality in incomes among identical individuals.

While these issues require more investigation, at least it is essential to dispel the impression that equivalent income is a measure that gives money a special value and assumes that everything should be for sale. It is true that equivalent income is a good measure of well-being only if variations in individual situations are commensurable to inequalities in income, in the concerned individuals' eyes—which excludes lexicographic preferences, for instance. Whether such commensurability is the case or not may be tested empirically.

More will be said about the equivalence approach in the next chapters, because of its relevance to the discussion of subjective well-being and capabilities.

CHAPTER 5

Is Happiness All that Matters?

The literature on subjective well-being has been soaring in the last two decades. Excellent syntheses on this new development can be found in Clark, Fritjers, and Shields (2008), Diener (2000), Diener, Helliwell, and Kahneman (2010), Dolan and White (2007), Di Tella and McCulloch (2006), Frey and Stutzer (2002), Graham (2009), Kahneman, Diener, and Schwarz (1999), Kahneman and Krueger (2006), and Oswald (1997). This literature has brought two important changes to the economic perspective on well-being.

First, it has shifted priorities. The idea that social welfare can be equated with the growth of GDP has been much more powerfully shaken by the Easterlin paradox that derives from happiness surveys, than by theoretical objections against its underlying assumptions. Easterlin (1974, 1995) observed that happiness scores in various countries seem quite flat in the long run in spite of a twofold or threefold increase in GDP over the last decades.[1] Figures 5.1 and 5.2, borrowed from Clark, Fritjers, and Shields (2008), illustrate this striking phenomenon for the United States and for five European countries. In addition, some happiness data suggest that employment, family, leisure, and pain are important aspects of well-being. Growth, therefore, can no longer be the only policy priority for economic advisors.

The other change to the economic perspective on well-being is methodological. A strong positivist tradition initiated by Robbins (1932) convinced

1. This claim is disputed by Stevenson and Wolfers (2008) and Sacks, Stevenson, and Wolfers (2010). More on this in this chapter.

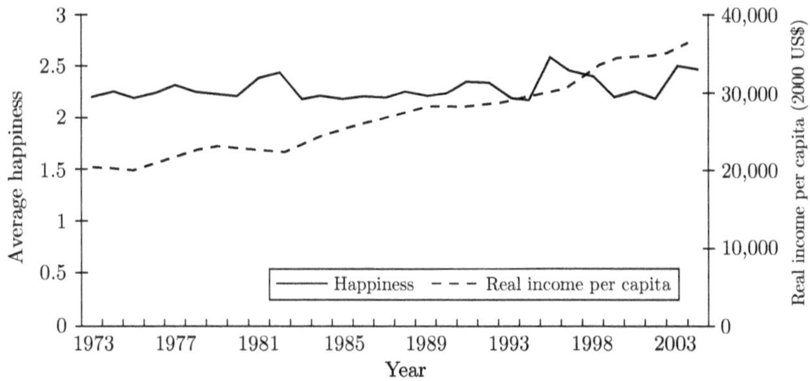

Figure 5.1
Happiness and Real Income Per Capita in the United States, 1973–2004
Source: Clark, Fritjers, and Shields (2008, fig. 1)

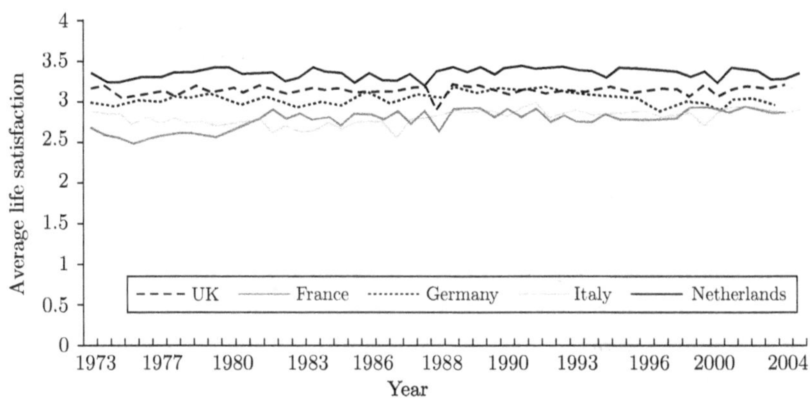

Figure 5.2
Life Satisfaction in Five European Countries, 1973–2004
Source: Clark, Fritjers, and Shields (2008, fig. 2).

economists for a very long time that choice behavior is the only source of relevant information about individual preferences and well-being. The concept of utility, which was central in the utilitarian tradition and was then considered almost as tangible a notion as money, became relegated to the status of a mathematical convenience making it easier to manipulate preference orderings. Interpersonal comparisons were viewed as a normative exercise not fit for a scientific discipline. What happiness studies have changed is that the practice of listening to people's verbal utterances is now becoming respectable. It has also greatly contributed to reviving interest in the measurement of well-being.

Beyond the methodological shift, the resurrection of the concept of utility is impressive. There are now papers that estimate the curvature of the utility function directly from happiness data (Layard, Mayraz, and Nickell 2008), and many authors argue that the similar behavior of various happiness and satisfaction scores suggests that they track the same underlying magnitude (e.g., Di Tella, McCulloch, and Oswald 2003), while others argue that clever observation techniques make it possible to measure an "objective" form of subjective well-being (Kahneman 1999). Bentham's views make an unexpected comeback (Kahneman, Wakker, and Sarin 1997; Layard 2005).

These developments make it possible to imagine a new and simple solution to the quest for a measure of social welfare. Happiness scores are not very costly to elicit and are now available for most countries of the world. Why not use such data to compute Gross National Happiness, and take this statistic as the new compass of nations and policymakers? While this idea is cautiously defended by some authors (e.g., Diener 2000; Dolan and White 2007; Kahneman et al. 2004; Oswald 1997), many refrain from doing so, and some firmly oppose it. The ongoing debate is partly reminiscent of a previous debate about subjective welfarism that took place in political philosophy about 30 years ago.

In this chapter we shall connect the two debates in order to better elucidate the normative underpinnings of a measure of social welfare centered on the notion of happiness. This chapter argues that happiness scores cannot be expected to reflect people's values and goals in life directly, although they can provide useful information if properly handled. Whether or not one endorses the view that a good measure of social welfare should reflect people's preferences, the implication is that happiness data should not be used without a careful processing that eliminates undesired biases and noises.

The first section reviews the main arguments from the happiness literature in favor of shifting the focus from material to subjective aspects of well-being and relates them to the classical debate on welfarism. The second section proposes a theory of subjective well-being as it appears in questionnaires, in relation to the standard concepts of utility and preference orderings that economists are familiar with, but also taking account of perspectives and insights from psychology. The third section examines how the collection of data could be improved and how such data can be used for the empirical application of different conceptions of well-being.

5.1 THE EASTERLIN PARADOX: HAVE WE BEEN WRONG FOR 70,000 YEARS?

Our species has considerably evolved since it left its African cradle some 70,000 years ago. It has progressively conquered the whole planet, assimilating or eliminating other human species, and has now gained an amazing and even self-endangering power over its surroundings. It has proliferated considerably, and about two-thirds of it has reached an unprecedented level of longevity, consumption, and sophistication. If happiness surveys had been conducted over this whole period, one would perhaps find a remarkable stability in happiness scores over the millennia. The Easterlin paradox is, one may think, not just a post-World War II phenomenon, but a more profound phenomenon of stability of subjective evaluations and feelings in our species.

The underpinnings and plausibility of such stability will be discussed in more detail in this chapter. The question to be raised in this paragraph is the following. If this conjecture about the stability of happiness scores over the whole human history were correct, would it imply that all that has been achieved is a loss of energy, a staggering waste of labor and research, a sequence of wrong-headed, narrowly materialistic endeavors?

This formulation is meant to highlight that the happiness literature advocates not just broadening the concept of well-being, but radically shifting the focus in the formulation of human goals. The shift from material achievements to subjective well-being potentially implies repudiating most of the golden calves that have been adored throughout history. Whether subjective well-being scores accurately record what one would like to promote at the individual and social level is the foundation-shaking question that policymakers should answer before using them as their new compass.

It must be noted here that the Easterlin paradox is itself being disputed. First, another claim by Easterlin was that happiness was more or less identical among the nonpoor countries, but the data from the Gallup World Poll have shown a rather neat logarithmic relation between the average satisfaction with life in countries and GDP per capita (Deaton 2008; Stevenson and Wolfers 2008). What is called the "Easterlin paradox" here only refers to the long-run stability of satisfaction scores. But even such stability is questioned in Sacks, Stevenson, and Wolfers (2010). These works will be examined in more detail in the next section. The purpose of this section is simply to argue that, *even if it were confirmed* over the very long run, the Easterlin paradox would not have the sweeping implications against growth and progress that are often derived by commentators.

5.1.1 Bentham is back

The literature on happiness is not just a cold-blooded observation of facts of the human psyche. For many authors, the "hope is that hedonic psychology will be relevant to policy," and subjective well-being statistics are meant "to provide a more direct assessment of the final outcome about which people are most concerned" (Kahneman, Diener, and Schwarz 1999, pp. xi–xii). "Economic things matter only in so far as they make people happier" (Oswald 1997, p. 1815). Putting happiness at the forefront of social goals raises a number of important questions. First, what is happiness at the individual level? Second, what is it at the social level? Third, why should it be the goal rather than something else, such as wisdom or control over one's life? Obviously, answers to the last question will depend on how happiness is defined in the previous two questions.

At the individual level, the psychology literature distinguishes many different aspects of subjective well-being (Diener et al. 1999). A key divide opposes cognitive evaluations (what people think *of* their life) to affective, emotional states (how they feel *in* their life). The affects themselves come in many shapes and colors, with a surprising independence between the positive and the negative affects, which seem to be connected to different mechanisms in the brain. Attempts to construct classifications of affects along two or more dimensions (e.g., positive/negative valence and high/low activation, as proposed by Russell 1980) or in terms of discrete categories (Ekman 1992) have triggered many debates, but it seems that no simple classification is able to distinguish all emotions (for instance, anger and fear are both intense negative emotions). These issues are well summarized by Frijda (1999).

In practice, it is also not trivial to separate affects from judgments. Ordinary language, which has to be used in questionnaires, is itself ambiguous, as it is not so obvious how to distinguish "to be happy in one's life" from "to be happy with one's life," for instance. When the General Social Survey in the United States asks "Taken all together, how would you say things are these days? Would you say that you are very happy/pretty happy/not too happy?" it is actually hard to tell for sure whether this refers to feelings or to an evaluation. As it turns out, moods are shown to have a strong influence on evaluative judgments (Schwarz and Strack 1999), and conversely, reports on personal emotions cannot avoid judgmental thoughts (Kahneman 1999). The happiness literature often appears to assume that there is a single object, like "utility," that operates behind the scene to generate the answers of respondents. The fact that econometric regressions of happiness scores and satisfaction scores are generally similar is often taken as an argument in favor of this assumption (Layard,

Mayraz, and Nickell 2008). There is, however, a growing evidence of a different pattern for affective scores and evaluative scores. Affective scores seem to be less sensitive to objective conditions of life, more prone to adaptation, than evaluative scores (Kahneman and Krueger 2006; Krueger and Schkade 2008; Kahneman and Deaton 2010).

An important finding of the psychology literature is that people are not very good at predicting their future feelings (Kahneman 1994; Kahneman and Thaler 2006). They typically underestimate how easily they can adapt to a change in their situation and exaggerate the effect of changes over future feelings. They also give too much weight to their current mood. This may lead them to badly organize the sequence of activities. Another phenomenon is that at a time of decision about a particular aspect of their life, people typically overestimate the importance of this aspect and do not anticipate that when this aspect drops from the center of attention, it will have much less impact on their well-being. Such phenomena create a wedge between "decision utility" and "experienced utility." From this standpoint, the Easterlin paradox, for instance, may be imagined to be due to the fact that people underestimate that their efforts to improve their standard of living will not have a long-lasting effect on their subjective well-being.

People also appear to have a peculiar memory about past episodes, giving more attention to the peak and the end of episodes than the overall content (Kahneman, Wakker, and Sarin 1997). This may be so strong that adding a mildly unpleasant end to a more severely unpleasant episode improves individuals' memories about it. This phenomenon makes it delicate to measure "experienced utility," because people's memories differ from a moment-to-moment recording of the episode.

There are also collective mistakes. Comparisons to others seem an important element of subjective well-being as reported in questionnaires, which suggests that there are large externalities, and therefore room for large inefficiencies. It may in particular happen that people make great efforts to improve their relative position in society. Most people doing the same, their relative position does not change much, but growth has ensued, without improving subjective well-being substantially. Economic growth could then be, at least in part, the residual waste of the fight for positions. The Easterlin paradox is explained by Clark, Fritjers, and Shields (2008) as a combination of this phenomenon and of the fact that people adapt to their improved standard of living.

The happiness literature has shown hesitations about whether to focus on affects or on satisfaction evaluations. The latter are cognitively demanding and appear fragile at the individual level. Schwarz and Strack (1999) emphasize that respondents are influenced by the order and wording of questions and by transient information, or simply by their current mood, and conclude that affects may be a more reliable source of information about subjective well-being. This is also the general tone of Kahneman's chapter in the same volume (Kahneman 1999), with the hope that a good measure of affects approaches an "objective" notion of happiness. On the other hand, the fact that adaptation seems stronger for affects makes indicators of affects less attractive if one wants a subjective indicator that has some good link with objective conditions of life. Affects may be easier to measure objectively, but may also give a less relevant perspective on people's lives.

Let us now turn to the definition of happiness at the social level. At the social level, the distribution of happiness across individuals has to be considered. Most studies focus on average scores and therefore neglect the distribution, but this is seldom defended as a definite neutral attitude about the distribution of happiness. Layard (2005), for instance, argues in favor of giving some priority to the most miserable. The average score has the advantage of eliminating noises and disturbances that are randomly distributed over the population. Estimating the distribution of happiness is statistically more demanding and requires more confidence about the possibility of comparing score levels across individuals. Truly enough, the average score also requires great confidence about the possibility of comparing score variations across individuals. The risk is that individuals with greater variations will sway the general movement of the indicator. At any rate, the important point here is that it is not obvious that "happiness" at the social level should be understood as the average score.

Then comes the key normative question: Why take happiness as the goal of society? The happiness literature is not always explicit about an answer, but when it is, the main argument is that this is the goal of the population, "the final outcome about which people are most concerned," as quoted in the first paragraph of this section. More specifically, many authors argue that happiness is the ultimate goal, and that everything else that is desired is only a means to this end (Diener 1994; Frey and Stutzer 2002; Layard 2005; Oswald 1997). Bentham's principle of the Greatest Happiness is then brought back to the fore. As one prominent author in this field writes: "I believe that Bentham's idea was right and that we should fearlessly adopt it and apply it to our lives" (Layard 2005, p. 112).

The general outlook emerging from this approach is the following, as well summarized in the preface of Kahneman, Ritov, and Schkade (1999):

> A scientific understanding of hedonic experience will allow for the development of valid hedonic indicators that reflect the pleasantness of life in the everyday experiences of people. At present, economic indicators hold the most sway in

> policy circles. Yet, the economic approach is limited in several ways. First, it focuses on those aspects of life that can be traded in the marketplace. Thus, desirable goods such as love, mental challenge, and stress are given little consideration. As people reach what Ronald Inglehart has labeled a "post-materialist" level in which basic physical needs are met, they become increasingly concerned with fulfillment in less materialistic realms. Second, the economic view presupposes that individuals will choose the greatest amount of utility for themselves; yet a great deal of evidence now contradicts this proposition. Third, economics assesses variables that are only indirect indicators of something else—of subjective fulfillment. (pp. xi–xii)

In other words, according to this literature the focus on material performance should give way to a focus on subjective well-being. When individuals and societies appear to strive for something else, such as territorial expansions, technical inventions, greater possessions, or more consumption, they ultimately seek subjective well-being and do so awkwardly. Their strategies actually fail to maximize experienced utility. The new focus on hedonic fulfillment will eventually give people what they have wrongly sought in material performance.

5.1.2 The debate about subjective welfarism

There are many other reasons than the Benthamite principle one may like the political conclusions derived by the happiness literature. The main political conclusions are indeed that one should have a greater concern for poverty alleviation, mental health, pain relief, social relations, leisure. But attractive policy implications do not necessarily make a good normative theory. It is important to assess the soundness of social objectives.

Moreover, real policy challenges may be lurking. Although this is not broadcast by the happiness literature, for instance, the impact of education and technical innovation on happiness is dubious and, from the point of view of happiness, one should wonder whether the high priority they currently receive is deserved. The same could be said about health care and medical research that deals with nonfatal conditions, because subjective well-being tends to adapt to bad health, except mental health and pain. Similarly, while poverty alleviation is important in the hedonist perspective because poverty is associated with low subjective well-being in various direct and indirect ways, one may wonder if inequalities in subjective well-being track the kind of inequalities that one should seek to eliminate. As Graham (2009) emphasizes in the title of her book, there are "happy peasants and miserable millionnaires." Therefore it is important to examine the arguments for and against the subjective approach to well-being measurement.

There was a philosophical debate about subjective "welfarism" in the 1980s, from which welfarism has not emerged unscathed, and it is interesting to rehearse the main ingredients of this debate.

Three objections have been raised against subjective welfarism. Dworkin (1981) has argued on grounds of fairness that people who are more difficult to satisfy because they have more expensive tastes cannot claim that they are worse off and should not request more resources than the others. A more ambitious goal in life cannot be presented as a handicap in the achievement of satisfaction and a reason for an extra amount of help from the other members of society.

Rawls (1982) has raised a similar point and moreover objected to subjective measures on the ground that they cannot provide a sensible method of interpersonal comparisons. Individuals have different goals in life that are incommensurable. One can compare the resources available to individuals but not their success in achieving their different goals. A measure of success that would operate across a diversity of goals would require an overarching notion of success, and such a notion does not exist and would not make sense.

Sen (1985) has objected that subjective well-being is too malleable and adaptable to serve as a good proxy for the conditions of life that people care about. One shouldn't count against a poor and oppressed individual that his subjective well-being is well adapted.

Importantly, these objections are not based on the rejection of individual preferences as a guide for the evaluation of personal situations. Sen's view probably introduces a distinction between people's actual preferences, which may be distorted by oppression and social conditioning, and the more authentic form of valuation they would have in better circumstances. Such a distinction is, however, rather standard. As we have seen, the happiness literature also introduces a (different) wedge between a misguided "decision utility" and an authentic "experienced utility" and wants to make people happy against their will if necessary. As Layard puts it, he is "advocating the promotion of good feelings, not the satisfaction of desires" (2005, p. 260). All in all, however, there is a general liberal consensus that in some form, people's perspective should be the ultimate guideline in the evaluation of individual situations, even if immediate preferences may not be trustworthy.

The above objections against subjective welfarism are therefore not based on the idea that people may be deeply mistaken about their own good, and that one should promote their good against their view. Rather, the objections have to do with the fact that subjective well-being does not provide a good metric of advantage for interpersonal comparisons. One may have a high level of subjective well-being and be disadvantaged, and conversely. The objections all turn around the idea of "happy peasants and miserable millionaires."

5.1.3 Is happiness the ultimate goal?

In the next section we will examine in more detail how it may happen that subjective scores fail to record a sensible notion of advantage. Let us here focus on a possible response from the happiness perspective. One may think of biting the bullet and arguing that a happy peasant is truly better off than a miserable millionaire, the reason being that happiness is really the ultimate goal of people in life.

If happiness is really the ultimate goal of people in life, the objections listed in the previous subsection are not compelling. Insofar as happiness is comparable across individuals, Rawls's objection misses the target because happiness provides the overarching measure of success that encompasses all the diversity of possible individual preferences. Sen's objection points to the real phenomenon of adaptation, but the correct attitude about this phenomenon is to worry about the ills to which people do not adapt, such as pain and noise, rather than insisting that the ills to which they do adapt are still priorities. Finally, if the person with expensive tastes could *benefit* from psychological counseling that would raise his well-being by adjusting his goals, this would invalidate Dworkin's view that this person is not disadvantaged.

The argument that happiness is the ultimate goal in life is so popular in the happiness literature that it deserves some scrutiny. The fact that happiness is multifaceted makes it difficult to assess. It may be true for some dimensions of subjective well-being and wrong for others. There may also be differences between individuals. And the picture is complicated by the fact that most people are mistaken, in their daily decisions, about what drives happiness.

There is an ambitious and a modest version of the argument. The ambitious form seeks to *prove* that happiness is the ultimate goal. One finds such an attempt in Layard (2005, p. 113): 'Happiness is that ultimate goal because, unlike all other goals, it is self-evidently good. If we are asked why happiness matters, we can give no further, external reason. It just obviously does matter.'

This argument has two weaknesses. First, it is not true that happiness cannot be sought for external reasons. People want to be happy, among other things, in order to carry out their tasks and duties unencumbered by depression and bad feelings. There are other good effects of happiness: it makes one more pleasant to one's family and relatives, it is good for health and longevity, and so on.

Second, and more importantly, even if happiness were the only aspect of life that is desirable only for itself, and all other aspects had some impact on happiness, this would not show that the other aspects are not also partly desirable for themselves. In economics, this is a familiar pattern. It is common, for instance, to consider the possibility that health is an argument of the utility function (it is desirable in itself) but is also an argument of the wage function (good health increases earnings) and is therefore indirectly desirable. The fact that health is indirectly desirable does not prove that it is not also directly desired. Likewise, the fact that many good things in life enhance happiness does not imply that people want them only for the purpose of a greater happiness. Therefore, the strong form of the argument fails.

The more modest form of the argument is that happiness *is* actually people's ultimate goal. This is a factual statement, which may be true or false. Presumably, it cannot be true simultaneously for all aspects of subjective well-being, and we will examine its application to hedonic scores and satisfaction scores successively.

Let us therefore first contemplate the thesis that people, in absence of psychological mistakes, would be most concerned, for themselves, with experiencing certain feelings (i.e., experiencing certain positive feelings, avoiding certain negative feelings, with a certain temporal pattern). This thesis is, however, factually wrong. There may be people who are, ultimately, exclusively interested in experiencing certain feelings but they most probably are a minority of the population. Most people are interested in other things than their own mental states and care about a variety of achievements. Taking happiness as the ultimate goal in life is far from normal and popular. It corresponds to an outlier in the range of life goals that ordinary people adopt, and an outlier that does not appear to deserve much praise in ordinary morality.[2] Psychologists have studied the link

2. Hedonism is often viewed as morally questionable. Assimilating a great life with a life of pleasant feelings appears rather mediocre. Very few people want to have good feelings all the time. What people typically want, as far as feelings are concerned, is to have the appropriate feelings for the circumstances they encounter. A good life is a life with strong social ties, which imply much pleasure and shared laughter, but also their full lot of mourning and bereavement. A good life is a life of daring enterprises, which

between goals and affects and noted the complexity of human goals and their multiple associations with affects and cognitions (Pervin 1983).

At this point, an advocate of hedonism may turn normative and say that people should care only about happiness (as far as they are concerned—they may of course also care about the others' happiness) and are mistaken if they do not. But it is hard to see what their mistake is, given that, as explained previously, there is no logical proof that happiness is the only ultimate value.

Let us therefore abandon the idea that people are most concerned with feelings, although this may be true for some, and turn to the alternative idea that people are most concerned with their life evaluation, that is, with the cognitive judgment they are requested to make in a satisfaction questionnaire. There is a sense in which the thesis then appears tautologically true. Life evaluation is supposed to synthesize what people care most about in their life, and therefore it is definitely *about* what they are most concerned with. There is, however, a difference. People are tautologically concerned ultimately about the *object* of their satisfaction. This is not the same as saying that they are concerned about their satisfaction. In a sense, their satisfaction is what they care the least about! It is not satisfaction that makes a good life, but a good life that gives satisfaction. Satisfaction is the consequence of having a life full of valuable things, but is not a source of value by itself.

Another way of explaining this point is that one must distinguish "obtaining what one wants" from "being satisfied," and realize that people are interested in the former, not in the latter. There are three ways to be satisfied, and obtaining what one wants is only one of them. One can also become satisfied by adapting one's aspiration level or by adapting one's preferences. Everyone can check for oneself if it is more attractive to obtain satisfaction by getting what one wants or by manipulating one's aspirations and preferences.[3]

There is, truly enough, a positive effect of feeling satisfied on emotions, self-confidence, and the like. This is why people do try also to manage their level of satisfaction by adopting modest aspirations and reasonable preferences. But even then satisfaction has an instrumental value, not an intrinsic value. The true source of value remains in feelings and objective achievements.

imply excitement but also fear, anxiety, and stress, all negative feelings without which courage could not be displayed (Nussbaum 2008).

3. Barry (2007) compares an individual who would seek to be satisfied per se—instead of getting what he wants—to a football fan who would support whatever team is most likely to win. What kind of football fan would that be?

Economists are used to describing individuals that "maximize $u_i(x)$," and this gives the profession a natural belief in the fact that utility is the ultimate goal of individuals. But if one thinks of $u_i(.)$ as a representation of the preference ordering, and of x as a comprehensive description of all things that the individual cares about, the maximizing model is compatible with an individual who does not care at all about $u_i(x)$ and only about x itself. In ordinary economic models in which x is a limited array of economic resources that have merely instrumental value in the achievement of higher goals, the situation is different because the true object of preference is not x. Then $u_i(x)$ may indeed capture other dimensions of life that are not covered by x and that matter a lot to the individual. Once x covers everything that matters, however, utility loses all value except being a representation of an ordering.

Similarly, when one says that an investor is ultimately concerned about the balance sheet, this is a misleading way of saying that he is really interested in the profit—an accountant that would cook a nice balance sheet that does not represent actual profit would not please the investor.

This line of reasoning shows that the argument that happiness is the ultimate value fails, no matter how one defines happiness. Feelings need not be the only source of value, and life satisfaction is not a source of intrinsic[4] value at all, but rather the valueless summary of all other things of value.

5.1.4 The key objection to subjective scores

The above discussion of happiness as the ultimate goal leads us to formulate a key objection to subjective welfarism. This objection has not been explicitly articulated in the classical debate on welfarism, but it seems more damaging than the classical objections because it undermines the core ambition of subjective welfarism to reflect people's own perspectives.

The objection is the following. Not only does subjective welfarism fail to capture real advantage and to provide a sensible metric for interpersonal comparisons, but by doing so, it betrays people's own concerns. When subjective welfarism focuses on affects, it betrays people's concerns when people are interested in achievements other than feelings. When subjective welfarism focuses on satisfaction, it also betrays people's concerns because it focuses on the *outcome* of the evaluation instead of the *object* of the

4. As explained, it may have instrumental value via its effect on feelings and other achievements.

evaluation. For instance, if it were possible to move to a situation in which people would have less of what they want but would have lower aspiration levels and end up being more satisfied, the welfarist approach would approve this change, but the people themselves would oppose it.

Layard acknowledges that "the thought that you can be happy in that way has led many people to reject altogether the idea of happiness as a goal" (2005, p. 73). His reply is that this way of raising happiness does not work in practice because people want to set themselves aspirations that are sufficiently challenging to avoid boredom. This reply is insufficient. First, the objection was a conditional. If one could make people happier by lowering their standards of satisfaction, that would be recorded as an improvement by the subjective well-being indicators. This reveals a flaw in such indicators even if this phenomenon never occurs. Second, a similar phenomenon does occur, on a very large scale, when satisfaction remains stable due to a shift in aspirations while conditions of life have changed tremendously.

The Easterlin paradox is, precisely, the best illustration of this problem. It appears most likely that people have a strong preference for the greater standard of living and longevity they enjoy now than 50 (or 70,000) years ago. The object of their satisfaction has improved and in this sense they are definitely more satisfied. But the level of satisfaction expressed in questionnaires may remain stable because the standards of answers shift with people's actual conditions of life. There is no paradox in the flatness of satisfaction curves because such curves do not reveal anything substantial about how much of people's goals is achieved.

An important caveat must be made here. These observations are compatible with the possibility that the direction of human development has been ill-chosen, that hubris and materialism have made the success of our species a catastrophe for the rest of the planet. Perhaps human goals and values are deeply questionable and should be radically revised. These are important moral issues that will not be discussed here at all. The point of this section is not to say that development has been good in spite of the stability of satisfaction curves. The point made here is that such stability, if confirmed, is not a proof that human development has been pointless or against human values and goals. Most probably, development has reflected actual human objectives. Such objectives may be wrong for moral reasons, but happiness data do not show it.

The "paradox" in Easterlin's paradox is that it has served to popularize the happiness challenge to the economic approach, whereas it is the best proof that the happiness approach is problematic. Subjective well-being indicators fail to accurately record the object of people's values and goals because they either focus on a narrow aspect of people's lives (their feelings) or focus on happiness and satisfaction scores that rely on standards of comparisons that are heterogenous across individuals (happy peasants, miserable millionaires) and drift along history (Easterlin's paradox).

This does not imply that happiness data are useless. Imagining a good use for them requires a little more exploration of how they are generated and can be processed. This is the topic of the next sections.

5.2 A THEORY OF SUBJECTIVE WELL-BEING

In this section we will try to construct a model of subjective well-being as it can be retrieved with typical questionnaires. This will put more flesh on some of the ideas put forth in the previous section and make it possible to think about how to make use of happiness data, which is the topic of the next section.

We will build on Schwarz and Strack (1999), who propose the following informal model—what is drawn in figure 5.3 is a simplified version, as their model also covers the evaluations of specific domains of life such as income or family life.

Their model reads as follows. When assigned the task of evaluating life, the individual considers if her current mood is informative. If not, she has to retrieve other relevant information, define what the target ("my life")

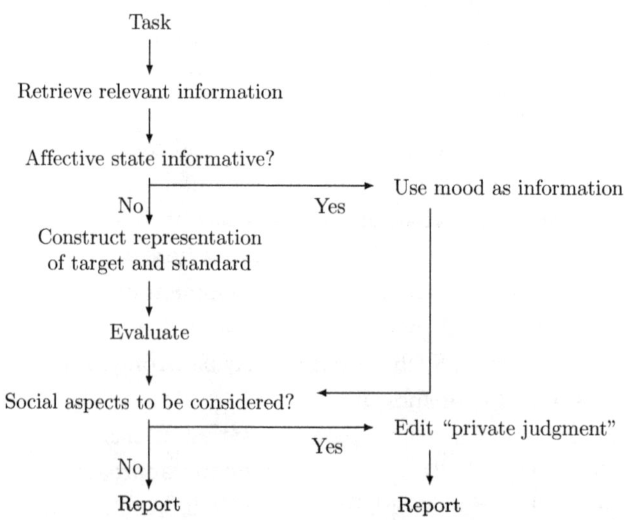

Figure 5.3
Schwarz and Strack's model of satisfaction answers (1999, p. 78)

consists of, and choose a standard of evaluation (e.g., "my neighbors"). A key element of the evaluation is that some elements may either be assimilated into the object of evaluation or act as contrasting background. After evaluation, she still has to see if the answer is appropriate in the context of the interview. If not, she can edit the initial judgment (e.g., make it more rosy).

5.2.1 Affects and judgments

Let us now develop our own model. First, let us think of the life of an individual i as a vector l_i of many dimensions that cover the diversity of states, activities, possibilities enjoyed or endured by the individual over the course of her life. At the time of answering a questionnaire, the individual is alive and not sure about her future life; therefore the dimensions of life include the various scenarios for the future that may unfold. Let us take the convention that beliefs about the probabilities of these scenarios are not part of life. This is convenient because it is not obvious that one should adopt the individual's own beliefs for the evaluation of life. For instance, if the individual is much too optimistic about her life expectancy, it may be advisable to use better expertise in order to evaluate her situation. This convention permits some flexibility about the choice of probabilities. Let l_{its} denote the subvector of life events that happen for i at time t in state (i.e., scenario) s. The individual's belief about the probability of state s is denoted π_{is}.

Where does subjective well-being find its place in the model? First, the feelings experienced at a particular date t form a subvector f_{its} of vector l_{its}. Importantly, feelings are multidimensional, and different people may put different weights on different feelings depending on their psychology or their values, and also depending on the circumstances. As explained in the previous section, for most people the desired feelings are not a constant sequence of intense exhilaration, or even of quiet contentment, but rather a sequence that fits the circumstances of life and enable the individual to cope with them in the best way according to her own values. It is interesting that the ranking of feelings cannot be "objective" because the feelings one considers fitting with the circumstances depend on how one wants to react to the circumstances. For instance, some people consider it weak to mourn for a long time, while others consider it the best way to pay tribute to the beloved deceased. Even something as simple as the distinction between negative and positive feelings is, in part, value laden and culture dependent. Some people like feeling proud, while others find it an uncharitable and egoistic emotion. Hatred is generally considered a negative feeling but is praised by some. Love and attachment for certain objects (animals, gold) is good for some and despicable for others.

In summary, we have $l_i = (l_{its})_{t,s}$ and $l_{its} = (f_{its}, \cdots)$. For present and past periods, there is only one state, and one simply writes $l_{it} = (f_{it}, \cdots)$.

It remains to find a place for life evaluation (as opposed to feelings). Here there are two possibilities. The simplest one assumes that the evaluation of life is not part of life, even though it is an act of the individual. When the individual i answers a happiness or satisfaction questionnaire, she looks at l_i and there is a function ξ_i that maps lives into the set of possible answers to the questionnaire. Therefore, i's answer is $\xi_i(l_i)$.

The more complex alternative takes the act of evaluating life as part of life. When the individual formulates the evaluation e_{it} at time t, this is a component of vector l_{it}. However, one may safely assume that the evaluation is not a function of itself but only of all other components of l_i, which means that there is a mapping ξ_i^* such that $e_{it} = \xi_i^*(l_i \backslash e_{it})$, where the notation $l_i \backslash e_{it}$ means that the component e_{it} is removed from vector l_i. What may happen, nevertheless, is that e_{it} has an impact on other components of l_i. For instance, a positive judgment may produce good feelings, or may give self-confidence that enhances future prospects. It would strange, however, if such effects were to make the computation of $e_{it} = \xi_i^*(l_i \backslash e_{it})$ problematic because of divergence.

We will work here with the first, simpler approach $\xi_i(l_i)$, which does not appear to miss much of the relevant phenomena. The question is now to understand how $\xi_i(l_i)$ is constructed by the individual.

The value of $\xi_i(l_i)$ must lie in a given scale, which can either be a verbal scale (e.g., very happy/pretty happy/not too happy, or very satisfied/fairly satisfied/not very satisfied/not at all satisfied), or a numerical scale (e.g., from 0 to 10). The cognitive problem for the individual is to put the many dimensions of l_i into one of a few ordered categories.

5.2.2 The three problems of the respondent

This problem can be decomposed into three problems: (1) the scope problem: what part of l_i is relevant? (this is what Schwarz and Strack call the target); (2) the ranking problem: how does l_i stand in the set of relevant possible lives? (3) the calibration problem: how does a position in the ranking translate into a category of the questionnaire? (this is what Schwarz and Strack call the standard). Schwarz and Strack do not distinguish the last two problems, but this distinction, familiar to the economist, appears crucial. Giving a grade from 0 to 10 to one's life involves first identifying where one's life stands in an *ordinal* ranking and then associating positions in the ordinal ranking to *grades* on the numerical scale. The two tasks are cognitively different.

The scope problem

The scope problem is shaped by the question itself and especially its ambiguities. Table 5.1, reproduced from Layard, Mayraz, and Nickell (2008), lists the various questions featuring in the main questionnaires.[5]

Most questions indicate that everything must be taken into account, but this does not dispel difficult boundary questions. A first and obvious difficulty for all such questions relates to the time frame. Does the expression "these days" or "nowadays" that appears in many of the questions refer to the time of evaluation (what is your judgment these days) or to the phase of life to be considered (your life in the current period)? Even when the expression is absent it is not obvious to decide whether one should think of one's whole life, or only of one's past life, or only of the current period. If the latter, the length of the period can go from a few days to several years.

Another difficulty has to do with relatives. Is the question purely personal, or should one incorporate one's family in the evaluation? Even if personal life partly depends on how one's relatives are doing, the weight attributed to their situation may greatly vary with how strongly the survey suggests that only the purely personal aspects are relevant for the question.

A third related ambiguity has to do with the general social context. It is part of a good life to be the member of a good polity, to be part of a world that goes well. For many people, what goes on in the world around them, or at least in their community, is like a public good or bad that directly affects their satisfaction. Whether this is part of their life or not is not easy to tell in the context of such a satisfaction question. Deaton (2012) observes that when the question is preceded by a question on politics, the level of satisfaction goes down substantially. This may due to the fact that the presence of the political question induces people to broaden the scope of their thoughts when answering the satisfaction question. As it is a popular thought to imagine that one's strictly personal situation is better than the situation of one's country and that the government's record is bad, the decrease in satisfaction level in this context is not surprising.

5. This list omits the ladder-of-life question used in the Gallup World Poll. This one will be discussed later on.

Table 5.1. HAPPINESS AND SATISFACTION QUESTIONS

Survey	Variable	Question
General Social Survey	Happiness	Taken all together, how would you say things are these days? Would you say that you are very happy, pretty happy, or not too happy?
World Values Survey	Life sat.	All things considered, how satisfied are you with your life as a whole these days? Please use this card to help with your answer. [Range of 1–10 with 1 labeled. "Very Dissatisfied" and 10 labeled. "Very Satisfied"]
European Social Survey	Happiness	Taking all things together, how happy would you say you are? Please use this card. [Range of 0–10 with 0 labeled. "Extremely unhappy" and 10 labeled. "Extremely happy"]
European Social Survey	Life sat.	All things considered, how satisfied are yon with your life as a whole nowadays? Please answer using this card, where 0 means extremely dissatisfied and 10 means extremely satisfied. [Range of 0–10 with 0 labeled. "Extremely dissatisfied" and 10 labeled. "Extremely satisfied"]
European Quality of Life Survey	Happiness	Taking all things together on a scale of 1 to 10, how happy would you say you are? Here 1 means you are very unhappy and 10 means you are very happy.
European Quality of Life Survey	Life sat.	All things considered, how satisfied would you say you are with your life these days? Please tell me on a scale of 1 to 10, where 1 means very dissatisfied and 10 means very satisfied.
German Socio-Economic Panel	Life sat.	In conclusion, we would like to ask you about your satisfaction with your life in general. Please answer according to the following scale: 0 means "completely dissatisfied," 10 means "completely satisfied." How satisfied are you with your life, all things considered?
British Household Panel Survey	Life sat.	How dissatisfied or satisfied are you with your life overall? [Range of 1–7 with 1 labeled. "Not satisfied at all" and 7 labeled. "Completely satisfied"]

Source: Layard, Mayraz, and Nickell (2008, p. 1849).

More generally, one may suspect that the ambiguity about scope is most likely to create a strong dependency of answers on the order of questions and various framing aspects of the questionnaire. When a question is ambiguous, people seek clues in the other aspects of the interview. The ambiguity of scope is likely to create uncontrolled diversity among respondents and to generate substantial noise.

Formally, let l_i^* denote the subvector of l_i that the individual considers relevant in the context of the questionnaire. For simplicity's sake, we can retain the same notation for the evaluation function and let $\xi_i\left(l_i^*\right)$ describe how the answer is determined.

The ranking problem

A happiness or satisfaction question does not expressly request the respondent to form a ranking. And one may suspect that very few people have well-formed preferences about their life in general. But when asked such a question, one is forced to shrink the complexity of a multidimensional life into an ordinal pattern, and this requires the prior construction of a ranking, no matter how coarse.

The cognitive complexity of this exercise may induce respondents to focus on some salient aspects of their situation and forget many relevant dimensions of their life. This is linked to the "focusing illusion," by which people tend to exaggerate the importance of aspects under consideration at the moment (Kahneman et al. 2006). Here again, the general structure of the questionnaire plays an important role. When the question is asked in the beginning, or after a series of questions that are not directly relevant, the construction of the ranking is particularly complex. When the question comes after a comprehensive examination of the various domains of life, the task is made somewhat less complex and the respondent should be less vulnerable to a focusing illusion—although the respondent may then be more vulnerable to the framing impact of the earlier questions.

Given that the scope problem has led the respondent to specify a subvector l_i^* of l_i to which attention is restricted, the respondent only needs an ordering of the possible vectors l_i^*. But the respondent is likely to have some preferences about the other components of l_i, and also about other aspects of the universe than l_i. Deriving a ranking of subvectors from the ranking of full vectors is easy if the excluded components are assumed to have a fixed value. One would naturally expect the respondents of a questionnaire to take the current values of these excluded components as the fixed value.

But fixed values for the excluded components may not be easy to assume in the context at hand, and this creates specific difficulties. Consider the case of a respondent from a rich country who has to imagine where to put her life on a 0–10 scale. Presumably, 0 is the grade of the worst life she can think of and 10 is the grade of the best life. But she may think that the worst life would consist of living in a destitute country with a lot of insecurity. Some aspects of this different situation would change the components of

$l_i \backslash l_i^*$, that is, the excluded components. Now, these different values for $l_i \backslash l_i^*$ may alter the ranking of l_i^*. For instance, in her quiet and affluent country she likes devoting her life to art, but if she were in the poor country she would prefer devoting her life to politics and would consider it scandalous to be an artist. It may therefore be that in her current situation she prefers l_i^* (artist) to $\tilde{l}_i^*$ (activist), but if she were in the poor country she would hold the opposite preference. It may, however, be the case that in the two contexts she would agree on what the worst life l^* is, but this cannot be guaranteed. In summary, while defining an ordering of l_i^* is in principle easy when one has an ordering of l_i and the excluded components are fixed, it may be unrealistic to assume that the excluded components are fixed when l_i^* takes all possible values. Then there may not be a well-defined ordering over l_i^*.

Expectations about the future are an interesting element to discuss at this point. If l_i^* includes the future, then the respondent's expectations over l_i, and in particular her beliefs π_{is}, will directly play a role. If l_i^* does not include the future, the respondent's preferences over her whole life l_i will make it tricky to define preferences over l_i^*. Very different values for l_i^* should, realistically, go with different expectations about the rest of life. Such different expectations may alter the preferences over l_i^*. For instance, if one expects to have a comfortable retirement one may want to adopt a safe lifestyle. If one's situation is so bad that one does not expect to live long, a less healthy lifestyle may become more attractive. It is then difficult to know what the preferences over l_i^* are, if this depends on how one revises expectations in the light of realizations in l_i^*.

This issue reveals that satisfaction indicators are, in a sense, much more informationally demanding than measures of well-being that are local in the preference space. The computation of an equivalent income, for instance, only requires information about the current indifference curve of the individual, and there is no need for the individual, is she were asked questions about this indifference curve, to imagine situations that are far away in the ranking, especially the extreme situations of the "best possible" and "worst possible" lives.[6]

Let us finally assume that the individual manages to construct an incomplete ranking of vectors l_i^*, and let R_i^* denote this reflexive and transitive but not necessarily complete relation (with associated strict preference

6. The equivalent income may require going far away "along" the indifference curve, and this may be cognitively demanding, too (e.g., imagining being healthy when one is chronically ill). But this is not the same problem as locating the current situation on a scale containing the best and the worst possible situations.

relation P_i^* and indifference relation I_i^*). Incompleteness must be limited in some way because it would be problematic if a subset of lives was completely incomparable to its complement subset. One may reasonably assume that for each life it is easy to find a similar life that differs only in a few dimensions and is clearly better or clearly worse. For a given vector l_i^*, let $L\left(l_i^*; R_i^*\right)$ denote the subset of vectors that are comparable to l_i^* and no better than l_i^*, that is, the set of l^* such that $l_i^* R_i^* l^*$, and let $H\left(l_i^*; R_i^*\right)$ denote the subset of vectors that are comparable to l_i^* and no worse than l_i^*, that is, the set of l^* such that $l^* R_i^* l_i^*$.

The calibration problem

The calibration problem is the most interesting in the context of questionnaires. Equipped with an incomplete ordering R_i^* of life vectors, how can the individual transform the position of his actual life l_i^* into a specific category $\xi_i\left(l_i^*\right)$ of the questionnaire?

Here there is a strong framing effect due to the fact that the scale offered in questionnaires is closed. While many aspects of life are open (there is no maximal possible income, and probably no worst possible pain) or have very fuzzy and remote physical limits (bodily and intellectual performance, as well as longevity, have no known limits), giving a closed scale to respondents forces them to move from a reasoning in terms of life content to a reasoning in terms of statistical distribution. They therefore have to determine where their situation lies in a particular distribution. The problem is then to choose which distribution.

Of course, this reference to a statistical distribution should not be taken too literally. Very few respondents will exactly identify the problem with finding a quantile in a distribution of possible lives. But it is clear that, given a fixed number of ordered categories, a respondent must choose a relative position for the grading of his life. It would be strange to hear a respondent saying that the human condition is appalling anyway, so that he chooses the worst category, or that life is the greatest gift, so that whatever happens he should pick the top of the categories. The ladder-of-life questions that explicitly refer to the "best possible" and the "worst possible" life most effectively force the respondent to think in relative terms. In the Gallup World Poll, the formulation is as follows:

> Please imagine a ladder with steps numbered from zero at the bottom to 10 at the top.
>
> The top of the ladder represents the best possible life for you and the bottom of the ladder represents the worst possible life for you.

On which step of the ladder would you say you personally feel you stand at this time? (ladder-present)

On which step do you think you will stand about five years from now? (ladder-future)

This approach was proposed by Cantril (1965), whose purpose was to devise a "self-anchoring scale" in which people would think in relative rather than absolute terms, with standards adjusted to their own perspectives and possibilities. It is interesting to note the ambiguities of the anchoring. The expression "best possible life for you" can mean "the best possible life *for a human being*, according to your preference ranking of lives," with a remaining ambiguity about whether "possible" refers to logical conceivability or to practical attainability in the current world; but it can also mean "the best possible life that *you* could achieve," here again with ambiguity about how the possible-impossible distinction is to be understood. These ambiguities introduce considerable noise in the data. How can one compare the answer of someone who defines the best possible life as the dreamed life of a human being in two millennia with the answer of someone who defines the best possible life as a moderately optimistic interpretation of his own possibilities? The same kind of ambiguity occurs for the "worst possible life."

In Cantril's study, there was no such ambiguity because the ladder question was preceded by the following questions:

1. All of us want certain things out of life. When you think about what really matters in your life, what are your wishes and hopes for the future? In other words, if you imagine your future in the *best* possible light, what would your life look like then, if you are to be happy? Take your time in answering; such things aren't easy to put into words.

2. Now, taking the other side of the picture, what are your fears and worries about the future? In other words, if you imagine your future in the *worst* possible light, what would your life look like then? Again, take your time in answering.

What is remarkable about Cantril's study is that it gives us an idea of what the best and worst life looks like for different people. Here are two contrasting examples about the best life, one from India and the other from the United States:

I want a son and a piece of land since I am not working on land owned by other people. I would like to construct a house of my own and have a cow for milk and ghee. I would also like to buy some better clothing for my wife. If I could do this then I would be happy.

I would like a reasonable income to maintain a house, have a new car, have a boat, and send my four children to private schools. (Cantril 1965, pp. 206 and 222)

It is a popular rebuttal of figures describing the Easterlin paradox that GDP is on an open scale whereas satisfaction scores are bounded by construction. But the real difficulty with satisfaction questions is that the true scale of life is more like GDP and is not naturally bounded. Respondents are therefore induced to reason in relative terms when they must describe an open-ended object, their lives, in a closed scale.[7]

Sometimes this does not look so artificial. There are dimensions of life that are bounded. One's social status, one's position in the distribution of income, and all similar relative positions are already cast in the relativistic frame. Health is also conceived in comparison to perfect health. Obviously, for individuals who care only about their relative position in their community, their task is made easier because they do not have to make a conversion to a relative scale as they already think in these terms.

In summary, the fact that life is made of a combination of open-ended and bounded dimensions makes it necessary to answer the satisfaction questionnaires in relative terms. This does not necessarily mean that a comparison to other members of society has to be made. But a comparison to some benchmark seems unavoidable, and the reference to the best and worst possible lives in the ladder questions makes it explicit.

Formally, thinking about life in relative terms amounts to defining a distribution over the set of l_i^*. Let μ_i denote the probability measure that the individual chooses. Then a natural way to evaluate the relative position of l_i^* is to compute $\mu_i\left(L\left(l_i^*; R_i^*\right)\right)$, or $1 - \mu_i\left(H\left(l_i^*; R_i^*\right)\right)$.

In the literature it is common to introduce relative terms that take the form of a ratio in which the denominator is an average value. This is a special case of what is described here. For a real random variable y that is uniformly distributed over an interval, the ratio $y/\bar{y}$, where $\bar{y}$ is the mean value, is an affine transform of the cumulative distribution function. For a distribution with unbounded support (such as the normal or the lognormal distribution), however, $y/\bar{y}$ is not a bounded variable and is not a convenient way of squeezing y into a bounded scale.

7. Note that the problem does not come from the limited number of rungs on the ladder. Nor would it be solved if the ladder had no upper bound, because people would still have to generate their own understanding of the gap between two rungs.

From $\mu_i\left(L\left(l_i^*; R_i^*\right)\right)$, or $1 - \mu_i\left(H\left(l_i^*; R_i^*\right)\right)$, to $\xi_i\left(l_i^*\right)$, it only remains to partition the [0, 1] interval into subintervals. This creates a secondary calibration problem, but we can assume that a uniform partition is adopted and that the main calibration operation does all the hard work.

Let us now examine the key task for the respondent, which is to define a standard, that is, the distribution μ_i that will do the calibration. Three natural possibilities arise. A first one is the distribution of possible lives as expected, some time earlier, by the respondent. The calibration is then driven by expectations or aspirations. A second possibility is to look at the distribution of other people's lives, in some reference group. The calibration is then driven by comparisons to others. A third possibility, which makes sense only when l_i^* only refers to the current live vector l_{it_0}, where t_0 is the time of interview, is to look at the past experience of the respondent. The calibration is then said to rely on the past. The past experience of the respondent is typically a degenerate distribution with which it is not possible to directly compute $\mu_i\left(L\left(l_i^*; R_i^*\right)\right)$ because l_i^* does not belong to its support. One must then define a distribution around the past experience in order to define what is a "small" or a "big" improvement or deterioration.

Note that for each of these three possibilities, there are many possible choices. Aspirations can be more or less ambitious, comparisons to others may refer to various reference groups, and reference to the past may look at different periods. The consequence for analysts using happiness data is that the calibration problem is a source of heterogeneity across individuals. Moreover, respondents can construct μ_i by mixing various sources of inspiration. Different measure functions can be combined easily to form a new measure function, simply by computing a weighted average. Some individuals may give a greater weight to comparison to others, while other respondents may primarily refer to their own aspirations, but all of them can give some positive weight to these different considerations.

Steffel and Oppenheimer (2009) study the comparisons standards used by respondents in the context of simple happiness questions ("How happy are you?"). First, their study confirms that, even for such a direct question that could be interpreted as referring to affects rather than life evaluation, people do make comparisons to calibrate their answers. Second, there is a variety of standards used, with a majority of intrapersonal comparisons (the reference distribution being "what is typical for me") over interpersonal comparisons in their study. Third, the respondents comparing themselves to others tend to give higher happiness scores than those making intrapersonal comparisons. One of the conclusions of their paper is that the surveys should try to eliminate the heterogeneity of standards that renders the answers hard to compare across respondents.

Finally, it must be emphasized that the model that is proposed here, and that can be summarized by the formula

$$\xi_i\left(l_i^*\right) = \mu_i\left(L\left(l_i^*; R_i^*\right)\right),$$

has variants. For instance, instead of going through the scope-ranking-calibration stages listed above, the respondent could do the three exercises at the level of life domains first, obtaining satisfaction scores for each life domain. In this case, global satisfaction can then be constructed as a weighted average of the scores of the various life domains. This has perhaps the advantage of making the ranking exercise easier because life domains contain less heterogeneous subdimensions. But the hard work of making life domains commensurable is then postponed to the last stage of aggregating scores and cannot be escaped completely. This variant is particularly plausible for questionnaires in which the respondent is indeed asked to give scores for life domains before being asked the overall satisfaction question.

Schwarz and Strack's model gives great importance to the role of mood as an informational shortcut. Given that current mood at the time of interview has been shown to influence satisfaction scores, it is indeed interesting to understand how that can happen. The hypothesis that mood makes the respondent bypass the whole reasoning and delivers an immediate score is a rather extreme possibility. Other hypotheses that might be worth exploring are that a good mood distorts the ranking phase by making the respondent focus on positive aspects of her situation (selective attention), or distorts the calibration phase by making the respondent take a less favorable reference distribution μ_i, or by inducing the computation of $\mu_i\left(L\left(l_i^*; R_i^*\right)\right)$ to be biased upward. All three mechanisms can be partly driven by the unconscious desire of the respondent to generate feelings that confirm the current mood. A good mood is reinforced by a good evaluation.

5.2.3 Heterogeneous and shifting standards

The model proposed in the previous subsection suggests that respondents give answers that are hard to compare when they use heteregeneous strategies or different sorts of information to cope with the scope, ranking, and calibration problems.

Although this is an empirical statement that has to be ultimately decided by the data, one may safely conjecture that the main source of heterogeneity lies in the calibration problem. A happy peasant and a miserable millionaire cannot diverge so much in the evaluation of lives because they focus on different aspects of their lives when they define l_i^* and construct R_i^*. They must take very different reference distributions μ_i in order to transform their presumably similar rankings into bounded scores. Their personal expectations, their community, their own past, all three typical sources of inspiration for the choice of the distribution μ_i can indeed differ exactly in the way that generate their different evaluation standards. One is more easily satisfied if one had low expectations, if one compares oneself to a less well-off community, and if one comes from a disadvantaged background. Cantril (1965) showed this very early on by eliciting free descriptions of the "best possible life." Loewenstein and Ubel (2008) and Graham (2009) emphasize such diversity, as induced in particular by the adaptation phenomenon (Brickman and Campbell 1971).

In particular, the stability of satisfaction scores as epitomized in the Easterlin paradox can easily be explained by the fact that all three sources of calibration tend to follow the evolution of people's actual situations. Along the development path, expectations move up, the rest of society moves up, and the past experience, if defined by a fixed lag to the present, also moves up. Therefore, if, due to these shifting references, the distribution μ_i follows the change in l_i^*, the stability of $\mu_i\left(L\left(l_i^*;R_i^*\right)\right)$ can be observed in spite of a constant improvement of the position of l_i^* in the ranking defined by R_i^*.

Di Tella and McCulloch (2006, p. 35) observe that "for both adaptation and relative income effects to be relevant explanations of the Easterlin (1974) paradox we would need a very specific pattern: it would have to be the case that individuals adapt to income, but do not adapt to their relative position." They go on to note that this pattern seems to be confirmed by the data. The model proposed here offers a simple explanation of this phenomenon. The relative position does not need a calibration operation, whereas an unbounded variable such as income does. Someone who is relatively well-off in her reference group can steadily give a higher satisfaction score, but the long-run increase in income shifts the distribution μ_i and therefore disappears in the satisfaction score.

Adaptation to relative position is, truly enough, logically compatible with the model. It could happen if the individual cares about her relative position as such and uses her recent past experience in the relative position to calibrate the score. But that requires a very specific pattern of ranking (caring about the relative position) and calibration (using the recent past about the relative position). In particular, it appears rather unnatural to recalibrate a variable that already comes in a relative form.

The model also suggests why it is possible for satisfaction scores to appear more sensitive to objective conditions of life than affective scores that record emotion flows, although emotions appear negatively affected by low income (Kahneman and Krueger 2006; Kahneman and Deaton 2010). Suppose that, outside the stressful conditions of deprivation, emotions are managed by individuals in such a way that they always come back to their set level, and that this set level depends on personality more than on the contents of life. Then affects are not very sensitive to conditions of life, except in seriously disadvantaged situations. In contrast, the shifting standards that reduce the sensitiveness of satisfaction scores to life do not attenuate the relative outcomes (except in the very special configuration described in the previous paragraph). Insofar as individuals care about their relative position or use it to calibrate their answers, their scores will therefore be stable at various unequal levels corresponding to their position in the distribution of objective outcomes.

A challenge to the idea that people use heterogeneous standards across space and time has been raised by Deaton (2008), Kahneman and Deaton (2010), Stevenson and Wolfers (2008) and Sacks, Stevenson, and Wolfers (2010). Consider figure 5.4, showing the average level of satisfaction in various countries against GDP per capita. This figure reveals a rather nice log-linear relation, although it also shows great variations of satisfaction at every level of income. Moreover, Sacks, Stevenson, and Wolfers (2010) show that the slope of this log-linear cross-section relation *between* countries is generally similar to the slope of the relation *within* countries. As far as change over time is concerned, they note that the long-run evolution of satisfaction in various countries has been quite diverse, with some countries exhibiting a negative relation in the long run between income and satisfaction. However, looking at the whole set of countries in their sample, they show that the data are, on average, compatible with a positive relation with income, with a similar slope as in the cross-section picture, although the degree of confidence is low because the data are still sparse for the long run.

The log-linear relation between income and well-being can interpreted in at least two ways. Kahneman and Deaton (2010) and Deaton (2012) refer to Weber's law. This law says that the smallest noticeable variation of a stimulus is proportional to the initial magnitude of the stimulus. The associated Fechner law implies that the relation between stimulus and response is log-linear (which derives from Weber's law if the response is linear with respect to perceptions). Although income is measured in monetary terms

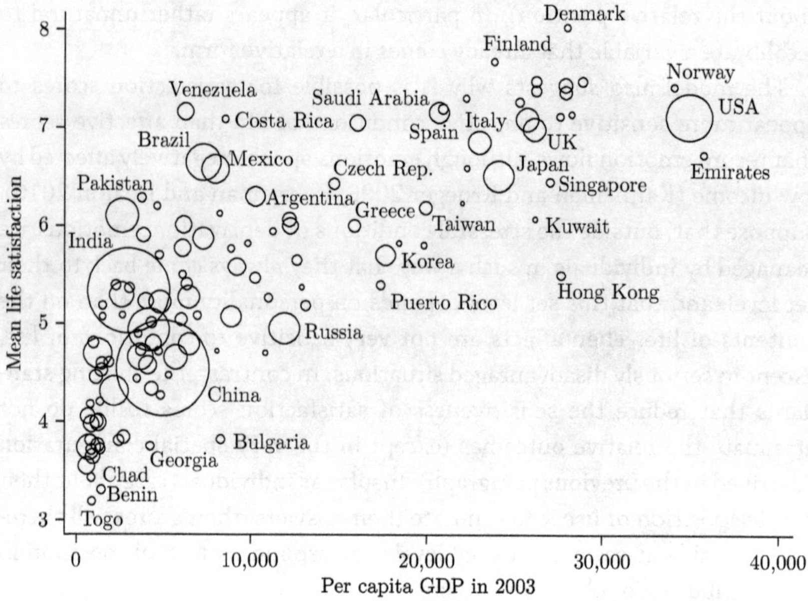

Figure 5.4
Life Satisfaction and Per Capita GDP around the World
Source: Deaton (2008, fig. 1).

and has objective smallest units, it is plausible that the stimulus variation that people feel is the percentage increase in income rather than the absolute increase. This is how a log-linear relation can be obtained.

This interpretation suggests a stable relation between income and satisfaction over time, but is compatible with substantial heterogeneity across individuals and countries.

Note that a logarithmic curve goes from $-\infty$ to $+\infty$, so that the Weber-Fechner laws cannot be the whole story for a bounded scale. Prolonging the curve drawn by Deaton (2008) would cross the 10 ceiling at about \$300,000.

There is, moreover, an alternative and not less natural interpretation of the logarithmic curve suggested by the figure. Such a curve is also the shape of a cumulative distribution function. In particular, the CDF of a distribution of income may easily display this shape. Figure 5.5, from Sala-i-Martin (2006), shows an estimation of the CDF of income in the world, with income measured in logarithmic scale.

The curve is not straight, but if one removes the levels of income below \$500 and above \$40,000, the 2000 curve is relatively straight. So the shape of satisfaction answers can also be explained by the fact that people take inspiration from their rank in the world distribution of income in order to

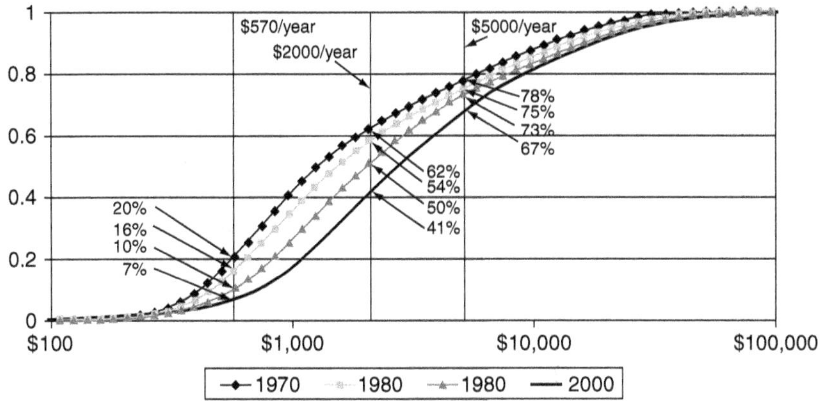

Figure 5.5
World Distribution of Income
Source: Sala-i-Martin (2006).

answer the satisfaction questionnaire. Of course, people's actual position in the distribution need not correspond to their perception, and it is the latter that would be the basis of their satisfaction.

We therefore have two conflicting interpretations of the shape of the satisfaction curve. They induce different predictions about long-term movements. With the Weber-Fechner interpretation, all countries move along the fixed curve. With the CDF interpretation, the curve moves horizontally across time as all countries grow and changes shape as the distribution changes.

The two interpretations are not exclusive and can be combined in the following way. One can imagine that the area of satisfaction below 5 is one in which subsistence concerns matter, giving a role to the Weber law, whereas the area of satisfaction levels above 5 is more influenced by comparisons with the current distribution. Therefore one could imagine that along history, there is an increase in the average satisfaction of countries that move out of dire poverty, whereas satisfaction in well-off countries remains stable. If the world evolved toward a less unequal distribution of income, the curve would move up above the 0–5 area, but would retain its CDF shape above that.

Imagine a scenario in which, over the next century, the situation of European countries stagnates, whereas Northern America benefits from a multiplication of its GDP per capita by 10, and the life expectancy of its population doubles (this would mimic the current gap between the rich countries and the poor countries). The Weber-Fechner interpretation would have it that European satisfaction would remain as high as it is nowadays. It appears more realistic to conjecture that, contemplating the much greater standard of living and longevity in Northern America, the Europeans would revise their view of what the "best possible life" is and would have a substantially lower satisfaction as a result.

Coming back to the question of whether calibrations are homogeneous and stable or heterogeneous and shifting, we make three concluding remarks. First, figure 5.4 reveals not only a general trend, but also a great variety. The countries are not on the same line. In particular, one sees that the intermediate levels of satisfaction are experienced by countries of vastly different levels of income. It is really hard to believe that Brazilians are on average better off than the Japanese, for instance. Therefore these data show not only a general pattern, but also a lot of noise that reveal the different calibrations used by respondents of different circumstances. Far from defeating the thesis that there are heterogeneous standards in the surveys, these data confirm it.

Second, the analysis of the long-run relationship between income and satisfaction in Sacks, Stevenson, and Wolfers (2010) reveals a great variety of situations over the world. Whereas the data are compatible with an average positive relationship, Sacks, Stevenson, and Wolfers (2010) emphasize that this relation is not robust to the composition of the sample and show that the situation is not a uniform move of all countries along the same slope. There is a great variety of slopes, and a sizable group of countries even experienced a negative relation between income and well-being. The circles in figure 5.4 are, therefore, not slowly moving along the average log-linear line, they are following complex patterns. Di Tella and McCulloch (2010) separate the sample into two subsets according to the rank of countries in 1960 in terms of GDP per capita and show that the satisfaction level in the poorer half did benefit from growth between 1960 and 2005, whereas the richer half did not show any significant impact of GDP growth on satisfaction. These authors interpret these results in a way that is similar to the combination, proposed earlier, of the Weber law for low levels of satisfaction with the CDF interpretation for high levels. Another possible explanation is that the CDF theory applies everywhere, with a sizable group of respondents in the poorer group of countries feeling that their rank in the distribution has improved.

Third, as explained in the previous section, these debates about whether satisfaction is stable over space and time or increases with growth are really about the quality of such surveys, not about the true evolution of well-being. If the data revealed no link between satisfaction and income, this should create suspicion about satisfaction surveys, primarily. If the data reveal some link between satisfaction and income, this is better but still does not prove that satisfaction surveys are reliable in tracking what people care about, especially if the link appears very noisy.

5.2.4 What do people care about?

The model proposed here also helps understanding how subjective well-being data relate to "the final outcome about which people are most concerned" (Kahneman, Diener, and Schwarz 1999, p. xii).

As we have said, individuals may care about many things, of which the components of l_i are just a part and those of l_i^* an even smaller part. Let us make abstraction of the excluded dimensions and focus on how individuals care about l_i^*. The question is whether $\xi_i\left(l_i^*\right)$ is a good representation of "the final outcome about which people are most concerned," and can be used to compare situations across time and across individuals and populations.

The fact that different people may focus on different parts of l_i when they address the scope problem, and on different parts of l_i^* when they try to make a synthetic ranking of lives, diminishes the comparability of answers, as we have seen. But the key problem is, once again, the heterogeneity of calibration strategies. Forgetting the excluded components, a good life is a good l_i^*, as assessed by R_i^*. If one takes two individuals, Abel and Bael, who share the same R^*, and they both agree that Abel has a better life, it seems reasonable to conclude that Abel is better off. Let us call this the "same-preference" principle (Fleurbaey et al. 2009):

Same-Preference Principle: If $R_i^* = R_j^*$ and $l_i^* P_i^* l_j^*$, then i is better off than j.

But it may happen that these individuals use different calibration strategies, so that Abel actually has a lower $\xi_i\left(l_i^*\right)$. Trusting the satisfaction score would betray the concerned individuals' views about the comparison. The violation of the same-preference principle is the formal way to capture this problem.

This is just a more precise formulation of the problem raised in the earlier discussion of the Easterlin paradox. The object of people's concern is what happens in their life, not how they calibrate the answer to fit their evaluation in a bounded scale. To be fully precise, people do care about the calibration and may engineer it so as to enhance their mood, as explained in subsection 5.1.3, or to appear honorable in front of an interviewer—this is the social consideration appearing at the end of Schwarz and Strack's model. But they do not care about it so much that a greater $\xi_i\left(l_i^*\right)$ is generally more important than a better l_i^*, when they have to choose between the two.

Are there approaches that satisfy the same-preference principle? The equivalence approach, epitomized in the equivalent income indicators for instance, does satisfy it. When two individuals have the same preferences, necessarily the one with a better life has a better equivalent life in the reference set, for example, a greater equivalent income. Intuitively, this is because, as they have the same preferences, the one with a better life has an indifference curve that is everywhere higher. This property carries over to the multireference equivalent income that is computed on the basis of several reference situations by taking the average (or generalized average, or lowest) value of the equivalent incomes obtained for each of them.[8]

Another example, closer to what has been studied in this section, is a measure that would rely on a fixed calibration, that is, on a given measure μ_0, can also satisfy the same-preference property. When two individuals have the same R^* and $l_i^* P^* l_j^*$, then $\mu_0\left(L\left(l_i^*; R^*\right)\right) > \mu_0\left(L\left(l_j^*; R^*\right)\right)$ provided that μ_0 is fine enough to be able to distinguish the two sets $L\left(l_i^*; R^*\right) \supsetneq L\left(l_j^*; R^*\right)$.

Interestingly, a measure $\mu_0\left(L\left(l_i^*; R_i^*\right)\right)$ is not very different, in its formal structure, from a multireference equivalent income. Indeed, the value of $\mu_0\left(L\left(l_i^*; R_i^*\right)\right)$ is a measure of the lower contour set $L\left(l_i^*; R_i^*\right)$. Now, assume that the model of this chapter can be linked to that of the previous chapter by setting $l_i^* = (x_i, y_i)$ and letting u_i be a utility representation of R_i^*. For instance, the average equivalent income

$$\int_{(\tilde{p},\tilde{y})} e_i\left(\tilde{p}, \tilde{y}, u_i(l_i^*)\right) f(\tilde{p}, \tilde{y}) d(\tilde{p}, \tilde{y})$$

is a measure of the lower contour set of situations (m, p, y) such that

$$v_i\left(m, p, y\right) \leq u_i(l_i^*).$$

(This set is the lower contour set in figure 4.8, for instance.)

There is one technical difference. The probability measure μ_0 is supposed to be bounded, whereas the equivalent income is more like a measure of volume of the set and is therefore unbounded. The former is a relative magnitude; the latter is expressed in monetary units. This difference is not essential because one could easily normalize equivalent incomes to make

8. Recall, however, that the equivalence approach has been defined for complete preference orderings. Extending it to incomplete orderings is not very complex, but it requires considering imprecise values for equivalent incomes.

them relative, or multiply $\mu_0 \left(L\left(l_i^*; R_i^*\right)\right)$ by some conventional magnitude in order to give an absolute meaning. However, the fact that life is intrinsically open-ended may be a reason to prefer an open-ended measure like the equivalent income to a bounded measure. In particular, it may be easier with a measure that is expressed in the natural units of a life dimension to think about inequality aversion than with a measure that has no units and already contains a reference to a distribution. This is an interesting issue that may deserve further analysis.

5.2.5 Comparisons across preferences

It is more important, with respect to the example of $\mu_0 \left(L\left(l_i^*; R_i^*\right)\right)$, to notice that there are not just one, but two important issues with ordinary subjective scores $\mu_i \left(L\left(l_i^*; R_i^*\right)\right)$. We have insisted in this chapter on one of these issues, namely, tracking what people care about, which is hampered by the heterogeneity in the calibrations μ_i. Such heterogeneity generates violations of the same-preference principle and makes it problematic to respect the views of individuals sharing the *same* preferences and values in life. This problem is indeed alleviated when one takes a uniform calibration measure μ_0.

The other important issue, which was highlighted in the classical debate on welfarism (subsection 5.1.2), is that comparisons across individuals with *different* preferences would not necessarily be well performed even if all individuals relied, in their expressions of subjective well-being, on the same calibration measure μ_0. Such a measure would correctly compare individuals with identical preferences R_i^*, but it might fail to suitably compare individuals with different preferences. As advocated by Rawls (1982), Dworkin (2000), and even Bergson (1954) earlier on, such comparisons require fairness principles, like the restricted dominance principle or similar notions as found in the theory of fair social orderings.

This additional issue reveals how difficult it may be for subjective data to provide good proxies of well-being for social evaluation. While the problem of heterogeneous calibrations may perhaps be roughly eliminated by the law of large numbers when one looks at average statistics, the estimation of the distribution of well-being for a population with heterogeneous preferences about life is much more demanding. It appears heroic to hope that spontaneous answers to subjective well-being questionnaires could directly deliver data for ethically reasonable interpersonal comparisons.

For instance, Fleurbaey, Schokkaert, and Decancq (2009) have compared the populations of the worst off (lowest quintile) in terms of satisfaction and the worst off in terms of equivalent income in a Russian sample and found that these populations differ widely—much more than when different reference parameters are adopted for the computation of equivalent incomes. Specifically, the worst off in subjective terms include people who are quite well off on all objective counts, even if they are not all millionaires.

5.3 MAKING USE OF HAPPINESS DATA

Equipped with the conceptual apparatus of the previous section, we can examine the various uses of subjective well-being data that have been proposed and explore various possibilities.

5.3.1 Proposed indicators

There is first the simple average score (of satisfaction or happiness), which is the most common statistic in the literature:

$$\frac{1}{n}\sum_i \mu_i\left(L\left(l_i^*;R_i^*\right)\right).$$

Such an indicator assumes that the individual scores $\mu_i\left(L\left(l_i^*;R_i^*\right)\right)$ are cardinally measurable and interpersonally comparable, and that social welfare increases when this average number increases. These two assumptions are distinct. The former is justified if $\mu_i\left(L\left(l_i^*;R_i^*\right)\right) = \mu_0\left(L\left(l_i^*;R_i^*\right)\right) + \varepsilon_i$, where $\mu_0\left(L\left(l_i^*;R_i^*\right)\right)$ is a cardinally meaningful measure and $\frac{1}{n}\sum_i \varepsilon_i$ does not fluctuate across measurement operations.

None of these assumptions is plausible. Variations in scores are not directly comparable across individuals when heterogeneity in calibrations involves more than a fixed individual shift; comparisons across populations (e.g., countries) are problematic when $\frac{1}{n}\sum_i \varepsilon_i$ varies with culture; and summing scores ignores inequality.

Introducing inequality aversion would require computing a generalized mean

$$\frac{1}{n}\sum_i \varphi\left(\mu_i\left(L\left(l_i^*;R_i^*\right)\right)\right),$$

with a concave transform φ. Unfortunately, the informational demands on individuals scores $\mu_i\left(L\left(l_i^*;R_i^*\right)\right)$ are then even greater, as they must be fully measurable and comparable.

There have been apparently less demanding uses of these data. The Gallup-Healthways Well-Being Index focuses on the percentage of respondents in various levels, considering in particular that on the 0–10 ladder, the respondents at 4 or below are "suffering" while those at 5–6 are "struggling." Such an approach is also advocated by Hammond, Liberini, and Proto (2011). This requires that individual score levels, rather than differences, be interpersonally comparable, and, for applications to social welfare, it also requires the additional ethical assumption that individuals with lower scores should be considered worse off than individuals with higher scores. Moreover, seeking to minimize the proportion of the population below a certain score would involve a form of maximin criterion with some aggregation at the bottom.

This approach is not compatible with the assumption $\mu_i\left(L\left(l_i^*; R_i^*\right)\right) = \mu_0\left(L\left(l_i^*; R_i^*\right)\right) + \varepsilon_i$, and it essentially requires that for all i, $\mu_i\left(L\left(l_i^*; R_i^*\right)\right) = \mu_0\left(L\left(l_i^*; R_i^*\right)\right)$, but without the assumption that $\mu_0\left(L\left(l_i^*; R_i^*\right)\right)$ is a cardinally meaningful measure. As suggested by the study of the worst-off population in Fleurbaey, Schokkaert, and Decancq (2009), it is not very likely that this approach suitably identifies the subgroup of the population that deserves the most priority in social policy.

Kahneman and Krueger (2006) have proposed a more parsimonious indicator, the U-index, which bears on emotions and records the average proportion of the day that people spend in a mood in which negative emotions predominate. The distinction between positive and negative emotions is perhaps the least controversial aspect of subjective well-being for comparisons across individuals. However, some interpersonal variations may occur in how people identify the dominant emotions (some may be more sensitive to negative emotions than others in their evaluation, in a way that makes comparisons difficult). Nevertheless, one can probably be more hopeful about coming up with interpersonally comparable indicators for emotions than for satisfaction judgments.

In conclusion, it appears that happiness and satisfaction scores cannot be used directly as representations of "the final outcome about which people are most concerned," because they involve calibrations that are heterogeneous in space and time and may not reflect ethical priorities. Measures of emotions may be more promising on the measurement side, but they cannot be taken to measure "the final outcome about which people are most concerned," because they represent only a part of what matters in life for the individuals who are not pure hedonists.

The fact that subjective well-being data do not deliver the desired output directly does not mean that they do not provide anything useful. If one would like to measure well-being on the basis of individual preferences, for instance with a measure like the equivalent income or like $\mu_0\left(L\left(l_i^*; R_i^*\right)\right)$, such data are useful if it is possible to filter the calibration variations and retrieve information about individual preferences.

In the remainder of this section, we briefly examine how to devise a strategy for the extraction of useful information from data on subjective well-being.

5.3.2 Putting affects in their place

Regarding affects, it is easy to conclude from what precedes that they should be treated as a life domain, along other domains like income or health. In fact, the boundary between emotions and mental health is fuzzy, which reinforces the idea that they belong to a domain of this sort.

The interesting research question that emerges from this perspective is to find out how much weight people give to this dimension of life in their global evaluation. This is not rendered easy by the correlation between emotions and other dimensions. Success in other dimensions produces positive emotions.

In a different vein, Kimball and Willis (2006) propose to use emotions as an indicator of preferences in a clever way. It is argued in psychology (Kahneman and Thaler 2006) that emotions are carried by events more than by states, that is, by changes rather than by stable situations. Suppose that an emotion score then reflects the change in satisfaction recorded in the most recent period. If one can regress an emotion score on the change in the vector of life dimensions that has occurred recently, one can interpret the relative weight of the various dimensions in such a regression as the relative weights they have in people's preferences.

The difficulty of this approach is to find data that have the right temporal pattern, and to be confident that emotions reflect variations in satisfaction. The risk is that emotions reflect changes in life domains that occur separately at different times, without a clear link between the intensity of the emotion and the weight of the life domain in the respondent's preferences. One may be happy after finding a job, then happy after marriage, then happy after having a child, but it may be very hard to retrieve weights from such a sequence.

5.3.3 Identification problems

With satisfaction and happiness scores, the estimation of preferences over life dimensions is rendered particularly arduous by identification problems.

An important characteristic influencing responses is the respondent's personality. Few data sets have information about personality, and it is often thought that panel data are preferable because they make it possible to isolate individual fixed effects. This, however, works well only if personality influences the answers only by moving them up or down by a constant (or by moving the probability of answering in a high category by a constant). If personality exacerbates or attenuates the variations of the score over time, this is not eliminated by fixed effects, and the typical regression will give a greater importance, in the estimation, to the individuals with a "sensitive" personality over the others.

Panel data have the drawback of eliminating not only fixed characteristics that appear irrelevant such as personality, but also the fixed characteristics that are objects of preference. A disability that is fixed over the waves of the survey and reduces well-being will be assimilated to a particularly gloomy personality. Only the people acquiring this disability over the survey will have a role in the estimation of its importance. And the individual characteristics that are fixed over one's life but may nevertheless have an impact on satisfaction, as objects of preferences or as influences on objects of preferences that are not recorded in the data, necessarily go unnoticed. One may think of social or ethnic background as examples of such characteristics.

The calibration problem also makes it very hard to determine whether relative variables have an impact as objects of preferences or are only due to the calibration. Consider Abel, whose preferences are not affected by comparisons with others, and are represented by the utility function

$$a_0 + a_1 \ln x_1 + a_2 x_2.$$

It may nevertheless happen that Abel, on a questionnaire with a bounded scale, gives a satisfaction score that reflects the quantile of this expression in the uniform distribution over some interval $[\bar{u} - A, \bar{u} + A]$, where $\bar{u}$ is the average value of $a_0 + a_1 \ln x_1 + a_2 x_2$ in a reference group and A is a constant. His satisfaction score is then equal to

$$\frac{a_0 + a_1 \ln x_1 + a_2 x_2 - \bar{u} + A}{2A}.$$

Compare Bael, who cares primarily about his relative position in the distribution of each good, and whose preferences are representable by the utility function

$$b_0 + b_1 \ln \frac{x_1}{\bar{x}_1} + b_2 (x_2 - \bar{x}_2),$$

where $\bar{x}_1$ is the geometric mean and $\bar{x}_2$ the arithmetic mean of these variables in a reference group. Because his preferences are already about relative magnitudes, Bael uses a simple affine transformation in order to calibrate his satisfaction grades for the questionnaire.

With satisfaction data, there is no way in which Abel, who does not care about comparisons at all in his preferences about life, can be distinguished from Bael, whose sole concern is his relative position with respect to the reference group. This example shows that it is very hard to derive from standard happiness and satisfaction questionnaires reliable information about how much people really care about comparisons to others. The same problem affects any estimation of adaptation over time. People who care mostly about the evolution of their situation are hard to distinguish from people who care about their current situation but look at the past to calibrate their answers.

In other words, the data may tell us more about the calibration strategies of the respondents than about their true preferences and values in life. Importantly, this does not mean that the distinction between preferences and calibration is metaphysical and cannot be observed in any way. It is rather easy to track preferences by making the respondents face trade-offs between improvements in their absolute situation and improvements in their relative position. This requires different questionnaires that ask directly about preferences over alternative options rather than about grading the current situation.

Tversky and Griffin (1991) and Benjamin et al. (2012) have explored such trade-offs in questionnaires about stated preferences. Moreover, they have asked respondents to estimate their satisfaction or happiness level with the various options. In a majority of cases respondents prefer the improvement in their absolute situation, even if some of them forecast that their happiness would be higher with an improvement in their relative position. The latter fact may be attributable to various possible factors. Respondents may not care that much about their relative position but forecast that their satisfaction, which is relative, will evolve otherwise. Or they may understand the question about future happiness as referring to feelings and know that their feelings are strongly influenced by their relative position. Or they may choose the absolute improvement because they care about the good externalities it has on their relatives, but their personal concern is about their relative position.

Coming back to happiness data, it may be reassuring to see that, whether people are more like Abel or more like Bael, if the average values for the reference groups do not vary much, the estimation of the coefficients is not necessarily biased. What is difficult is to know whether respondents care about absolute or relative values of the variables. But for personal trade-offs about the absolute values of these variables, the estimation is indicative of the relative weight that respondents assign to them and of the choices they would make if they had to choose.

In other words, ordinary estimations with happiness data do not tell us much about problems like the Easterlin paradox, because shifting calibrations are not distinguishable from the presence of relative variables in preferences, but they do tell enough about personal indifference curves to know if people give a great weight to health or to employment, as opposed to income. They may therefore be useful to estimate the indifference curves that are needed to compute equivalent incomes or similar measures of well-being. They must, however, be supplemented with additional data in order to know whether people care about comparisons and how much.

Another consideration that must be borne in mind is that many variables in happiness or satisfaction regressions are not truly exogenous. For instance, income may be influenced by personality, which also influences happiness. The influence of income on happiness may then be overestimated. Marital status may be influenced by happiness as much as happiness is influenced by it. Panel data and natural experiments are generally thought to provide partial solutions to this difficulty. Ideally, one would need a structural model of the choices made by the individuals and of the various influences of such choices before one starts deriving equations to be estimated. So far, the structural approach has not been tried much. It is obviously quite hard to develop a realistic structural model in a model with multiple life dimensions.

5.3.4 Can happiness data be improved?

There are two doctrines about the design of happiness questionnaires. One doctrine says that the question must be as little prepared as possible and as vague as possible, so that respondents are left free to flesh out the notion of happiness with whatever they care about and are submitted to little framing by preparation questions. The opposite doctrine is that the question should be as precise as possible, leaving no ambiguity about the target concept, and come after a series of questions helping the respondent to recap the various relevant aspects of her life.

The former doctrine is convincing if happiness for herself is something that each respondent has a clear idea of and can give an answer right away. The latter doctrine fits better with the observation that the evaluation of one's life is a cognitively demanding exercise and is not something that people have in mind, ready to be uttered. As argued by Schwarz and

Strack (1999), the answer to a satisfaction question is actually constructed on the spot, with the various elements at the respondent's disposal.

Answering a satisfaction question is not a completely novel exercise for most respondents. People generally have a rough idea about whether their life is going well. They also have rough preferences about the contents of their life, as they are used to making decisions repeatedly, which forces them to think about what they want. Even in life domains over which little choice is possible, the human mind is accustomed to fantasize and imagine how nice or bad a different situation would be. Finally, people make comparisons to others, or reference to their aspirations, sufficiently often so that the exercise of calibrating answers by reference to a distribution is not a totally new exercise. Nevertheless, it is hard to deny that helping the respondents with sufficient time and occasions to think about the various life domains before giving a global evaluation seems the most reasonable way to proceed.

It would be particularly interesting to see if the quality of answers varies with the kind of questionnaire that is administered. The test-retest robustness of happiness data is rather weak compared to more objective data (Krueger and Schkade 2008), and it would be natural to seek to determine if giving more time and preparation to respondents improves the test-retest quality.

Another direction of potential improvement has to do with calibration. As in Steffel and Oppenheimer (2009), it is possible to ask respondents how they construct their answer and what elements of comparison, if any, they use. A more radical move is to guide the calibration by asking the respondents to refer to a particular standard. One can also control the calibration by the use of vignettes. That is, one can describe a list of lives and indicate what grades they should have, or in what category they fall.[9] This may be the most promising route if one hopes to obtain happiness data that have an absolute value in spite of the bounded scale. It is then sufficient to keep the vignettes unchanged across waves of the survey. This may be untenable over a long period of time because changes in techniques and vocabulary may render the descriptions outdated. Imagine vignettes conceived in the seventeenth century and used nowadays. A good life would probably involve a noble status, many servants, and feats of arms. But for one century static vignettes may be possible. They would make it possible to test the true meaning of the Easterlin paradox.

9. Another possibility, as exemplified by Kapteyn, Smith, and Van Soest (2009), is to ask respondents to freely grade lives described in vignettes and then use the answers to recalibrate satisfaction scores afterward. These authors show that American and Dutch respondents have different grading patterns (but the difference is not a simple shift).

Similarly, the scope problem can be alleviated if the question makes it precise what part of life is relevant. The most interesting question is probably about the whole life rather than the current period, but this may depend on the purpose of the survey. Asking two questions, one about the whole life and one about the current period, might be the best strategy. It would also be useful to somehow specify the boundaries of "personal" life, as opposed to the rest of society and the whole universe.

Finally, happiness data can be supplemented with direct questions on preferences. Asking such questions would make it possible to check if the relative weights of life domains obtained through satisfaction scores are similar to what is obtained directly from stated preferences.

5.4 CONCLUSION

Happiness data provide an invaluable source of information on the population's preferences and values in life. While there remains a great potential for improving the quality and meaningfulness of the data, the great achievement of this field is the methodological recognition of verbal expressions as relevant for the evaluation of welfare. Such data make it possible to go beyond the very limited domain of preferences revealed by choices, epitomized by the classical economic analysis of market demand. Looking back at chapter 3, one can appreciate the progress made in seeking to widen the scope of well-being considerations beyond the narrow economic aspects of life.

However, happiness data have often been offered as the promise of a direct measure of well-being. "These kinds of statistics are probably the only ones available to us if we wish to measure well-being," writes Oswald (1997, p. 1827). "Self-reported happiness has turned out to be the best indicator of happiness.... It exhibits considerable intrapersonal stability and interpersonal comparability and therefore can be used without major problems for many purposes," write Frey and Stutzer (2002, pp. 26 and 28).

As we have seen in this chapter, the calibration problem makes it impossible to use such data directly. Doing so is likely to betray people's actual concerns with the contents of their life, as the Easterlin paradox—if confirmed—suggests. It is very implausible that people are indifferent to the growth in living standards and longevity that has been witnessed in the last decades. A stability in the satisfaction curves would reveal more about the shifting calibrations of the answers than about how people really feel about the issue.

Some authors in the literature have seen that there is an apparent contradiction between preferences and subjective well-being scores and that this cannot be simply attributed to mistakes in "decision utility." "Obviously, everyone would choose to be healthy rather than paraplegic, and rich rather than poor. But it is not obvious how to demonstrate that the rich are actually happier than the poor if both groups report the same level of well-being. At the same time, it is clear that an adequate measure of well-being must distinguish between rich and poor, and between paraplegic and quadriplegic" (Tversky and Griffin 1991, p. 724). "Assuming that future research provides a deeper understanding of hedonic adaptation, is it likely that such information would cause people to conduct their lives differently? Would they stop wearing seatbelts with the assurance that they would get used to being paralyzed? Would they exploit an embezzlement opportunity knowing that prison wouldn't be all that bad in the long run? We suspect not" (Frederick and Loewenstein 1999, p. 320).

As we have seen, the problem appears simple once one understands that subjective well-being indicators give information either about a calibrated $\xi_i\left(l_i^*\right)$, or about feelings f_{it} (a part of l_i), whereas people actually care about l_i.

The fascination of the happiness literature for the magnitude of subjective well-being indicators may come from the meeting of two disciplines by coincidence. Psychology seeks to understand mental states and behaviors, and emotions as well as life evaluations are mental states that are certainly worth studying and explaining. Economics has been constructed around the concept of utility, and it is apparently easy for economists to forget that when the economic model makes the individual maximize $u(x)$, this means that the individual cares about x, not $u(x)$. If individuals cared about $u(x)$, they would spend their time working on their mind-set rather than changing the world around them.

The simple model that has been proposed in this chapter to describe the mental operations that respondents have to perform when they face a happiness question has shown that the calibration problem is pervasive, making it hard to compare individuals who use different calibration strategies, and making it impossible, for instance, to identify from such data how much the individuals actually care about their relative position versus their absolute situation.

The calibration problem comes from the gap between the open-ended nature of many dimensions of life and the bounded scale imposed by questionnaires. The violation of the "same-preference" principle shows how, precisely, this problem may make the measure go against the concerned people's views about their own situations.

We have seen that taking a fixed calibration would eliminate the problem. But, as explained in this chapter, it would not eliminate the difficulty of making ethically sound comparisons between individuals with different preferences about the dimensions of life. Interpersonal comparisons involve not only respectfully tracking what people care about, but also adjudicating conflicts of interests in order to determine who deserves greater priority in social evaluation. The capability approach, studied in the next chapter, is the prominent example of an approach that is primarily based on such considerations.

CHAPTER 6

Empowering Capabilities

After having discussed the pricing approach, the equivalent-income approach, and the happiness approach, we now turn to an approach that has an equally fascinating intellectual history. The "capability approach" (CA) was introduced by Sen and Nussbaum in the 1980s (Sen 1985; Nussbaum 1988; see also, among many other references, Sen 1999a; Nussbaum 2000), taking inspiration in particular from the basic needs approach[1] and from certain ideas about well-being going back to Aristotle and Smith. In a nutshell, this approach advocates focusing on a *comprehensive* list of functionings (activities, states) that people are *able to* achieve, rather than on specific achievements like income or happiness.

In less than 30 years, this approach has attracted considerable interest and enthusiasm, so much so that it now has its own association, its own journal, and a variety of specific scholarly, developmental, and political activities. It is most conspicuously associated with the Human Development Index published since 1990 by the United Nations Development Program. Its basic tenets can now be found in a textbook (Deneulin and Shahani 2009) and in a thick collection of essays (Comim, Qizilbash, and Alkire 2008; see also Alkire 2002 for a detailed presentation, as well as Kuklys 2005). Important critical discussions have been made in handbook chapters by Schokkaert (2009) and Basu and Lopez-Calva (2011).

The main reason for the appeal of the CA in the last decades is probably that it offers the perspective of shifting the focus, especially in development policy debates, from narrow economic indicators to broader

1. See, e.g., Streeten et al. (1981). In Sen (1980), the focus is on "basic" capabilities. The link between the basic needs approach and the CA is highlighted in Alkire (2002).

considerations of human flourishing. As such broadening is exactly what this book is about, it is important to examine how this approach compares to the others and how it can help us make progress toward a better measurement of individual well-being and social welfare.

There are many thoughtful discussions of the CA (in particular the references already provided), and the purpose of this chapter is much more specific. We are in this book in search of good measures of well-being, and we will therefore focus on what the approach proposes in this domain. As it turns out, the measurement issue is generally considered one of the weak parts of the CA, most of the writing about the approach dwelling on more general philosophical questions. Philosophical questions are not to be neglected, as it is important to get them right before embarking on applied projects. However, the pressure of applications is often very useful because it brings to the fore the most relevant issues. We will here follow the lead of the measurement objective.

The question that underlies this chapter is whether the CA is an alternative to the approaches discussed in the previous chapters or whether it can rely on these approaches for its applications. Several CA authors have faced the question of whether subjective well-being questionnaires could be a vehicle for the application of the CA (in particular Anand, Hunter, and Smith 2005). We will argue here that the equivalent-income approach provides a more promising way of putting numbers on the CA. This, however, requires modifying some basic pillars of the CA as articulated by Sen and Nussbaum, because the classical writings on the CA reject the idea of allowing individual-specific weights for the different dimensions of capabilities. This may, after all, be a point of reasonable disagreement. The conclusion will therefore be that, although the CA can mingle with the happiness approach and the equivalent-income approach for applications, it is also possible to think of it as a third approach that is more objective than both in the sense that it relies less on subjective perceptions by the concerned populations.

A preliminary remark is in order. The CA has been introduced in the "equality of what?" debate,[2] as a forerunner for the equality of opportunity theories, and many arguments about the approach and its contenders rely on egalitarian considerations. We will have to follow the pattern of the debates in this chapter and will therefore often discuss the capability metric as something to equalize across individuals, rather than just a measure of individual advantage.

2. See Sen (1980, 1985, 1992).

The chapter is organized as follows. The first section recalls the background concepts of functionings and capabilities, explaining how they compare to classical notions. The second section argues that, insofar as the CA insists on capabilities viewed as opportunity sets, as opposed to achievements, it could find interesting material in the literature on equality of opportunity that has developed recently, but it would also meet some challenges there. Beyond the opportunity-achievement distinction, the CA has to address the basic index problem like any other theory of well-being, and the third section questions key ideas that Sen defended in this respect. If one accepts the objections made in that section, the equivalent-income approach appears a more promising application of the CA than the typical methodologies that are found in the empirical CA literature. The last section concludes with the question introduced in a previous paragraph: Is the CA a separate approach, or can it rely on other approaches for applications?

6.1 THE CAPABILITY APPROACH

6.1.1 From basic needs to capabilities

The CA appeared in a preliminary form in the debate among theories of social justice that asked, "Equality of what?" In his Tanner Lectures bearing this title, Sen (1980) rejected both the utility metric (utilitarianism and welfare egalitarianism) and the resource metric (Rawls) and argued that basic needs were not fully captured by either approach. He coined the definition "basic capabilities: a person being able to do certain basic things" in order to tackle the case of a disabled person who has low marginal utility, high utility level, decent resources, but severely limited bodily functions. Such a person would be given low priority by utilitarianism, welfare egalitarianism, and resource egalitarianism even though his life possibilities appear dramatically insufficient.

The proximity between the basic needs approach and the CA has been important in the field of development analysis and is well documented in Alkire (2002). The focus on basic capabilities has remained a key feature of Nussbaum's version of the CA. In her approach, a list of essential dimensions of human flourishing should be elaborated, and once a good list has been obtained after proper expertise and collective deliberation, it could be used to request that social institutions guarantee every member of society the possibility of achieving a basic level in each of these dimensions.

There are two important restrictions in this formulation. First, only the *possibility* of certain achievements would be guaranteed, not the achievements themselves. The main motivation here is the fact that it may be part of reasonable life plans not to develop even minimal levels in certain dimensions. The most obvious example is that while the possibility of having children should be guaranteed to all, many individuals choose not to procreate without this implying that they are disadvantaged.

The second restriction is that only *minimal* levels are to be guaranteed. This may seem harder to justify, but imagine that a high level were offered to all members of society. Then it becomes important to decide where to set the levels in the various dimensions, and debates about the implied trade-offs would have to be concluded before practical decisions could be made. In contrast, insisting on basic levels reduces the scope for weighting problems, as one can require every dimension be treated satisfactorily without one being forced to make a judgment on the relative importance of the various items in the list.

With this issue, we are already at the heart of the difficulties with the CA. Unlike Nussbaum, Sen has quickly abandoned the focus on basic needs. Restricting attention to basic levels has one important drawback. It makes it impossible to develop a full theory of individual well-being and social welfare (i.e., covering all levels of well-being and not just situations of poverty and subsistence) and to address the wide array of policy issues that welfare economics usually covers.

In later versions of his approach, Sen introduces functionings as all sorts of doings and beings, at any level of affluence and development, that may matter to defining a flourishing life. The focus is then put on the difference between the space of functionings and the space of utility or the space of resources that form the settings of other classical approaches.

Sen's approach is therefore more straighforwardly in the tradition of welfare economics and social choice theory. It aims at elaborating a notion of individual advantage that can serve to compare various individuals and social groups at all levels of affluence and that can feed studies of inequalities as well as normative evaluations of societies and public policies. Recall that Sen's view of social choice theory is that it needs to introduce interpersonally comparable indexes of individual well-being in order to escape Arrow's impossibility, and that such indices need not be utilities or resources, but can be other measures that better assess individual situations (Sen 2002, pp. 341–343).

6.1.2 Functionings, between "opulence" and "utility"

The main idea, then, remains to avoid the utility metric as well as the resource metric. In particular, the latter is epitomized not only in Rawls's theory, but in all economic analyses of living standards. Both the utility metric and the resource metric are primarily criticized by Sen for being too narrow and reductionist. The proposal is then to broaden the space of dimensions of life that are to be considered, and such dimensions are called "functionings"—capabilities are then the sets of combinations of functionings that individuals are able to achieve. The word "functioning" is a confusing term that has often been interpreted as referring to activities. In fact, functionings are meant to encompass all "doings and beings," that is, not just actions and behaviors but also states of the person, such as being free from the threat of malaria or of political repression.

For many scholars who are suspicious of economic theory and monetary measures, the move from income to functionings (e.g., from GDP to HDI) probably represents the greatest attraction of the CA. Qizilbash (2008, p. 53) introduces the approach as "a, if not the only, major alternative to standard welfare economics." As noted in Schokkaert (2009), many self-proclaimed applications of the CA approach appear to be merely more or less comprehensive studies of living conditions incorporating nonmarket data. Interestingly, in his review of *Commodities and Capabilities* (Sen 1985), Basu (1987) introduces the book primarily as a defense of the use of nonmarket data.

Given that functionings encompass all that a person "manages to do or to be," the weighting issue comes back with a vengeance. Sen assumes that every individual can be endowed with a "valuation function" that assesses the quality of functioning vectors. One may wonder how much at this point hinges on the function itself, as opposed to an ordinal ranking, and it is worth checking if the theory could be developed in a parallel way with a valuation preordering that ranks the various functioning vectors (i.e., the various lives) that the individual could conceivably achieve.

Until now, we are on familiar grounds. The nonmarket dimensions of life discussed in the previous chapters can include all relevant functionings, and the valuation preordering is very similar to the preference ordering that has been invoked previously. A small difference is that Sen insists on the likely incompleteness of the valuation preordering, whereas we have generally assumed so far that the preference relation is complete, that is, an ordering. Sen also emphasizes that the valuation relation does not derive from ordinary preferences but is based on a deeper assessment of what makes a good life. This is perfectly in line with a rather standard view of preferences as the best judgment that individuals make about life.

According to Sen (1985), subjective well-being (happiness, satisfaction) does not provide an appropriate measure of well-being because mental states (in particular hedonic states) form only a subset of the functionings, while satisfaction with life, as ordinarily expressed by individuals, is too dependent on aspiration levels that adapt to actual circumstances. This view appears quite consistent with our critical discussion of the subjective well-being approach in the previous chapter.

6.1.3 From functionings to capabilities

But functionings are only the beginning. A more accurate picture of individual advantage, Sen argues, includes the opportunities offered to people, not just their ultimate well-being. (In the previous chapters of this book, no such distinction between *well-being* and *advantage* was made, and well-being was the catchword for the relevant notion of individual advantage.) Functionings constitute the adequate space to describe well-being, but capabilities, it is argued, are a better description of advantage. Formally, individual advantage is then to be examined in terms of the capability set of the individual, that is, the set of functioning vectors accessible to the individual.

In a recent synthesis on the topic, Sen (2009) puts forth three reasons to move from the space of functionings to the space of capabilities. The first has repeatedly been very explicit in the literature and corresponds to the incorporation of freedom as an important element of advantage. The main argument here is that two individuals with identical functionings but very different capability sets cannot be considered equally well off. Fasting is different from starving, says a famous example.

The second reason is the importance of letting people choose between different possible affiliations and cultures. This can be read as another application of the idea that freedom is an essential aspect of advantage. More broadly, people's freedom to follow their own goals in life might appear to require an approach in terms of opportunities rather than achievements, as argued by Nussbaum (2000, p. 87): "If we were to take functioning itself as the goal of public policy, pushing citizens into functionings in a single determinate manner, the liberal pluralist would rightly judge that we were precluding many choices that citizens may make in accordance with their own conceptions of the good, and perhaps violating their rights."

The third reason is that focusing on opportunities rather than achievements is consonant with making room for the exercise of personal responsibility in the final distribution of well-being. Giving access to health care, Sen suggests as an example, is a more appropriate policy goal than making sure that everyone makes use of health care facilities.

Another potential benefit is seldom mentioned directly in the CA literature but is quite relevant here. Focusing on capabilities rather than functionings makes the weighting problem less pressing. Indeed, when individuals are offered substantial opportunities, they are free to choose as they wish, and therefore the choice of particular weights for various dimensions of functionings has fewer consequences. The final distribution of functionings may even reflect the diversity of individual valuations even when a uniform weighting system is used in the evaluation of capabilities. In fact, the move to the capability space is typically considered in the CA literature as compounding the measurement difficulty rather than alleviating it, because in addition to the valuation of functioning dimensions, one must assess opportunity sets.

To conclude this brief introduction of the background, it may be worth emphasizing that the CA has been versatile in part due to Sen's insistence that it mostly consists of advocating working in the space of functionings and capabilities and refrains from recommending particular measures and methodologies. At the limit, the CA could be summarized as merely stating that nonincome dimensions of life and freedom are important aspects of the evaluation of well-being and advantage. Such vagueness has made the approach attractive to many scholars, but it may also have hindered potential developments.

In particular, even though Sen (1985) introduces some basic formalism to describe how functionings and capabilities relate to commodity consumption, modeling has played almost no role in the CA literature, especially in its applications. This could mean that the CA is capturing certain aspects of well-being that welfare economics and its mathematical tools are unable to grasp. Or it could mean that some work remains to be done to reconcile the insights from the CA with rigorous concepts.

6.2 CAPABILITIES AS OPPORTUNITIES

6.2.1 Valuing sets

In the perspective of connecting the CA approach to economic theory, it is interesting to read Muellbauer's (1987) reaction to the CA. The main aspect Muellbauer retains is the focus on opportunity sets (although he discusses other themes that are less directly linked to the CA, such as habits and equivalence scales). As alluded to in subsection 4.3.1, the reference to opportunity sets was already the argument used by Deaton and Muellbauer (1980) to justify the use of money-metric utility in interpersonal comparisons (see also Deaton 1980).

There is now a sizable literature on the ranking of sets (see surveys in Barberà, Bossert, and Pattanaik 2004; Foster 2011), and it seems directly relevant to the evaluation of capability sets. In his Arrow Lectures (Part VI of Sen 2002), Sen critically discusses this literature, comparing the approaches that involve preference orderings over elements of the sets and the approaches that are based on the cardinality of the sets. Most of this literature is very abstract. It deals with a nondescript universe Z, the problem being to rank a collection of subsets $A \subset Z$.

To give an example, Sen draws attention to the possibility of seeking unanimity among several valuation orderings R_i (the set of i may coincide with the population if the valuation orderings are the individuals') that rank elements of Z. This can be done in two ways.

1. One can first define the intersection ordering: $zR^{\cap}z'$ if and only if zR_iz' for all i. Then one can say that A is at least as good as B if there is $z \in A$ such that $zR^{\cap}z'$ for all $z' \in B$.[3]
2. One can be less demanding and directly play with the variety of R_i when comparing elements of sets. For instance, one can say that A is at least as good as B if for every i, there is $z \in A$ such that zR_iz' for all $z' \in B$.[4]

As can be seen, the first approach is very conservative, as a set is not comparable to another as soon as there is a dissenting R_i in the comparison of $z \in A$ to $z' \in B$. The second approach may seem too lenient, in contrast, because it is enough for set A to contain a few extreme options that together suit all R_i, even if each of them is terrible for some R_i, whereas set B contains many intermediate options that would each be reasonable choices for all R_i.

Muellbauer (1987) considers a slightly more concrete framework with subsets of $\mathbb{R}_+^\ell$ that are generalizations of budget sets. He proposes to evaluate sets by measuring the distance of their boundary from the origin along a particular ray or the distance from the origin of a hyperplane that is tangent to their boundary. He also proposes averaging such measures over a collection of reference rays or reference slopes for the tangent hyperplane. Such proposals have been echoed in more recent work by Xu (who axiomatizes the surface of sets) and Gaertner and Xu (who take the minimum distance from the origin or from a minimum bundle, rather than the average).[5]

3. A variant says that A is at least as good as B if for all $z' \in B$, there is $z \in A$ such that $zR^{\cap}z'$.

4. Again, a variant says that A is at least as good as B if for every i, and for all $z' \in B$, there is $z \in A$ such that zR_iz'.

5. See Xu (2004) and Gaertner and Xu (2008).

Note that these last approaches are less far from Sen's analysis than it seems. The distance from the origin along a particular ray coincides with evaluating sets by their best element according to Leontief preferences. The distance from the origin of a tangent line coincides with evaluating sets by their best element according to linear preferences. Taking an average or a minimum over possible indexes obtained with various preferences is not the same, however, as considering the intersection over different preferences. There is apparently an endless variety of possibilities.

At this stage, two difficulties appear. First, the direction taken by these evaluations of sets seems to abandon the idea of respecting individual valuations for every personal situation, even when valuation orderings are allowed to play a role in the assessement of capability sets. This is an issue that will be discussed in detail in the next section.

The other difficulty is that there seems to be a lack of ethical principles to feed the elaboration of a ranking of opportunity sets. The only considerations that appear in this literature refer to the quantity and sometimes the diversity of options in the sets, and to the value of the options for some valuation or preference orderings, as exemplified by the criteria listed above in points 1–2. This seems to miss an important part of what makes opportunities a key issue in distributive justice. Consider for instance opportunities for consumption and leisure or effort. There are debates about whether it is fair to offer the opportunity of a decent income without working, or whether it is fair to have considerable differences in consumption between those who work and those who do not work. Such considerations seem absent from criteria that primarily check if some persons would rather choose from one set than from the other, or if there are more options in one set than in another.

In this context, it seems natural to make the connection with the economic literature on equality of opportunity that was inspired by the philosophical debate, "Equality of what?" In this debate, several authors advocated some form of equality of opportunity in a fashion that is not too different from the CA. Indeed, in the philosophical arena the CA belongs to a broader class of theories that define justice in terms of opportunities rather than achievements. Prominent authors include Arneson, Cohen, Dworkin, Van Parijs in addition to Nussbaum and Sen.[6] Between these authors, there are variations in the arguments used to defend the metric of opportunities as a basis for interpersonal comparisons, but from the point of view of applications these differences do not matter much.

6. A useful introduction to the philosophical literature, for economists, can be found in Roemer (1996).

In welfare economics, a variety of modeling strategies have been proposed to incorporate these ideas in the definition of new types of social objectives. These different strategies are discussed and compared in Fleurbaey (2008) and Fleurbaey and Maniquet (2011a). As it turns out, this literature contains three insights that are worth examining here.

6.2.2 The relevant aspects of opportunities

The first insight is that it is possible to give a structure to capability sets that makes them amenable to ethically relevant interpersonal comparisons. In fact, two different approaches have been proposed.

First, Roemer (1993, 1998) has proposed relying on an interpersonally comparable measure of functioning achievement coupled with a measure of effort. An opportunity set is then defined as a set of pairs (u, e), where u is a synthetic measure of functioning achievement, and e effort, which is calibrated to be a real number in the unit interval.

Let us assume that individual i's achievement is determined as a function of his circumstances, denoted y_i, and his effort e_i. While circumstances are fixed, effort is supposed to possibly take different values in a set E that is equally accessible to all. The achievement function can be denoted $u\left(y, e\right)$, and it is the same function for all individuals if all relevant characteristics are described either in y or in e. The opportunity of an individual is then depicted as

$$\left\{\left(u\left(y, e\right), e\right) \mid e \in E\right\}.$$

Roemer also proposed a practical way to construct such sets, which goes as follows. First partition the population into subgroups who have similar circumstances and can be assumed to have similar opportunities. Such subgroups he calls "types." Then construct the CDF of achievement for each type and measure every individual's level of effort as his percentile position in the distribution of achievement of his respective type. For instance, if education is the achievement under consideration, it may be that the child of an executive at the median of her type has 19 years of education whereas the child of a clerk at the median of her type has only 16 years, but they are then considered to have exerted the same level of effort, given their respective circumstances. A variant of this methodology directly looks at a proxy measure for effort and defines effort as the percentile in the distribution of the proxy in one's type. For instance, if health is the achievement, the proxy for effort may be years of smoking, and as different types have different patterns of smoking, effort is calibrated to reflect these patterns. Twenty years of smoking for a factory worker may represent the same "effort" as 16 years for a teacher, and this is evaluated by their rank in their type-specific distribution of smoking.

It is important to see that the general idea of defining opportunity sets as $\{(u(y,e),e) \mid e \in E\}$ is independent of the practical methodology by which it is applied. We focus here on this $\{(u(y,e),e) \mid e \in E\}$ general form. The added value of structuring sets in this way is that it summarizes the ethically relevant information in a convenient way. While the CA is confronted with assessing a myriad of life options that individuals can choose, this approach simplifies the task by pointing to two relevant dimensions: each option is summarized by the amount of achievement u that it brings, and the amount of effort e that it requires.

Relying on a synthetic measure of achievement is well in line with the use of valuation functions or orderings suggested by Sen.[7] In addition, the notion of effort makes it possible to evaluate how accessible the various options are. Indeed, two individuals may have access to the same achievement levels, but the best level may be easy to obtain for one and cost a lot of effort to the other. This is obviously very relevant information.

Equipped with this structured information, one is able to formulate a key egalitarian principle, which says that ideally, "equal effort should give equal achievement." This is called the "compensation principle" in the literature, in view of the fact that it offers a guide about how much compensation for disadvantageous circumstances one should provide.

When the compensation principle is fully satisfied, all individuals have the same opportunity sets $\{(u,e)\}$. Equality of sets, when they are defined in this way, therefore makes good sense. This is in contrast with requiring complete physical equality of capability sets, which is much less compelling because one can have equally good sets that offer quite different options. This may be viewed as an important contribution of this literature. While physical equality of capability sets is not particularly attractive, seeking equality of the sets $\{(u(y,e),e) \mid e \in E\}$ is a sensible idea.

The other approach is somewhat similar to Roemer's definition of opportunity sets but has interesting differences that will appear important in the next subsection. Proposed independently by Fleurbaey (1994) and Bossert (1995), it does not require an interpersonally comparable measure of achievement (although it obviously does not exclude it). It consists in describing the situation of an individual by three components: x, a scalar measure of resource transfers incurred by the individual, y, a description

7. Roemer advocates applying his approach to specific dimensions of achievement such as education or income, but it seems natural to apply it as well to a synthetic measure of functionings.

of circumstances that cannot be changed, and e, a description of characteristics for which the individual is deemed responsible (for instance, because he can choose their values). The idea of this threefold structuration of individual situations is to separate the role of the three factors that determine the fate of individuals: social policy (via transfers), history and nature (circumstances), and the individual (personal responsibility). Most theories of justice as equality of opportunity advocate using social policy to compensate for inequalities due to circumstances while remaining neutral regarding the influence of responsibility characteristics, and the CA does not depart from this general perspective. The variables y and e can be interpreted as being essentially the same as in Roemer's general approach (but e is not measured as Roemer suggests in typical applications of this alternative approach).

How does this relate to capability sets? When a social policy is minimally impartial, it only depends on the characteristics (y, e) of the individual. Now assume again that any individual is considered to have access to a set E of possible values of e. This triggers an opportunity set

$$\{(x(y,e), y, e) \mid e \in E\},$$

where y is fixed and e takes all values in E.

Make the additional assumption that any given e implies a specific ordering R_e of the pairs (x, y). This can, for instance, be derived from an achievement function $u(x, y, e)$, but such a function is more than what is needed for the specification of such an ordering. For instance, e may simply be a preference characteristic, and for a given e the individual has a well-defined preference ordering over the life perspectives offered by pairs (x, y). With these elements in hand, we can once again define the compensation principle as requiring that individuals with identical e should have equally good (x, y) for R_e. This again corresponds to the correct calibration of social help (x) needed to compensate for disadvantageous circumstances (y).

This means that instead of requiring equality of the sets $\{(x(y,e), y, e) \mid e \in E\}$, what is sought in this approach is to equalize the sets $\{(I(y,e), e) \mid e \in E\}$, where $I(y, e)$ is an indifference set for R_e in the space of pairs (x, y). In other words, there is no need to offer exactly the same pairs (x, y) to individuals with identical e, but they should have equally good pairs as evaluated by R_e.

In conclusion, the first insight here is that one can structure capability sets in such a way as to make their equality a sensible objective, because accessibility of the various options, as well as their value, is explicitly described.

6.2.3 Shaping opportunity sets

The second insight is that fairness considerations can help evaluate the content of opportunity sets, for instance when one has to decide what combinations of leisure and consumption are suitable. This is sometimes called the "reward problem," and it pops up as soon as one sees that the compensation principle can be fully satisfied in many different ways. For instance, in the $\{(u(y,e),e) \mid e \in E\}$ setting, compensation is complete when u is equalized across all individuals, regardless of effort, but it can also be achieved by rewarding the individuals with high e and punishing those with low e. In other words, the compensation principle can only be part of the theory. The ideal of equalizing opportunities does not completely determine how they should be shaped.

Here again, the two branches of the economic literature have proposed different approaches. Following the philosophical literature, the Fleurbaey-Bossert approach has adopted the principle that individuals sharing the same circumstances (i.e., the same characteristics y) should be submitted to the same transfers. This idea has not only been advocated by resourcist theories such as Rawls's and Dworkin's, but also by proper theories of equality of opportunity such as Arneson's and Cohen's. This principle of equal transfer for equal circumstances, which motivates the explicit presence of resources in the corresponding framework, is based on the idea that differences in responsibility characteristics between individuals do not provide any reason for transfers. Redistribution is only assigned the role of compensating inequalities due to circumstances. This approach has been dubbed "liberal" in Fleurbaey (2008) because it involves a neutral noninterventionist attitude with respect to responsibility differences.

One then obtains a rather precise prescription about the shape of opportunity sets, because if transfers are insensitive to e, the opportunity sets take the form $\{(x(y),y,e) \mid e \in E\}$, for which the impact of e on achievements is the direct impact of e without any interference from transfers. For instance, if e is a preference characteristic, this means that individuals will have to make do with a fixed transfer that does not punish or reward their preferences.

What is interesting for CA specialists is that adopting a reward principle provides a way to evaluate arbitrary opportunity sets. For instance, taking account of the fact that the liberal ideal is to have x independent of e, and retaining the egalitarian inspiration of the CA, one can, when the resource transfer $x(y,e)$ is a scalar, focus on the worst possible situation $\min_e x(y,e)$ in order to evaluate the possibilities offered to an individual. What needs to be evaluated is then simply the pair $(\min_e x(y,e),y)$. This can be done, for instance, by picking a reference value for e, which can be denoted $\tilde{e}$, and then the pairs $\left(\min_e x\left(y,e\right),y\right)$ can be ranked by $R_{\tilde{e}}$.

In a typical economic model, maximizing the worst $\left(\min_e x\left(y,e\right),y\right)$ for $R_{\tilde{e}}$ will generally imply, in the first-best context (i.e., with no incentive constraints due to imperfect information about individual y characteristics), adopting a policy $x(y)$ and making $\left(x\left(y\right),y\right)$ equal across all individuals for $R_{\tilde{e}}$. This allocation is known as "conditional equality," this label coming from the fact that it guarantees everyone an equally valuable pair $\left(x,y\right)$ provided that the person adopts $e=\tilde{e}$. The consequences of any deviation from $\tilde{e}$ are fully borne by the individuals. For instance, if $R_{\tilde{e}}$ corresponds to nonfasting preferences, conditional equality makes sure that everyone achieve good nutrition (compensating differential needs y by suitable transfers $x(y)$) with such preferences, and does not care if people have fasting preferences that induce them to have a lower nutritional achievement.

It is, of course, also possible to combine different values of $\tilde{e}$ either with some averaging method, or by the intersection approach (which generally yields a partial ordering).

The Roemer approach proposes another conception of reward, which is based on the simple idea that inequalities in individual achievement within types (i.e., between individuals with the same circumstances) do not matter, so that only the sum of achievement levels needs to be examined for every type. This provides a very simple methodology of set evaluation when the particular statistical measure of effort proposed by Roemer is adopted. The value of $\left\{\left(u\left(y,e\right),e\right) \mid e\in E\right\}$ for an individual is then equal to the average achievement over the possible values of e that are accessible to this individual, which, when effort is measured as suggested by Roemer, coincides with the average achievement in the individual's type. Given this summing form of evaluation, one can call this approach to reward "utilitarian." Of course, it is not straight utilitarian, because it combines utilitarianism within types with egalitarianism across types.

It is interesting that Roemer's approach provides a justification for a specific form of the "number-crunching" cardinality valuation method that Sen (2002) discusses with little sympathy. Indeed, consider the case in which the set $\left\{\left(u\left(y,e\right),e\right) \mid e\in E\right\}$ is delineated by the graph, in e space, of the function $u(y,e)$. Assume that $u(y,e)$ takes nonnegative values, and that one can consider that it is always possible for an individual to achieve any nonnegative value below $u(y,e)$—this is a sort of free disposal assumption. The average value of $u(y,e)$ over possible values of e is then equal to the surface below the graph of the function $u(y,e)$, and therefore to the cardinality measure of the opportunity set for the case of a continuum of values.

This observation is also valid when e itself takes a finite number of values (cardinality then corresponds to the sum of segment lengths).

In other words, when a suitable structuration of capability sets is adopted, not only does it make sense to seek equality of sets, but evaluating sets by their cardinality can also be defended as a viable (but certainly not the only) methodology.

6.2.4 Equality against set valuation

It is, however, noteworthy that this equality-of-opportunity literature has not insisted on the possible use of its outputs for the evaluation of opportunity sets. This perhaps contributes to explaining why the connection with the CA literature has not been made, as the CA scholars have been used to thinking in terms of capability sets to be evaluated and compared across individuals. If anything, the economic literature on equality of opportunity has warned against such a set-valuation approach. There are two deep problems with proceeding in terms of set valuations. One is that it is hard to reconcile set valuation with a respect for individual values and preferences. This will be developed in the next subsection and the next section.

The other problem is that this approach clashes with the compensation principle. The literature first identified a clash between liberal reward and compensation (see Fleurbaey 1994; Bossert 1995; and subsequent literature), then identified a similar clash for the utilitarian approach to reward (Fleurbaey 2008). More recently, Fleurbaey and Peragine (2010) argue that underlying such problems there is a deeper tension between an ex ante evaluation of opportunities and an ex post approach.

The clash between liberal reward and compensation relies on the simple observation that if one forces $x(y, e)$ not to depend on e, it becomes hard or even impossible to reduce inequalities between individuals having the same e but different y, for *all* values of e. For instance, if R_e evaluates pairs (x, y) by the function xy, equality between individuals sharing this same e requires $x(y) = k/y$ for some constant k. But if for another e', $R_{e'}$ evaluates pairs (x, y) by the function $x + y$, equality between individuals sharing this same e requires $x(y) = k' - y$ for some constant k'. To obtain equality within the e subgroup and the e' subgroup simultaneously, one would need the function $x(.)$ to depend on e as well, which goes against the liberal reward principle.

The clash between utilitarian reward and compensation involves the observation that reducing the gap between the average outcome levels of two different types may be obtained by increasing inequalities between individuals having the same effort. This is illustrated in figure 6.1. The

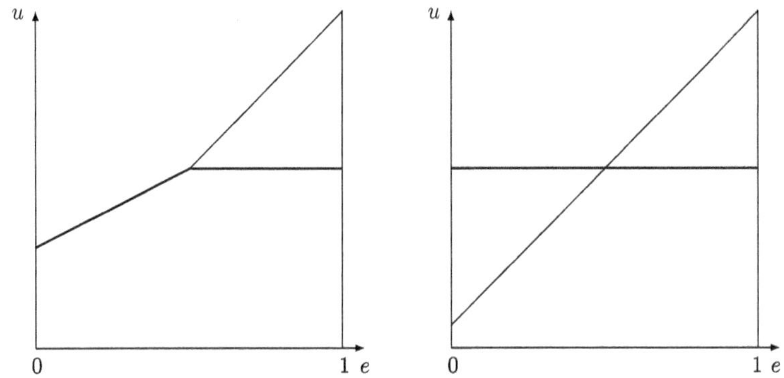

Figure 6.1
Equalizing sets versus equalizing set values

right-hand panel displays a situation that is equal in terms of average u for two types, but the left-hand panel is preferable in view of the compensation principle because it has less inequalities across individuals with same e.

This figure can also be described in the simple language of set comparisons. The right-hand panel displays sets of equal surface, that is, of equal value if set valuation is made in terms of surface, but the two sets are less dissimilar in the left-hand panel. Equalizing the value of sets may contradict the goal of giving identical sets to all individuals.

But the problem is even more serious than suggested by this picture. Consider the following example, inspired by Fleurbaey and Peragine (2010). Achievement is determined by the function

$$u = x + ye,$$

where x, y, e are scalars and x denotes a resource transfer, while y denotes a circumstance variable. For instance, one may think of y as a market wage rate and of e as a quantity of labor—the achievement variable u is then posttransfer income. To simplify the discussion, let e only take the values 0, .5, and 1.

Suppose there are four types in the population, induced by four values of y: 10, 12, 30, 32. In the status quo, the transfers are uniform within each type and are equal to +10, +12, 0, +2, respectively.

Compare the first two types. The $y = 10$ type faces the opportunities

$$u = 10 + 10e,$$

whereas the $y = 12$ type faces the opportunities

$$u = 12 + 12e.$$

In all terms, and no matter how one thinks of reward and set valuation, the latter is advantaged (greater transfer, better circumstances). One way to reduce the gap is to transfer one unit from the $e = 1$ individuals of the second type to the $e = 0$ individuals of the first type. The opportunities are then described for the two types as

$$u = \begin{cases} 11 & \text{if } e = 0 \quad (\text{with } x = 11) \\ 15 & \text{if } e = .5 \quad (\text{with } x = 10) \\ 20 & \text{if } e = 1 \quad (\text{with } x = 10) \end{cases}$$

$$u = \begin{cases} 12 & \text{if } e = 0 \quad (\text{with } x = 12) \\ 18 & \text{if } e = .5 \quad (\text{with } x = 12) \\ 23 & \text{if } e = 1 \quad (\text{with } x = 11). \end{cases}$$

No matter how one evaluates sets, this is a reduction in the inequality of opportunities.

Similarly, for the third and fourth types, one can reduce the gap between

$$u = 30e \quad \text{and} \quad u = 2 + 32e,$$

by transferring one unit from the $e = 0$ individuals of the last type to the $e = 1$ individuals of the other type. One then obtains the following situation:

$$u = \begin{cases} 0 & \text{if } e = 0 \quad (\text{with } x = 0) \\ 15 & \text{if } e = .5 \quad (\text{with } x = 0) \\ 31 & \text{if } e = 1 \quad (\text{with } x = 1) \end{cases}$$

$$u = \begin{cases} 1 & \text{if } e = 0 \quad (\text{with } x = 1) \\ 18 & \text{if } e = .5 \quad (\text{with } x = 2) \\ 34 & \text{if } e = 1 \quad (\text{with } x = 2). \end{cases}$$

Let us now conclude. The two transfers introduced reduce the inequality between the opportunities of types, no matter how one evaluates opportunities. But consider the distribution of outcomes for the $e = 0$ individuals. It was initially $(0, 2, 10, 12)$ and it is now $(0, 1, 11, 12)$. This is a clear increase in inequalities. Similarly, for the $e = 1$ individuals one records a change from $(20, 24, 30, 34)$ to $(20, 23, 31, 34)$, again an increase in inequalities. From the standpoint of the compensation principle, the situation has unambiguously worsened.

In other words, reducing the gap between types that incur cumulative inequalities in transfers and circumstances, which is a clear form of compensation operated over opportunities, may produce an increase in inequalities between individuals who have exerted the same effort, and therefore go against the compensation principle itself.

This difficulty can also be described as a conflict between an ex ante and an ex post perspective on compensation. Imagine a dynamic story in which individuals are first offered opportunity sets and only later choose e and end up in final situations. Before they choose e, one can look at their opportunity sets and declare that an individual who enjoys better circumstances and the guarantee of greater resources than another individual is clearly advantaged. Ex ante compensation would organize transfers between individuals unequally advantaged in this way. In contrast, ex post compensation looks at individuals after they have chosen their effort. It compares the achievements of individuals having exerted the same effort and seeks to reduce inequalities between them. Ex post compensation only compares individuals within the same "tranche" of effort (a tranche is a subgroup of individuals sharing the same e, in a terminology introduced by Peragine 2004). The conflict between the ex ante and the ex post perspectives comes from the fact that an individual who is ex post advantaged compared to a second individual may be ex ante disadvantaged compared to a third individual, and so on, generating a cycle.

The difference between the example presented in figure 6.1 and the last numerical example is important. In the former example, one could see a clash between equalizing the value of sets and making the sets identical. In the latter, the ex ante form of compensation is a move toward identical sets, not just toward sets of equal value. What this example shows is that trying to make sets identical may sometimes make them more dissimilar. There is an internal tension between various ways of making sets identical.

The economic literature on equality of opportunity has explored how to give priority to ex post compensation when there is a clash with reward principles or with ex ante compensation. One way to do this consists in defining social welfare not in terms of a distribution of sets, but by looking at the intersection of all the individual opportunity sets. When opportunity sets are defined in terms of pairs (u, e), trying to make this intersection as large as possible, as evaluated according to the suitable reward principle, gives priority to the worst-off individuals in every tranche, which is well in line with the compensation principle. For instance, Roemer's approach computes the surface of this intersection of sets (or equivalently, the average achievement of the worst off from all tranches).

Note that the intersection of opportunity sets may not correspond to the opportunity set of anyone in the population (such coincidence occurs only when there is a worst-off type that is dominated for all values of e).

The compensation principle requires going beyond a simple evaluation in terms of individual opportunity sets.

The liberal reward approach has another way to satisfy the compensation principle, which also departs from a simple set evaluation. It consists in looking at a hypothetical situation in which inequalities in y have been eliminated and all individuals have the same reference $\tilde{y}$. In such a situation the optimal allocation gives the same transfer to all individuals, regardless of their e. The current situation is equivalent to such a hypothetical situation for a certain hypothetical distribution of transfers $\tilde{x}(y,e)$:

$$(x(y,e),y,e)\, I_e \,(\tilde{x}(y,e),\tilde{y},e) \quad \text{for all } y, e.$$

Observe that in a given e tranche, the worst-off individuals (as evaluated by R_e) have the lowest $\tilde{x}(y,e)$ of the tranche. Maximizing the lowest $\tilde{x}(y,e)$ over the whole population therefore guarantees the satisfaction of the compensation principle.

In the hypothetical situation, the individual opportunity sets

$$\left\{\left(\min_e \tilde{x}(y,e),\tilde{y},e\right) \mid e \in E\right\}$$

are easy to compare when x is a scalar because all R_e agree on how to compare $\left(\min_e \tilde{x}(y,e),\tilde{y}\right)$ across different y. Namely, the worst set corresponds to $\left(\min_{y,e} \tilde{x}(y,e),\tilde{y}\right)$, which is congruent with the idea of applying the maximin criterion to $\tilde{x}(y,e)$. This approach shows that it may be reasonable to look at equivalent hypothetical opportunity sets, rather than actual opportunity sets, in order to evaluate a social situation and properly identify the worst off. This is another illustration of the usefulness of the equivalence approach introduced in subsection 4.3.1.

The lesson from these observations is that one should be cautious before embarking on interpersonal (or intertype) comparisons in terms of opportunity sets. Even if one accepts the ideal of equalizing opportunity sets, there is an important difference between equalizing sets and equalizing the value of sets. Moreover, even if sets are structured in a way that makes their full equalization meaningful, problems and dilemmas in the search for such equality are hard to avoid.

6.2.5 Why capabilities?

But one may also question the evaluation of individual advantage in terms of opportunity sets and therefore object to the ideal of equalizing opportunity sets. There has been a wave of criticism against the theories of justice defined as equality of opportunity (see in particular Anderson 1999; Arneson 1998; 2000; Fleurbaey 1995; Wolff 1998). The most vivid criticism is perhaps that focusing on opportunity sets may be harsh on the low achievers, especially when risk is involved and one wants to let individuals bear the consequences of bad luck when they could have ensured against the risk. Another important criticism is that an exclusive concern with opportunities may fail to cater to what people really want, when there is a trade-off between enhancing opportunities and improving achievements.

Although the CA is just one branch of a broader class of equal-opportunity approaches, it may be interesting here to focus on what the CA literature says about the adoption of a capability metric rather than a functioning metric.

What one reads in this literature seems, quite interestingly, insufficient to justify its exclusive focus on capabilities. Consider first the key example used by Sen to illustrate why capabilities are relevant. Fasting is different from starving, because it involves a possibility of greater nutritional achievement that is absent from a starvation situation. This example shows that opportunities are relevant, but it does not show that opportunities are the only thing that matters. In order to show that the capability metric is the good one, one does not need an example with equal functionings and different capabilities such as fasting versus starving, but an example with equal capabilities and different functionings.

As a matter of fact, one does not need just one example, but a general rule that all such examples should be treated in the same way. For instance, it is not sufficient to say that there is no inequality concern between the fasting bourgeois and the epicurean bourgeois (who have, supposedly, equal capabilities but different functionings). One must also say that there is no inequality concern between the starving surfer who could work and the hardworking employee, between the school dropout who could have studied and the devoted student, between the drug addict who could have avoided dependence and his healthy brother, between the unemployed person who failed to accept a job and the worker who took it. Or, to take an example from Sen himself (2009, chap. 11), between the sick individual who failed to obtain health insurance and cannot afford his treatment and the individual who did not fail to obtain insurance.

Another intriguing argument that one repeatedly finds in Sen's writings is that there is no informational loss in focusing on capabilities rather than achievements, if one is concerned about the latter. As the capability set contains the functioning vector that is actually enjoyed by the individual, the argument goes, it is always possible to take account of achievements when one looks at capabilities. "Even if we are ultimately concerned only with achievements, not with freedoms (except instrumentally as means to the achievement), the capability set can in fact still be used for evaluation. The capability set gives us more information than we need, but the chosen combination is a part of the capability set" (1992, p. 51). This argument seems to involve a basic logical mistake. Knowing the set from which the individual chooses is insufficient to know what the individuals actually chooses. If one is concerned about individual achievements (exclusively or inter alia), one should not accept being given information about capabilities only.

Sen's line of reasoning is actually more complex and must be examined in detail here, because it connects to issues discussed in the next section. The reasoning refers to the most basic form of evaluation of capability sets, called "elementary evaluation" by Sen, which consists in evaluating a set by computing the value of the best element of the set for the valuation ordering that is used to rank functioning vectors. Note that elementary evaluation corresponds to the case in which no intrinsic importance is attached to the possibility of choosing from a set, because the value of a set does not increase when options of equal or lesser value than the best element are added to the set. Now, if the individual chooses from the capability set by maximizing the valuation ordering under consideration, the value of the best element in the set coincides with the value of the element that is actually chosen. Therefore, focusing on sets and using elementary evaluation is equivalent to focusing on the chosen functionings and ignoring opportunities. The conclusion of the argument is then that set evaluation is more general and encompasses the special case of achievement evaluation.

This reasoning shows that there is indeed one case in which set evaluation is equivalent to achievement evaluation. It is this case that Sen uses to prove that set evaluation is more general, or informationally more inclusive, than achievement evaluation. But this reasoning is not successful because the assumption that the individual always picks the best element for the valuation ordering that the analyst uses is quite restrictive. It involves assuming that the individual's immediate preferences coincide with her valuation ordering (an assumption that Sen expressly rejects when discussing desire satisfaction as a metric of well-being) and that the analyst's valuation ordering coincides with the individual's valuation ordering, which requires the analyst adopt multiple valuation orderings when individuals disagree on values (an option that is also rejected by Sen, as explained in the next section).

Therefore, not only would it be incorrect to say abruptly that capability sets contain information about achieved functionings, but it is also appears insufficient to refer to the special case of elementary evaluation in order to support this conclusion.

Another instance of this difficulty appears when Sen argues that it would be equally good to consider "refined functionings" rather than capabilities. The refined functioning vector is defined as the standard functioning vector to which one adds additional components describing the extent of freedom that the individual enjoyed and the amount of choosing that she practiced. Obviously, there is much more information in refined functionings than in the capability set. It is very tempting to think that refined functionings are, actually, more in line with the arguments offered by the CA literature in favor of taking account of freedom and choice than capabilities are.

In conclusion, the CA appears as keen to proclaim that capabilities provide the appropriate metric for the evaluation of advantage as it is reluctant to classify achievements as irrelevant. It seems impossible to find any clear statement in the CA literature that the capability metric induces neglecting what individuals actually achieve. There is a tension, perhaps even a contradiction, in this literature between its explicit focus on capabilities as the relevant metric and its claim to include achievements in the evaluation.

For the critics of justice as equality of opportunity, this inconsistency in the CA should be welcome. The CA is more attractive if it is not really an opportunity approach, and if it makes it possible to look at what happens to low achievers, as well as at how much value individuals attribute to freedom and choice in their life. Renaming the approach the "human flourishing" approach would perhaps better capture what it is really after.

6.3 THE VALUATION ISSUE

In this section we examine how the CA seeks to respect the population's values and preferences. The CA literature insists that capabilities and functionings must be evaluated not in a mechanistic ("number-crunching") way, but by referring to what people value or "have reason to value." This is very important in order to deflect basic objections.

One such objection is that many functionings and capabilities are trivial and cannot count as much as basic necessities. Another objection is that adding more options to an opportunity set is not always a good thing, as it may complicate the task of choosing, or even create a danger of foolish choice. The CA answers that indeed it is important to use weights and some selection in order to track what really enhances people's lives.

It then becomes essential to determine where the value system should come from. The concerned population is one potential source, but other sources include philosophers, cultural and literary references, or religious texts or authorities. There is a well-known difference between Nussbaum and Sen in this respect. The former, who focuses on basic capabilities, seeks a substantial degree of universality for the list of relevant dimensions, even if some flexibility is allowed to cater to cultural variation in the exercise of various capabilities. The latter, who is interested in a more general form of social evaluation, makes more room for variations across countries and perhaps social groups or smaller communities.

Generally speaking, however, the CA appears to endorse the principle that once a valuation system is chosen (which may be partial and allow for some incommensurability), all individuals in the relevant constituency should have their situation evaluated with the same weighting system. The extreme example, which may not be fully representative of the CA ideal, is the HDI, which uses the same weighting system for all countries of the world to combine data about income, education, and health. This is in stark contrast with the classical principle, in welfare economics, of respecting preferences at the individual level.

The purpose of this section is to examine whether this issue marks a doctrinal difference between the CA and the liberal tradition in welfare economics, or whether one could adjust the CA to make room for variations at the individual level in the valuation system.

6.3.1 The intersection approach

It is helpful to start this exploration by looking at the "intersection approach," which is a central element in Sen's analysis of the valuation problem. This approach has already been discussed in subsections 4.2.2 and 4.3.5. It makes use of individual valuation orderings and considers that the intersection of these orderings provides robust interpersonal comparisons. Let $z_i \in Z$ denote the situation (which can include functionings and capabilities) of individual $i \in N$, and R_i denote her valuation ordering over Z. The intersection approach, applied to the set of orderings of the population, defines the intersection ordering $R^{\cap}$ as follows: $z_i R^{\cap} z_j$ if and only if $z_i R_k z_j$ for all $k \in N$.

Let us mention in passing that what have been called preferences in the previous chapters can be considered to be essentially the same as what Sen calls valuation orderings. When the assessment of personal well-being and social welfare relies on individual preferences, one has to decide whether these are ordinary preferences (the preferences underlying ordinary choices) or deeper, ideal preferences that individuals would have under suitable conditions of information and deliberation. What Sen calls valuation orderings is closer to the latter. It makes good sense to rely on deep, authentic preferences rather than immediate desires, even if this complicates the informational requirements of the approach, as it is much harder to elicit authentic preferences than the immediate preferences that govern observed choices.

The intersection ordering never disagrees with an individual's personal evaluation of his own situation in the sense that $z_i R^\cap z_i'$ always implies that $z_i R_i z_i'$. But, as explained in subsection 4.3.5, the intersection ordering is nevertheless incompatible with respecting individual personal evaluations (the nonpaternalism principle), because there is generally no ordering that coincides with each R_i on personal situations and extends $R^\cap$ on interpersonal comparisons. This problem occurs even if the personal valuation relations and the interpersonal relation are allowed to be incomplete. It does not come from a requirement of completeness.

As already suggested in 4.3.5, the origin of this difficulty is that the intersection approach uses personal rankings on $z_i \in Z$ to construct an interpersonal ordering over situations (z_i, R_i) and neglects that z_i is just one element of advantage, the other being the "fit" between z_i and R_i. It is instructive to see that if one extends the intersection approach to the pairs (z_i, R_i), the problem vanishes.

This extension can be made as follows. The pair (z_i, R_i) is said to doubly dominate the pair (z_j, R_j) if:

i) z_i intersection dominates z_j: $z_i R^\cap z_j$, and either

ii-a) at z_i, the lower contour set of R_i contains the lower contour set of R_j

$$\{z \in Z \mid z_i R_i z\} \supseteq \{z \in Z \mid z_i R_j z\},$$

or

ii-b) at z_j, the upper contour set of R_j contains the upper contour set of R_i:

$$\{z \in Z \mid z R_j z_j\} \supseteq \{z \in Z \mid z R_i z_j\}.$$

Part (ii) of this definition captures the fit between z and R. In (ii-a), the fit of z_i with either preferences is examined, whereas in (ii-b) the fit with z_j is at stake. Figure 6.2 illustrates a configuration of double dominance in which (ii-a) but not (ii-b) is satisfied.

Note that these conditions compare different preferences at the same z. There is a better fit at z with R than with R' when the lower contour set of the former is larger (in terms of set inclusion) or if the upper contour set of the latter is larger. This seems the most natural way to compare,

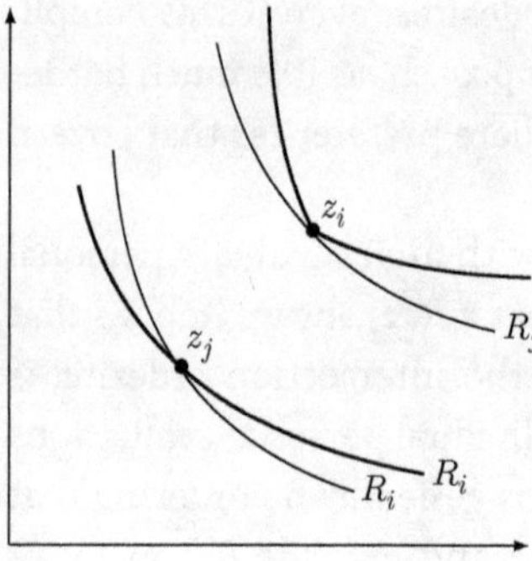

Figure 6.2
Double dominance

for two preference relations, the fit between preferences and the object of preferences.

But one could think of a direct comparison of fit across z as well, saying that z_i better fits R_i than z_j fits R_j when

$$\{z \in Z \mid z_i R_i z\} \supseteq \{z \in Z \mid z_j R_j z\}$$
$$\text{or } \{z \in Z \mid z R_j z_j\} \supseteq \{z \in Z \mid z R_i z_i\}.$$

For standard economic preferences, the two lines in this definition are equivalent.

It is straightforward to check that when (z_i, R_i) doubly dominates the pair (z_j, R_j), necessarily z_i better fits R_i than z_j fits R_j. Indeed, assume for instance that (ii-a) is satisfied, as in figure 6.2. Take any z such that $z_j R_j z$. Necessarily, $z_i R_j z$ because $z_i R^{\cap} z_j$ implies $z_i R_j z_j$. By (ii-a), $z_i R_j z$ implies $z_i R_i z$. This means that we have shown

$$\{z \in Z \mid z_i R_i z\} \supseteq \{z \in Z \mid z_j R_j z\}.$$

Similarly, with (ii-b) one would derive the other inclusion.

What is most important for this discussion is that there exist orderings that coincide with each R_i on personal situations and that are compatible with the relation induced by double dominance. All the orderings from the equivalence approach (including equivalent income) provide examples. Therefore, the double dominance principle seems to better capture the original idea of the intersection principle when the objective is to construct an index of well-being that takes account of the fit between personal orderings and personal situations.

6.3.2 Disagreement and respect for diversity

Understanding interpersonal comparisons as bearing on pairs (z, R) rather than on vectors z is key to our analysis of the valuation problem in the CA. The consequence is that the interpersonal ordering that ranks pairs (z, R) is not the same thing as the individual valuation relations that rank z for personal purposes. It has different objects and derives from different considerations.

Individual valuation orderings reflect personal goals in life. In this context, an evaluation of personal advantage can make room for a diversity of values and preferences. Some people may have a strong preference for living close to nature, while others may put a high value on social interactions or value work highly, or certain cultural achievements, or certain hobbies.

Sen is right to use the word "value" to mark the contrast with pure whimsical tastes, in the context of the evaluation of life functionings and capabilities. Although some particular goals in life may have no deep meaning, there is no serious life plan that does not involve important values about what makes life worthy and meaningful.

However, it does not appear problematic if different individuals endorse different values, or put different weights on the same values. Making different life plans does not always involve serious moral conflicts. Even in cases that carry potential conflicts (such as when different views on what makes a family come into opposition), it still makes sense to seek to accommodate the diverse views in a peaceful society. Individuals may despise or abhor the lifestyle of some of their fellow citizens without being willing to interfere directly. They may even accept that respecting a diversity of views on the good life is an important aspect of a good society.

By focusing on capabilities rather than achievements, the CA is generally interpreted as allowing for such a diversity of life plans. Being given equal capabilities, individuals can make use of them (or not) in many different ways.

In contrast, the interpersonal ordering on (z, R) involves ethical principles that cannot be left to vary within the ordering itself. For instance, if the principle of respecting individual preferences is adopted, the following condition (similar to the nonpaternalism principle from 4.3.5 and the same-preference principle introduced in 5.2.4) will be applied:

Respect principle: (z, R) is at least as well off as $\left(z', R\right)$ if and only if zRz'.

This condition is not a matter of personal values of the concerned population; it is an ethical choice of the evaluator who constructs the interpersonal ordering. It would be inconsistent to apply it to some individuals and not to others.

Of course, disagreements about the ethical principles underlying the interpersonal ordering will generate a diversity of orderings. For instance, some orderings will seek to respect individual preferences, while others will impose the same weights uniformly on the population. But a disagreement about interpersonal comparisons means that, ultimately, either one is chosen or some compromise in policy in areas of disagreement will be introduced. For instance, if there is a disagreement about who the worst off are in the population, social policy may end up helping all the social groups that are deemed worse off for at least one relevant interpersonal ordering. Another possibility is to apply the intersection ordering to interpersonal orderings (as opposed to personal orderings R) and decide that those who are really worst off are those who are identified as such by all relevant orderings.

There are many possibilities. But none of them involves applying to every individual the interpersonal ordering that this individual would favor if she were to take the role of the evaluator and construct such an ordering. This would be meaningless, because an interpersonal ordering is meant to apply to different individuals. Two individuals who disagree on the interpersonal ordering could not be compared consistently if one wanted to apply one individual's ordering when this individual is involved and the other's ordering when the other individual is involved. As both are involved in the comparison between them, an inconsistency arises when they disagree about who is better off.

The problem with Sen's analysis of the valuation issue is that he ignores the difference between personal orderings over z and interpersonal orderings over (z, R), because the fit between z and R is not part of his theory. As the interpersonal ordering is, in his approach, an ordering R that applies directly to z, Sen applies the argument of the previous paragraph to this ordering:

> If different people's valuations do differ, then we have a *disagreement* as to what the appropriate valuations are. We may try to argue out which valuation is correct; or take only the intersection partial order as non-controversial; or even possibly take the view that there is nothing "right" or "wrong" about these valuations (I personally won't, but some people clearly would). But there is, in none of these cases, the possibility of using one valuation function for one person, another for the second, and then make *inter-valuation-functional* comparisons of the relative well-beings of the two persons. (1985, pp. 57–58)

This argument, applied to R that compares $z \in Z$, rather than to the interpersonal ordering that compares pairs (z, R), cannot easily be made compatible with the liberal view that people may adopt different values in life and pursue them jointly and peacefully along their own track. This argument seems to be the source of the standard view in the CA that the weights for different functionings and capabilities have to be decided collectively by the concerned population rather than adjusted to every individual or subgroup of the population. In this approach, there may be a diversity across communities, but not within the population that will be submitted to inequality evaluation. In case of irreducible disagreement (e.g., between those who like the countryside and those who like the city), a partial order based on the intersection approach is the only recommendation.

This approach raises an intriguing issue. If different communities can choose different valuations for their own purposes, there will be a problem when comparisons of living standards or advantage have to be made across communities. For instance, if the HDI is applied to make intercountry comparisons, it may be quite inconsistent with the evaluations of inequalities that are made within every country.

But this kind of difficulty is avoided if one makes the distinction between personal orderings over z and interpersonal orderings over (z, R). Diversity of the former is compatible with full consistency for the latter. Take, for instance, the equivalent income index. It can consistently be compared across individuals, but it also coincides with every individual's ordering R over the personal dimensions of life.

In summary, understanding that interpersonal comparisons consist in constructing an ordering on (z, R), not z, makes it possible and meaningful to respect the diversity of preferences R over z, and also makes it possible to define the intersection principle in a way (the double dominance principle) that does not clash with such respect.

6.3.3 Implications of respect for personal preferences

Respecting individual relations R over z, in the elaboration of an interpersonal ordering over (z, R), has two interesting implications. In this subsection we assume that each R is an ordering, for the sake of simplicity.

First, contrary to what might appear at first glance, it does not leave interpersonal comparisons completely undetermined. Consider again the respect principle introduced in the previous subsection. This principle is naturally applied to the comparison of two different lives for a given individual. But it is just as compelling for the comparison of two individuals who share the same ordering R, an idea captured by the same-preference principle introduced in the previous chapter.

What this principle leaves blank is the comparison of situations involving different preferences. Fleurbaey and Tadenuma (2012) propose the following monotonicity principle:

Monotonicity principle: (z, R) is at least as well off as (z, R') if $\{q \in Z \mid qRz\} \subseteq \{q \in Z \mid qR'z\}$.

This principle says that a change in R induces an improvement if the upper contour set at the contemplated z shrinks, reflecting the fact that z moves up, unambiguously, in the ranking of elements of Z. (This idea already inspired the analysis of fit between z and R in subsection 6.3.1.)

This principle can also be defended as embodying the ideal of respecting preferences. When the situation z unambiguously moves up in the valuation ordering, how could we declare this to reflect a worsening of the situation and to mean that the individual is worse off as a consequence?

Combining the respect principle and the monotonicity principle does not yield a precise interpersonal ordering, but it does imply that the interpersonal ordering must be compatible with double dominance. Even more than that, whenever

$$\{q \in Z \mid qRz\} \subseteq \{q \in Z \mid qR'z'\}$$

(which means that z better fits R than z' fits R'), necessarily (z, R) is at least as well off as (z', R').

This implication holds true in any framework such that when

$$\{q \in Z \mid qRz\} \subseteq \{q \in Z \mid qR'z'\},$$

there is z'' such that

$$\{q \in Z \mid qRz\} \subseteq \{q \in Z \mid qRz''\} \subseteq \{q \in Z \mid qR'z''\} \subseteq \{q \in Z \mid qR'z'\}.$$

Indeed, by the respect principle, (z, R) is at least as well off as (z'', R), and (z'', R') is at least as well off as (z', R'), while by the monotonicity principle, (z'', R) is at least as well off as (z'', R'). This is illustrated in figure 6.3.

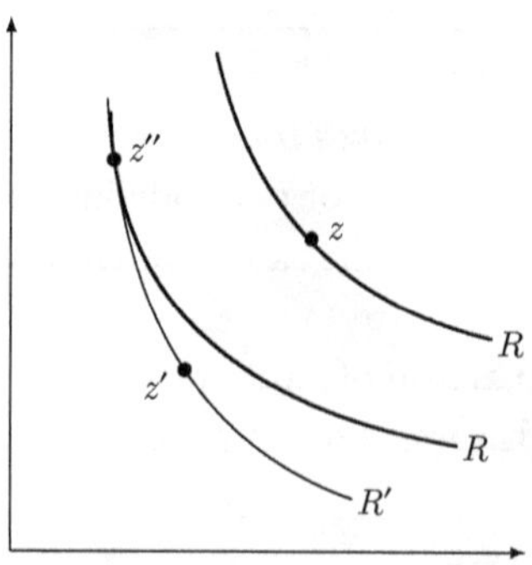

Figure 6.3
Respect and monotonicity principles and fit

These implications also hold true with standard continuous and monotonic preferences over $\mathbb{R}^{\ell}_{+}$. In this framework the domain condition introduced in the previous paragraph is not satisfied (think of asymptotic indifference curves for z and z' in $\mathbb{R}^2_+$). But what happens is that when the existence of a z'' as described in the previous paragraph is not satisfied, necessarily

$$\{q \in Z \mid qRz\} \cap \{q \in Z \mid z'R'q\} = \varnothing,$$

which means that the indifference curves do not cross and therefore there is R'' that shares the two indifference curves, that is, such that

$$\{q \in Z \mid qR''z\} = \{q \in Z \mid qRz\}$$

and

$$\{q \in Z \mid qR''z'\} = \{q \in Z \mid qRz'\}.$$

In this case, (z, R) and (z', R') are respectively as well off as (z, R'') and (z', R'') by the monotonicity principle. And (z, R'') is better off than (z', R'') by the respect principle.

We propose the respect principle and the monotonicity principle as the two basic principles that any reasonable interpersonal ordering should satisfy. An intuitive way to remember both of them that summarizes the previous paragraphs is that whenever an indifference curve is everywhere above another indifference curve, it corresponds to a better situation.

In order to obtain a more specific interpersonal ordering, one needs additional principles, such as the principles identifying objective situations that are equally good for all preferences (this sort of principle justifies the equivalence approach, as explained in subsection 4.3.5). This is a field in which more research is needed in order to map out the various possibilities and axiomatic justifications. In appendix A the respect principle and the monotonicity principle are combined with the requirement that an individual who becomes indifferent to a dimension of y, other things equal, is not deemed worse off as a consequence, and this implies using the personalized minimum equivalent income introduced in subsection 4.3.5.

The second implication of respecting individual orderings R over z is that this may solve the problem of deciding whether one should focus on capabilities or on functionings. Recall that an important criticism of equality-of-opportunity theories is that, in certain trade-offs, opportunities may be less important than achievements in the eyes of the concerned individuals. Also recall that the concept of refined functionings enables us to describe individual situations in a way that includes a description of the possibilities that were offered and of the choice process. Once a methodology that respects individual preferences is available, it can be applied, at the individual level, to decide how much importance to attribute to freedom and choice in the assessment of well-being and advantage.

Theories of justice in terms of equal opportunities would object to this proposal, arguing that focusing on opportunities rather than achievements is not a matter of personal taste (or even value) but a matter of fairness. Their view is that individuals should assume responsibility for seizing opportunities, and that others cannot be requested to pick up the tab for the low achievers. This is a reasonable conception of social justice, but it is not palatable to all scholars in the field. It encourages social interactions of an inimical sort ("Don't count on me to help you, you'd better pick yourself off the ground").

In this context, it is interesting to see that in general Sen insists on freedom rather than responsibility as the primitive value that justifies looking at opportunities rather than achievements. Fleurbaey (2008, chap. 10) argues that one can forget responsibility as a primitive value and the moralizing attitudes that go with it, and focus on freedom and respect for individual goals in life. This still implies substantial individual responsibilities, in a derivative way, because the diverse goals of people are then implemented in their own lives and induce important differences in achievements. But along this route, opportunities are considered only insofar as they matter to the concerned individuals. The opportunities-versus-achievement issue then becomes, indeed, a matter of personal values and preferences.

6.4 IS THE CA A SEPARATE APPROACH?

The main message of the CA is that one should avoid narrow evaluations of individual well-being, in particular resourcist measures and welfarist measures. Resources are at best an indication of some possibilities in the domain of consumption, and fail to capture important functionings. Subjective well-being is either a small part of the relevant functionings (mental states) or, in the case of satisfaction judgments, an unreliable proxy of well-being for interpersonal comparisons because of the adaptation phenomenon.

Beyond this critical message, what the CA has proposed consists primarily in a list of basic capabilities (Nussbaum's list) and in Sen's intersection principle about how to aggregate discordant valuations in the concerned population. Many empirical applications have used various strategies to fill in the gaps, but one cannot say that a particular methodology has become sufficiently prominent to be representative of the CA, except perhaps the practice of using deliberation in communities in order to make the selection of the relevant functionings and capabilities. One cannot even say that the CA recommends looking at capabilities and ignoring achievements in functionings completely.

In this chapter, however, we have found that there is an explicit opposition, in Sen's work, to letting the measure of well-being vary at the individual level. This is linked to the idea that interpersonal judgments cannot mix different valuation orderings. This creates a strong contrast with the tradition of welfare economics, which seeks to respect individual preferences in all their diversity.

The CA is here at a crossroads. If it sticks to the principle that only one valuation system for functionings can consistently be used in interpersonal comparisons of functioning achievements and capabilities, then it faces the problem of avoiding the drawbacks of perfectionism and paternalism. Various elements of the CA make sense in this perspective, as they can be read as strategies to alleviate such drawbacks. The intersection approach takes account of the diversity of people's valuations by emitting a clear judgment only when everyone agrees. Focusing on capabilities rather than functionings offers people the freedom to choose in their own opportunity set according to their own values, even if their situation is assessed with other values. Encouraging deliberative procedures for the selection of dimensions and the choice of weights may also induce convergence of values in the community, make the imposition of a single weighting system look more democratic, and make the intersection approach less incomplete.

The other route is to accept that the consistency requirement for interpersonal comparisons applies only to the interpersonal ordering on pairs (x, R), and that a single ordering on such pairs can accommodate the respect principle, that is, adjust the evaluation of each individual's situation to this particular individual's values and goals in life. There is nothing in the basic principles of the CA that seems to preclude taking this alternative route. This is, however, a route that goes back to classical principles of welfare economics. The equivalent-income approach can then be proposed as a possible methodology for the application of the CA, making it possible to cast the net on any list of dimensions of life that matter to people (including freedom and choices processes) and synthesize it into a well-being index that respect individuals as the primary source of valuation of their own situation.

We have argued here that the latter route exerts a strong appeal. The main reason is not just that the other route fails to respect individual values fully, in their diversity, but also that it misses an important element of well-being, namely, the fit between personal values and personal situation. By omitting this aspect of well-being, the CA can be criticized as too narrow, like the resourcist and welfarist approaches. Well-being is not just a matter of functionings and capabilities, but also a matter of how the functionings and capabilities correspond to what the individual seeks in her life.

In conclusion, it is possible for the CA to remain more objective than the happiness approach and the equivalent-income approach and adopt weights for the different dimensions of functionings and capabilities that are not adjusted to individual valuation orderings. If it sticks to this line, it is truly a separate approach, and will follow its own way along the other two. It can produce measures like the HDI.

If, on the contrary, it decides to incorporate the fit between personal values and personal situation in its assessment of individual advantage, then it may consider the other approaches as potential implementation tools. The happiness approach is unlikely to help much, however, because the criticisms raised by Sen against subjective welfarism remain as strong as ever. In contrast, the equivalent-income approach, which, unlike the happiness measures, satisfies the respect principle and the monotonicity principle, seems compatible with the basic ideas of the CA and may be proposed as a way to implement it.

CONCLUSION

How to Converge on a Multiplicity

WHY SYNTHETIC INDICATORS?

Let us try to wrap up the main lessons from our exploration of alternatives to GDP. Several routes have been explored, from which we returned with a mix of positive and less positive messages. It is time to formulate them in a simple and consistent fashion, to suggest further explorations or to help pave the way for more operational roads. Yet, first of all, it is useful to insist again a little on the motives for such an exploration. Challenging GDP is not a goal in itself. One must be as explicit as one can on reasons for doing so and on the kind of requirements that alternatives to GDP should comply with.

The ultimate purpose is to have at hand reliable information that tells whether a society is currently on a path of socioeconomic development, or whether it is instead on a regressive track. In both cases, one also wants to know at what speed progress or regression occurs. This must be done in a way that allows cross-country comparisons: do some countries progress faster than others, how far behind are the laggards, are gaps narrowing, or do they increase? Also, for those countries whose paths look positively oriented, can one expect this good orientation to last, or are there clues that this is no more than a temporary window, with future generations threatened with again descending the ladder of socioeconomic development?

There was only moderate hope of answering these questions with just a small collection of numbers, and very little hope of doing so with *a* unique magical number able to capture the quintessence of all the factors that are at stake, as GDP has been too often believed to do. The reason is that these factors are complex and highly multidimensional, with strong individual variability.

Statisticians are surely not the last ones to be aware of this. Heterogeneity is a common characteristic of all the raw statistical material they have to cope with, and describing this heterogeneity is part of their core activity. Neither do they adhere by nature to the one-dimensional view of development said to be conveyed by GDP. As a matter of fact, it is seldom the case that a statistician feels statisfied with single-valued characterizations of any given object.

Let us consider unemployment figures as an example. Global unemployment rates are one thing and there are guidelines that allow measuring them in a way that is roughly comparable across countries. But they are just one dimension of the phenomenon, and it is common statistical practice to quantify other dimensions: the share of *long-term unemployment*—because it is not the same to have many persons experiencing short spells of unemployment or a few people durably caught in unemployment; the number of *underemployed* people—those working only a few hours per week but who would like to work more if they could; *discouraged workers*—those formally not considered as unemployed because they have completely abandoned efforts to seek employment, but who would still prefer being at work rather than inactive. All these concepts can then be produced at more or less disaggregated levels, by socioeconomic groups or geographical areas.

The situation is comparable for national accounts. They do not reduce to the production of GDP. National accounts are self-described as a "system," that is, a very large set of consistent monetary statistics on many aspects of economic activity: production, savings, final and intermediate consumptions, wealth, and so on. The fact that GDP has progressively become the yardstick for the comparison of national performances should not hide the set of all these associated or underlying statistics.

So, if multiplicity is the common lot statisticians are used to deal with, why not just be satisfied with the abundance of data provided by statistical organizations? What precludes stopping there is that there is an inescapable need for relatively global assessments, whatever the implied losses of information. Details are a necessity when one seeks expertise on a specific domain, but systematically forcing users of statistics to deal with overabundant tables of numbers cannot be a solution. We also need bird's-eye views, hence a permanent back-and-forth movement between detailed statistics and aggregate summaries. There is a time for synthesizing information, and a time for having it unfolded. The question of this book was about the synthesis phase, with a clear consciousness of its limits: it is known that what is complex is not operational, but also that what is synthetic is wrong. But when one tries to be synthetic, one's duty is to be as little wrong or misleading as possible. It is with this aim in mind that our successive explorations have proceeded.

What are the messages, then?

First message: trying to be synthetic does not mean that one absolutely needs to be *one-dimensional*. Limits of our human minds are not such that one cannot consider more than one figure at the same time when one compares countries or periods of time. When some dimensions are strictly irreducible to each other, there is no reason to force oneself to boil them down to only one. From chapter 2, one can retain that there is at least one domain where this principle of nonaggregation should be firmly respected. This domain is the assessment of sustainability. If one is concerned both with the present and with the future—and the present generation has a moral duty to be so vis-à-vis future generations—it clearly misses the point to build indicators collapsing the two dimensions into one. There is admittedly some tradition of building and using aggregate measures of intertemporal well-being that proceed in such a way, mainly for theoretical uses or for addressing specific policy issues. But useful theoretical concepts do not always translate into interesting statistical indicators that meet social demand. Claiming such intertemporal aggregations to be *the* answer to the sustainability question would be as incongruous as having a meteorologist satisfied with providing only *averages* of temperatures observed today and expected for the next days. It is not the average of present and future conditions that one wants to know, it is the comparison between the two that matters. We definitely need to distinguish the situations of a country A that lives particularly well, but is burning up its assets in a way implying that this happy state of affairs will not last for long, and a country B that seems to benefit a little less from its various consumption possibilities, but that, in doing so, gives to future cohorts the possibility of keeping the living standards of their parents. Both countries can exhibit the same level of discounted intertemporal well-being—at least for some value of the discount factor—but underlying time profiles are completely different. Characterizing these profiles requires at least two numbers, not one. Such a point seems to go without saying and was clearly incorporated in the seminal Nordhaus-Tobin endeavor quoted at length throughout this volume. Yet it has been often forgotten by large segments of the "alternatives to GDP" industry that has followed this initial attempt. Having it recalled was not superfluous.

From there, our problem splits up into two subproblems. Once one admits the principle of separate measures applied to the present and the future, how should one proceed in both cases, and here again the question of aggregation is at the forefront: how, and how far, can aggregation proceed at the two levels?

Let us start with the measurement of *current* well-being. At this level too, one option is to reject any idea of a scalar approach and rather opt for an intermediate level of aggregation, that is, the choice of a small set of numbers as representative as possible of the main dimensions of development. Two branches of social choice theory seem to come in support of such a position. The first one is the famous Arrow result according to which, under allegedly mild conditions, it is impossible to provide a social ordering over a set of heterogenous items that respects the whole set of individual preferences. The second is Sen's approach that argues in favor of assessing well-being (or advantage) in terms of capabilities, which avoids imposing constraining norms about the way such potentialities should be translated into effective achivements by individuals.

Yet the aspiration for much more synthetic views remains strong. What to do and what not to do if one wants to meet it? These have been the main questions asked throughout this book.

SHORTCUTS AND PITFALLS

Chapter 1 warned about the limits of a purely statistical way of performing such an aggregation, the route of composite indicators. Widespread availability of socioeconomic series of any kind makes that route tempting and relatively easy and, for this reason, somewhat congested. Two objections are raised against this approach. First, the weighting of the components of the indicator involves a lot of arbitrariness. This remark applies not only to composite indexes aiming at challenging GDP but to the whole industry of composite indicators that currently proliferate for cross-country benchmarkings of all types. This is perhaps a temporary situation, but up to now, no serious proposal has been made to articulate a theory of the weights. Individual preferences cannot be relied upon because they do not bear on such objects (who could express a personal preference over unemployment versus inflation?), and therefore there is no hope of making the population vote or express preferences in a meaningful way about the construction of such indicators. One could think instead of looking at the choices actually made in a country, but the implicit preferences revealed by societies in their recent history are unlikely to carry any normative value. This is why, currently, the art of building such indicators still evokes the culinary metaphor of adding up apples and oranges.

The second problem with the composite approach is that it fails to track what happens at the individual level. Adding up domain indicators misses the important phenomenon that disadvantages (low income, bad health, low status, isolation, low-quality environment, etc.) are generally accumulated by the most deprived subgroups of the population. Obviously, data limitations make it difficult to know the joint distribution of all aspects of life at the most detailed level. Nevertheless, the methodology should rely on a theory that captures individual situations first before aggregating in order to produce a summary indicator. Only when going to the data may one think of how best to approximate the theory. In contrast, the composite approach is generally[1] conceived in such a way that it first aggregates by domain before adding up the domain contributions, and this seems a radical shortcoming.

What about the other route, consisting in just asking people how they value the lives they are having? Of all those we have explored, this route could be the most direct. The problem is that it is not certain that this approach delivers what it promises. It has exerted a strong fascination on the economic profession over the last decade, but scepticism is also widespread. There is no objection against collecting and analyzing subjective data. What is problematic is their direct use for the assessment of global well-being, because it is unclear what these data really reveal about how our world goes. The main reason for doubt is illustrated by the well-known Easterlin paradox, that is, the apparent long-run stability of these subjective data despite many improvements of living conditions that are far from being exclusively material.

Admittedly, the Easterlin result is not as robust as initially believed. Especially in cross-section, one cannot say that all forms of subjective well-being are independent of income beyond a certain level. For long-run trends the jury is still out. But the adaptation phenomenon is sufficiently well documented that it is clear that the levels of subjective well-being (not just hedonic scores but also satisfaction judgments) do not reliably reflect the evaluative comparisons of situations made by the population itself. When calibration scales shift with the situations to be compared, the variations of raw indicators are no longer meaningful, and they fail to reflect the population's views. If one had long-run data on subjective well-being, the raw indicators would probably suggest that past efforts by our parents to improve our living conditions have been, by and large, a waste of time and energy. Still more embarassing, they would suggest that efforts to maintain these living conditions for our descendants are not such a priority: whatever the deteriorated conditions that we shall leave to them, they will ultimately adapt without any major change in their perceived level of satisfaction.

More precisely, we have seen that subjective well-being indicators are vulnerable to two problems. First, they do not reflect people's values

1. The recent form of the HDI can be viewed as an exception.

and preferences when they mix heterogeneous calibration strategies with expressions of preferences. They may thus run against the common evaluations made by people sharing the same values and preferences, for example, considering that these people are equally well off while these people themselves all rank their situations in a consensual, strict order. Second, they are unlikely to provide ethically sound comparisons of the situations of individuals with different goals in life. Theories of fairness, in various forms, suggest that objective conditions of life are important for such comparisons, and subjective indicators cannot be expected to be consistent with any single theory of fairness.

Given the prevailing consensus in our society, as well as in theories of fairness, on the importance of living standards, we seek approaches that give a positive value to the notion of progress and a negative value to the idea of regression, and raw subjective indicators appear too unreliable. Understanding the mental processes that govern these subjective assessments is undoubtedly a fascinating issue, one that chapter 5 has discussed at length, but we do not come back from this exploration with the feeling that a new statistical paradigm is at hand with this new material. This does not close the door to using information of this kind, quite the contrary: they represent important sources of useful data. But they do not offer the radical shortcut that would make all the other routes unnecessary to explore.

VICES AND VIRTUES OF MONETARY INDICATORS

In view of all these skeptical messages, the defense of standard GDP might appear to recover some of its strength. If the difficulty is to add up consumptions of apples and oranges without a priori knowing the relative tastes that people have for both, the reference to market values may seem to be a good idea: a high price for oranges will reveal a strong preference by people in their favor, and adding up *values* of apples and oranges is a natural way to take these relative valuations into account.

Yet the message of chapter 3 was that this brings us much less far than expected on the road to measuring something akin to social well-being. Some of the reasons for this are familiar and were certainly known to the reader before opening this book: the fact that this method is silent on arguments of well-being for which no exchanges take place and for which no prices are observed, and the fact, that, being a simple sum of incomes, it is completely silent about the way resources are shared in the population. But there is more than that. Even when these problems do not arise, it appears that GDP is a much poorer indicator of well-being than one could have expected. It is at best *changes* in GDP that inform us whether well-being increases or decreases, only under particular conditions, and without any indication of how large these increases or decreases are. A fortiori, comparisons of GDP at distant dates or across different populations with different tastes cannot be considered informative about variations in social welfare. All this does not tell us that GDP is an indicator to be thrown away: it remains a relevant measure of what it has been coined for, that is, global economic activity. But it is only by mental laziness that the idea that it could *also* measure well-being has slowly crept in.

Yet these arguments are often identified with the idea that it is the monetary valuation of components of well-being that is intrinsically flawed. Such a conclusion is not correct, and chapter 4 intended to show that there exist ways to put values on things that escape most of the criticisms that apply to GDP. Monetary valuation does not have to be rejected per se. As a matter of fact, whatever one does, aggregation implies putting relative values upon very different items, and doing so in monetary units is no less respectable than the apparently dimensionless valuations implicit in composite indexes. And the main message of chapter 4 has been that the toolbox of economists precisely offers instruments that permit monetary evaluations in much more satisfactory ways than the simple sum of individual incomes performed by GDP, allowing treatment of preference heterogeneity and nonmarketed goods. The key element is the notion of equivalent incomes, that is, incomes leading to the same utility level as the one currently attained but for given reference values of nonmarket aspects—health, leisure, social interactions, environment, and so on. This concept provides an indirect way to assess who is more or less advantaged in a society—and this is what one ultimately needs—without requiring more than the choice of a reference bundle for the nontraded goods and some knowledge of how people are ready to trade these goods against monetary income, that is, only some information on elasticities of substitution of the kind we measure when we assess willingness-to-pay for various nonmarket goods.

Let us explain again the idea as simply as possible. Imagine that country A is an Eden whose inhabitants benefit from a lot of natural amenities. Imagine that country B faces much harsher conditions and that its inhabitants compensate for this by engaging in intense market activities, whence large monetary incomes. GDP statistics tell that inhabitants of country B are better off that those of country A. If one rather opts for subjective indicators, it may be that inhabitants of country A will express more satisfaction about their lives than those of country B, but this is unfortunately unwarranted: it may be that people are so much used to their good or bad living conditions that they ultimately express the same feelings about how pleasant their lives are.

A composite indicator combining GDP with an index of these natural amenities can eventually provide a more adequate message, but its does so in a normative way with a priori assumptions about how monetary incomes and natural amenities can substitute for each other, and it assumes that this substitutability assumption applies in the same terms to both populations.

The equivalent income approach works differently. Let us assume that the natural conditions of country A are taken as the reference. Then the approach consists in asking how much of their monetary income inhabitants of country B would be ready to abandon to benefit from the natural amenities of country A. The resulting corrected income now allows comparisons between the two countries, and it does so in a way that can take into account differences in tastes. If inhabitants of country B indeed love their way of life, they will not express so much willingness-to-pay for moving to the milder climate of country A. The resulting correction, in that case, will not strongly modify the initial message delivered by monetary incomes.

If one chooses to venture on this track, Arrow's impossibility is still in ambush, but much less dangerously than generally believed. Computing individual equivalent incomes depends upon the choice of a common (or preference-specific) reference basket for nonmarketed items, which indeed violates one of Arrow's axioms. But the axiom this violates is the most disputable of the three well-known requisites of Arrow's theorem: Weak Pareto, Nondictatorship, and Independence of irrelevant alternatives. The first two do not suffer discussion if individual preferences are worthy of equal respect.

In contrast, the third requirement excessively restricts the amount of information considered relevant for designing social orderings. As it goes, this third postulate says that two states x and x' must be ranked without any reference to how people judge any other state x''. This assumption is indeed violated when one introduces the notion of a reference bundle common to all individuals. But this transgression is relatively mild and could even be welcome. As demonstrated in chapter 4, it simply amounts to saying that willingness-to-pay or elasticities of substitution also matter. Such an idea has traditionally been considered reasonable in welfare economics. More intriguing is the fact that the Independance axiom has been accepted for so long and so easily by a large part of Arrow's posterity.

Of course, getting rid of this postulate does not mean that all difficulties vanish. Principles have to be adopted for the choice of appropriate reference parameters-appendix A makes a proposal—and properly measuring willingness-to-pay is a difficult empirical task, but developing efforts in such a direction is certainly far better than stalling in the present status quo. Empirical attempts have already been made and further efforts are under way.

A MULTIPLICITY OF SYNTHETIC INDICATORS

This is, however, the time to explain the title of this conclusion. Advocating a single alternative indicator is not our goal. In the debate opposing dashboards and synthetic indicators, we want to avoid the extreme view that a single synthetic alternative to GDP should be sought, as much as the opposite view that no synthetic indicator should be investigated. Our view is that a multiplicity of synthetic indicators must be considered because there are several reasonable philosophical approaches that are able to propose aggregation methodologies and that cannot converge to a single indicator.

We believe that the equivalent income (and, more generally, the equivalence approach developed by the theory of fair allocation) provides an attractive way of incorporating people's values and preferences in the evaluation of their own situations, but we do not ultimately advocate that it should be the only methodology for aggregation. Moreover, the equivalence approach is a general methodology that can deliver many indices depending on how the reference parameters are chosen, and we have noted that different ethical views may justify different choices of reference parameters.

More important, there are at least two other substantially different views, examined in this book, that deserve to be part of the public debate about the assessment of social progress. Happiness indicators and capability indicators should still be produced because they embody respectable views about human flourishing.

We have sought to debunk the pretention of these alternative approaches to respect people's values and preferences. We believe that they are inherently paternalist or perfectionist. But this is not a sufficient reason to exclude these approaches from the public forum, because their arguments must be listened to. Happiness indicators track mental states that are not the sole concern of the population, but the various forms of hedonist philosophies argue that they should be the sole concern, and that the currently prevailing interest in material achievements is morally wrong. One may disagree with this view but not reject it from the public debate.

Similarly, in their current form, capability studies cannot be presented as respecting the diversity of values and preferences in the population, but they can be defended as embodying values that can emerge in a form of democratic consensus about the good life. For instance, education may be given a large weight in the assessment of a population's state, even if some members of that population care little about intellectual achievements. This can be based on the view that education is important for a good life in some form of perfectionist ideal. Truly enough, we have argued in chapter 6 that some branches of the capability approach could easily adopt the equivalence approach and evolve toward a more liberal (i.e., respectful of individual values in their diversity) assessment of individual situations. But this is unlikely to eradicate the perfectionist approach, which is based on a very old and venerable philosophical tradition.

The idea of respecting people's values and preferences is, at any rate, complex. Every individual has several layers of values and preferences, from the most immediate to the deepest, from the most conventional to the most authentic. Happiness advocates sometimes argue that immediate preferences cannot be trusted and that experienced utility is more relevant. Orthodox economists typically favor immediate preferences because they do not want to interfere with individual choices that are governed by immediate preferences. But their libertarianism is challenged by behavioral studies showing that immediate preferences are malleable and inconsistent. Why not conclude that when the goal is to respect people's values and preferences, it is most natural to ask them what layer they themselves consider to be the most respectable? Presumably, their answer will not point to immediate preferences but instead to some deeper and more authentic layer. The discussion of possible improvements to subjective well-being questionnaires in chapter 5 has been inspired by the hope that, with suitable time and preparation, statements of satisfaction and preference could touch the level of what really matters to the respondents.

SUSTAINABILITY WARNINGS

Let us finally come back to the sustainability issue. The question has been examined in chapter 2 and not discussed again in the following chapters. As stated in the general introduction to the volume and restated in the opening of this general conclusion, this should not at all be understood as a form of minimization of the issue, quite the contrary. The point is rather that this issue is so large that it would deserve another volume. Here, our objective has been more modest. It has been to stress the specific difficulties of the problem and to show in what sense it differs from measuring current well-being—in a somewhat less formal way than in the other chapters, leaving more in-depth examinations for future work.

What are the messages on this aspect of the debate about GDP? Once we have admitted that the sustainability question is about quantifying whether tomorrow will be worse or better than today, what is the right way to proceed? One point on which agreement must be easy to reach is the idea that well-being tomorrow depends upon resources that the present generation leaves to future generations for arranging their own lives. Some link can incidentally be made with the capability approach. It is not a *level* of well-being or *functionings* that the present generation can or must transmit to future generations, but rather an opportunity set that they will use to build their own living conditions, and that they will then pass on to their own descendants, restructured, expanded, or contracted depending upon the way they will have managed it.

All this provides the basis for the so-called "capital-based" approach to sustainability. At this point, the same kind of semantic problem may arise as with the "monetary" approach to current well-being, as the same mercantile connotation affects the two expressions. Yet the core of the problem is not here. The main question is neither the wording nor the choice of such and such aggregation metric, it is once again to know how and how far such an aggregation is possible.

The problem is often presented as a debate between advocates of "weak" and "strong" sustainability, the former arguing that what matters is only the global amount of these assets, without any minimum requirements concerning some of them, the latter arguing, on the contrary, the necessity of preserving separate sufficient levels of some of them, due to limited substitution possibilities across all these assets, most particularly between natural and human-made assets: building new machines or investing in scientific discoveries cannot indefinitely compensate for losses in biodiversity, a deteriorating climate, depleted fossil resources, and so on.

To some extent, this debate between weak and strong sustainability is exaggerated. If some resources become really crucial for the maintenance of living conditions, it is always possible to imagine strongly increasing price signals for these assets, making "weak" sustainability indicators completely dominated by negative trends in these assets. The difficulty is rather that, in this field, it is definitely not on markets' price signals that one can count, except maybe in the very last moments before full economic and environmental collapse, when it is too late to react. Correct and sufficiently forward-looking shadow price signals are required, meaning that imputation much more than observation is needed, and it is here that the problem reveals its true nature and its true difficulty. There is no miracle, and it could have gone without saying: delivering messages about the future does not only involve observation, it requires prediction. Giving relative weights to assets that matter for sustainability means projections of how their relative scarcity will evolve and affect future well-being. This implies many more unknown parameters than when it was just *current* well-being that was at stake: physical or technical parameters that govern the dynamics of assets, preferences of future generations describing how they can benefit from these assets, and so forth. The necessity of such predictive exercises is beyond this discussion. The point is that it brings us far beyond the realm of standard statistical production within which the quest of "alternatives to GDP" remains generally confined.

Truly enough, making progress on a synthetic indicator of current well-being is helpful in the perspective of sustainability evaluation. Once an indicator of well-being is designed, one can indeed ask if future generations will have the means to maintain it at a certain level, which is a rather clearcut way of defining sustainability. In view of the uncertainty surrounding predictions of the future, however, a better formulation of the question is probabilistic: how likely is it, given the information now available, that future generations will have the means to maintain social welfare at a certain level? But here one sees two ways in which multidimensionality creeps in.

First, one should really ask the question for different levels of social welfare. Suppose that current welfare can be maintained with the same probability whether the current generation adopts policy x or policy x'. It might happen, however, that policy x is riskier and is such that the induced probability that future social welfare will be reduced by more than half is much greater with x than with x'. This can be seen only if the sustainability question is not only asked for the current level of welfare, but also for lower levels. In summary, what one would like to know is the distribution of probability of the various levels of welfare that can be sustained.

The second way in which multidimensionality is hard to avoid is that the sustainability question can, in practice if not in theory, be considered only for a given horizon. It is known almost for sure that the human species will disappear some day, even if it manages to leave the earth before it becomes inhospitable. It probably makes little sense to ask whether the current level of welfare can be maintained for the next billion years. Therefore one should consider asking the sustainability question for a list of different horizons. One may want to accept great risks of unsustainability for the very distant future, due to the high probability of natural disasters, but not for the next few generations that depend on more controllable conditions.

Finally, the practical difficulty of making probabilistic predictions about the evolution of the future technology and about the ability of future generations to derive social welfare from given conditions makes us wary of the capacity of theory to deliver applicable methodologies to address the sustainability questions. In the context of *current* welfare, it is known that dashboards remain useful because they help us see where efforts should be put in order to improve the situation as summarized by synthetic indicators. In the prediction of *future* welfare, it may be that we are not yet able to go beyond dashboards and early warning indicators by domain. Doubts about our ability to build an all-purpose scalar index of sustainability are too strong. What does not seem unreachable for the assessment of current well-being looks far more remote in the context of sustainability. This suggests concentrating efforts on a well-defined set of warning indicators covering separately the various dimensions of sustainability. Practically, one needs signals about which of the relevant instruments deserves current action. To this aim, a reasoned set of domain indicators might do a much better job than any currently feasible synthetic indicator.

In short, if we were to briefly sketch out our preferred solution for a "beyond GDP" or "GDP and beyond" program, a reasonable compromise between relevance and syncretism could be the following: (*a*) keep GDP for what it has been built for, that is, the measurement of economic activity; (*b*) try to have it completed with a short list of synthetic indicators of current well-being that reflect prevailing philosophical conceptions; (*c*) include in this list equivalent income indicators based on the best estimate of people's values and preferences about marketed and nonmarketed goods; and (*d*) accept the idea of having more than one number to tell whether the current state of affairs is likely to last or not, not forgetting that such indicators can only inform us about probabilities of things turning bad. The power of statistics stops here: all information about the future cannot be encapsulated in a small set of numbers. In the end, it is the purpose of such a set of indicators to avoid the realization of the risks that they are asked to reveal.

APPENDIX A

A Theory of the Reference for Equivalent Incomes

A.1 THE MODEL

We retain one of the main models used in this book. Individual i consumes market commodities $x_i \in \mathbb{R}^{\ell}_{+}$ available at price $p \in \mathbb{R}^{\ell}_{++}$, and enjoys nonmarket goods (or bads) $y_i \in Y$, where $Y \subset \mathbb{R}^m$. His preference ordering R_i (strict P_i, indifference I_i) on (x_i, y_i) is represented by a utility function $u_i(x_i, y_i)$ and an indirect utility function

$$v_i(p, y_i, m_i) = \max \left\{ u_i(x_i, y_i) \mid px_i \leq m_i \right\}.$$

The expenditure function for i is defined by

$$e_i \left(\tilde{p}, y_i, u_i \right) = \min \left\{ \tilde{p}x' \mid u_i(x', y_i) \geq u_i \right\}.$$

The direct equivalent income (or money-metric utility) is then

$$e_i \left(\tilde{p}, \tilde{y}, u_i(x_i, y_i) \right) = \min \left\{ \tilde{p}x' \mid u_i(x', \tilde{y}) \geq u_i(x_i, y_i) \right\},$$

and the indirect one is

$$e_i \left(\tilde{p}, \tilde{y}, v_i(p, y_i, m_i) \right) = \min \left\{ m \mid v_i(\tilde{p}, \tilde{y}, m) \geq v_i(p, y_i, m_i) \right\},$$

which is also the solution m_i^* to

$$v_i(\tilde{p}, \tilde{y}, m_i^*) = v_i(p, y_i, m_i).$$

Recall that the value of equivalent income only depends on ordinal properties of R_i and not on the choice of functions.

The problem is to choose $\tilde{p}, \tilde{y}$.

A.2 REFERENCE OPERATORS

In chapter 4 (subsection 4.3.5) we introduce a generalization of the equivalent income that involves multiple references and a weighted average of equivalent incomes computed with the different possible references. A further generalization should be considered.

Let Ξ be the set of admissible references $(\tilde{p}, \tilde{y})$. For a given individual i with given preferences R_i, and a given bundle (x_i, y_i), the equivalent income defines a mapping $m_i^* : \Xi \to \mathbb{R}_+$ by

$$m_i^* \left(\tilde{p}, \tilde{y}\right) = e_i \left(\tilde{p}, \tilde{y}, u_i(x_i, y_i)\right).$$

A reference operator is a functional $\xi : \mathbb{R}_+^{\Xi} \to \mathbb{R}_+$ that, for every mapping $m_i^* (.,.) \in \mathbb{R}_+^{\Xi}$, defines a level of equivalent income $\xi \left(m_i^*\right) \in \mathbb{R}_+$ that summarizes the various levels attained by m_i^* for different reference parameters. Two key properties are required of an operator, monotonicity and homogeneity.

Monotonicity: If $m_i^* \left(\tilde{p}, \tilde{y}\right) \geq m_i^{*\prime} \left(\tilde{p}, \tilde{y}\right)$ for all $\left(\tilde{p}, \tilde{y}\right)$, then $\xi \left(m_i^*\right) \geq \xi \left(m_i^{*\prime}\right)$; if $m_i^* \left(\tilde{p}, \tilde{y}\right) > m_i^{*\prime} \left(\tilde{p}, \tilde{y}\right)$ for all $\left(\tilde{p}, \tilde{y}\right)$, then $\xi \left(m_i^*\right) > \xi \left(m_i^{*\prime}\right)$.

Homogeneity: For all $\lambda \in \mathbb{R}_{++}$, $\xi \left(\lambda m_i^*\right) = \lambda \xi \left(m_i^*\right)$.

These two properties guarantee that the application of an operator to m_i^* produces an equivalent income that still reflects the preference ordering R_i and that is still commensurable with money. The latter is important for applications in inequality-averse social welfare functions. Note that the convex combination of two operators is still an operator.

Here are the main examples of operators we will focus on.

1. A single-reference operator picks a single value of $\left(\tilde{p}, \tilde{y}\right)$:

$$\xi \left(m_i^*\right) = m_i^* \left(\tilde{p}, \tilde{y}\right).$$

2. A weighted average operator relies on a measure f on Ξ and is defined as

$$\xi \left(m_i^*\right) = \int_{\Xi} m_i^* \left(\tilde{p}, \tilde{y}\right) df \left(\tilde{p}, \tilde{y}\right).$$

3. The min operator is defined as

$$\xi\left(m_i^*\right) = \min m_i^*\left(\Xi\right),$$

where $m_i^*\left(\Xi\right)$ is the range of m_i^* on the domain Ξ.

4. The transformed average operator is intermediate between the previous two, applying a concave transform ($\rho > 0$):

$$\xi\left(m_i^*\right) = \left(\int_{\Xi}\left(m_i^*\left(\tilde{p},\tilde{y}\right)\right)^{1-\rho} df\left(\tilde{p},\tilde{y}\right)\right)^{\frac{1}{1-\rho}}.$$

5. The max operator is defined as

$$\xi\left(m_i^*\right) = \max m_i^*\left(\Xi\right).$$

It is possible to combine these operators on different components of the vector $\left(\tilde{p},\tilde{y}\right)$. For instance, one may pick a single $\tilde{p}$ and a weighted average for $\tilde{y}$:

$$\xi\left(m_i^*\right) = \int_{\Upsilon} m_i^*\left(\tilde{p},\tilde{y}\right) df\left(\tilde{y}\right),$$

where Υ is the projection of Ξ on the set of nonmarket goods (Y)—this is actually equivalent to taking a standard weighted average operator, with a measure on Ξ that puts zero weight on other prices than $\tilde{p}$.

Another example would take a weighted average for $\tilde{p}$ and the min for $\tilde{y}$:

$$\xi\left(m_i^*\right) = \int_{\Gamma} \min_{Y} m_i^*\left(\tilde{p},Y\right) df\left(\tilde{p}\right),$$

where Γ is the projection of Ξ on the set of price vectors ($\mathbb{R}_{++}^{\ell}$), and $m_i^*\left(\tilde{p},\Upsilon\right)$ the range of $m_i^*\left(\tilde{p},.\right)$ on the domain Υ.

These various possible combinations allow us to study the choice of the reference separately for $\tilde{p}$ and for $\tilde{y}$.

A.3 NONMARKET GOODS

Let us start with nonmarket goods, for which the relevant considerations are intuitive. As explained in chapter 4, the special property of the reference is that individuals who enjoy the reference can be compared directly in terms of incomes, without asking about their preferences.

This property is appealing when the reference corresponds to a "normal" value to which everyone aspires. The main example for this is health (Fleurbaey 2005). Good health is not always an unambiguous notion (especially for individuals at different ages), but by and large it is well defined, and, more important, it is something that is considered a "normal" state. In this state, people are generally compared with respect to other aspects of life, and it would be strange to argue that of two healthy individuals, the one who is less worried about keeping a good health is pro tanto less well off than the one who cares more about health.

In such a case, picking the normal value as the single reference makes good sense. Then the equivalent income systematically measures the loss for those who do not reach the normal state. This is typically how one would like to reason with respect to health. Of two equally unhealthy individuals, the comparison is never framed in terms of how much each of them gains with respect to a worse health condition, but how much each of them loses with respect to good health.

This discussion can be summarized in the following principle: *When there is a "normal" value of y_k (for a dimension k) to which everyone aspires, this value should be taken as the reference.*

Unemployment is like sickness and provides another example in which everyone aspires to avoiding it, which suggests a natural reference.

The example of leisure is similar but not identical.[1] When work is considered a definite bad by all, it makes sense to take zero labor as the reference. Equivalent income is then suitably sensitive to the situation of those with a strong aversion to work.

But work is not always unpleasant, and many people derive many nonincome benefits from working. One could of course try to measure these benefits separately (social relations, status, self-accomplishment, sense of purpose), but this may be hard to do, and, even then, certain pleasant types of work would retain intrinsic attraction.

Applying the min operator, in this context, is particularly appealing. As shown in figure A.1, it is equivalent to computing the level of income that would suffice (in replacement of the current work-earnings situation) if working did not bring any earnings. This neatly separates the nonincome benefits due to working from the income benefits.

For those who are averse to work (e.g., because they only have access to unpleasant jobs), the value of zero labor remains the reference implied by the min operator, whereas for those who genuinely like working (e.g., the

1. Recall that leisure-labor is best dealt with among the nonmarket goods because it is not transferable between unequally skilled individuals.

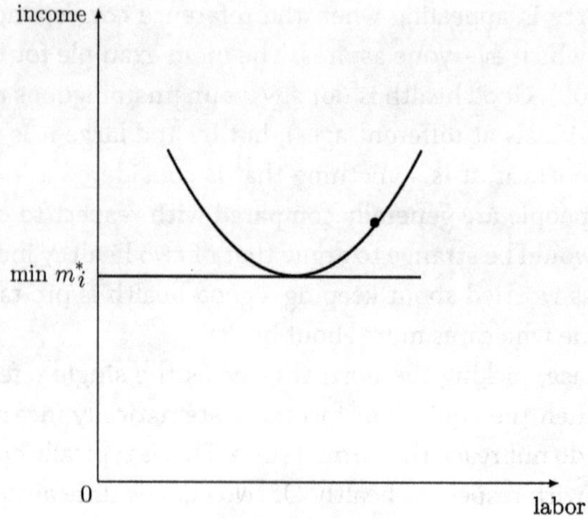

Figure A.1
The min operator is equivalent to a flat equivalent budget

iconic researcher), the implied reference is maximum labor time. For those who prefer an intermediate balance between work and leisure, the implicit reference is then the quantity of work they would perform for free—this is the configuration illustrated on figure A.1.

These considerations show that choosing the min operator is compatible with picking the "normal" value as the single reference and is an intuitive generalization of the previous principle: *When "normal" values of y_k differ across individuals, the min reference tracks this diversity by taking the person-specific normal value as the reference for each individual.*

Assuming that there is only one market commodity, the equivalent income computed with the min operator is the only measure of well-being that satisfies the following properties:

1. It is equal to income when the individual is indifferent to y_i.
2. Respect (subsection 6.3.2): It does not decrease when the individual moves to a bundle that is at least as good as the initial bundle.
3. Monotonicity (subsection 6.3.3): It does not decrease when the upper contour set at (x_i, y_i) shrinks.
4. It does not decrease when the individual becomes indifferent to y_i.

Condition 1 is a minor calibration condition, given that condition 2, combined with anonymity, already implies that when two individuals are indifferent to y, the one with a greater income is better off. Conditions 2–3 have been discussed at length in chapter 6. Condition 4 is the key property that induces a focus on the cost to individuals not enjoying their preferred y, rather than on the gain to individuals not enduring their most dispreferred y.

The proof of the characterization statement goes as follows. Take an arbitrary (m_i, y_i) (recall the assumption that there is only one market commodity, which is therefore identified with income). Consider the equivalent $(m_i^*, \tilde{y}_i)$, chosen so as to minimize m_i^*. By condition 2, the individual is equally well off with $(m_i^*, \tilde{y}_i)$. Suppose the individual becomes indifferent to y_i. By condition 4, he is at least as well off. But as this corresponds to an expansion of the upper contour set, the individual is at most as well off by condition 3. Therefore he is equally well off, and by condition 1 his well-being is then measured by m_i^*.

As argued in subsection 4.3.5, one may criticize the single-reference equivalent income for failing to be sensitive to certain improvements in the fit between preferences and the individual's situation. The min operator does not escape the criticism because it still focuses on a single reference, even if this reference varies across preferences.

Taking the average weighted operator would, however, go too far in the direction of granting a good index to individuals who are very sensitive to a nonmarket dimension. Consider figure A.2, where two indifference curves are depicted, one for an individual who cares little about health and the other for an individual who care a lot. Given that they are equally unhealthy

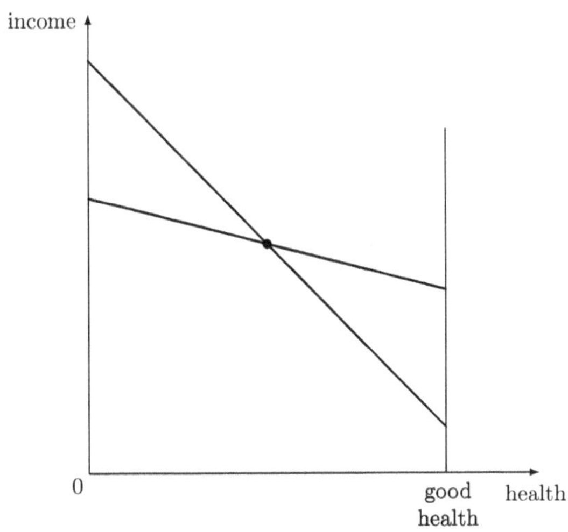

Figure A.2
The individual who cares more about health is worse off

(and have the same income), it seems necessary to conclude that the individual who cares more should be considered worse off. In contrast, a simple average over all possible values of reference health would declare them equally well off.

Therefore the best approach would probably be to take a transformed average operator with a strong focus on the lower values (i.e., a high parameter ρ). This produces maximum sensitivity to the shape of indifference curves while keeping a focus on the values of nonmarket goods to which people aspire.

It can be argued that the min operator is an imperfect (because it is less sensitive) but suitable approximation. It has the special practical advantage of making the choice of the reference $\tilde{y}$ completely endogenous to each individual's preferences and, therefore, avoids any (justified or unjustified) impression of arbitrariness.

It is standard in social evaluation to put a special focus on the most disadvantaged populations. Taking the min operator is just an extension of this idea, by adopting, for every individual, the worst possible evaluation of his or her situation. In this way one respects the individual's aspirations and one measures how frustrated they are.

In practice, one difficulty with the min operator is that preferences are estimated locally, whereas the lowest equivalent income may be obtained for a reference that is far away. The worst configuration is when some unbounded variable is estimated to have a positive effect on satisfaction. Then the min operator would suggest taking an infinite reference value for this variable, inducing unrealistically low (possibly negative) equivalent incomes. A pragmatic solution to this problem may consist in bounding the range of this variable for application of the min operator, so that only reasonable estimates of the preferences are relied upon in the computation of the equivalent income.

A.4 MARKET PRICES

The choice of a reference for market prices is less intuitive.[2] In particular, the min operator then depends significantly on the normalization of

2. Here one touches issues that are addressed in the literature on PPP indexes (Deaton 2010; Deaton and Heston 2010; Neary 2004). However, this literature seldom considers using equivalent incomes with heterogenous preferences. The typical view in the field is well summarized as follows: "In so far as data on real income have any meaning, it is that they provide an answer to the question: 'How well off would the same reference consumer be in different countries?' " (Neary 2004, p. 1425).

prices that is retained in the set Ξ. A different normalization changes the reference parameter $\tilde{p}$ for the min in a way that is harder to understand. Moreover, it is very easy to obtain very low values of equivalent incomes by taking extreme values for $\tilde{p}$. Finally, the axiomatic analysis of the previous section is not applicable to prices viewed as y parameters, because individuals with monotonic preferences in commodities cannot be indifferent to prices for a given nominal income.

We consider a setting in which different individuals may face different market prices. If we want to evaluate several different allocations for the same population, we consider the concatenated allocation in which every individual is represented by several clones, one for each allocation. If we want to make international comparisons, the allocation under consideration is the world allocation.

Interestingly, the max operator, not the min, already plays an important role in the economics of market commodities. In particular, the max operator appears in a social ordering studied by Fleurbaey and Maniquet (2011b). Consider a simple economy with only market commodities and bundles x_i, that is, without nonmarket dimensions y_i. Suppose that the prices are normalized by the total consumption X, that is, $\tilde{p}X = 1$. Pick any inequality-averse and Paretian social welfare function applied to equivalent incomes and apply the max operator to social welfare (rather than each individual's utility):

$$\max_{\tilde{p}:\,\tilde{p}X=1} W\left(e_1\left(\tilde{p}, u_1(x_1)\right), \ldots, e_n\left(\tilde{p}, u_n(x_n)\right)\right). \tag{A.1}$$

This expression induces an ordering over allocations, with the particular property that the reference price $\tilde{p}$ depends on the considered allocation. Fleurbaey and Maniquet show that maximizing this ordering over all allocations that distribute X implies that the best allocations are exactly the set of competitive equilibria from equal split (i.e., the competitive equilibria reached when the endowment X/n is given to every $i = 1, \ldots, n$).

The argument is simple. For all allocations such that $\sum_i x_i = X$ (where X is fixed), all p such that $pX = 1$,

$$\sum_i e_i\left(p, u_i(x_i)\right) = \sum_i \min\left\{px \mid xR_i x_i\right\} \leq 1.$$

For all allocations that are not competitive equilibria from equal split, and all vectors p, either $\sum_i \min\left\{px \mid xR_i x_i\right\} < 1$ (in case the allocation is inefficient or p is not a supporting price when the allocation is efficient), or $\sum_i \min\left\{px \mid xR_i x_i\right\} = 1$ and there is inequality in $\min\left\{px \mid xR_i x_i\right\}$ between agents (in case the allocation is efficient, p is the supporting price, but the budgets are not equal).

In both cases, for the inequality-averse W,

$$W\left(e_1\left(\tilde{p},u_1(x_1)\right),\ldots,e_n\left(\tilde{p},u_n(x_n)\right)\right) < W\left(1/n,\ldots,1/n\right).$$

Now, for any competitive equilibrium from equal split with price p^*, one has $e_i\left(p^*,u_i(x_i)\right) = 1/n$ for all i, so that

$$W\left(e_1\left(p^*,u_1(x_1)\right),\ldots,e_n\left(p^*,u_n(x_n)\right)\right) = W\left(1/n,\ldots,1/n\right).$$

Therefore, such an allocation is strictly preferred to all allocations that are not competitive equilibria from equal split.

This approach is, obviously, different from applying the max operator at the individual level. But applying the max operator individually, with the same normalization $\tilde{p}X = 1$, is also worth considering because it implies taking the ray utility function (defined in section 4.1) as the representation of individual well-being, with X as the reference bundle. This is shown as follows. For any $\tilde{p} \in \mathbb{R}^{\ell}_{++}$ supporting i's indifference curve at a bundle αX, one has $\tilde{p}\alpha X/\tilde{p}X = \alpha = u_X\left(x_i\right)$. For all vectors $\tilde{p}$ that support i's indifference curve at a bundle q that is not proportional to X, one has $\tilde{p}\alpha X \geq \tilde{p}q$ and therefore $\tilde{p}q/\tilde{p}X \leq \alpha$. This proves that $\max_{\tilde{p}:\,\tilde{p}X=1} e_i\left(\tilde{p},u_i(x_i)\right) = u_X\left(x_i\right)$.

Both observations single out the normalization $\tilde{p}X = 1$ as worthy of consideration. In terms of reference parameters for the computation of individual equivalent incomes, the first idea gives us a single-reference[3] $\tilde{p}$ and the other one the max operator.

These ideas have shortcomings, however. Nonmarket goods have disappeared and must be reintegrated in the analysis. The extension is easy to do for the ray utility,[4] but is harder for the competitive equilibrium approach.

In absence of y, there was a nice connection with the ideal of equality of endowments. In the presence of y, one would presumably want to

3. Presumably, for consistency, the social welfare function that serves in the computation of $\tilde{p}$ should also be the social welfare function that is later used in social evaluation.

4. One then measures well-being by the solution α^* to the equation

$$\left(\alpha^* X,\tilde{y}\right) I_i \left(x_i,y_i\right),$$

where $\tilde{y}$ is the suitable reference for i. Note that $\tilde{y}$ may be individual specific, e.g., if the min operator is used.

seek equality of $e_i\left(\tilde{p},\tilde{y},u_i(x_i,y_i)\right)$ across individuals[5] by a competitive distribution of X. But this means giving individuals unequal endowments in this equilibrium, and therefore it would not make sense to focus on the expression

$$\max_{\tilde{p}:\,\tilde{p}X=1} W\left(e_1\left(\tilde{p},y_1,u_1(x_1,y_1)\right),\ldots,e_n\left(\tilde{p},y_n,u_n(x_n,y_n)\right)\right) \tag{A.2}$$

for an inequality-averse W.[6]

Note that if, in (A.1), one dropped inequality aversion, the same results would be obtained except that egalitarian competitive allocations would not be the *only* best allocations for the induced social ordering. We will now propose some arguments in favor of considering the expression (A.2) with an inequality-neutral W (e.g., the sum).

Maximizing the sum $\sum_i e_i\left(\tilde{p},y_i,u_i(x_i,y_i)\right)$ with respect to $\tilde{p}$ under the constraint $\tilde{p}X=1$ implies solving the system of equations

$$\frac{\sum_i \partial e_i/\partial\tilde{p}_k}{X_k}=cst \quad \text{for all } k,$$

which by Shepard's lemma can also be written as

$$\frac{X_k^c}{X_k}=cst \quad \text{for all } k,$$

where X_k^c is the total compensated demand for good k at price $\tilde{p}$.

The reference price vector $\tilde{p}$ that emerges from this maximization is the supporting price of the bundle $X^c=\lambda X$ that belongs to the lower boundary of the Scitovsky set. See figure A.3 for an illustration. Let us call this reference price vector the Scitovsky reference price.

We propose three arguments in favor of this inequality-neutral approach. First, the best distribution of endowments, if one wants to equalize $e_i\left(\tilde{p},\tilde{y},u_i(x_i,y_i)\right)$ across individuals, depends on the distribution of y_i in a

5. Here, for simplicity, we ignore the lesson from the previous section that different individuals may have different $\tilde{y}$.

6. Alternatively, maximizing

$$\max_{\tilde{p}:\,\tilde{p}X=1} W\left(e_1\left(\tilde{p},\tilde{y},u_1(x_1,y_i)\right),\ldots,e_n\left(\tilde{p},\tilde{y},u_n(x_n,y_n)\right)\right)$$

over all feasible distributions of X produces an allocation that makes sense, but it does not produce an egalitarian competitive allocation in which all individuals enjoy the same budget at price $\tilde{p}$ (and the same $\tilde{y}$). It is then hard to argue that in the obtained allocation one should take $\tilde{p}$ as the reference rather than the prevailing equilibrium market price.

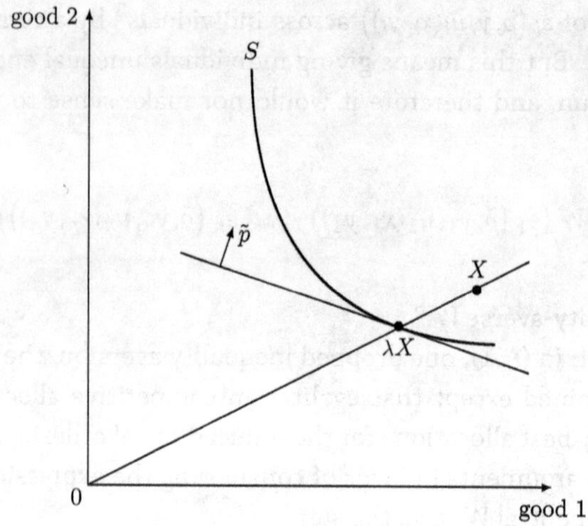

Figure A.3
Choosing a reference price vector

complex way. For the sake of picking a reference $\tilde{p}$, one can ignore this issue by focusing on the efficiency of the market allocation, so that the reference price will be compatible with *any* desirable distribution of endowments. Focusing on efficiency in the limited exercise of choosing $\tilde{p}$ reduces the amount of information needed to find this reference price, while keeping it possible to incorporate fairness considerations elsewhere in the analysis.

The second argument is that this approach seeks to minimize the distance between the reference $\tilde{p}$ and the actual market price vectors p that prevail in the allocations to be evaluated. Such distance can be evaluated in an economically meaningful way by seeking to maximize the ratio $\sum_i e_i\left(\tilde{p}, y_i, u_i(x_i, y_i)\right)/\tilde{p}X$ in the concatenated allocation (which gathers all allocations to be evaluated). For every i, the ratio $e_i\left(\tilde{p}, y_i, u_i(x_i, y_i)\right)/\tilde{p}x_i$ is less or equal to 1, with equality to 1 obtained when $\tilde{p}$ is (proportional to) the market price at which the bundle x_i has been bought. Similarly, the ratio $\sum_i e_i\left(\tilde{p}, y_i, u_i(x_i, y_i)\right)/\tilde{p}X$ is less or equal to 1, with equality when $\tilde{p}$ is proportional to the market price vectors at which the bundles x_i have been bought. Now, maximizing the ratio $\sum_i e_i\left(\tilde{p}, y_i, u_i(x_i, y_i)\right)/\tilde{p}X$ with respect to $\tilde{p}$, and normalizing the solution so as to have $\tilde{p}X = 1$, is the same as maximizing $\sum_i e_i\left(\tilde{p}, y_i, u_i(x_i, y_i)\right)$ with respect to $\tilde{p}$ under the constraint $\tilde{p}X = 1$. Therefore this implies choosing the Scitovsky reference price as well.

Another, axiomatic justification of this reference can also be provided. A nice property of the approaches discussed earlier in this section is that the reference prices depend only on the direction of X and on the upper contour sets of the individuals at the (concatenated) allocation under consideration.

But they fail to satisfy a property that seems very appealing in practice. When all individuals face price vectors that are proportional to each other, one would like to take a common reference $\tilde{p}$ that is also proportional to these price vectors. In this way, one can directly compare them in terms of their effective budget sets. To illustrate this point, imagine that $m_i = m_j$ but that the price vector faced by i on his own market is half the price vector for j: $p_i = p_j/2$. If one takes $\tilde{p} = \lambda p_i$ for an arbitrary positive λ, one obtains that $e_i\left(\tilde{p}, y_i, u_i(x_i, y_i)\right) = 2e_j\left(\tilde{p}, y_j, u_j(x_j, y_j)\right)$, thereby correctly depicting their unequal budget sets.

Now the Scitovsky reference price proposed here can be characterized as follows: It is (up to a scaling factor) the only reference price that depends only on the direction of X and on the upper contour sets at the allocation (property 1) and that is equal to p when p is the common market price vector faced by all individuals (property 2). Indeed, by property 1, one can move from the original allocation to another allocation in which total consumption is λX and the Scitovsky reference price is the common market price faced by all individuals, which remain on the same indifference curve. Property 1 applies because λX is proportional to X and the upper contour sets are not changed. By property 2, in this new allocation the reference price must be the common market price, which is the Scitovsky reference price.

Observe that the Scitovsky reference price satisfies not only property 2—a weak property chosen for lean axiomatics—but is indeed proportional to individual price vectors when these vectors are all proportional to one another.

In conclusion, price parameters cannot be dealt with like true nonmarket parameters y, the min operator being unapplicable in this case. The Scitovsky reference emerges as a simple solution, clearly motivated by the goal of having a reference situation that is as close as possible to the actual market situation faced by individuals.

A difficult practical problem raised in the PPP literature (in particular Deaton 2010) is the fact that different populations from distant regions may actually consume very different commodities, so that it is hard to estimate their preferences over the whole set of commodities available in the world. Many empirical studies deal with composite commodities (food, clothes, lodging, transportation, etc.) for which this problem apparently does not arise, except that it plagues the construction of the composite commodities. There is no simple solution to this problem if one wants to respect people's preferences over *commodities*, because such preferences are hard to estimate and may not even exist (when people have never tried commodities that are not available to them). A more promising idea might be to work in the space of universal human *functionings* rather than commodities. After all, individual preferences over commodities probably derive from preferences over such functionings.

A.5 THE HOUSEHOLD PROBLEM

In the literature on equivalence scales (see, e.g., Lewbel 1997), it is common to take the single person as the reference household. The traditional approach to equivalence scales assumes the unitary model of the household, in which household utility depends on income and size. It appears preferable to compute the equivalent income at the individual level, as suggested by Browning, Chiappori, and Lewbel (2006), who refer to "indifference scales" in this case.

Following the same idea, Fleurbaey and Gaulier (2009) note the following fact. If individuals are identical in the household, and if household expenditures maximize their identical utility and are always equally split between private expenditures and local public goods, the OECD equivalence scale that divides total income by the square root of household size coincides with the equivalent income that any member of the household would need, as a single, to reach the same satisfaction from consumption.

This is due to the fact that constant expenditure shares reveal an underlying preference represented by a Cobb-Douglas function $\sqrt{xg}$, where x denotes private consumption and g public consumption. As the n members of the household are identical, each of them consumes $\left(x/n, g\right)$, meaning that their common preferences are represented by $\sqrt{(x/n)\,g}$. Indeed, maximizing cg under the budget constraint $nc + pg = m$ (we take c as the numeraire) implies $x = nc = pg$. Their indirect utility is then $m/\left(2\sqrt{pn}\right)$, in which the equivalence scale $m/\sqrt{n}$ is singled out.

This is easily generalized to the formula m/n^{β} if β is the constant share of private expenditures. Although this may be viewed as a justification of the OECD scale, it also points out the restrictive assumptions that underlie this particular formula, especially the assumption of identical individuals. Another limitation is that this approach ignores the social amenities (as opposed to economic amenities) brought by living in a family.

Moreover, one may question the reference to the single household. In international comparisons, corrections to equivalent incomes due to household size are huge because average household size is much greater than 1. One could accept it if theory justified this reference. But the single household is not the aspiration of most people, therefore it is hard to relate this reference to the theory proposed above. Living alone is not uncommon, but is hardly considered normal or desirable by most people.

Another issue is that local (intrahousehold) public goods do not easily fit in the x, y dichotomy because they are ordinary market commodities but display special sharing properties within a household as a function of the number of people using them (a room for two cannot be used by five, for instance, but it can be used by one person).

We propose to take as a model the configuration of a household in which all adults earn equal amounts and in which younger members are taken care of by the altruistic feelings of the adults. This means that the indirect utility of an individual takes as arguments total household income divided by the number of adults, and the y variables that include the composition of the household (adults, children and sharing possibilities): $v_i\left(p, y_i, M_i/a_i\right)$, where M_i is total income in i's household, and a_i the number of adults in the household.

Equivalent income for a given reference $\tilde{y}$ is then the solution m_i^* to the equation

$$v_i\left(p, \tilde{y}, m_i^*\right) = v_i\left(p, y_i, M_i/a_i\right).$$

We argue that, under these assumptions, it makes sense to apply the min operator, opening the possibility that different individuals may have different household types as their reference. Intuitively, with the min operator every individual will pick as a reference the household type in which his per adult share of income would be the lowest and this alternative situation would still give him the same satisfaction as in his current situation.

This implies interpersonal comparisons of the following sort. Two adults are deemed equally well off if they would be indifferent between their current situation and bringing the same per capita income contribution m^* to the household of their own preferred type (under the condition that every adult contributes m^* to the household income). This implies that a society in which all adults earn the same income and belong to households of their choice is considered to be perfectly egalitarian.[7] Conversely, it also implies that a society in which all adults earn the same income but not all of them belong to households of their choice will consider that those who would rather be in a different type of household are worse off than those who are satisfied with the composition of their household.

7. We assume away any other source of inequality between people.

Consider for instance the simple model introduced earlier, with identical members consuming two goods and not caring about social amenities. For each of them one computes

$$v\left(p, n, M/n\right) = .5\frac{M}{n}\sqrt{n/p},$$

which, for a fixed M/n, is increasing in n, reflecting the economic amenities obtained from sharing consumption of local public goods. Therefore the lowest possible equivalent income is obtained for the largest possible reference household. For individuals who only care about their consumption standard, their aspiration is indeed, for a given income per capita, to be in the largest possible household.

Such preferences are not very realistic. Many adults in developed countries, for instance, seem to prefer living in a nuclear family with about four or five members (two adults, two or three children). It is therefore likely that for many people this would be the implicit reference type induced by the min operator.

As mentioned above, we propose to deal with children by imposing altruistic preferences on the adults who take care of them. This is meant to guarantee that adults enjoy the company of well-catered children only. We do not have a specific proposal for how to calibrate the impact of children's consumption on the adults' utility.

APPENDIX B

Proofs

B.1 A PARETIAN RANK-DEPENDENT CRITERION

The consumption set of all individuals is $\mathbb{R}_+^\ell$, for $\ell \geq 2$, and individual preferences are assumed to be strictly convex and strictly monotone. All (individual utility and social welfare) functions are assumed to be differentiable. The notation $px_{(i)}$ refers to the ith component of the vector $(px_1, \ldots, px_n)$, by increasing order.

Proposition B.1 *(Hammond 1978) The partial ordering of allocations generated by the criterion*

$$\sum_{i=1}^{n} \alpha_i px_{(i)} \geq \sum_{i=1}^{n} \alpha_i px'_{(i)}$$

for fixed rank-order weights[1] $\alpha_1 > \ldots > \alpha_n$ *is compatible with a Paretian social welfare function* $\overline{W}(x_1, \ldots, x_n) = W(u_1(x_1), \ldots, u_n(x_n))$ *if and only if all individual Engel curves are linear and identical.*

The proof of the "only if" part goes as follows. Let $v_i(p, m_i)$ denote i's indirect utility function (m_i is i's income) and define the function

$$w\left(p, m_1, \ldots, m_n\right) = W(v_1(p, m_1), \ldots, v_n(p, m_n)).$$

1. Hammond considers the special case $\alpha_i = n - i + 1$.

The rank-order weights require that for all $(m_1, \ldots, m_n)$ that are ranked in increasing order,[2]

$$\frac{\partial w / \partial m_i}{\partial w / \partial m_j} = \frac{\alpha_i}{\alpha_j},$$

which implies that there is a function F such that[3]

$$w(p, m_1, \ldots, m_n) = F\left(p, \sum_{i=1}^{n} \alpha_i m_i\right).$$

For a particular p_0, there is no restriction in assuming that F is linear in the second argument because only the ordinal properties of w matter. Therefore one can write, for this particular p_0, and after a suitable rescaling of W,

$$W(v_1(p_0, m_1), \ldots, v_n(p_0, m_n)) = \sum_{i=1}^{n} \alpha_i m_i.$$

This expression implies that W, thus rescaled, can be written

$$W(u_1, \ldots, u_n) = \sum_{i=1}^{n} \alpha_i e_i\left(p_0, u_i\right),$$

where $e_i\left(p_0, u_i\right)$ is the expenditure function. Let us rescale the utility functions so that one can write, on the domain in which $(m_1, \ldots, m_n)$ is ranked in increasing order,

$$W(u_1, \ldots, u_n) = \sum_{i=1}^{n} \alpha_i u_i.$$

One then has, for all p and not just for p_0,

$$\sum_{i=1}^{n} \alpha_i v_i(p, m_i) = F\left(p, \sum_{i=1}^{n} \alpha_i m_i\right).$$

2. Hammond derives this equation with arguments that implicitly assume an interior allocation, but no such assumption is needed.

3. In his proof, Hammond writes a similar equation that covers all income distributions. But one cannot assume that F takes the same form in all subspaces corresponding to different rankings of individual incomes, even if by continuity the different functions for different subspaces must coincide when incomes are equal.

Differentiating with respect to m_i, this implies, letting F_2 denote the derivative of F with respect to its second argument,

$$\alpha_i \frac{\partial v_i}{\partial m_i} = F_2\left(p, \sum_{i=1}^{n} \alpha_i m_i\right)\alpha_i,$$

which means that $\partial v_i/\partial m_i$ does not depend on i. As it cannot depend on the second argument of F_2 because it cannot depend on m_j for $j \neq i$, one then obtains that, in this normalization of utilities, $\partial v_i/\partial m_i$ depends only on p. Therefore

$$v_i(p, m_i) = \gamma_i(p) + \beta(p) m_i.$$

From Roy's identity, one derives that individual i's demand is

$$-\frac{\partial v_i/\partial p_k}{\partial v_i/\partial m_i} = -\frac{\frac{\partial \gamma_i}{\partial p_k} + \frac{\partial \beta}{\partial p_k} m_i}{\beta(p)},$$

which clearly shows that the Engel curves are linear (and parallel).

Extending the argument to all possible orderings of $(m_1, \ldots, m_n)$, one obtains that

$$w(p, m_1, \ldots, m_n) = \varphi_\sigma\left(\sum_{i=1}^{n} \alpha_{r(i)}\left[\gamma_i(p) + \beta(p) m_i\right]\right), \tag{B.1}$$

where $r(i)$ is the rank of m_i and φ_σ is a continuous increasing function that is specific to the ordering σ of the individuals in terms of income.

By continuity of w, the expression in (B.1) corresponding to the orderings $\sigma_1 : m_1 \leq \ldots \leq m_i \leq m_{i+1} \leq \ldots \leq m_n$ and $\sigma_2 : m_1 \leq \ldots \leq m_{i+1} \leq m_i \leq \ldots \leq m_n$ tends to the same value when $m_i - m_{i+1} \to 0$ (the values of m_t for $t \neq i, j$ being fixed). When $m_i - m_{i+1} \to 0$ from below (i.e., $m_i < m_{i+1}$), it tends to $\varphi_{\sigma_1}\left(z + (\alpha_{i+1} - \alpha_i)\, \gamma_{i+1}(p)\right)$; when $m_i - m_{i+1} \to 0$ from above (i.e., $m_i > m_{i+1}$), it tends to $\varphi_{\sigma_2}\left(z + (\alpha_{i+1} - \alpha_i)\, \gamma_i(p)\right)$, for

$$z = \sum_{t \neq i, i+1} \alpha_t \left[\gamma_t(p) + \beta(p) m_t\right] + \alpha_i \left[\gamma_i(p) + \gamma_{i+1}(p)\right] \\ + (\alpha_i + \alpha_{i+1})\, \beta(p) \lim m_i.$$

The identity $\varphi_{\sigma_1}\left(z + (\alpha_{i+1} - \alpha_i)\, \gamma_{i+1}(p)\right) \equiv \varphi_{\sigma_2}\left(z + (\alpha_{i+1} - \alpha_i)\, \gamma_i(p)\right)$ is constraining. Let $(\alpha_{i+1} - \alpha_i)\, \gamma_i(p') = (\alpha_{i+1} - \alpha_i)\, \gamma_i(p) + \varepsilon$. One must then have

$$\begin{aligned}\varphi_{\sigma_2}\left(z-\varepsilon+(\alpha_{i+1}-\alpha_i)\,\gamma_i(p')\right) &= \varphi_{\sigma_2}\left(z+(\alpha_{i+1}-\alpha_i)\,\gamma_i(p)\right) \qquad \text{(B.2)}\\ &= \varphi_{\sigma_1}\left(z+(\alpha_{i+1}-\alpha_i)\,\gamma_{i+1}(p)\right)\\ &\quad \text{by the identity with the right-hand term of (B.2)}\\ &= \varphi_{\sigma_1}\left(z-\varepsilon+(\alpha_{i+1}-\alpha_i)\,\gamma_{i+1}(p')\right)\\ &\quad \text{by the identity with the left-hand term of (B.2),}\end{aligned}$$

which implies, comparing the last two lines, that

$$(\alpha_{i+1}-\alpha_i)\,\gamma_{i+1}(p') = (\alpha_{i+1}-\alpha_i)\,\gamma_{i+1}(p)+\varepsilon,$$

and thus that $\gamma_{i+1}(p)-\gamma_i(p)$ does not depend on p. Therefore the individuals have identical preferences. This achieves the argument.

Note that if one writes $\gamma_i(p)$ as a sum $\gamma_i(p)=\gamma(p)+\delta_i$, one can rewrite (B.1) as

$$w\left(p,m_1,\ldots,m_n\right)=\psi_\sigma\left(\sum_{i=1}^{n}\alpha_{r(i)}\left[\gamma(p)+\beta(p)m_i\right]\right),$$

by incorporating $\sum_{i=1}^{n}\alpha_{r(i)}\delta_i$, which only depends on the ordering σ, in the function. The same argument as in the previous paragraph then implies that the ψ_σ functions must be identical. Therefore there is a normalization in which individual utilities are identical and the social welfare function is symmetric. Of course, there exist other normalizations for which this is not the case.

B.2 REFERENCE-PRICE INDEPENDENCE

The framework is the same as in the previous section. We assume differentiability of welfare and utility functions, but also of compensated demand functions.

Proposition B.2 *(adapted from Roberts 1980, prop. 10)*[4] *The criterion*

$$W\left(e_1\left(\tilde{p},v_1(m_1,p)\right),\ldots,e_n\left(\tilde{p},v_n(m_n,p)\right)\right)$$

4. Roberts does not introduce Strong Pareto and considers the possibility of social welfare not depending on some individuals.

satisfies Strong Pareto and is independent of the reference price $\tilde{p}$ if only if individual preferences are identical and homothetic.

We focus on the "only if" part. It has been shown in the text that, under reference-price independence,

$$\begin{aligned} &W\big(e_1\left(\tilde{p}, v_1(m_1,p)\right),\ldots,e_n\left(\tilde{p}, v_n(m_n,p)\right)\big) \\ &\quad\geq W\big(e_1\left(\tilde{p}, v_1(m_1',p)\right),\ldots,e_n\left(\tilde{p}, v_n(m_n',p)\right)\big) \end{aligned}$$

if and only if

$$W(m_1,\ldots,m_n) \geq W\big(m_1',\ldots,m_n'\big).$$

One can therefore write

$$W\big(e_1\left(\tilde{p}, v_1(m_1,p)\right),\ldots,e_n\left(\tilde{p}, v_n(m_n,p)\right)\big) = F\left(G\left(W\left(m_1,\ldots,m_n\right),p\right),\tilde{p}\right),$$

with F and G being increasing in their first argument. Moreover, one has, for all w,

$$F\big(G(w,p),p\big) = w.$$

Differentiating w.r.t. $\tilde{p}_k$ (for some $k = 1,\ldots,\ell$), one gets

$$\sum_{i=1}^{n} \frac{\partial W}{\partial e_i}\frac{\partial e_i}{\partial \tilde{p}_k} = \frac{\partial F}{\partial \tilde{p}_k}, \tag{B.3}$$

and recall that by Shepard's Lemma,

$$\frac{\partial e_i}{\partial \tilde{p}_k} = x_{ik}^c\left(\tilde{p}, v_i(m_i,p)\right),$$

where $x_{ik}^c\left(\tilde{p}, v_i(m_i,p)\right)$ denotes i's compensated demand in good k.

Independence of $\tilde{p}$ also implies that W is homothetic, because $e_i\left(\lambda\tilde{p}, v_i(m_i,p)\right) = \lambda e_i\left(\tilde{p}, v_i(m_i,p)\right)$, so that

$$\begin{aligned} &W\big(e_1\left(\tilde{p}, v_1(m_1,p)\right),\ldots,e_n\left(\tilde{p}, v_n(m_n,p)\right)\big) \\ &\quad\geq W\big(e_1\left(\tilde{p}, v_1(m_1',p)\right),\ldots,e_n\left(\tilde{p}, v_n(m_n',p)\right)\big) \end{aligned}$$

if and only if

$$\begin{aligned} &W\big(\lambda e_1\left(\tilde{p}, v_1(m_1,p)\right),\ldots,\lambda e_n\left(\tilde{p}, v_n(m_n,p)\right)\big) \\ &\quad\geq W\big(\lambda e_1\left(\tilde{p}, v_1(m_1',p)\right),\ldots,\lambda e_n\left(\tilde{p}, v_n(m_n',p)\right)\big). \end{aligned}$$

We can normalize W so that $W(e,\ldots,e)=e$.

Let

$$a_i = \frac{\partial W}{\partial e_i}(0,\ldots,0,e_i,0,\ldots,0),$$
$$b_i = \frac{\partial W}{\partial e_i}(e,\ldots,e).$$

As W is homothetic, a_i and b_i are constant;[5] by Strong Pareto they are positive; and by the normalization of W, one has $a_i < 1$, $\sum_i b_i = 1$. One also has (by Euler's homogeneous function theorem):

$$W(0,\ldots,0,m,0,\ldots,0) = a_i m.$$

If $m_i = 0$, $e_i\left(\tilde{p}, v_i(m_i,p)\right) = 0$ and $x_i^c\left(\tilde{p}, v_i(m_i,p)\right) = 0$. Applying (B.3) to the distribution $(0,\ldots,0,m,0,\ldots,0)$, one obtains

$$a_i x_{ik}^c\left(\tilde{p}, v_i(m,p)\right) = \frac{\partial F}{\partial \tilde{p}_k}\left(G(a_i m,p),\tilde{p}\right).$$

Applied to a distribution $(m,\ldots,m)$ and at $\tilde{p}=p$, which implies that one also has equality of $e_i\left(\tilde{p}, v_i(m_i,p)\right)$, one obtains

$$\sum_{i=1}^{n} b_i x_{ik}^c\left(p, v_i(m,p)\right) = \frac{\partial F}{\partial \tilde{p}_k}\left(G(m,p),p\right).$$

Combining the two equations (and inserting $\tilde{p}=p$ in the first one), one obtains

$$\sum_{i=1}^{n} \frac{b_i}{a_i}\frac{\partial F}{\partial \tilde{p}_k}\left(G\left(a_i m,p\right),p\right) = \frac{\partial F}{\partial \tilde{p}_k}\left(G(m,p),p\right). \tag{B.4}$$

If $\frac{\partial F}{\partial \tilde{p}_k}\left(G(m,p),p\right)$ is linear in m for all k, this equation is satisfied. This implies that $x_{ik}^c\left(p, v_i(m,p)\right)$, which is equal to the uncompensated demand $x_{ik}\left(m,p\right)$, is linear in m for all k, and therefore that preferences are homothetic. Moreover they must be identical, as one then has, for all i,

$$x_{ik}\left(m,p\right) = \frac{\partial F}{\partial \tilde{p}_k}\left(G(m,p),p\right).$$

5. Contrary to what Roberts writes (p. 293), in general $a_i \neq b_i$.

It remains to show that $\frac{\partial F}{\partial \tilde{p}_k}\left(G(m,p),p\right)$ is linear in m for all k.[6] Fix k. By differentiability of $x^c_{ik}\left(p, v_i(m,p)\right)$ w.r.t. v_i, and of v_i w.r.t. m, the function $\frac{\partial F}{\partial \tilde{p}_k}\left(G(m,p),p\right)$ is differentiable in m, which implies that $\frac{\partial F}{\partial \tilde{p}_k}\left(G(m,p),p\right)/m$ is continuous in m, including at $m=0$, by L'Hospital's rule. Therefore[7]

$$\begin{aligned}
\frac{\frac{\partial F}{\partial \tilde{p}_k}\left(G(m,p),p\right)}{m} &= \sum_{i=1}^{n} b_i \frac{\frac{\partial F}{\partial \tilde{p}_k}\left(G\left(a_i m,p\right),p\right)}{a_i m} \\
&= \sum_{i=1}^{n} b_i \sum_{j=1}^{n} b_j \frac{\frac{\partial F}{\partial \tilde{p}_k}\left(G\left(a_j a_i m,p\right),p\right)}{a_j a_i m} \\
&= \dots
\end{aligned}$$

Replicating this decomposition, one sees that the right-hand term tends to $\lim_{m\to 0}\frac{\partial F}{\partial \tilde{p}_k}\left(G(m,p),p\right)/m$. Therefore $\frac{\partial F}{\partial \tilde{p}_k}\left(G(m,p),p\right)/m$ is a constant in m.

B.3 A SIMPLE PROOF OF ARROW'S THEOREM IN AN ECONOMIC FRAMEWORK

The framework is similar to that chapter 3. There are $n \geq 2$ individuals, $\ell \geq 2$ commodities. Individual preferences are denoted R_i (strict preference, P_i). The set of alternatives to be ranked is the set Z of allocations $(x_1,\dots,x_n)$ such that for all i, $x_i \in \mathbb{R}^\ell_+ \setminus \{0\}$. A social ordering function associates every profile of preferences $(R_1,\dots,R_n)$ with an ordering (complete and transitive binary relation) of Z. The domain of profiles D is the n-Cartesian product of the set of self-centered preferences that are continuous, monotonic and convex.

6. This last part of the argument is incorrect in Roberts (1980) and Slesnick (1991). Both take for granted that $x^c_{ik}\left(p, v_i(m,p)\right)/m$ is continuous in m at $m=0$, and Slesnick handles a vector of demands as if it was a scalar.

7. Continuity of $\frac{\partial F}{\partial \tilde{p}_k}\left(G(m,p),p\right)/m$ at $m=0$ is needed. Consider for instance the case $b_i = 1/n$ and $a_i = a$ for all i. Then (B.4) boils down to

$$\frac{1}{a}\frac{\partial F}{\partial \tilde{p}_k}\left(G(am,p),p\right) = \frac{\partial F}{\partial \tilde{p}_k}\left(G(m,p),p\right),$$

and a violation of linearity in m is possible if the function $\frac{\partial F}{\partial \tilde{p}_k}\left(G(m,p),p\right)$ is not differentiable in zero.

Weak Pareto $(x_1, \ldots, x_n)$ is better than $(x'_1, \ldots, x'_n)$ under profile $(R_1, \ldots, R_n)$ if for all i, $x_i P_i x'_i$.

Arrow Independence Assume that for all i, R_i and R'_i coincide on $\{x_i, x'_i\}$. Then $(x_1, \ldots, x_n)$ is better than $(x'_1, \ldots, x'_n)$ under profile $(R_1, \ldots, R_n)$ if and only if it is better under profile $(R'_1, \ldots, R'_n)$.

Nondictatorship There is no i_0 such that $(x_1, \ldots, x_n)$ is better than $(x'_1, \ldots, x'_n)$ under profile $(R_1, \ldots, R_n)$ whenever $x_{i_0} P_{i_0} x'_{i_0}$.

Proposition B.3 *(Arrow) There is no social ordering function on D that satisfies Weak Pareto, Arrow Independence, and Nondictatorship.*

To shorten the notations, let $(x_1, \ldots, x_n)$ be denoted x_N and $(R_1, \ldots, R_n)$ be denoted R_N.

Step 1. By an extension of the Condorcet paradox, for a given profile R_N^* there must exist two allocations x_N^*, y_N^* such that $\exists i_0$, $x_{i_0}^* P_{i_0}^* y_{i_0}^*$, $\forall i \neq i_0$, $y_i^* P_i^* x_i^*$, and $x_N^* P^* y_N^*$, where P^* denotes the social ordering under R_N^*.

This is shown as follows. Take a bundle $q \in \mathbb{R}_{++}^{\ell}$. Consider the allocations x_N^m, for $m = 0, \ldots, n$, defined by

$$\begin{aligned}
x_N^0 &= (q, \ldots, q)\\
x_N^1 &= (q/2^n, 2q, \ldots, 2q)\\
x_N^2 &= (q/2^{n-1}, q/2^{n-1}, 2^2 q, \ldots, 2^2 q)\\
&\vdots\\
x_N^{n-1} &= (q/2^2, q/2^2, \ldots, q/2^2, 2^{n-1} q)\\
x_N^n &= (q/2, q/2, \ldots, q/2, q/2).
\end{aligned}$$

Observe that for all $i = 1, .., n$, $x_i^{i-1} P_i x_i^i = x_i^{i-1}/2^n$ and $x_j^i P_j x_j^{i-1} = x_j^i/2$ for all $j \neq i$.

If there is $i = 1, \ldots, n$ such that $x^{i-1} P^* x^i$, we are done.

If not, one has $x^n R^* x^0$ by transitivity. By Weak Pareto, $x^0 P^* x^n$, a contradiction.

Step 2. By Arrow Independence, there is no loss of generality in assuming that the indifference sets at x_N^*, y_N^* touch the axes. Let $a_N, b_N \in (\mathbb{R}_{++} \times \{0\}^{\ell-1})^n$ (only good 1 is consumed) be such that

$$\begin{gathered}
a_{i_0} P_{i_0}^* x_{i_0}^* P_{i_0}^* y_{i_0}^* P_{i_0}^* b_{i_0};\\
\forall i \neq i_0,\ y_i^* P_i^* b_i > a_i P_i^* x_i^*.
\end{gathered}$$

Let R_N be any profile (R the associated social ordering), and x_N, y_N be two allocations such that $x_{i_0} P_{i_0} y_{i_0}$. By Arrow Independence, there is no loss of generality in assuming that the indifference sets at x_N, y_N touch the axes.

Let $c_N, d_N \in \left(\{0\} \times \mathbb{R}_{++} \times \{0\}^{\ell-2}\right)^n$ (only good 2 is consumed) such that

$$x_{i_0} P_{i_0} c_{i_0} > d_{i_0} P_{i_0} y_{i_0};$$
$$\forall i \neq i_0,\ d_i > c_i,\ x_i P_i c_i,\ d_i P_i y_i.$$

There exist preferences R'_N such that

$$c_{i_0} P'_{i_0} a_{i_0} > b_{i_0} P'_{i_0} d_{i_0};$$
$$\forall i \neq i_0,\ b_i P'_i d_i > c_i P'_i a_i.$$

By Weak Pareto, $a_N P^* x^*_N$ and $y^*_N P^* b_N$, implying $a_N P^* b_N$. By Arrow Independence, $a_N P' b_N$.

By Weak Pareto, $c_N P' a_N$ and $b_N P' d_N$, implying $c_N P' d_N$. By Arrow Independence, $c_N P d_N$.

By Weak Pareto, $x_N P c_N$ and $d_N P y_N$, implying $x_N P y_N$. This contradicts Nondictatorship.

BIBLIOGRAPHY

Afsa C., D. Blanchet, V. Marcus, M. Mira d'Ercole, P.A. Pionnier, G. Ranuzzi, L. Rioux, P. Schreyer 2008, "Survey of existing approaches to measuring socio-economic progress," Joint Insee-OECD document prepared for the first plenary meeting of Commission on the Measurement of Economic Performance and Social Progress, http://www.stiglitz-sen-fitoussi.fr/documents/.

Ahlheim M. 1998, "Measures of economic welfare," in S. Barberà, P.J. Hammond, C. Seidl (eds.), *Handbook of Utility Theory*, vol. 1, Dordrecht: Kluwer.

Alkire S. 2002, *Valuing Freedoms: Sen's Capability Approach and Poverty Reduction*, New York: Oxford University Press.

Anand P., G. Hunter, R. Smith 2005, "Capabilities and well-being," *Social Indicators Research* 74: 9–55.

Anderson E. 1999, "What is the point of equality?" *Ethics* 109: 287–337.

Arneson R.J. 1989, "Equality and equal opportunity for welfare," *Philosophical Studies* 56: 77–93.

Arneson R.J. 1998, "Real freedom and distributive justice," in J.F. Laslier, M. Fleurbaey, N. Gravel, A. Trannoy (eds.), *Freedom in Economics: New Perspectives in Normative Analysis*, London: Routledge.

Arneson R.J. 2000, "Luck egalitarianism and prioritarianism," *Ethics* 110: 339–349.

Arrow K.J. 1951, *Social Choice and Individual Values*, New York: Wiley.

Arrow K.J., P.S. Dasgupta, L. Goulder, G. Daily, P. Ehrlich, G. Heal, S. Levin, K.G. Mäler, S. Schneider, D. Starrett, B. Walker 2004, "Are we consuming too much?" *Journal of Economic Perspectives* 18: 147–172.

Arrow K.J., P.S. Dasgupta, K.G. Mäler 2003a, "Evaluating projects and assessing sustainable development in imperfect economies," *Environmental and Resource Economics* 26: 647–685.

Arrow K.J., P.S. Dasgupta, K.G. Mäler 2003b, "The genuine savings criterion and the value of population," *Economic Theory* 20: 217–225.

Asheim G.B. 2007, *Justifying, Characterizing and Indicating Sustainability*, Berlin: Springer.

Asheim G.B., K.A. Brekke 2002, "Sustainability when capital management has stochastic consequences," *Social Choice and Welfare* 19: 921–940.

Asheim G.B., W. Buchholz, C. Withagen 2003, "The Hartwick rule: Myths and facts," *Environmental and Resource Economics* 25: 129–150.

Atkinson A.B. 1970, "On the measurement of inequality," *Journal of Economic Theory* 2: 244–263.

Atkinson A.B., J.E. Stiglitz 1980, *Lectures on Public Economics*, London: McGraw-Hill.

Aubin J.P. 1991, *Viability theory*, Birkhaüser: Springer Verlag.

Barberà S., W. Bossert, P.K. Pattanaik 2004, "Ranking sets of objects," in S. Barberà, P.J. Hammond, C. Seidl (eds.), *Handbook of Utility Theory*, vol. 2, Dordrecht: Kluwer.

Barry B. 2007, "Rationality and want-satisfaction," in M. Fleurbaey, M. Salles, J. Weymark (eds.), *Justice, Political Liberalism and Utilitarianism: Themes from Harsanyi and Rawls*, Cambridge: Cambridge University Press.

Basu K. 1987, "Achievements, capabilities, and the concept of well-being," *Social Choice and Welfare* 4: 69–76.

Basu K., L. Lopez-Calva 2011, "Functionings and capabilities," in K.J. Arrow, A.K. Sen, K. Suzumura (eds.), *Handbook of Social Choice and Welfare*, vol. 2, Amsterdam: North-Holland.

Baumgärtner S., M.F. Quass 2009, "Ecological-economic viability as a criterion of strong sustainability under uncertainty," *Ecological Economics* 68: 2008–2020.

Becker G., T. Philipson, R. Soares 2005, "The quantity and quality of life and the evolution of world inequality," *American Economic Review* 95: 277–291.

Bene C., L. Doyen, D. Gabay 2001, "A viability analysis for a bio-economic model," *Ecological Economics* 36: 385–396.

Benjamin D., O. Heffetz, M. Kimball, A. Rees-Jones 2010, "What do you think would make you happier? What do you think you would choose?" *American Economic Review*, 102: 2083–2110.

Bergson (Burk) A. 1938, "A Reformulation of Certain Aspects of Welfare Economics," *Quarterly Journal of Economics* 52: 310–334.

Bergson A. 1954, "On the Concept of Social Welfare," *Quarterly Journal of Economics* 68: 233–252.

Blackorby C., D. Donaldson 1988, "Money metric utility: A harmless normalization?" *Journal of Economic Theory* 46: 120–129.

Blackorby C., D. Donaldson 1990, "A review article: The case against the use of the sum of compensating variations in cost-benefit analysis," *Canadian Journal of Economics* 23: 471–494.

Blackorby C., F. Laisney, R. Schmachtenberg 1994, "Ethically-consistent welfare prescriptions are reference price-independent," in R. Blundell, I. Preston, I. Walker (eds.), *The Measurement of Household Welfare*, Cambridge: Cambridge University Press.

Blanchet D., J. Le Cacheux, V. Marcus 2009, "Adjusted Net Savings and other approaches to sustainability: Some theoretical background," INSEE DESE Working Paper G 2009/10.

Bleys B. 2005, "Alternative welfare measures," photocopy, Vrije Universiteit Brussel.

Blundell R., I. Preston, I. Walker 1994, "An introduction to applied welfare analysis," in R. Blundell, I. Preston, I. Walker (eds.), *The Measurement of Household Welfare*, Cambridge: Cambridge University Press.

Boadway R., N. Bruce 1984, *Welfare Economics*, Oxford: Basil Blackwell.

Boarini R., A. Johansson, M. Mira d'Ercole 2006, "Alternative measures of well-being," OECD Social, Employment and Migration Working Papers 33.

Bommier A. 2006, "Uncertain lifetime and intertemporal choice: Risk aversion as a rationale for time discounting," *International Economic Review* 47: 1223–1246.

Bommier A., S. Zuber 2008, "Can preferences for catastrophe avoidance reconcile social discounting with intergenerational equity?" *Social Choice and Welfare* 31: 415–434.

Bossert W. 1995, "Redistribution mechanisms based on individual characteristics," *Mathematical Social Sciences* 29: 1–17.

Brickman P., D.T. Campbell 1971, "Hedonic relativism and planning the food society," in M.H. Appley (ed.), *Adaptation-level theory*, New York: Academic Press.

Browning M., P.A. Chiappori, A. Lewbel 2006, "Estimating consumption economies of scale, adult equivalence scales, and household bargaining power," Boston College Working Paper No. 588.

Brundtland G.H. 1987, *Our common future*, New York: Oxford University Press.

Cairns R.D., N.V. Long 2006, "Maximin: A direct approach to sustainability," *Environment and Development Economics* 11: 275–300.

Cantril H. 1965, *The Pattern of Human Concerns*, New Brunswick, N.J.: Rutgers University Press.

Champsaur P., G. Laroque 1981, "Fair allocations in large economies," *Journal of Economic Theory* 25: 269–282.

Chichilnisky G., W. Thomson 1987, "The Walrasian mechanism from equal division is not monotonic with respect to variations in the number of consumers," *Journal of Public Economics* 32: 119–124.

Clark A.E., P. Fritjers, M.A. Shields 2008, "Relative income, happiness, and utility: An explanation for the Easterlin paradox and other puzzles," *Journal of Economic Literature* 46: 95–144.

Cobb C.W., J. Cobb 1994, *The Green National Product*, Lanham, Md.: University Press of America.

Cobb C.W., C. Rixford 1998, *Lessons Learned from the History of Social Indicators*, San Francisco: Redefining Progress.

Cobb J., H. Daly 1989, *For the Common Good: Redirecting the Economy toward Community, the Environment and a Sustainable Future*, Boston: Beacon Press.

Cohen G. A. 1989, "On the currency of egalitarian justice," *Ethics* 99: 906–944.

Comim F., M. Qizilbash, S. Alkire (eds.) 2008, *The Capability Approach: Concepts, Measures and Applications*, Cambridge: Cambridge University Press.

Commission of the European Communities 2009, *GDP and Beyond: Measuring Progress in a Changing World*, Communication from the Commission to the Council and the European Parliament, http://www.beyond-gdp.eu/index.html.

Costantini, V., S. Monni 2004, "Sustainable human development for European Countries," *Fourth International Conference on the Capability Approach: Enhancing Human Security*, University of Pavia, Italy.

Costanza R., M. Hart, S. Posner, J. Talberth 2009, "Beyond GDP: The need for new measures of progress," Pardee Papers No. 4, Boston University.

d'Aspremont C., L. Gevers 1977, "Equity and the informational basis of collective choice," *Review of Economic Studies* 44: 199–209.

Dasgupta P.S. 2001, "Valuing objects and evaluating policies in imperfect economies," *Economic Journal* 111: C1–C29.

Dasgupta P.S., G.H. Heal 1974, "The optimal depletion of exhaustible resources," *Review of Economic Studies* 41: 3–28.

Dasgupta P.S., K.G. Mäler 2000, "Net national product, wealth, and social well-being," *Environment and Development Economics* 5: 69–93.

Deaton A. 1979, "The distance function in consumer behaviour with applications to index numbers and optimal taxation," *Review of Economic Studies* 46: 391–405.

Deaton A. 1980, "The measurement of welfare: Theory and practical guidelines," Living Standards Measurement Study Working Paper No. 7, World Bank.

Deaton A. 2008, "Income, health, and well-being around the world: Evidence from the Gallup World Poll," *Journal of Economic Perspectives* 22: 53–72.

Deaton A. 2010, "Price indexes, inequality, and the measurement of world poverty," *American Economic Review* 100: 5–34.

Deaton A. 2012, "The financial crisis and the well-being of Americans," *Oxford Economic Papers*, 64: 1–26.

Deaton A., A. Heston 2010, "Understanding PPPs and PPP-based national accounts," *American Economic Journal: Macroeconomics* 2: 1–35.

Deaton A., J. Muellbauer 1980, *Economics and consumer behaviour*, Cambridge: Cambridge University Press.

Debreu G. 1951, "The coefficient of resource utilization," *Econometrica* 19: 273–292.

Deneulin S., L. Shahani 2009, *An Introduction to the Human Development and Capability Approach: Freedom and Agency*, London: Earthscan.

Desai M. 1994, "Greening the HDI?" in A. Macgillivray, S. Zadek (eds.), *Accounting for Change*, London: New Economic Foundation.

Diener E. 1994, "Assessing subjective well-being: Progress and opportunities," *Social Indicators Research* 31: 103–157.

Diener E. 2000, "Subjective well-being: The science of happiness and a proposal for a national index," *American Psychologist* 55: 34–43.

Diener E., J.F. Helliwell, D. Kahneman 2010, *International Differences in Well-Being*, Oxford: Oxford University Press.

Diener E., E.M. Suh, R.E. Lucas, H.L. Smith 1999, "Subjective well-being: Three decades of progress," *Psychological Bulletin* 125: 276–302.

Dietz S., E. Neumayer 2004, "Genuine savings: A critical analysis of its policy-guiding value," *International Journal of Environment and Sustainable Development* 3: 276–292.

Diewert W.E. 1976, "Exact and superlative index numbers," *Journal of Econometrics* 4: 115–145.

Diewert W.E. 1983, "Cost-benefit analysis and project evaluation," *Journal of Public Economics* 22: 265–302.

Diewert W.E. 1992a, "Exact and superlative welfare change indicators," *Economic Inquiry* 30: 565–583.

Diewert W.E. 1992b, "Fisher ideal output, input, and productivity indexes revisited," *Journal of Productivity Analysis* 3: 211–248.

Di Tella R., R. McCulloch 2006, "Some uses of happiness data in economics," *Journal of Economic Perspectives* 20: 25–46.

Di Tella R., R. MacCulloch 2010, "Happiness adaptation to income beyond 'basic needs,'" in E. Diener, J.F. Helliwell, D. Kahneman (eds), *International Differences in Well-Being*, Oxford: Oxford University Press.

Di Tella R., R. McCulloch, A. Oswald 2003, "The macroeconomics of happiness," *Review of Economics and Statistics* 85: 809–827.

Dolan P., M.P. White 2007, "How can measures of subjective well-being be used to inform public policy?" *Perspectives on Psychological Science* 2: 71–85.

Donaldson D. 1992, "On the aggregation of money measures of well-being in applied welfare economics," *Journal of Agricultural and Resource Economics* 17: 88–102.

Dow J., S. Werlang 1988, "The consistency of welfare judgments with a representative consumer," *Journal of Economic Theory* 44: 269–280.

Dworkin R. 1981, "What is equality? Part 2: Equality of resources," *Philosophy & Public Affairs* 10: 283–345.

Dworkin R. 2000, *Sovereign Virtue: The Theory and Practice of Equality*, Cambridge: Harvard University Press.

Easterlin R.A. 1974, "Does economic growth improve the human lot? Some empirical evidence," in P.A. David, M.W. Reder (eds.), *Nations and Households in Economic Growth: Essays in Honor of Moses Abramovitz*, New York: Academic Press.

Easterlin R.A. 1995, "Will raising the incomes of all increase the happiness of all?" *Journal of Economic Behaviour and Organization* 27: 35–48.

Ekman P. 1992, "An argument for basic emotions," *Cognition and Emotion* 6: 169–200.

Estes R., M. Levy, T. Srebotnjak, A. de Shrebinin 2005, *2005 Environmental Sustainability Index: Benchmarking National Environmental Stewardship*, New Haven: Yale Center for Environmental Law and Policy.

Everett G., A. Wilks 1999, "The World Bank genuine savings indicator: A useful measure of sustainability?" Bretton Woods Project, http://brettonwoodsproject.org/topic/environment/gensavings.pdf

Feldstein M. 1972a, "Distributional equity and the optimal structure of public prices," *American Economic Review* 62: 32–36.

Feldstein M. 1972b, "Equity and efficiency in public sector pricing: The optimal two-part tariff," *Quarterly Journal of Economics* 86: 175–187.

Fisher I. 1922, *The Making of Index Numbers*, Boston: Houghton Mifflin.

Fleurbaey M. 1994, "On fair compensation," *Theory and Decision* 36: 277–307.

Fleurbaey M. 1995, "Equal opportunity or equal social outcome?" *Economics and Philosophy* 11: 25–56.

Fleurbaey M. 2005, "Health, wealth and fairness," *Journal of Public Economic Theory* 7: 253–284.

Fleurbaey M. 2007, "Social choice and the indexing dilemma," *Social Choice and Welfare* 29: 633–648.

Fleurbaey M. 2008, *Fairness, Responsibility, and Welfare*, Oxford: Oxford University Press.

Fleurbaey M., G. Gaulier 2009, "International comparisons of living standards by equivalent incomes," *Scandinavian Journal of Economics* 111: 597–624.

Fleurbaey M., F. Maniquet 2006, "Fair income tax," *Review of Economic Studies* 73: 55–83.

Fleurbaey M., F. Maniquet 2011a, "Compensation and responsibility," in K.J. Arrow, A.K. Sen, and K. Suzumura (eds.), *Handbook of Social Choice and Welfare*, vol. 2, Amsterdam: North-Holland.

Fleurbaey M., F. Maniquet 2011b, *A Theory of Fairness and Social Welfare*, Cambridge: Cambridge University Press.

Fleurbaey M., P. Mongin 2005, "The news of the death of welfare economics is greatly exaggerated," *Social Choice and Welfare* 25: 381–418.

Fleurbaey M., V. Peragine 2010, "Ex ante versus ex post equality of opportunity," *Economica*, DOI: 10.1111/j.1468-0335.2012.00941.x

Fleurbaey M., E. Schokkaert, K. Decancq 2009, "What good is happiness?" CORE Discussion Paper 2009/17.

Fleurbaey M., K. Suzumura, K. Tadenuma 2005, "The informational basis of the theory of fair allocation," *Social Choice and Welfare* 24: 311–342.

Fleurbaey M., K. Tadenuma 2012, "Universal social orderings. An integrated theory of policy evaluation, inter-society comparisons, and interpersonal comparisons," photocopy.

Foster J.E. 2011, "Freedom, opportunity, and well-being," in K.J. Arrow, A.K. Sen, and K. Suzumura (eds.), *Handbook of Social Choice and Welfare*, vol. 2, Amsterdam: North-Holland.

Freeman III A.M. 1992, *The Measurement of Environment and Resource Values*, Washington, D.C.: Resources for the Future.

Frederick S., G. Loewenstein 1999, "Hedonic adaptation," in D. Kahneman, E. Diener, N. Schwarz (eds.), *Well-Being: The Foundations of Hedonic Psychology*, New York: Russell Sage Foundation.

Frey B., A. Stutzer 2002, *Happiness and Economics: How the Economy and Institutions Affect Human Well-Being*, Princeton: Princeton University Press.

Frijda N.H. 1999, "Emotions and hedonic experience," in D. Kahneman, E. Diener, N. Schwarz (eds.), *Well-Being: The Foundations of Hedonic Psychology*, New York: Russell Sage Foundation.

Gadrey J., F. Jany-Catrice 2006, *The New Indicators of Well-Being and Development*, London: Macmillan.

Gaertner W., Y. Xu 2008, "A new class of measures of the standard of living based on functionings," *Economic Theory* 35: 201–215.

Global Footprint Network. 2010, Annual report 2010, http://www.footprintnetwork.org/images/uploads/2010_Annual_Report_spread.pdf.

Gollier C. 2012, *Pricing the Planet's Future: The Economics of Discounting in an Uncertain World*, Princeton: Princeton University Press.

Graaff J. de V. 1977, "Equity and efficiency as components of the general welfare," *South African Journal of Economics* 45: 362–375.

Graham C. 2009, *Happiness around the World: The Paradox of Happy Peasants and Miserable Millionaires*, Oxford: Oxford University Press.

Guesnerie R. 2005, "Calcul économique et développement durable," *Revue Économique* 55: 363–382.

Hamilton K., M. Clemens 1999, "Genuine saving in developing countries," *World Bank Economic Review* 13: 33–56.

Hammond P.J. 1978, "Economic welfare with rank order price weighting," *Review of Economic Studies* 45: 381–384.

Hammond P.J. 1994, "Money metric measures of individual and social welfare allowing for environmental externalities," in W. Eichhorn (ed.), *Models and Measurement of Welfare and Inequality*, Berlin: Springer.

Hammond P.J., F. Liberini, E. Proto 2011, "Individual Welfare and Subjective Well-Being: Commentary Inspired by Sacks, Stevenson and Wolfers," Warwick Economic Research Papers No. 957.

Hansson B. 1973, "The independence condition in the theory of social choice," *Theory and Decision* 4: 25–49.

Hartwick J.M. 1977, "Intergenerational equity and the investing of rents from exhaustible resources," *American Economic Review* 66: 972–974.

Heal G.M., B. Kriström 2005, "National income and the environment," in K.G. Mäler, J.R. Vincent (eds.), *Handbook of Environmental Economics*, vol. 3, Amsterdam: North-Holland.

Hicks J.R. 1941, "Consumer's surplus and index numbers," *Review of Economic Studies* 9: 126–137.

Hicks J.R. 1946, *Value and Capital: An Inquiry into Some Fundamental Principles of Economic theory* (2nd edition), Oxford: Clarendon Press.

Hicks J.R. 1956, *A Revision of Demand Theory*, Oxford: Clarendon Press.

Hoekstra A.Y. 2009, "Human appropriation of natural capital: A comparison of ecological footprint and water footprint analysis," *Ecological Economics* 68: 1963–1974.

Hotelling H. 1931, "The economics of exhaustible resources," *Journal of Political Economy* 39: 137–175.

Jany-Catrice F., S. Kampelmann 2007, "L'indicateur de bien-être économique: Une application à la France," *Revue Française d'Économie* 22: 107–148.

Jerison M. 2006, "Nonrepresentative representative consumers," photocopy, SUNY Albany.

Jones C.I., P.J. Klenow 2010, "Beyond GDP? Welfare across countries and time," NBER Working Paper No. 16352.

Jorgenson D.W. 1990, "Aggregate consumer behavior and the measurement of social welfare," *Econometrica* 58: 1007–1040.

Jorgenson D.W., B. Fraumeni 1989, "The accumulation of human and non-human capital, 1948–1984," in R.E. Lipsey, H.S. Tice (eds.), *The Measurement of Saving, Investment and Wealth*, Chicago: University of Chicago Press.

Kahneman D. 1994, "New challenges to the rationality assumption," *Journal of Institutional and Theoretical Economics* 150: 18–36.

Kahneman D. 1999, "Objective happiness," in D. Kahneman, E. Diener, N. Schwarz (eds.), *Well-Being: The Foundations of Hedonic Psychology*, New York: Russell Sage Foundation.

Kahneman D., A. Deaton 2010, "High income improves evaluation of life but not emotional well-being," *Proceedings of the National Academy of Sciences* 107: 16489–16493.

Kahneman D., E. Diener, N. Schwarz (eds.) 1999, *Well-Being: The Foundations of Hedonic Psychology*, New York: Russell Sage Foundation.

Kahneman D., A.B. Krueger 2006, "Developments in the measurement of subjective well-being," *Journal of Economic Perspectives* 20: 3–24.

Kahneman D., A.B. Krueger, D. Schkade, N. Schwarz, A.A. Stone 2004, "Toward national well-being accounts," *American Economic Review* 94: 429–434.

Kahneman D., A.B. Krueger, D. Schkade, N. Schwarz, A.A. Stone 2006, "Would you be happier if you were richer? A focusing illusion," *Science* 312: 1908–1910.

Kahneman D., I. Ritov, D. Schkade 1999, "Economic preferences or attitude expressions? An analysis of dollar responses to public issues," *Journal of Risk and Uncertainty* 19: 203–235.

Kahneman D., R.H. Thaler 2006, "Anomalies. Utility maximization and experienced utility," *Journal of Economic Perspectives* 20: 221–234.

Kahneman D., P. Wakker, R. Sarin 1997, "Back to Bentham? Explorations of experienced utility," *Quarterly Journal of Economics* 112: 375–405.

Kannai Y. 1970, "Continuity properties of the core of a market," *Econometrica* 38: 791–815.

Kapteyn A., J.P. Smith, A. Van Soest 2009, "Comparing life satisfaction," Working Papers 623-1, Rand Corporation Publications Department.

Kelley A.C. 1991, "The human development Index: Handle with care," *Population and Development Review* 17: 315–324.

Kimball M., R. Willis 2006, "Utility and happiness," photocopy, University of Michigan.

King M. 1983, "Welfare analysis of tax reforms using household data," *Journal of Public Economics* 21: 183–214.

Kirman A.P. 1992, "Whom or what does the representative individual represent?" *Journal of Economic Perspectives* 6: 117–136.

Kolm S.C. 1968, "The optimal production of social justice," in H. Guitton, J. Margolis (eds.), *Economie publique*, Paris: Ed. du CNRS.
Kolm S.C. 1972, *Justice et équité*, Paris: Ed. du CNRS. Trans. as *Justice and Equity*, Cambridge: MIT Press, 1999.
Kolm S.C. 2004, *Macrojustice: The Political Economy of Fairness*, New York: Cambridge University Press.
Krueger A.B., D. Schkade 2008, "The reliability of subjective well-being measures," *Journal of Public Economics* 92: 1833–1845.
Kuklys W. 2005, *Amartya Sen's Capability Approach: Theoretical Insights and Empirical Applications*, Berlin: Springer.
Kuznets S. 1934, *National Income, 1929–1932: A report to the U.S. Senate*, 73rd Congress, 2nd Session, Washington, D.C.: U.S. Government Printing Office.
Lasso de la Vega M.C., A.M. Urrutia 2001, "HDPI: A framework for pollution sensitive human development indicators," *Environment, Development and Sustainability* 3: 199–215.
Layard R. 2005, *Happiness: Lessons from a New Science*, London: Allen Lane.
Layard R., G. Mayraz, S. Nickell 2008, "The marginal utility of income," *Journal of Public Economics* 92: 1846–1857.
Lewbel A. 1997, "Consumer demand systems and household equivalence scales," in M.H. Pesaran, P. Schmidt (eds.), *Handbook of Applied Econometrics*, vol. 2, Oxford: Blackwell.
Loewenstein G., P.A. Ubel 2008, "Hedonic adaptation and the role of decision and experience utility in public policy," *Journal of Public Economics* 92: 1795–1810.
Malmquist S. 1953, "Index numbers and indifference surfaces," *Trabajos de Estadistica* 4: 209–242.
Maniquet F., Y. Sprumont 2004, "Fair production and allocation of an excludable nonrival good," *Econometrica* 72: 627–640.
Martinet V., L. Doyen 2007, "Sustainability of an economy with an exhaustible resource: A viable control approach," *Resource and Energy Economics* 29: 17–39.
Max-Neef M. 1995, "Economic growth and quality of life: A threshold hypothesis," *Ecological Economics* 15: 115–118.
Mayston D.J. 1974, *The Idea of Social Choice*, London: Macmillan.
McGillivray M. 1991, "The human development index: Yet another redundant composite development indicator?" *World Development* 19: 1461–1468.
McGillivray M., H. White 2006, "Measuring development? The UNDP's human development index," *Journal of International Development* 5: 183–192.
McKenzie G.W. 1983, *Measuring Economic Welfare: New Methods*, Cambridge: Cambridge University Press.
McKenzie G.W., I.F. Pearce 1976, "Exact measures of welfare and the cost of living," *Review of Economic Studies* 43: 465–468.
McKenzie G.W. 1982, "Welfare measurement: A synthesis," *American Economic Review* 72: 669–682.
McKenzie L.W., I.F. Pearce 1957, "Demand theory without a utility index," *Review of Economic Studies* 24: 185–89.
Meadows D.H., D.L. Meadows, J. Randers, W.W. Behrens 1972, *The Limits to Growth*, New York: Universe Books.
Miringoff M., M.L. Miringoff, S. Opdyke 1999, *The Social Health of the Nation: How America is Really Doing*, New York: Oxford University Press.
Moulin H., W. Thomson 1988, "Can everyone benefit from growth?" *Journal of Mathematical Economics* 17: 339–345.

Muellbauer J. 1987, "Professor Sen on the standard of living," in A. Sen (G. Hawthorn ed.), *The Standard of Living*, Cambridge: Cambridge University Press.

Neary J.P. 2004, "Rationalizing the Penn World Table: True multilateral indices for international comparisons of real income," *American Economic Review* 94: 1411–1428.

Neumayer E. 2000, "On the methodology of ISEW, GPI and related measures: Some constructive suggestions and some doubts on the 'threshold' hypothesis," *Ecological Economics* 34: 347–361.

Neumayer E. 2004, *Weak versus Strong Sustainability: Exploring the Limits of Two Opposite Paradigms*, Cheltenham: Edward Elgar.

Nordhaus W., J. Tobin 1972, "Is growth obsolete?" in *Economic Research: Retrospect and Prospect*, Vol. 5: *Economic Growth*, NBER, http://www.nber.org/chapters/c7620.

Nussbaum M.C. 1988, "Nature, function, and capability: Aristotle on political distribution," *Oxford Studies in Ancient Philosophy*, suppl. vol., 145–184.

Nussbaum M.C. 2000, *Women and Human Development: The Capabilities Approach*, Cambridge: Cambridge University Press.

Nussbaum M.C. 2008, "Who is the happy warrior? Philosophy poses questions to psychology," *Journal of Legal Studies* 37: S81–S113.

OECD 2011, *How's life? Measuring well-being*, Paris: OECD.

OECD/JRC 2008, *Handbook on Constructing Composite Indicators: Methodology and User's Guide*, Paris: OECD.

Osberg L., A. Sharpe 2002, "An index of economic well-being for selected countries," *Review of Income and Wealth* 48: 291–316.

Oswald A.J. 1997, "Happiness and economic performance," *Economic Journal* 107: 1815–1831.

Pazner E. 1979, "Equity, nonfeasible alternatives and social choice: A reconsideration of the concept of social welfare," in J.J. Laffont (ed.), *Aggregation and Revelation of Preferences*, Amsterdam: North-Holland.

Pazner E., D. Schmeidler 1974, "A difficulty in the concept of fairness," *Review of Economic Studies* 41: 441–443.

Pazner E., D. Schmeidler 1978, "Egalitarian equivalent allocations: A new concept of economic equity," *Quarterly Journal of Economics* 92: 671–687.

Peragine V. 2004, "Measuring and implementing equality of opportunity for income," *Social Choice and Welfare* 22: 1–24.

Pearce D.W., K. Hamilton, G. Atkinson 1996, "Measuring sustainable development: Progress on indicators," *Environment and Development Economics* 1: 85–101.

Perret B. 2002, *Indicateurs sociaux: État des lieux et perspectives*, Report for the Conseil Supérieur de l' Emploi, des Revenus et de la Cohésion sociale, Paris.

Pervin L.A. 1983, "The stasis and flow of behavior: Toward a theory of goals," in M.M. Page (ed.), *Personality: Current Theory and Research*, Lincoln: University of Nebraska Press.

Pezzey J.C.V. 1997, "Sustainability constraints versus optimality versus intertemporal concern, and axioms versus data," *Land Economics* 73: 448–466.

Pezzey J.C.V. 2004, "One-sided sustainability tests with amenities, and changes in technology, trade and population," *Journal of Environmental Economics and Management* 48: 613–631.

Pezzey J.C.V., M.A. Toman (eds.) 2002, *The economics of sustainability*, London: Ashgate Press.

Pezzey J.C.V., M.A. Toman 2003, "Progress and problems in the economics of sustainability," in T. Tietenberg, H. Folmer (eds.), *International Yearbook of Environmental and Resource Economics, 2002–3*, Cheltenham: Edward Elgar.

Pillarisetti J.R., J.C.J.M. van den Bergh 2010, "Sustainable nations: What do aggregate indexes tell us?" *Environment, Development and Sustainability* 12: 49–62.

Pollak R.A. 1981, "The social cost of living index," *Journal of Public Economics* 15: 311–336.

Posner, S.M., R. Costanza 2011, "A summary of ISEW and GPI studies at multiple scales and new estimates for Baltimore City, Baltimore County, and the state of Maryland," *Ecological Economics* 70: 1972–1980.

Prinz A., B. Bünger 2009, "Living in a material world: Happy Income and Happy Life Years," CAWM Discussion Paper No 15.

Qizilbash M. 2008, "Amartya Sen's capability view: Insighful sketch or distorted picture?" in F. Comim, M. Qizilbash, S. Alkire (eds.), *The Capability Approach: Concepts, Measures and Applications*, Cambridge: Cambridge University Press.

Ramsey F.P. 1928, "A mathematical theory of saving," *Economic Journal* 38: 543–559.

Ravallion M. 2010a, "Mashup indexes of economic development," Policy Research Working Paper 5432, World Bank, Washington, D.C.

Ravallion M. 2010b, "Troubling tradeoffs with the Human Development Index," Policy Research Working Paper 5484, World Bank, Washington DC.

Rawls J. 1971, *A Theory of Justice*, Cambridge: Harvard University Press.

Rawls J. 1982, "Social unity and primary goods," in A.K. Sen, B. Williams (eds.), *Utilitarianism and Beyond*, Cambridge: Cambridge University Press.

Robbins L. 1932, *An Essay on the Nature and Significance of Economics*, London: Macmillan, 2nd edition, 1937.

Roberts K.W.S. 1980, "Price independent welfare prescriptions," *Journal of Public Economics* 13: 277–298.

Roemer J.E. 1993, "A pragmatic theory of responsibility for the egalitarian planner," *Philosophy & Public Affairs* 22: 146–166.

Roemer J.E. 1996, *Theories of Distributive Justice*, Cambridge: Harvard University Press.

Roemer J.E. 1998, *Equality of Opportunity*, Cambridge: Harvard University Press.

Russell J.A. 1980, "A circumplex model of affect," *Journal of Personality and Social Psychology* 39: 1161–1178.

Sacks D.W., B. Stevenson, J. Wolfers 2010, "Subjective well-being, income, economic development and growth," NBER Working Paper 16441.

Sagara A.D., A. Najam 1998, "The human development index: A critical review," *Ecological Economics* 25: 249–264.

Sala-i-Martin X. 2006, "The world distribution of income: Falling poverty and . . . convergence, period," *Quarterly Journal of Economics* 121: 351–397.

Samuelson P.A. 1947, *Foundations of Economic Analysis*, Cambridge: Harvard University Press.

Samuelson P.A. 1956, "Social Indifference Curves," *Quarterly Journal of Economics* 70: 1–22.

Samuelson P.A. 1961, "The evaluation of 'social income': Capital formation and wealth," in F.A. Lutz and D.C. Hague (eds.), *The Theory of Capital*, London: Macmillan.

Samuelson P.A. 1974, "Complementarity: An essay on the 40th anniversary of the Hicks-Allen revolution in demand theory," *Journal of Economic Literature* 12: 1255–1289.

Samuelson P.A. 1977, "Reaffirming the existence of 'reasonable' Bergson-Samuelson social welfare functions," *Economica* 44: 81–88.

Samuelson P.A., S. Swamy 1974, "Invariant economic index numbers and canonical duality: Survey and synthesis," *American Economic Review* 64: 566–593.
Schokkaert E. 2009, "The capabilities approach," in P. Anand, P.K. Pattanaik, C. Puppe (eds.), *The Handbook of Rational and Social Choice*, Oxford: Oxford University Press.
Schwarz N., F. Strack 1999, "Reports of subjective well-being: Judgmental processes and their methodological implications," in D. Kahneman, E. Diener, N. Schwarz (eds.), *Well-Being: The Foundations of Hedonic Psychology*, New York: Russell Sage Foundation.
Sen A.K. 1970, *Collective Choice and Social Welfare*, San-Francisco: Holden-Day.
Sen A.K. 1976, "Real national income," *Review of Economic Studies* 43: 19–39.
Sen A.K. 1979, "The welfare basis of real income comparisons: A survey," *Journal of Economic Literature* 17: 1–45.
Sen A.K. 1980, "Equality of what?" in S. McMurrin (ed.), *Tanner Lectures on Human Values*, Cambridge: Cambridge University Press. Rep. in *Choice, Welfare and Measurement*, Oxford: Basil Blackwell.
Sen A.K. 1985, *Commodities and Capabilities*, Amsterdam: North-Holland.
Sen A.K. 1992, *Inequality Re-examined*, Oxford: Clarendon Press.
Sen A.K. 1999a, *Development as Freedom*, New York: Knopf.
Sen A.K. 1999b, "The possibility of social choice," *American Economic Review* 89: 349–378.
Sen A.K. 2002, *Rationality and Freedom*, Cambridge: Belknap, Harvard University Press.
Sen A.K. 2009, *The Idea of Justice*, London: Allen Lane.
Slesnick D.T. 1991, "Aggregate deadweight loss and money metric social welfare," *International Economic Review* 32: 123–146.
Slesnick D.T. 1998, "Empirical approaches to the measurement of welfare," *Journal of Economic Literature* 36: 2108–2165.
Slivinsky A.D. 1983, "Income distribution evaluation and the law of one price," *Journal of Public Economics* 20: 103–112.
Solow R.M. 1974, "Intergenerational equity and exhaustible resources," *Review of Economic Studies* 41: 9–45.
Srinivasan T. N. 1994, "Human development: A new paradigm or reinvention of the wheel?" *American Economic Review* 84: 238–243.
Steffel M., D.M. Oppenheimer 2009, "Happy by what standard? The role of interpersonal and intrapersonal comparisons in ratings of happiness," *Social Indicators Research* 92: 69–79.
Stern N. 2007, *The Economics of Climate Change: The Stern Review*, Cambridge: Cambridge University Press.
Sterner T., U.M. Persson 2008, "An even Sterner review: Introducing relative prices into the discounting debate," *Review of Environmental Economics and Policy* 2: 61–76.
Stevenson B., J. Wolfers 2008, "Economic growth and subjective well-being: Reassessing the Easterlin paradox," *Brooking Papers on Economic Activity* 1: 1–87.
Stiglitz J., A. Sen, J.P. Fitoussi 2009, *Report by the Commission on the Measurement of Economic Performance and Social Progress*, www.stiglitz-sen-fitoussi.fr.
Stone R. 1975, *Towards a System of Social and Demographic Statistics*, New York: United Nations.

Streeten P., with S.J. Burki, M. ul Haq, N. Dicks, F. Stewart 1981, *First Things First: Meeting Basic Human Needs in Developing Countries*, London: Oxford University Press (for the World Bank).

Talberth J., C. Cobb, N. Slattery 2006, *The Genuine Progress Indicator 2006: A Tool for Sustainable Development*, Oakland: Redefining Progress (available at www.rprogress.org).

Thomson W. 1994, "Notions of equal, or equivalent, opportunities," *Social Choice and Welfare* 11: 137–156.

Thomson W. 2011, "Fair allocation rules," in K.J. Arrow, A.K. Sen, and K. Suzumura (eds.), *Handbook of Social Choice and Welfare*, vol. 2, Amsterdam: North-Holland.

Tversky A., D. Griffin 1991, "Endowments and contrast in judgments of well-being," in R.J. Zeckhauser (ed.), *Strategy and Choice*, Cambridge: MIT Press. Reprinted in D. Kahneman and A. Tversky (eds.), *Choices, Values, and Frames*, Cambridge: Cambridge University Press, 2000.

UN Department of Economic and Social Affairs 2007, *Indicators of Sustainable Development: Guidelines and Methodologies* (3rd edition), New York: United Nations.

UNDP 1990, *Human Development Report 1990*, New York: Oxford University Press.

UNDP 2010, *Human Development Report 2010. The Real Wealth of Nations: Pathways to Human Development*, New York: Oxford University Press.

UNDP 2011, *Human Development Report 2011. Sustainability and Equity: A Better Future For All*, London: Palgrave Macmillan.

UNECE/OECD/Eurostat 2008, "Report on measuring sustainable development: statistics for sustainable development, commonalities between current practice an theory," Working Paper ECE/CES, 2008–29.

Usher D. 1973, "An imputation to the measure of economic growth for changes in life expectancy," in M. Moss (ed.), *The Measurement of Economic and Social Performance*, Studies in Income and Wealth, No. 38, NBER.

van de Kerk G., A. Manuel 2008, "A comprehensive index for a sustainable society: The Sustainable Society Index," *Ecological Economics* 66: 228–242.

Vanoli A. 2005, *A History of National Accounting*, Fairfax: IOS Press.

Varian H. 1974, "Equity, envy and efficiency," *Journal of Economic Theory* 9: 63–91.

Varian H. 1976, "Two problems in the theory of fairness," *Journal of Public Economics* 5: 249–260.

Varian H. 1992, *Microeconomic Analysis*, New York: Norton.

Veenhoven R. 1996, "Happy Life-Expectancy, a comprehensive measure of quality of life in nations," *Social Indicators Research* 39: 1–58.

Wackernagel M., W. Rees 1995, *Our Ecological Footprint: Reducing Human Impact on the Earth*, Gabriola Island, BC: New Society Publishers.

Weitzman M.L. 1976, "On the welfare significance of national product in a dynamic economy," *Quarterly Journal of Economics* 90: 156–162.

Weitzman M.L. 1988, "Consumer's surplus as an exact approximation when prices are appropriately deflated," *Quarterly Journal of Economics* 102: 543–553.

Weitzman M.L. 2001, "A contribution to the theory of welfare accounting," *Scandinavian Journal of Economics* 103: 1–23.

Weymark J.A. 1985, "Money-metric utility functions," *International Economic Review* 26: 219–232.

Wiedmann T., J. Barrett 2010, "A review of the Ecological Footprint indicator: Perceptions and methods," *Sustainability* 2: 1645–1693.

Wiedmann T., J. Minx 2008, "A definition of carbon footprint," in C.C. Pertsova (ed.), *Ecological Economic Research Trends*, Hauppauge: Nova Science Publishers.
Willig R.D. 1981, "Social welfare dominance," *American Economic Review* 71: 200–204.
World Bank 2011, *The Changing Wealth of Nations: Measuring Sustainable Development in the New Millenium*, Washington, D.C.: World Bank.
Wolff J. 1998, "Fairness, respect, and the egalitarian ethos," *Philosophy & Public Affairs* 27: 97–122.
Xu Y. 2004, "On ranking linear budget sets in terms of freedom of choice," *Social Choice and Welfare* 22: 281–289.
Yaari M.E. 1965, "Uncertain lifetime, life insurance and the theory of the consumer," *Review of Economic Studies*, 32: 137–150.
Zolotas X. 1981, *Economic Growth and Declining Social Welfare*, New York: New York University Press.

SUBJECT INDEX

NAME INDEX